COURT, COUNTRY AND CULTURE

Essays on Early Modern British History
in Honor of Perez Zagorin

Perez Zagorin
Wilson Professor Emeritus of History – University of Rochester
Photograph by James Montanus, University of Rochester

COURT, COUNTRY AND CULTURE

Essays on Early Modern British History
in Honor of Perez Zagorin

EDITED BY

Bonnelyn Young Kunze   and   Dwight D. Brautigam

with a preface by Donald R. Kelley

UNIVERSITY OF ROCHESTER PRESS

First published 1992

University of Rochester Press
200 Administration Building, University of Rochester
Rochester, New York 14627, USA
and at PO Box 9, Woodbridge, Suffolk IP12 3DF, UK

ISBN 1 878822 05 5

Library of Congress Cataloging-in-Publication Data
Court, country, and culture : essays on early modern British history
in honor of Perez Zagorin / edited by Bonnelyn Young Kunze and
Dwight D. Brautigam ; with a preface by Donald R. Kelley.
   p.   cm.
Includes bibliographical references.
ISBN 1–878822–05–5 (alk. paper)
1. Great Britain – History – Tudors, 1485–1603. 2. Great Britain
– History – Stuarts, 1603–1714. I. Zagorin, Perez. II. Kunze,
Bonnelyn Young. III. Brautigam, Dwight D., 1956– .
DA300.C78 1992
942.05–dc20   92–2727

British Library Cataloguing-in-Publication Data
Court, Country and Culture : Essays on Early Modern
British History in Honor of Perez Zagorin
I. Kunze, Bonnelyn Young
II. Brautigam, Dwight D.
941
ISBN 1–878822–05–5

Contents

Preface

Dear Perez:

When I met you over twenty years ago (at that memorable and, for some, revolutionary meeting of the American Historical Association in Washington in December 1969), I had no idea that I would soon be joining you at the University of Rochester as colleague and (shortly thereafter) friend who would share the ups and downs of life in the Rochester history department. Before then I had heard of you only in two connections. First, I knew that you were the author of *A History of Political Thought in the English Revolution*, a pioneering survey of radical, "communist," and republican ideas which had impressed not only American novices like myself but also some of the most exacting of English historians (from left to right). Second, I had heard of you as a scholar who had made his own trek across the ideological spectrum of mid-century America. Even then I wondered how these two Zagorins fit together.

The answer to this question came in part in the new book that you were just finishing at this time – *The Court and the Country*, which broadened your exploration of seventeenth-century English history and joined it to more theoretical questions, especially the "causes of the English Revolution." In this connection you were also confronting the larger issue of the nature of revolution in general, which you see both as a central topic of early modern history and as the dominant myth of our own century. Your conclusions about this double question, together with a treasure-lode of insights drawn from a lifetime of teaching, are the basis of your *Rebels and Rulers (1500–1660)*, which offered both a synthesis of modern European history and a nominalist critique of the modern concept of revolution, portrayed by you as a long-term western phenomenon predating the "industrial Revolution," eluding simple class analysis, and transcending the French and Russian models. So you not only moved across the channel but also raised your conceptual sights and, I think, drew us closer together.

A further, more unexpected expansion of your aims appeared more recently, as you left the *terra firma* of socio-political history for a largely unexamined aspect of European underground culture – that is, the mysteries of human behavior, thought, and self-justification under conditions of repression and persecution. Like your earlier work on revolutions, *Ways of Lying* reflects and provides a deeper perspective on one of the central predicaments of twentieth-century society in an age disfigured by totalitarian regimes – and specifically how outlawed minorities survive and preserve their integrity against ethnic and ideological assault. Besides throwing light on my initial question, I think you have added a new dimension to our view of early modern history by an original and sensitive study of deep structure, probing beneath the surface of the historical process, examining what is to many historians (by definition) an almost inaccessible and unintelligible aspect of human behavior. I was moved by the adventurousness as well as the acumen of your explorations, and I'm almost ready to accept your redefinition of an "age of Revolution" as an "age of dissimulation."

Your work had always reflected a spirit of adventure and willingness to take on large challenges, including those in the philosophy of history. Nor have you avoided the role of polemicist, having published in *Science and Society* as well as that austere organ of the historical profession, the *American Historical Review*. You have opposed, in public and in private, vulgar Marxist interpretations of the historical process, intellectual surrender to destructive attitudes of relativism, indulgence in the textualist excesses of new fashions in intellectual history – and indeed any position that, on epistemological grounds, would deny the intelligibility or accessibility of the human past. In particular you have taken Carl Becker to task for unreflective skepticism, Christopher Hill for his partisan readings of English texts, Sir Isaiah Berlin for a lack of rigor in his analysis of Vico's famous identification of the scientifically true (*verum*) and the humanly created (*factum*), and Frank Ankersmit for his reduction of history to "discourse." Yet you have done this with unfailing good humor and wit as well as impressive learning and acumen, and you have taught many younger scholars, myself included, not only how to argue but also how to behave.

At Rochester our lives have intersected at many points. We started out by sharing a few of our Harvard recollections – some of your teachers I had heard (Wilbur K. Jordan, Crane Brinton, Carl Friedrich, David Owen, and of course Myron Gilmore), others I had only heard about (C. H. McIlwain, A. P. Ussher) – and I'm sure these overlapping experiences contributed to the common ground we cultivated, including mutual interests in philosophy, history, and literature. Not that we agreed on all issues, as our students in the philosophy of history course we shared soon found out. Yet this served only to enhance the cooperative and (what I, but certainly not you, might call the) dialogical character of history. I think this was further in the colloquium we shared for fifteen years and in the Friday evening seminar on early modern history which (with the unpaid support of colleagues and friends) we maintained in the 1970s and '80s.

Over the years we have also read each other's work, served on committees, attended scholarly conferences, seminars, and Ph. D. exams together, discussed editorial problems, competed in the writing of limericks,* and, with our wives, Honoré Sharrer and Bonnie Smith, travelled together in strange and warmer places. You have instructed my students in the "ways of lying," and I have retaliated by telling yours about the mysteries of Postmodernism; you have made me read Hilary Putnam, as I have tried to turn you to Heidegger – and through it all neither of us has ever given up on the other. If we have not spoken much about our childhood experiences in Chicago or our respective encounters with working-class culture, we have endlessly argued (and sometimes agreed) about Hegel and Marx, Proust and Pound, Vico and Wittgenstein, Deconstruction and the Covering Law, Geoffrey Elton and Lawrence Stone, Gene Genovese and Hayden White, Wagner and Surrealism (though here I defer to you and especially to Honoré) – though never (I think) have we argued about politics, religion, editorial policy, or how to bring up children.

All this is in the way of not of farewell but only of fond recollection, for I have no doubt that this friendship, dialogue, and collaboration will continue for many years. So, of course, will your work, and we all look forward to your new book, which goes back to your first investigations – the political face of Milton. I hope you like this volume, as I know you enjoyed the scholarly conference on which it is based; both of these tributes do no more than justice to a distinguished career and to a superlative human being. Stay in touch with all of us.

In all collegiality and friendship,

Don Kelley

* I have an old friend named Zagorin,
   Who knows the familiar and foreign,
    He's learned and he's taught
    and written a lot:
   Than he takes out, he always puts more in.

Introduction

The original idea for this volume, *Court, Country, and Culture: Essays on Early Modern British History in Honor of Perez Zagorin*, emerged from a conference honoring Professor Perez Zagorin at his retirement, held at the University of Rochester in November 1989. This collection of essays is by design an eclectic group. It covers an array of subjects on the historiography of early modern Britain, in terms of the political, intellectual, cultural, and religious currents in the period. These essays, taken together, present an argument for the need for historical research and writing that does not reduce the complexity and diversity of the historical process to either overly general or overly narrow interpretations.

Given the wide variety of research specialties among this volume's participants, the usual arbitrary nature of editors may seem even more obvious in the arrangement of the essays here. Still, we have attempted to group the essays in a somewhat coherent fashion. The first part of the book groups articles that will be of greatest interest to historians of politics and constitutional thought, though such a designation is not quite accurate either. Certainly the raging debates initiated by Conrad Russell and the revisionists are broader than politics and the constitution, but the first several essays will capture the attention of those scholars who have been following or participating in that debate. How we actually do history is at stake in that debate, and these essays touch on such questions.

The opening piece both captures the continuing significance of Professor Zagorin's scholarship and raises some fascinating aspects of our comprehension of ideas in history. Gordon Schochet's essay pays particular attention to Professor Zagorin's earliest book, *A History of Political Thought in the English Revolution*. Schochet seeks to resurrect many of that book's main arguments and demonstrate their relevance to current debates about the place of political philosophy, or more broadly, ideas, in the shaping of events. Thus, after a fervent defense of the work undertaken by historians of ideas, he sets out to examine the English Revolution as an example of a time where clashes of ideas produced political, religious, social, and cultural ferment that grew into a revolution. Schochet has produced a stirring defense of the preeminence of ideas within a culture, rather than allowing them to be merely products of language or other cultural expressions.

Not only must we evaluate our understanding of ideas, but we must also examine our methods. William H. Dray's essay on Christopher Hill is a fine example of historiographical exploration. In a fascinating and tightly-argued piece, Dray draws attention to issues that should concern all humanists and especially historians. How we understand and utilize causation can create problems for us all, and Dray's penetrating look at Hill's methodology should serve as both caution and inspiration to all of us. While the "neo-Whig"/revisionist debate attracts many who will read this volume, numerous other areas of inquiry are also caught up in debates in which the participants would do well to avoid the kinds of errors philosophers of history, such as Dray, may find in historians' work. Dray's essay is a caution that we must all pay careful attention to our methods as well as our conclusions.

Assumptions, conclusions, and methods are all significant, to be sure, and these are nowhere more important than in building those broad historical constructs on which we hang our more specialized research. In that regard, John Guy's contribution provides an outstanding example of broad, informed scholarship. He manages to draw together an extremely impressive amount of material in his "resynthesis" of key English constitutional ideas spanning the Tudor and Stuart periods. Beginning with the Magna Carta, Guy examines such significant concepts as the divine right of kings, the privileges of the subject under statute and common law, and the necessarily vague entity known as the English Constitution. That constitution underwent considerable change during the period Guy has chosen, with especially great impact done by the Bill of Rights at the end of the Stuart period. His article helps us retain that ever crucial long view without which our work loses meaning.

Four articles follow which more closely focus on particular historical questions, each illustrating the fascinating complexity of the historian's more detailed work. Joseph Levine's contribution on Sir Walter Ralegh gives the reader an intriguing example of historical investigation. It is an especially appropriate essay since it also examines Tudor/Stuart historiography. Levine's fine account of Ralegh's construction of his *History of the World* allows us special insight into the complex world of historical authorities combined with Christian faith and its relationship to understanding historical sources. The battle between the "ancients" and the "moderns" finds particular focus in Levine's well organized account of Ralegh's historical scholarship. All humanists can share in Levine's depiction of Ralegh as he faces the joys and limitations of scholarship.

Scholars were (and are) dependent on help, of course, and the interconnected nature of early modern English society is reflected in Linda Levy Peck's paper on patronage in the early seventeenth century. This essay offers illuminating insights into early Stuart court activities while affording us a penetrating analysis of the early modern English rationale for the "benefits" of patronage, combining classical, theological, and economic considerations for the justification of the common court practice. With her examples we gain particular knowledge of the cultural complexities inherent in the traditional understanding of patronage as it was undergoing change during the career of the Duke of Buckingham. Buckingham's oversight of patronage for James I affords useful information both about patronage in general, but also about the tensions between king and subjects that increased during the Duke's career; his management of patronage had something to do with that conflict, as Peck demonstrates. Peck does an admirable job of drawing together Tudor/Stuart expressions of classical rhetoric, social order, and economic activity.

Those tensions found expression in a number of ways, and many historians have evaluated them, including Professor Zagorin in his seminal *The Court and the Country*. Dwight Brautigam's essay on the usefulness of the terms "court" and "country" reflects Professor Zagorin's continued influence in the revisionist-inspired debate about the roots and nature of the English Revolution and Civil War. While many scholars have concluded that such terminology only obscures or even distorts the historical picture, Professor Brautigam argues for the continued relevance of ideas in early Stuart society. As the work of J.P. Sommerville and others has demonstrated, English men knew of and debated theories of sovereignty. Hence, with ideological awareness high, Englishmen could easily apply such theories to their own practical difficulties with both James I and Charles I. Brautigam argues that the revisionists have chosen to ignore or misinterpret this entire area of disagreement between English monarchs and their subjects, particularly in Parliament, though as the recent works of Richard Cust and Thomas Cromwell bear out, disgruntled Englishmen were not confined to Westminster. This assertion gains even more weight when one includes the burgeoning conflict over the nature of Anglicanism, a conflict that grew dangerously during the 1620s. Brautigam reminds us that such levels of argument and debate over constitutional issues are sufficient reason to retain Professor Zagorin's apt terms, "court" and "country."

The broad significance of the English Revolution attracts not only early Stuart specialists, of course. William Hunt's "View from the Vistula" on that revolution is a valuable addition to this collection. Hunt's comparative approach illuminates some significant characteristics of Tudor/Stuart political culture. His comparisons of views of liberty between English aristocrats and their Polish counterparts is especially striking. The implications for the nature of the English Revolution are certainly broad, and issue a further challenge to the revisionists on this count. Furthermore, Professor Hunt's lively presentation allows even readers with no knowledge of early modern Poland to grasp some of the salient differences between developments in these two early modern societies.

British historiography of the early modern period has been deeply influenced by the works and methods of social history. The work of Professor Paul S. Seaver has demonstrated an important influence on the construction of seventeenth-century urban life in England, specifically in London. Seaver illustrates in his study, "Declining Status in an Aspiring Age: The Problem of the Gentle Apprentice in Seventeenth-Century London," the ideological and cultural context of a seventeenth-century younger son of gentry status, who because of the effects of primogeniture, could claim little of the power, status, or privileged treatment as seen in the London world of work. Professor Seaver analyzes the "key institution" of apprenticeship, which, he maintains, acculturated both the newcomers streaming into London from rural parts, and the following generations of journeymen and masters, "to the realities of responsible economic and civic life." On the one hand, apprenticeship appears as an "obvious institution performing an obvious set of social and economic functions." On the other hand, the author sees complexities and ambiguities in the institution for it experienced close to a fifty percent attrition rate, despite its contractual basis. His close study of 269 litigated cases between master and apprentice affords us some fascinating insights into the "social realties which surround that rather puzzling institution."

The importance of religion in seventeenth-century England in court and countryside, in local and national conflict, and in the role of nonconformity, is a subject of enduring importance that continues to gain the attention of historians of early modern England. Emphasis often has been placed on Puritan developments up to and during the mid-seventeenth century Great Rebellion. Professor Peter Lake has analyzed the deep tension and ambiguity of the Laudian Anglican developments prior to and during the English Revolution. He has examined the Laudian approach to religion, not only in terms of its arguments vis-à-vis Puritan casuistry, but also in terms of its own inherent mixture of arguments over religious questions regarding good order in the Church of England. In untangling the Laudians' multifaceted arguments on the subject of rites and ceremonies, Professor Lake has pointed out that the "relative weight" the Laudians gave to their authorities varied at different points, according to the issues at hand. Lake's paper expertly illuminates a tidy hierarchy of arguments which the Laudians believed were entirely compatible with their view of the universal Catholic church. Thus, as Professor Lake expressed it, the Laudians wanted "to have their polemical and eat it too."

Because politics and religion were intertwined in the regimes of early modern England, another important manifestation of Protestantism in this period was nonconformity. In the years following the domination of Laudian church politics, a plethora of sectarian groups emerged, among which were the Quakers. The Quakers engaged in evangelizing across England, and beyond its shores, shortly after the sect emerged as a coherent religious group in England in the 1650s. Professor Bonnelyn Young Kunze has examined the peculiar role allotted to women in Quakerism. The Quakers distinguished themselves from most other groups of their era by assigning a prominent role to women in their community. Although actual practice did not match their early theory of Quaker women in the "Light" having equality to men, they did allow women to lead active evangelizing lives, conduct their own business meetings, collect money, and dispense their own charity. Kunze's study analyzes the connections, durability, and influence of a transatlantic female sectarian network, and its beliefs, which is based in part on a collection of Anglo-American correspondence of Quaker women's religious meetings between 1675 and 1758. The collection of letters offers an internal picture of the nature of the religious women's network and why it endured for generations, much longer than natural family ties were maintained among English kin who migrated to the new world.

Moving to the thought world of early modern England, there existed powerful intellectual forces that made a deep and lasting impact upon the life and thought of the times. Professor Paolo Pasqualucci's study, "Metaphysical Implications in Hobbes Theory of Passions," offers a fresh contribution to the history of ideas. It begins with an overview of Hobbes' materialistic and mechanistic account of the nature of human sensation, thought, and passion or affection, and shows that the concept of motion is, indeed, crucial in Hobbes' theory of the passions. Pasqualucci compares Hobbes' general argument on motion to that of Zeno of Elea. He points out that, remarkably, Hobbes and Zeno used the same assumption, that for there to be motion over any space or distance, there must first be motion over or in all possible segments or subdivisions of it in order to reach diametrically opposed conclusions. While Hobbes used it to prove the possibility of motion in infinitesimal spaces, Zeno used it to deny the possibility of any kind of motion at all. Hobbes denied Zeno's notion of infinite divisibility by concluding that "infinite divisibility" simply meant that something was divisible "into as many parts as any man will." Pasqualucci's essay offers striking insights into the Hobbesian solution to the problem of Zeno's infinite divisibility paradox.

The English Renaissance flourished throughout the sixteenth century and well into the seventeenth century, although it was in competition with other values. It was deeply influenced by Italian intellectual currents, especially the humanist movement that set the tone of Renaissance culture in Italy since the fourteenth century. Professor Antonio D'Andrea's long-term interest in the influence of the Italian Renaissance in England (and France) is the subject of his article, "Aspiring Minds: A Machiavellian Motif from Marlowe to Milton." D'Andrea points out a deep tension in the assimilation of Italian Renaissance ideas by English writers of the period. While the English borrowed Italian Renaissance ideas, they also demonstrated an aversion to, even a stated rejection of, the influences of Italian Renaissance culture. According to Professor D'Andrea, Nicolo Machiavelli presented a special problem to English Renaissance authors, for Machiavelli both "horrified them [the English], instructed them, entertained them – in fact he affected them over the whole attraction, repulsion spectrum." This illuminating philological study illustrates a "small fragment in this long history of contradictory images coming out of Italy to England." He examines the word "aspire," and its derivatives, in the writings of three English writers – Marlowe, Ralegh, and Milton – and probes the Machiavellian themes threaded through their works. D'Andrea holds that the "lexical coincidence" of these word links in Marlowe, Ralegh, and Milton may well shed more light on the mysteriously ambivalent and powerful character of Satan in Milton's work. D'Andrea's work offers some interesting insights into the uses of literature in early modern historiography.

Another contribution to the intellectual and cultural history of England is Professor Edward Hundert's study, "Performing the Enlightened Self: Henry Fielding and the History of Identity." Professor Hundert presents a richly-textured analysis which discusses a topic of significance, both for the history of ideas in general, and the history of literary genre in particular. Hundert observes how Hobbesian philosophy on human action as self interest influenced a newly-emerging literary genre in the seventeenth and eighteenth centuries. He begins with a discussion of the notion of social behavior as role playing. Normally we distinguish between our everyday actions or behavior, which we take to be the natural and spontaneous expression of our inward feelings and thoughts, and our formal and ritualized behavior which we recognize as consciously-learned and rule-governed behavior. The author points out that this distinction between natural and artificial behavior is blurred when we view a culture or society removed from us in distance and time. Hundert analyzes the development of the emerging idea of self in his discussion of the writer, Henry Fielding. Fielding could rely on his readers' awareness of the notion of role distance as a category of public perception. According to Hundert, Fielding used the notion of a theatricized public domain to develop this new literary genre, that of the "comic prose epic," which provided a new vehicle for social satire. Fielding's new genre put the reader in the position of an "impartial spectator," one who was distanced enough from an agent to gain the impartiality necessary for moral evaluation, yet knowledgeable enough of the social codes governing action to be able to interpret the agent's action as signs of the inner thoughts and intentions of the agent. Hundert cogently argues that in the creation of this new genre, Fielding was responding to an important eighteenth century phenomenon.

This volume pays tribute to a master historian and an unusual man. The *Preface* to this volume, written by Professor Donald R. Kelly, his colleague and long-time friend, attests to the fact that Professor Zagorin has expanded and deepened in a significant way the scholarly field of early modern British and European history.

Perez Zagorin's career has exhibited the marks of academic excellence, from his doctoral work at Harvard, completed in 1952, to his various teaching appointments. He taught at Vassar and Amherst Colleges from 1947 to 1953, and was Professor of History at McGill University from 1955 to 1965. Professor Zagorin held a visiting professorship in English History at the University of Pittsburgh in 1964, and the Johns Hopkins University in 1964–65. He has made many contributions at the University of Rochester serving as Professor of History from 1965 to 1982, and as the Joseph C. Wilson Professor of History from 1982 to 1989. Perez Zagorin has been the recipient of numerous awards and honors, including a Fulbright year in the United Kingdom and a Sheldon Travelling Fellowship. He was a senior Fellow at the Folger Shakespeare Library and held a Fellowship at the National Humanities Center. Professor Zagorin also has held fellowships from the J.S. Guggenheim Memorial Foundation, the Center for Advanced Study in the Behavioral Sciences, and the National Endowment for the Humanities.

An outstanding scholar, he has also been an equally superb teacher, as the editors can and do assert, both having been Ph.D. students under him. Perez Zagorin has spent a major portion of his academic life in the role of teacher, educator, and mentor to his students, and as Wilson Professor Emeritus of History at the University of Rochester still acts in that capacity. In the classroom, Professor Zagorin always presented his ideas with clarity, precision, and coherence, without being overbearing. His vast wealth of knowledge, his bibliographic genius, his breadth of coverage and depth of analysis of the historical subject at hand, combined with his approaches to historical thinking, were and are qualities deeply appreciated by his students.

As an inspiring teacher, with a wide breadth of interests, it is not doubted that this is due, in part, to his exceptional wife, Honoré Sharrer, whose own outstanding accomplishments as an artist have given Perez an even wider range of intellectual and aesthetic pursuits. Both are not only unceasing workers in their respective professions, but also combine hard work with friendliness, personal warmth, humor, and charm. The Zagorins' frequent hosting of student seminars at the end of semester classes was an especially pleasant experience. As a result, Perez and Honoré both have touched the lives of his students in a personal and unforgettable way.

As students, colleagues, peers, and friends of Perez Zagorin, we present this Festschrift as a symbol of esteem with best wishes for many more years of scholarship, good health, and happiness. Although Perez Zagorin has recently retired from active teaching, he has not retired as a historian. His students, colleagues, and friends are anticipating more scholarly work forthcoming from the pen of Perez Zagorin.

Bonnelyn Young Kunze and Dwight Brautigam

The English Revolution in the History of Political Thought*

GORDON J. SCHOCHET

"Political philosophy is not, characteristically, the product of the study or laboratory," George H. Sabine wrote in the opening of the Introduction to his 1941 edition of *The Works of Gerrard Winstanley*. "It occurs rather as an incident or a by-product of action, and even when it is produced by scholars, its authors have one eye on the forum. When political philosophy is produced in quantities, it is a sure symptom that society is going through a period of great stress and strain. . . . Of this there is no better illustration than the period of the Puritan Revolution."[1]

Indeed, the two revolutionary decades stretching between the first meeting of the Long Parliament and the coronation of Charles II comprehend one of the most momentous epochs in early-modern English history. That period witnessed two civil wars, the execution of a king, radical restructurings of the political and ecclesiastical constitutions, the growth of a remarkable volume of public debate about politics, religion, and social structure — including the publication in 1651 of what has been called "the greatest, perhaps the sole, masterpiece of political philosophy written in the English language,"[2] Thomas

* My title is an obvious play on Perez Zagorin's *A History of Political Thought in the English Revolution* (London, 1954), and this essay is written in equally obvious appreciation of and indebtedness to that work, which seems not to enjoy the scholarly prestige it deserves. Following Zagorin, I use the term "English Revolution" to refer to the entire period between the Long Parliament and the Restoration and have generally avoided "Civil Wars," "Puritan Revolution ('Rebellion')," and "Interregnum."

The larger body of work out of which this paper has grown owes much to the stimulating company of my colleagues at the Folger Institute Center for the History of British Political Thought – Lena Cowen Orlin, John Pocock, and Lois G. Schwoerer – and has enjoyed the generous support of the Research and Fellowship Divisions of the National Endowment for the Humanities.

[1] George H. Sabine, ed., *The Works of Gerrard Winstanley* (Ithaca, 1941), p. 1. In an unintended commentary on Sabine's nearly reductionist account of the nature of "political philosophy," the original owner of the copy of this work in the Alexander Library of Rutgers University wrote in the margin at this point, "Superstructure."

[2] Michael Oakeshott's characterization in the Introductions to his edition of *Leviathan*, Blackwell's Political Texts (Oxford, 1957), p. viii.

Hobbes's *Leviathan* — the full flowering of the English literary renaissance in the poetry of John Milton, and the unleashing of unprecedented religious sectarianism, to cite only some of the most familiar bench marks. For many, the Revolution emancipated that race of "masterlesse men," who, knowing no law and without a "coercive Power to tye their hands from rapine, and revenge,"[3] had "turned the world upside down."[4] From this perspective, it was a time of intense anxiety.

It is no wonder that Sabine should have seen in the Revolution a veritable prototype for the conditions that give birth to and fully nourish engaged political philosophy. However else it may be conceived and characterized, political philosophy responds as well as contributes to changes in the ordering of the social and political world. In this sense, it is inevitably rooted in historical circumstances. As Perez Zagorin remarked:

> It has often been held that the problems of philosophy are eternal and unchanging, and the history of any of its branches is merely the record of how these same problems have been dealt with down the ages. . . But further reflection, I think, will disclose the illusory character of this notion. . . the political theorist does not meditate on The State as such. His concern is rather with some historically-determined political order, which is the only state he can know. So the problems of political philosophy are not the same but different problems, and the state of Plato's meditations is not the state of Aquinas or of Hobbes.[5]

At the same time, however, there is something of an enduring (although not necessarily "timeless" and "eternal") quality to the *activity* of philosophizing (or theorizing) about politics as well as, to a considerably lesser extent, its specific pronouncements and judgments. As Sabine suggests, political philosophy is a consequence of injustice, disruption, and crisis that seems to be nearly inevitable; it is equally an enterprise that is vital to social and political continuity.[6]

---

3 Thomas Hobbes, *Leviathan: or The Matter, Forme, and Power of Commonwealth Ecclesiastical and Civil* (1651), ed. C. B. Macpherson (Harmondsworth, 1968), ch. 18 (p. 238); the phrase is repeated in ch. 21 (p. 266).

4 Acts.xvii.6, and, of course, Christopher Hill, *The World Turned Upside Down: Radical Ideas During the English Revolution* (New York, 1973), for whom this Biblical passage is an epigraph. "Masterless men" are discussed in ch. 3. The anxieties created by the specific turmoil of the Revolution were hardly new. John Donne had long ago complained of decay and disorder; "All coherence gone" was his plaintive cry in *The Anatomie of the World* (1611).

5 Zagorin, *History*, p. 2.

6 This claim is defended and expanded below when I discuss the characteristic conceptual vocabulary in which a society and its institutions are legitimated and/or attacked. For a general statement about the unavoidability of political theory, see Isaiah Berlin, "Does Political Theory Still Exist?" in *Philosophy, Politics, and Society,*

As standards of justice and stability cross temporal and international boundaries[7] — which they do by their natures – they establish the *appearance* of persistent discussions that defy and transcend temporal isolation. Yet, these standards are undoubtedly altered in the mere process of being applied to new or "alien" circumstances, and the implication of this recasting of Zagorin's claim is that historical analysis must begin by focusing on the *results* of those alterations. Only subsequently can it actually appreciate and then focus on the alterations themselves. There is an obvious and irreducible interpretative tension here between the perception of political philosophies as the functional artifact of specific societies and analyzing them in terms of trans-cultural borrowings and apparent continuities and innovations.[8]

Conceived in these terms the political thought of the English Revolution can be approached from numerous perspectives and interpreted in many different ways. The Revolution itself marked a period of profound disruption and innovation that, at the same time, was continuous with much that had been occurring in England for the previous century. Its political thought was equally Janus-faced, demanding restructurings of the social and political fabrics and anxiously condemning the disorder.

No epoch in English history has so captured the fancies of analysts and attracted historians, and none has given rise to more passionate and intense scholarly disagreement. These divergent accounts reflect the concerns and interests of the commentators as well as warying interpretative fashions. The definition of a subject and the way it is conceived will determine both the content and the method of study. In this particular instance, there is a pair of crosscutting issues, competing views of the history of political thought and divergent understandings of the Revolution itself.

This essay deals with the intersection of these two concerns, the former conceptual and historiographic, the latter rather more substantive. Using Sabine's and Zagorin's observations as points of departure and employing examples drawn primarily from the period of the English Revolution, Part I discusses some of the theoretical questions that have recently engaged historians of political thought as they debated the contours of their field. Part II turns to

2nd ser., ed. Peter Laslett and W. G. Runciman (Oxford, 1962), pp. 1–33 (reprinted in his *Concepts and Categories: Philosophical Essays*, ed. Henry Hardy [New York, 1979], pp. 143–172).

[7] The relationship between historical and cultural analyses (as well as present-day misuses of the past) is intriguingly discussed in David Lowenthal, *The Past Is a Foreign Country* (Cambridge, 1985).

[8] I take this phrase from the subtitle of Shelden S. Wolin, *Politics and Vision: Continuity and Innovation in Western Political Thought* (Boston, 1960), which, even though it has been out of print for some time remains for political scientists one of the most popular and influential textbooks in the history of political thought.

analyses of the Revolution and examines varying accounts of its political thought, ultimately suggesting a possible coherence provided by the doctrine of sovereignty.

I

The History of Political Thought

In the fifty years since Sabine wrote, few subjects have experienced such profound and self-conscious conceptual alterations as what he called "political philosophy." Conspicious among these changes has been the emerging importance of the history of political thought – a development to which Sabine himself made significant contributions with his classic and magisterial textbook, A History of Political Theory[9] — and its increasing identity as what can be called a *historical* subject.

What the history of political thought is taken to be — how the subject is defined in terms both of content and method — is, however tacitly and/or unconsciously, conceptually prior to any particular study. Such a notion will determine what is studied and how it is analyzed, in the process eliminating some elements from purview and prejudging the legitimacy of admitting others. Conventionally, the subject was directly related to what Sabine called "political philosophy," constituting the account of its history or "development" and emphasizing the major or "canonical" (as they are now called) writers and the most important or "key" philosophic concepts in the political lexicon. At its best, this approach became an abstract and often trans-historical study of the various appearances of specific ranges of political ideas over time, tracing and recording changes (usually called "developments"), rarely attempting to root those varying expressions in narrow historical circumstances, and frequently imposing an artificial coherence and unity on the created "histories." The aim was often to discover the philosophic and conceptual "origins" of the scholar's own present. At its worst, this approach resulted in the chronological presenta-

---

[9] Originally published in 1937, with subsequent editions in 1950, 1961, and 1973, Sabine's text is one of a small number of works that helped to define and legitimize the history of political thought as a distinct field of inquiry. It is ironic that it now seems to represent some of the limitations of the subject as it was conventionally practiced. Much of the contemporary sense of the nature and scope of the history of political thought was developed in opposition to Sabine's comprehensive sweep and his frequent lack of firm, "historical" moorings. His use of the terms "philosophy" and "theory" rather than "thought," which is preferred by contemporary historical scholars, is as much a consequence of his having been a philosopher (rather than an historian or political scientist) as it is a reflection of changing academic fashions.

tion and philosophic analysis of the leading ideas of the leading theorists or philosophers.

To speak of these approaches in the past tense and to characterize them so negatively — apart from revealing my own prejudices – is to suggest that they have been supplanted by newer and historically more "acceptable" methods, but that is not altogether true. The somewhat outdated history of ideas mode still survives, sometimes in the more acceptable guise of "conceptual history" and adorned by the fashionable appeal to an understanding of politics as "a linguistically constituted activity."[10] And the "leading thinkers" approach continues to prosper.[11] In general, however, the intrusion into the subject of self-consciously historical concerns along side and sometimes in place of the older philosophic and theoretical categories of analysis has transformed many aspects of the ways the history of political thought is conceived.

Among the most interesting of these recently-adopted, historicizing considerations is attention to the "languages," "vocabularies," and "discourses" in which political thought is expressed.[12] Because the verbalization of concepts is linguistically constrained and because a language is ultimately inseparable from its surrounding and supporting culture, the various elements that together comprise the history of a society's political thought, at crucial points – albeit in ways that may in fact be indeterminate — are themselves culturally-rooted. Put simply, they are to some irreducible degree historically determined. Further, they are parts of a discourse of more or lesser coherence that many members of the society share and (differentially) understand. That discourse, which is itself composed of varying and perhaps diverging elements, conveys meanings

[10] Terrence Ball, James Farr, and Russell L. Hanson, eds., *Political Innovation and Conceptual Change*, (Cambridge, 1989), p. ix. See also Reinhart Koselleck, "Begriffsgeschichte and Social History," in his *Futures Past: On the Semantics of Historical Time*, trans. Keith Tribe (Cambridge, Mass., 1985), pp. 74–91; Melvin Richter, "Conceptual History (*Begriffsgeschichte*) and Political Theory," *Political Theory*, XIV (1986), 604–637; Jeremy Rayner, "On *Begriffsgeschichte*," *ibid.*, XVI (1988), 496–501; and Richter, "Reconstructing the History of Political Languages: Pocock, Skinner, and the *Geschichtliche Grundbegriffe*," *History and Theory*, XXIX (1990), 38–70.

[11] Most evidently in the successive editions of *History of Political Philosophy*, ed. Leo Strauss and Joseph Cropsey (Chicago, 1963, 1973, etc.). The title is especially noteworthy in this context (note the absence of the indefinite article). See also, David Muschamp, ed., *Political Thinkers* (London, 1986), especially pp. 6–7 (a chart listing authors and political groups according to their responses to the question, "What, if anything, transforms political power into political authority?"). Brian Redhead, ed., *Political Thought from Plato to NATO* (London, 1984), tends in same direction but avoids some of the non-historical shortcomings inherent in the other two works.

[12] This innovation, related to recent work in literature and theories of interpretation, owes much to J. G. A. Pocock and Quentin Skinner. For excellent methodological accounts and substantive examples, see *The Languages of Political Theory in Early-Modern Europe*, ed. Anthony Pagden (Cambridge, 1987).

throughout the society, and is the principal means by which historical continuities and the very identity of the society are established and maintained.

Among the tasks confronting the historian of political thought for whom the field is defined so as to include these linguistic concerns is the identification and analysis of the structured discourses that contain the society's political thought. At this level, that is a *historical* task that requires attention to minor political writers, pamphleteers and propagandists, ideologues, and anyone else who may have employed the relevant discourse — including religious and literary figures — as well as to official pronouncement and responses to them as the means of discovering and establishing meanings, of comprehending what was at stake in political debates, of seeing how the expression of those stakes changed over time, and of explaining all this. This approach to the history of political thought should be especially fruitful for the analysis of so complex and rapidly changing a period as the English Revolution and should carry with it a growing attention to authors of relatively minor status.

What has occurred in fact is that the focus has remained on the major writers,[13] who are interpretatively "historicized" or "contextualized."[14] In the process, their relative statuses may actually be enhanced, as the contrasts with

[13] Note, for instance, that of the previously cited works in the history of political thought that claim comprehensive coverage – Sabine, Wolin, Strauss and Cropsey, Muschamp, and Redhead – only Sabine devotes specific chapters to writers and issues from the period of the Revolution other than Hobbes.

[14] A significant exception here – but one that so far stands virtually alone – is Conal Condren, *George Lawson's "Politica" and the English Revolution* (Cambridge, 1989). The concluding chapters argue for Lawson's historical and conceptual importance by showing his relationship to Hobbes and Locke. See also Julian Franklin, *John Locke and the Theory of Sovereignty: Mixed Monarchy and the Right of Resistance in the Political Thought of the English Revolution* (Cambridge, 1978), ch. 3, which is on Lawson and argues for his importance as a possible source of Locke's theory of dissolution. (Condren disagrees with Franklin's interpretation.) The Lawson-Locke relationship was first suggested in A. H. Maclean, "George Lawson and John Locke," *Cambridge Historical Journal*, IX (1947), 68–77.

Jack R. McMichael and Barbara Taft, eds., *The Writings of William Walwyn* (Athens, Ga., 1989), is an excellent edition with a valuable but brief historical and interpretative introduction that is not especially self-conscious about language. George M. Schulman, *Radicalism and Reverence: The Political Thought of Gerrard Winstanley* (Berkeley, 1989), is rather a different category of book: Winstanley already enjoys considerable status, and Schulman is more concerned with the twentieth century than he is with the seventeenth. Although sensitive to Winstanley's language, he does not attempt to situate it in a mid-seventeenth-century context and is not interested in its historical roots, treating it instead as if its subtleties were transparent to the twentieth-century reader. Schulman writes of Winstanley in the present tense, frequently interprets him in terms of Marx, and argues that "Winstanley's theory represents an alternative to Hobbes's and thus a road not taken in our history" (p. 256).

their contemporaries and their relationships to the events of their own times add new dimensions to our senses of their accomplishments.[15]

This continuing emphasis upon canonical texts and their authors[16] is a consequence of economic factors,[17] academic and professional ideologies and prejudices,[18] and — closely related and most important for present purposes – a persisting (but declining) disregard by the discipline of history itself of those conceptual cousins of the history of political thought, "intellectual history" and the "history of ideas." There lingers in much historical and social science explanation a quasi-sociology of knowledge/"materialist" conception of the world that sees thought and ideas as somehow less important than [other] institutional structures. Ideas are often viewed as consequences, perhaps super-ficial residues and/or rationalizations, of those institutions, which, however, dimly or imperfectly, they reflect or represent. Something like this notion is implicit in Sabine's assertion that political philosophy is an "incident or by-product of action."

Thus, historians of ideas have often had to justify their endeavors and to argue for their legitimacy. Several justifications are available: that ideas have significant histories of their own, that they provide means of understanding the other institution with which they share the world, and that in realm of politics and political thought, the expression of ideas is as much a political act as parliamentary meetings, revolutions, and executions. Ironically, all these claims help to sustain the canon, for they provide criteria for seperating the important from the commonplace.

At some point, the history of political thought cannot resist a nearly inevi-table invasion by the conceits of "transcendence" and at least the search for "truth." It is often maintained that the individual authors were able to over-come the constrictions of temporal circumstance that generated their thoughts and to which they were, in some sense, responding. And as historians of

---

[15] Cf. Leo Strauss, *Natural Right and History* (Chicago, 1953), Introduction and ch. 1, for a forceful insistence that "historicism" is reductive and "relativistic" and that it trivializes political philosophy by viewing its various expressions as (nothing more than) the consequences of their own times. Strauss's attack on "modernity" – Max Weber was the principal methodological target of this part of his argument – has been updated and transformed into a broadside against the modern American university in Alan Bloom, *The Closing of the American Mind* (New York, 1987).

[16] There is, of course, occasional attention paid to those of mere beatific status, i.e., those whose association with the major writors or with significant ideas qualifies them for partial inclusion.

[17] Books and articles about obscure and "unimportant" authors and/or subjects are generally not "marketable"; hence, works of this sort that are published usually include claims about the previously "unappreciated" significance of their subjects.

[18] As has been made clear by the somewhat inlikely combination of feminist and ethnic minority scholarship, on the one hand, and Thomas S. Kuhn, *The Structure of Scientific Revolutions*, 2nd ed. (Chicago, 1970), on the other.

political thought turn increasingly to "language" and from there to "traditions of discoure," they also turn away from specific contexts and conditions to categories that cut across and survive identifiable historical conditions.

One of the fascinating things that occurred in the political thought of the English Revolution was the revival of traditional "resistance theory" in support of the entitlement of parliament to discipline the King. This doctrine had substantial roots in the Conciliar theorists of the fourteenth and fifteenth centuries,[19] was adopted by the Marian Exiles,[20] and was an important ingredient in the sixteenth-century French Wars of Religion, many of the pamphlets from which were read and cited by English theorists of the 1640s and 1650s.[21] The sources of these doctrines were not lost on the apologists for King Charles. As one of the King's favorites, John Maxwell, Bishop of Tuam, Ireland, remarked, the doctrine of popular sovereignty had its origins in the conciliar theory of papal accountability that was enunciated by Gerson, John of Paris, and William of Occam, all of whom "were prior to Luther or Calvin. Our rabbies then have drawn Doctrines out of their polluted cisternes."[22] And Sir Robert Filmer, with equal self-consciouness, attacked the doctrine of natural, human freedom as a "new, plausible and dangerous opinion" that was "first hatched in the schools for good Divinity." He appealed instead to "the plain mind of Aristotle" to support his arguments for patriarchal absolutism and to fortify his attacks on Philip Hunton's defense of "mixed monarchy."[23]

All this presents rather an interesting if conceptually puzzling picture, for we

[19] Francis Oakely, "On the Road from Constance to 1688: The Political Thought of John Major and George Buchanan," Journal of British Studies, Number 2 (May, 1962), 1–31, esp. pp. 6–9 for the relevance to the mid-century revolutionary decades, and Zofia Rueger, "Gerson, The Concilliar Movement, and the Right of Resistance (1642–1644)," Journal of the History of Ideas, XXV (1964), 467–486.

[20] See for the most recent treatments Donald R. Kelley, "Ideas of Resistance before Elizabeth," in The Historical Renaissance: New Essays on Tudor and Stuart Literature and Culture, ed. Heather Dubrow and Richard Strier (Chicago, 1988), pp. 48–76 (also in Law, Literature, and the Justification of Regimes, Proceedings of the Folger Institute Center for the History of British Political Thought, ed. Gordon J. Schochet, II [Washington, D.C., 1990], pp. 5–28), and Jane Dawson, "Revolutionary Conclusions: The Case of the Marian Exiles," History of Political Thought, XI (1990), 257–272.

[21] J. H. M. Salmon, The French Religious Wars in English Political Thought (Oxford, 1959), chs. 5 and 6.

[22] [John Maxwell], Sacro-Sancta Regum Majestas: or, The Sacred and Royal Prerogative of Christian Kings (Oxford, 1644), p. 16. See also J. W. Allen, English Political Thought, 1603–1660, I: 1603–1644 [vol. II never published] (London, 1938), pp. 509–511, and Gordon J. Schochet, The Authoritarian Family and Political Attitudes in 17th-Century England: Patriarchalism in Political Thought, 2nd ed. (New Brunswick, 1988), pp. 109–110.

[23] Sir Robert Filmer, Patriarcha and Other Political Works, ed. Peter Laslett (Oxford, 1949), pp. 53, 229, and 299–301; the reference are to his Patriarcha (c.1640; published 1680), Observations upon Aristotle's Politiques (1652), and The Anarchy of a Limited or Mixed Monarchy (1648).

have specific and circumstantially-bounded historical exchanges that draw upon and comment on a mode of discourse that at least one of the participants clearly recognizes and correctly identifies as constituting what we might call a "tradition." In terms of the political thought of the Revolution, it is important to know both that the participants in the debates adapted older categories to deal with present concerns and that there was some self-conciousness about these borrowings. From here we can move to a consideration of the Revolution's uses of and contributions to the discourses of resistance and absolutism, looking at the alterations that were made and therefore at the form and content of the discourses that were passed on. What this illustrates is not so much the prescience of Maxwell and Filmer as it is the closeness of a historical conception of political discourse to trans-histroical analysis.

In a fundamental sense, structures of discourse and political language help to define society. At some point in the development of a civic or public order, this political vocabulary becomes the vehicle through which the society can be characterized by its members and in terms of which they can manipulate its institutions, for the public discourse contains the terms and categories of legitimation. People's collective conciousness of their status as participants in a particular civil society is simultaneously dependent upon and contributory to that political language.[24] These modes of self-expression and sources of verbal control are not hardened and unchangeable; neither are they univocal or altogether consistent. The discourse conveys varieties of meanings to different parts of the society and under different circumstances. Those differences plus the very acquisition and expansion of this civic self-conciousness all result in debates and legitimation conflicts, which themselves eventually contribute to changes in the discourse that has brought them into being. These phenomena sometimes are or lead to struggles for the control and possession of public power and for the ownership of the legitimating vocabulary, and when such struggles become prolonged and severe, it is a sure sign that the society is experiencing great stress and is possibly headed for revolution or civil war.

---

[24] This entire discussion is a gloss on and borrowing from some of the older, theoretical writings of J. G. A. Pocock, in particular "The History of Political Thought: A Methodological Enquiry," in *Philosophy, Politics, and society*, 2nd ser., ch. 9, and "Languages and Their Implications: The Transformation of the Study of Political Thought," in his *Politics, Language, and Time: Essays on Political Thought and History* (New York, 1971), ch. 1.

For the specific idea of civic consciousness, see also Stephen L. Collins, *From Divine Cosmos to Sovereign State: An Intellectual History of Consciousness and the Idea of Order in Renaissance England* (Oxford, 1989), pp. 149–168, *et passim*, and Donald W. Hanson, *From Kingdom to Commonwealth: The Development of Civic Consciousness in English Political thought* (Cambridge, Mass., 1970), esp. pp. 182–335.

II

The English Revolution

It would be impossible to provide a simple or single characterization of the political thought of so momentous and portentous an era as that of the revolution. Like the social and political forces that generated it, the political thought of the 1640s and 1650s went off in myriad directions, constantly feeding back upon itself and engaging new problems and questions. The issues debated during that cataclysmic twenty-year period were constitutional, religious, and socio-economic, and I shall suggest below that a concern with sovereignty ran through and united them.

They did not spring full-blown from the profound discontents and frustrations unleashed by the King's dismissal of the Short Parliament of 1640 but had been endemic in English society for some time. They manifested themselves, initially, in the constitutional impasse that resulted from the Long Parliament's considerations of the inherent vagaries of the "fundamental law,"[25] the composition of the "estates of the realm," and "mixed monarchy."[26] This "crisis of the constitution," as Margaret Judson termed it,[27] had festered — and occasionally erupted — beneath the unhappy and little-understood mythic accommodation that the English called "King-in-Parliament." It was a fused bomb waiting to be ignited by the doctrine of sovereignty.

Mingled with the discussion of the "estates" were the religious concerns that led to the exclusion of the bishops from the House of Lords and opened the door to the reorganization of the Church of England. These reforms were not part of a design to secularize England's civil society. Quite the contrary; they were attempts by the English Presbyterians to conclude the work of religious reformation that had been curtailed by the Elizabethan Settlement. The papist predilections of the Laudian reforms added to the burden of ancient discontents and increased the likelihood of religious opposition.[28] This religious

[25] J. W. Gough, *Fundamental Law in English Constitutional History* (Oxford, 1955), pp. 80–115.

[26] Michael Mendle, "Politics and Political Thought, 1640–1642," in *The Origins of the English Civil War*, ed. Conrad Russell (London, 1973), pp. 218–245, and the same author's *Dangerous Positions: Mixed Government, the Estates of the Realm, and the "Answer to the xix Propositions"* (University, Alabama, 1985), chs. 1 and 8.

[27] Margaret Atwood Judson, *The Crisis of the Constitution: An Essay in Constitutional and Political Thought in England, 1603–1645* (New Brunswick, New Jersey, 1949). For more recent, somewhat different, but compatible and often parallel accounts, see Mendle, *Dangerous Positions*, and J. P. Sommerville, *Politics and Ideology in England, 1603–1640* (London, 1986).

[28] See Conrad Russell, *The Causes of the English Civil War* (oxford, 1990), pp. 111–130.

theme was so strong a precipitant of the Civil War, John Morrill argues, that the crisis should be renamed "England's Wars of Religion."[29] What should not be forgotten in any event is the deep religious foundation on which the civil society of seventeenth-century England was built; religious concerns did not exist either in opposition to or in isolation from social and political ones. They were all part of one fabric, and any significant conflict was bound to find religious expression.[30] In this sense, the Revolution was utterly unremarkable, for it did little more than pull back the veneer of control and regulation that had covered over and contained religious discontent and, at least until 1642, had kept England free of the disastrous sectarian conflict that so much of Europe had experienced.

The third set of factors, socio-economic stresses and discontents, like the constitutional and religious problems, was the expression of forces that had been present in English society for some time prior to the Revolution. In this case, however, they were not dormant. A persistent sense of disequilibrium accompanied and was fostered by the expropriations and rapid economic growth of the English commonwealth that were among the consequences of enclosure.[31] Debated about the extent of the "underclass" in English society by the 1640s and the degree to which the Revolution itself was an expression of class-based antagonisms[32] can remain unresolved for present purposes. What cannot be questioned, however, is that the radical Digger[33] and agrarian repub-

[29] John Morrill, "Rhetoric and Action: Charles I, Tyranny, and the English Revolution," in *Religion, Resistance, and Civil War*, Proceedings of the Folger Institute Center for the History of British Political Thought, ed. Gordon J. Schochet, III (Washington, D.C., 1990), p. 104. See also his "The Religious Context of the English Civil War," *Transactions of the Royal Historical Society*, 5th ser., XXXIV (1984), 155–178, and cf. William Lamont, "The Religious Origins of the English Civil War," *Religion, Resistance, and Civil War*, pp. 1–11.

[30] See William M. Lamont, *Godly Rule: Politics and Religion 1603–1660* (London, 1969), which is primarily about millenarianism, but the general thesis is applicable here.

[31] Lawrence Stone, *The Causes of the English Revolution, 1529–1642* (New York, 1972), pp. 72–79, provides a concise account.

[32] For a full statement of this view, see Christopher Hill and Edmund Dell, eds., *The Good Old Cause: The English Revolution of 1640–1660; Its Causes, Course, and Consequences (Extracts from Contemporary sources)*, 2nd ed. (New York, 1969). Among Hill's many other writings on the subject, *The World Turned Upside Down* and "A Bourgeois Revolution?" in *Three British Revolutions: 1641, 1688, 1776*, ed. J. G. A. Pocock (Princeton, 1980), pp. 109–139, should also be consulted. Hill's interpretations are appreciatively assessed in Geoff Eley and William Hunt, eds., *Reviving the English Revolution: Reflections and Elaborations on the Work of Christopher Hill* (New York, 1988).

The works of David W. Petegorsky and C. B. Macpherson, cited below, are also relevant to the general question of class in the mid-century revolution.

[33] Zagorin notes Winstanley's "momentous realization that freedom requires more than a formal political equality if it is to have its full substance." *History*, p. 56. See also

lican[34] calls for reforms in the ownership and regulation of land and the Leveller demands that political power be redistributed were all grounded in complaints against an oppressive and/or outmoded economic and social structure.[35]

These accounts of what the Revolution was *about* — what was at stake in the mid-seventeenth-century ideological and military struggles — provide ways of understanding the political thought and public debates of the period. What is perhaps most striking about that political thought is how much it differed from that of the sixteenth and earlier seventeenth centuries. But like so much else, these changes had begun earlier and were not so much caused by the Revolution as they were hastened by it.

Although none of the parties seems to have appreciated the gravity of the dispute at the start, the Revolution began as a conflict among rival claims of entitlement to exercise sovereign power. At base, it continued to be a dispute about sovereignty, but the categories were widened to include the relationship of political sovereignty to the "rights," "liberties," and, by extension, "proprieties"[36] of the subjects. The Levellers (and others as well) insisted that subjects had inherent claims to such rights and liberties and that they were not granted by the ruler but actually conditioned the exercise of political power. This was a radical and dangerous doctrine with distinctly democratic portents. As Zagorin observes, "The Levellers at the very birth of political democracy stated its full theoretical implications."[37]

Sabine, "Introduction" to *The Works of Gerrard Winstanley, passim*, and David W. Petegorsky, *Left-Wing Democracy in the English Civil War: A Study of the social Philosophy of Gerrard Winstanley* (London, 1940).

[34] The allusion is to Harrington, whose concept of the "balance," as Zagorin observes, took "economic facts as primary and political facts as secondary." *History*, p. 136. Cf. J. G. A. Pocock, Introduction to *The Political Works of James Harrington*, ed. Pocock (Cambridge, 1977), p. 54. this Introduction is a thorough analysis of Harrington and has superseded all previous work. It should be consulted in conjunction with Pocock's *The Machiavellian Moment: Florentine Political Thought and the Atlantic Republican Tradition* (Princeton, 1975) for a wider account of the context and history of republican political thought both before and after the English Revolution.

[35] C. B. Macpherson, *The Political Theory of Possessive Individualism: Hobbes to Locke* (Oxford, 1962), is the leading work here; chs. 3 and 4 deal with the Levellers and Harrington in these terms. To Macpherson belongs the credit for having legitimated the use of class-based categories of analysis in the study of seventeenth-century English political thought.

[36] "Propriety," of course, was the early term for "property." It was just beginning to appear regularly in English-language politics in the mid-seventeenth century, and its meaning was not at all clear or consistent.

[37] Zagorin, *History*, p. 41. This volume of Leveller tracts and the secondary literature are immense. Zagorin, chs. 2 and 3, provides a good and sympathetic starting point that places Leveller theory and practice in a wider context and discusses the most interesting and important tracts. More recent literature is considered in Austin Woolrych, "Political Theory and Political Practice," in *The Age of Milton: Backgrounds to Seventeenth-Century Literature*, ed. C. A. Patrides and Raymond B. Waddington (Man-

This position terrified even those who had once supported the Levellers and was a contribution to intense and continuing debates about political principles. For the most part, as was appropriate to a preoccupation with these notions, the arguments were conducted in a legalistic or "juridical" framework. This mode of arguing had been supplanting the "humanist" concerns with "virtue" and "counsel" that were characteristic of sixteenth-century England[38] at least since the time of Hooker's *Laws of Ecclesiastical Polity*. Coming from a variety of sources — most notably the common law[39] — it was particularly evident in the parliamentary debates surrounding the Petition of Right in 1628. However, its debut in systematic English-language political thought — at least its most conspicuous and significant early appearance — is probably marked by the publication of Hobbes's *Leviathan* in 1651,[40] one chapter of which, twenty-five was an attack on the courtly discourse of counsel.[41]

Sovereignty is about power and authority as a coherent and *legal* singularity; it is, as Bodin said, "the most high, absolute, and perpetual power ouer the citizens and subjects in a Commonweale, . . . that is to say, The greatest power to commaund." The "principall point of soueraigne maiestie, and absolute power" consists "in giuing laws vnto the subjects in generall, without their consent."[42] The doctrine of sovereignty developed in France in the context of and in response to the problems inherent in "estates" theory. It was a codifica-

---

chester, 1980), pp. 34–70 (and see the "Bibliography of Secondary Sources," pp. 393–427), and in his *Soldiers and Statesmen: The General Council of the Army and Its Debates, 1647–1648* (Oxford, 1987), esp. ch. 1.

[38] For the humanist politics of the early Tudor period, see Alistair Fox and John Guy, *Reassessing the Henrician Age: Humanism, Politics, and Reform, 1500–1550* (Oxford, 1986), and Geoffrey Elton, "Humanism in England," in *The Impact of Humanism on Western Europe*, ed. Anthony Goodman and Angus MacKay (London, 1990), ch. 11. See also, in general, Richard Tuck, "Humanism and Political Thought," *ibid.*, ch. 3.

[39] J. G. A. Pocock, *The Ancient Constitution and the Feudal Law: A Study of English Historical Thought in the Seventeenth Century*, 2nd ed. (Cambridge, 1987), is the work most responsible for establishing this understanding of the transition. See also Brian P. Levack, *The Civil Lawyers in England, 1603–1641: A Political Study* (Oxford, 1973), ch. 4.

[40] Hobbes, of course, had written his earlier *Elements of the Law* (c. 1640) and *De Cive* (1642) in that same idiom, but *Leviathan* is the work by which his contemporaries best knew him. See Richard Tuck, *Natural Rights Theories: Their Origin and Development* (Cambridge, 1979), ch. 6, and the same author's *Hobbes* (Oxford, 1989), pp. 18–25. Cf. Gigliola Rossini, "The Criticism of Rhetorical Historiography and the Ideal of Scientific Method: History, Nature, and Science in the Political Language of Thomas Hobbes," in *Languages of Political Theory*, ed. Pagden, ch. 13.

[41] I am indebted to John Guy for having called the importance of this chapter to my attention.

[42] Jean Bodin, *The Six Bookes of a Commweale*, trans. Richard Knolles (London, 1606), facsimile reprint, ed. with an Introduction by Kenneth D. McRae (Cambridge, Mass., 1962), I, viii, pp. 84 and 98.

tion of historical experiences and emerging practices as well as a prescription for resolving existing conflicts and preventing the rise of others in the future.

In general, it was an innappropriate response to the *facts* of English politics, to which the "estates" had an anomalous relationship at best. Its most able and forceful defenders in the English Revolution were Robert Filmer and Thomas Hobbes, the latter of whom had considerably greater subtlety and theoretical acumen. When the broken-backed doctrine of King-in-Parliament had been exposed for the conceptual fraud that it was, Filmer and Hobbes appreciated that only a doctrine of strong, unified authority take its place and remedy the damage that England's "mixture" had generated.

Charles had acknowledged in his "Answer" to the "Nineteen Propositions" presented to him by the Long Parliament in June, 1642, before the first Civil War had erupted, that the government of England was a "Mixture" of "Absolute Monarchy, Aristocracy, and Democracy." He further acknowledged that the monarchy was one of the three "estates" of the realm — the other two were the lords temporal and the commons[43] — that jointly shared in the government, and insisted that this form of government gave "to this Kingdom (as far as humane Prudence can provide) the Conveniences of all three, without the Inconveniences of any one, as long as the Ballance hangs even between the three Estates."[44] It was on that basis and in order to preserve the "Ballance" that the King refused to grant parliament's demands for what he regarded as legislative supremacy.

That "Ballance" was precarious, as Charles appreciated, and was a dangerous source of political paralysis, as the inability of king and parliament to resolve their differences had already shown. But by claiming to be one of the estates — however important and determinative – and by admitting that the English government was "mixed," Charles (or whoever put the words into his mouth) ensured that the rupture would become ever more serious. Of course, it is hardly likely the theoretically neater and more coherent insistence upon the absolute power of the monarchy would have had different results. The stakes were actual power, not its theoretical elucidation or representation, and, as is usually the case in politics, theory was being used to *serve* and justify practice

[43] On one view, the three estates were the Lords Temporal, the "Lords Spiritual" (that is the bishops), and the Commons, with the King presiding over them all. The doctrine of Charles's "Answer" was not entirely innovative, however, for the claims that England was a "mixed government" and that the monarchy was one of the estates went back at least to the Elizabethan period. However, it seems not to have been the source of constitutional struggle until the 1640s. See Mendle, *Dangerous Positions*, chs. 2 and 3; Zagorin, *History*, pp. 190–196; and Woolrych, "Political Theory and Political Practice," pp. 35–36 and refs.

[44] Charles I, "His Majesty's Answer to the Nineteen Propositions of both Houses of Parliament, Tending Towards a Peace," in John Rushworth, *Historical Collection: The Third Part*, (London, 1721), IV, 725–735, quotations from 731. The text of "The Nineteen Propositions" precedes Charles's "Answer," *ibid.*, 722–724.

not to determine or direct it. The resulting impasse was one of the precipitants of the Civil War that led, eventually, to the assertion of doctrines of strict and undivided sovereignty by Hobbes and Filmer.[45] And it is possible to observe in the debates a growing movement on both sides toward acknowledgment of the indivisibility of sovereign power among the estates.

Some of the problems inherent in all this are well-illustrated by Filmer's attack on Philip Hunton, who, following King Charles, had insisted that it was "a clear and undoubted Truth, that the Authority of this Land is of a compounded and mixed nature in the very roots and constitution thereof."[46] Clearly, Filmer had the better of the theoretical *debate*, but in terms of practice and established institutions, Hunton's "mixture," for all its anomalies, would carry the day. It was the accommodations of 1688–89 and – eventually — John Locke's "constitutionalist" political theory and an implicit *legislative* supremacy that would triumph. Although Filmer accepted Bodin's notion that sovereign power was "indivisible" and could not be shared among the estates, he went further than the theory alone could sustain and insisted that rule had to be in the hands of a monarch. This latter claim he defended with his Biblical, patriarchal account of the unity of fatherhood and kingship as the expression of God's will. Hunton had no such further ground of appeal but was forced back on an attenuated doctrine of resistance and revolution as the only possible resort when the accommodation came unstuck.[47] And it was precisely that recourse and its inevitable and widespread chaos that were anathema to Filmer and Hobbes and to which the doctrine of sovereignty served as a response.

More faithful to the theory itself, Hobbes did not go quite so far as Filmer. He acknowledged the possibility of what Parliament and the Levellers had aimed at in the 1640s and what the Regicide and the abolition of the monarch had established, the sovereignty of the "people," whose *authorized* delegates

[45] "The location of legislative power, Filmer saw, was really the constitutional issue . . . at stake in the revolution." Zagorin, *History*, p. 197. James Daly, *Sir Robert Filmer and English Political Thought* (Toronto, 1979), ch. 2, discusses sovereignty with particular reference to Filmer's theory.

[46] [Philip Hunton], *A Treatise of Monarchy . . . Also a Vindication of the Said Treatise* (originally published in 1643 and 1644), reprinted (London, 1689), p. 32, citing the King's "Answer to the 19 Propositions."

Hunton has not been given the recognition he deserves. He is discussed in Franklin, *John Locke and the Theory of Sovereignty*, pp. 39–49, Charles H. McIlwain, "A Forgotten Worthy: Philip Hunton and the Sovereignty of King in Parliament," in his *Constitutionalism and the Changing World: Collected Essays* (Cambridge, 1939), pp. 196–230, and Allen, *English Political Thought*, pp. 449–455. Excerpts from the *Treatise* are reprinted in *Political Ideas of the English Civil Wars, 1640–1649: A Collection of Representative Texts with a Commentary*, ed. Andrew Sharp (London, 1983), pp. 153–161, and in *Divine Right and Democracy: An Anthology of Political Writing in Stuart England*, ed. David Wooton (Harmondsworth, 1986), pp. 175–211. Schochet, *Authoritarian Family*, pp. 117–118, 124, 137–8, and 146 discusses Filmer's attack.

[47] *Treatise*, pp. 41–46.

15

exercised power for them and in their name (but with the proviso that it could be taken back if it were abused). This was a very complex matter for Hobbes, and not at all the right of an organized revolution that other writers advocated. For him, it was only a right of personal resistance when the fundamental end for which sovereign power had been delegated, the preservation of one's own life, was frustrated or violated. In that case alone, an individual subject could resist. In general, however, Hobbes insisted that once sovereign entitlement had been conveyed, its exercise could not be questioned. To permit any questioning would be to admit a sharing of sovereign power, which was imprudent — for the bloody Civil Wars, only recently concluded when the *Leviathan* was published in 1651, were caused in part precisely by such a dangerous doctrine — as well as theoretically and politically impossible.[48]

The abolition of the monarchy after the Regicide was the final rejection by the residue of the parliamentary interests of the doctrine of mixed government. The Commonwealth that replaced the monarchy created its own practical and theoretical problems, principally, the legitimation of what was clearly a new and conventionally-established regime and persuading its members that they owed it their loyalty. One doctrine served both ends, the so-called *de facto* theory, which extracted political obligation from the efficacy of governmental protection and claimed that the Commonwealth was due the obedience of its subjects "merely because it was the power *de facto*." Perez Zagorin is owed the credit for identifying this important body of principle.[49]

The best-known spokesman for *de facto* obligation was Thomas Hobbes,[50] who ingeniously used the theory to unite the doctrine of sovereign entitlement

---

[48] This is the point of ch. xxix of *Leviathan*, "Of Those Things That Weaken, or Tend to the DISSOLUTION of Commonwealth," which is one of the central chapters of the book.

[49] See Zagorin, *History*, ch. 5. The quotation is form p. 63. In a previous article, I failed to give Zagorin credit for this discovery, and I am delighted now to have the opportunity to correct that egregious oversight.

For subsequent discussion of the *de facto* theory, see, in order of publication, John M. Wallace, "The Engagement Controversy, 1649–1652: An Annotated List of Pamphlets," *Bulletin of the New York Public Library*, LXVIII (1964), 384–405; Quentin Skinner, "History and Ideology in the English Revolution," *Historical Journal*, VIII (1965), 151–178; Wallace, *Destiny His Choice: The Loyalism of Andrew Marvell* (Cambridge, 1968), ch. 1; Philip A. Knachel, Introduction to his edition of Marchamont Nedham, *The Case of the Commonwealth of England, Stated* (Charlottesville, 1968 [originally published London, 1650]); and Margaret A. Judson, *From Tradition to Political Reality: A Study of the Ideas Set Forth in Support of Commonwealth Government in England, 1649–1653* (Hamden, Conn., 1980).

[50] Quentin Skinner, "The Context of Hobbes's Theory of Political Obligation," in *Hobbes and Rousseau*, ed. Maurice Cranston and Richard Peters (Garden City, N.Y., 1972), pp. 108–142, and "Conquest and Consent: Thomas Hobbes and the Engagement Controversy," in *The Interregnum: The Quest for Settlement, 1646–1660*, ed. G. E. Alymer (London, 1972), ch. 2. Cf. Glenn Burgess, "Usurpation, Obligation and Obe-

with consent.[51] This union was necessitated by the Engagement that the Commonwealth attempted to impose on "all men whatsoever . . . of the age of eighteen years and upward," each of whom was ordered to "*declar and promise, that I will be true and faithful to the Commonwealth of England as it is now established, without a king or House of Lords.*"[52] The problem was that people who remained loyal to the heirs of the executed King "scrupled" at the Engagement, but an insistence, as Hobbes put it, upon "the mutuall Relation between Protection and Obedience"[53] would dissolve their reluctance and, in the language of the day, "resolve their consciences." On this basis, even so staunch a royalist as Filmer could accept the Engagement.[54]

The Commonwealth was short-lived. Cromwell replaced it with the Protectorate and assumed the office of Lord Protector,[55] acts that alienated many of his previous supporters. Republicans were denied the victory that had seeemed within their grasp, and their response was overt advocacy.[56] Again, older doctrines were borrowed, refitted, and made applicable to mid-century England.[57] James Harrington's resolution of the problem of sovereignty used Machiavellian and classical republican notions to tie political entitlement to economic power and the possession of land.

In this appropriation of an older mode of discourse, Harrington undoubtedly voiced views and interests peculiar to his own socio-economic location.[58] Politics is always about stakes and interests and the possession and exercise of public power. Whether consciously or not and however much they may be structured in general and theoretical terms, the verbalized doctrines that arise from and/or superintend politics — which we call "political thought" — repre-

dience in the Thought of the Engagement Controversy," *Historical Journal*, XXIX (1986), 515–536.

[51] Gordon J. Schochet, "Intending (Political) Obligation: Hobbes and the Voluntary Basis of Society," in *Thomas Hobbes and Political Theory*, ed. Mary G. Dietz (Lawrence, 1990), ch. 4.

[52] "An Act for Subscribing the Engagement, 2 January 1650," from *The Stuart Constitution: Documents and Commentary*, ed. J. P. Kenyon (Cambridge, 1966), p. 341 (italics in Kenyon's text). The Engagement was not widely subscribed and apparently not strongly enforced (see Kenyon, p. 330) but it was intensely debated.

[53] Hobbes, *Leviathan*, Review and Conclusion, p. 728.

[54] See his *Directions for Obedience to Government in Dangerous and Doubtful Times* (1652), in his *Political Works*, p. 234.

[55] See Austin Woolrych, *From Commonwealth to Protectorate* (Oxford, 1982). Woolrych's opening sentence could serve as an epigraph for any work on the Revolution: "The History of the Great Rebellion in England is the story of unforeseen consequences" (p. 1).

[56] Zagorin, *History*, p. 88. See also p. 149.

[57] Pocock, *Machiavellian Moment*, Parts I and II.

[58] The significance of his having rested the weight of political power on the distribution of landed wealth is central in precisely this respect and is the point of departure for Macpherson. See *Possessive Individualism*, ch. 4.

sent these interests. Part of Harrington's intention was to recast and control the defining vocabulary in which the English state was portrayed. No less than the absolutism of Hobbes and Filmer, his republicanism was an aspect (or reflection) of the ideological structure that helps to maintain the distribution of power and the rule of an elite in any society. It was equally a sign of the political struggles and ideological conflicts that continued to characterize England.

What of the lower orders of society, the socially deprived and the politically excluded? After the end of the Commonwealth, we find little expression of their interests in literature of political thought, although they certainly continued to exist. In the 1640s and early 1650s, there had been an increasingly "radical" strain of political theorizing that seemed to understand and sympathize with the needs of "ordinary" people. That radicalism was ultimately frustrated. Since they rarely spoke for themselves, the lower orders seem eventually to have lost their voice. This apparent silence is to be expected, for, on the whole, people near the bottom of society lack the overt self-consciousness that lends itself to literary expression and do not have access to the means of disseminating their views and concerns. The absence of consciousness and voice are a substantial part of what is meant by the "lower social orders" and constitute the principle instruments by which relative deprivations are perpetuated.

What we do know about these people comes largely from such episodes as occasional "seeker," "Ranter," "Fifth Monarchy" (and other millenarian) outbursts, and Baptist and Quaker complaints about the Cromwellian establishment,[59] for, although they may have lost their voice, they did not lose their place. In other words, we know of these people largely as religious *sectarians* rather than, as was the case with Winstanley and his "digger" followers and their Leveller predecessors, as people who protested against conditions that were more conventionally social and political. In this respect, it is well to keep in mind that religion and politics were not so distinct in seventeenth-century England. At the same time, however, the limited religious "toleration" that the Protectorate established (including the readmission of Jews to England)[60] had the effect of making the separation more operational.

[59] See, in general, Michael Watts, *The Dissenters: From the Reformation to the French Revolution* (Oxford, 1978), I, ch. 2. More specifically, see P. G. Rogers, *The Fifth Monarchy Men* (London, 1966), A. L. Morton, *The World of the Ranters: Religious Radicalism in the English Revolution* (London, 1970), Lamont, *Godly Rule*, and, of course, Hill, *World Turned Upside Down*.

[60] The monumental work of W. K. Jordan remains as the standard reference. See *The Development of Religious Toleration in England*, 4 vols. (Cambridge, 1932–1940), Vol. IV of which is entitled "Attainment of the Theory and Accommodations in Thought and Institutions (1640–1660." However, "toleration" does not correctly describe the situation. Quakers, for instance, were badly abused; see Watts, *The Dissenters*,

There remains, then, a continuing undercurrent of deprivation and exclusion that is only implicitly a part of the theory of sovereignty. The third estate was never intended to include the genuinely common people, and Colonel Thomas Rainborough's declamations at Putney on behalf of the interests of "the poorest he that is in England"[61] went unheeded. Nonetheless, the concerns of these relatively inarticulate — although certainly not silent — lower orders must ultimately be assessed from the perspective of the Revolution's political thought; their place in the structural scheme that generated the Revolution and its ideology must be determined before any account of the political thought of mid-century England can be considered complete.[62]

In the short run, the Revolution did little to improve the status of the members of the lower orders. In 1660, Charles II was restored to the throne of his father, and the Anglican Church was reestablished. By 1662, sectarian religion was effectively outlawed; on the surface, things looked very much as they had before the Revolution. The objective of a government rooted in the sovereignty of the people had long since been frustrated, overcome by Cromwell himself and by the very theory from which it had emerged. Although they had not been intended to comprehend everyone, ideologies that were radically democratic by the standards of mid-seventeenth-century England had lived brief lives in the closing days of the Civil War and during the Commonwealth. But they were derailed long before Charles, the House of Lords, and the Anglican Church were restored.

Ultimately, that democratic impulse — which seems in so many respects to be a product of the exclusion, deprivation, and oppression it opposes — would fly in the face of and overcome the theory of sovereignty. When they appear in

pp. 209–212, for a discussion of James Nayler, who suffered more than most. On the treatment of Jews, see David Katz, *Philo-Semitism and the Readmission of the Jews to England, 1603–1655* (Oxford, 1982), ch. 5.

For the beginnings of a corrective to Jordan's relatively whiggish and somewhat uncritical appraisal of the Protectorate, see Balir Worden, "Toleration and the Cromwellian Protectorate," *Studies in Church History,* XXI: *Persecution and Toleration,* ed. W. J. Sheils, Ecclesiastical History Society Publications (1984), pp. 199–233.

[61] *Puritanism and Liberty: Being the Army Debates (1647–9),* ed. A. S. P. Woodhouse (London, 1938), p. 53.

[62] For one identifiable group, women, the necessary research is proceeding. Kieth Thomas, "Women in the Civil War sects," *Past and Present,* 13 (April, 1958), 42–62, is a pioneering work that remains central. To it should be added, among others, Hilda Smith, *Reason's Disciples: Seventeenth-Century English Feminists* (Urbana, 1982), esp. chs. 1–3, and Margaret J. M. Ezell, *The Patriarch's Wife: Literary Evidence and the History of the Family* (Chapel Hill, 1987).

It is important to note, however, that the women about whom we are learning, by and large, were not members of the lower orders but had access to the tools of literary and social expression. This is not to deny that women were excluded from politics – quite the contrary – but to suggest that class- and gender-based exclusion must be differentiated.

opposition to absolutist pretensions, as they did in the 1640s and would again in 1688–89 and 1776, democratic conceptions of rights and liberty are concerned with the *limits* of legitimate political action; sovereignty, by contrast, is concerned with its *extent*. Eventually, the theoretically incoherent doctrine of democratic constitutionalism would triunph over the more consistent principle of sovereignty, but that would not be until the English Revolution had long been over.[63]

What then is the immediate legacy of the English Revolution? In some senses, of course, it failed in all its myriad and contradictory objectives and left England with nothing more than a negative standard that would be hurled against champions of liberty well into the next century.

Structurally, its bequest to the future was religious sectarianism.[64] The English Presbyterians, who were virtually reborn with the meeting of the Long Parliament and who had held power in the Church in the 1640s and 1650s, were forced back into a submissive role in 1660. They and their Independent cohorts — for whom they actually had as little regard as did the Anglican Establishment — were given the choice of quietly (re)entering the restored Church or facing penalties for practicing their own religions. The Independents objected, wanting only to be "tolerated" and, with the Quakers, insisted upon their "rights" of conscience. The Presbyterians desperately wanted reunion with the Anglicans, but the price of conformity was higher than they would pay, and so they endured the Penal Statutes while working for comprehension throughout the Restoration and the reign of James II. In the end, the official persecution of the Clarendon Code gave way to the Parliamentary indulgence of the 1689 Act of Toleration, which had the effect of legally establishing religious diversity, eventually forcing the English-speaking world to grant the religious liberty that is fundamental to modern democracy.

This is the true legacy of the English Revolution.

---

[63] See Gordon J. Schochet, "Constitutionalism, Liberalism, and the Study of Politics," NOMOS XX: *Constitutionalism*, ed. J. Roland Pennock and John Chapman (New York, 1979), pp. 1–15. Zagorin remarks, "The programme the Levellers announced for their own day took more than two hundred and fifty years to achieve. . . . the beliefs they voiced did not die, and rose from the ashes into which the hopes of revolutionary England were consumed. Long afterwards, they were taken up by new forces, by the Chartists and the trade unions, to become the battle-cry of new struggles." *History*, p. 42.

[64] This discussion is based on two essays on the problems of religious persecution and toleration in the period 1660–1690: Gordon J. Schochet, "From Persecution to 'Toleration,' " in *Liberty Secured? British Liberty before and after 1688*, ed. J. R. Jones, The Making of Modern Liberty, Volume II (Stanford, 1992), and "The Act of Toleration and the Failure of Comprehension: Persecution, Non-Conformity, and Religious Indifference," in *The World of William and Mary*, ed. Dale Hoak and Mordechi Feingold (Berkeley, forthcoming).

Causes, Individuals and Ideas in Christopher Hill's Interpretation of the English Revolution

WILLIAM H. DRAY

I

Few controversies in English history have generated as rich and extensive a literature as the controversy over the nature, causes, and consequences of those events in the middle decades of the seventeenth century now commonly referred to as the English Revolution. Few of those presently involved in this controversy would hesitate to accord a very special place in it to the writings of Christopher Hill. Hill's erudition is legendary. His research has uncovered for the first time a whole stratum of radical thought and action in early Stuart England lying below the level of what was traditionally seen as the political nation. He has repeatedly emphasized the interconnectedness of things, ranging boldly across the frontiers separating political, economic, social, religious and intellectual aspects of the past. He has offered distinctive overall interpretations that contrast especially with the Whig approach which held the field when he began to write. At the same time, he has played a considerable part in training the next generation of English historians, most of whom, however, while acknowledging his influence, have gone on to reject his most treasured theses.

What has been rejected is often connected with his Marxism. The English Revolution, unlike the French, and despite the fact that both Marx and Engels produced interpretations of it, has attracted only a few native Marxist interpreters. Of these, Hill is without doubt the most celebrated. His interest in the period began in the thirties, when he translated analyses of it by Soviet historians. In 1940 on the three hundredth anniversary of the calling of the Long Parliament, he published a survey of the years 1640–1660 under the title *The English Revolution* which many have considered the classic statement of an extreme Marxist view.[1] In it a rising bourgeoisie, spearheaded by its repre-

---

[1] Christopher Hill, *The English Revolution*, 3rd edn. (London: Lawrence & Wishart, 1955).

sentatives in Parliament, is pictured as smashing the feudal fetters held in place by a reactionary Stuart monarchy and Laudian Church, and setting England on the road to full-fledged capitalist development. Given the overall Marxist vision of history, this makes the upheaval of the mid-seventeenth century one of the most important events in modern European history. Since 1940, Hill's Marxism has grown more subtle and flexible. His highly-praised monograph, *Economic Problems of the Church*, which appeared in 1956, and which examined for the first time in depth what was happening to the Church of England as an economic, social and political institution in the hundred years before 1640, was welcomed even by some of his strongest critics as revealing the dogmatic theoretician making way for the meticulous scholar.[2] Later works on Puritanism and other aspects of early seventeenth century English life have also been described as containing little more than "wisps and fumes of dogma."[3] Yet Hill has never admitted to having given up the fundamental framework of ideas which he brought to his study of seventeenth century history in the first place. He has always insisted that, in his later work, he has simply been filling in this framework.

In the present paper, my prime concern will not be with Hill's Marxism as such, but rather with the theory of historical causation that is either stated or implied in his writings on the English Revolution. I can hardly ignore, the Marxist ambience, however, and I should not want to, since it contributes a special dimension of interest. For one thing, although the idea that historians apply theory in their work is hardly one that enjoys great popularity in the historical profession at large, it would be strange to find a Marxist historian repudiating it; and Hill does so neither in theory nor in practice. The aspects of his theory of historical causation on which I want to concentrate concern two sorts of claims that any theory of causation can be expected to make. Any such theory will, first, formulate some idea of what the causal relation consists in, what counts as being historically caused. And it will, second, express some conception of how causal processes in history go, some notion of what generally causes what. What I propose to do is to isolate and examine a little two things that Hill's writings seem to me to convey with respect to each of these issues. With regard to his idea of a historical cause, I shall look at the close connection he affirms between causal analysis and explanation, and at his denial that there is any necessary connection between the ideas of historical causation and of human intention. With regard to his general theory of the causal process, I shall consider some things he says or implies, first about the role played in historical change by individual human agents, and then about

[2] Christopher Hill, *Economic Problems of the Church* (Oxford: Clarendon Press, 1956).

[3] Review of *Economic Problems of the Church* by A. Simpson, *Journal of Modern History* 29 (1957), 262.

the role played by ideas. All four of these issues are important for determining the nature and extent of a historian's Marxism. But they are important also for determining the theoretical stance of any historian whatever.

Just one further preliminary word about how I view my own involvement in all this. I am, by profession, a philosopher, not a historian; and my interest in what I find Hill saying is, in the first instance at any rate, that of a philosopher. I am therefore not primarily interested in appraising Hill's historical work as such, or even *primarily* interested in finding out how, in general, the English Revolution should be interpreted, although I confess to a secondary and entirely amateur fascination with that question. My first concern is with historical thinking as a genre, as an instance of inquiry, with a view, ultimately, to locating it on the map of knowledge. Philosophers, of course, have had that kind of interest in history for a long time — at least since the time of Hume and Vico — but it is only quite recently that they have paid much attention, while pursuing it, to the ways in which historians actually argue. For this "a priorism" they have been roundly and properly criticized by hard-nosed practitioners of the historian's art like Geoffrey Elton and J. H. Hexter, and the approach taken in this paper may be regarded as exemplifying the way at least some philosophers of history are currently trying to respond positively to such criticism. Not that, in consequence, they are likely to renounce their claim to judge, as well as to characterize, what they find historians doing whenever they think themselves in a position to do so. And they will, of course, continue to ask their own questions – although these seem often enough to be of interest to historians as well, and are, indeed, sometimes independently raised by them. How causation should be thought about in history is a prime example of this range of questions; and what follows is offered as an attempt to sink a philosophical probe into an ongoing historical controversy with a view to deriving some ideas for profitably discussing it. There is a special appropriateness, it seems to me, in undertaking such a task in a paper which appears in a volume intended to honour Perez Zagorin, for no historian of the early modern period has shown greater understanding and appreciation of the mutual relevance of historical and philosophical reasoning.

II

To turn, then, to the first of the four aspects of Hill's idea of historical causation that I want to consider, namely, his implied conception of what counts as a historical cause: there seems to be little doubt that he sees a close conceptual connection between the ideas of causation and of explanation. It often appears to be his view, indeed, that to offer explanation in history *is* to point to causal connections: that is what explanation *means*. It is causal analysis, for example, that he contrasts with mere narration when he complains that Veronica Wedgwood's popular accounts of peace and war under Charles I tell us only *what* happened, not *why* it did — this despite the assumption one might normally make that telling a story is one way of explaining things, and that in history it is often the most natural, and even sometimes an indispensable way of doing it.[4] In fact, neither in his practice nor in his theoretical asides does Hill himself succeed in maintaining an absolute distinction between causal analysis as explanatory and narrative as not. Indeed, he sometimes so far forgets his principle of separation as to claim it as one of the virtues of his Marxist approach that, more than any other, it provides us with "a coherent story which makes sense."[5] In his *Century of Revolution*, he tries to highlight the opposition between non-explanatory narrative and explanatory causal analysis by assigning them to separate chapters, the narratives intended as mere introductions to the analyses.[6] But the narrative accounts are so terse and so elementary that, if they fail to explain, it seems more reasonable to attribute this to their defectiveness as narratives than to their being narratives at all.

In considering Hill's apparent contention that the only way we can "make sense" of the past is by causal explanation, it is of interest to note, too, that not all the non-narrative explanations he offers himself are obviously causal in nature. In *God's Englishman*, for example, he tells us, surely with explanatory intent, that what "made possible the wide-reaching Presbyterian-royalist plot" of 1651 was a "spirit of disillusion among the radicals."[7] And in *The Century of Revolution* he observes at one point that it was "the division between court and country" that "made possible the Civil War."[8] To explain something by indicating what made it possible is, of course, a perfectly respectable and quite common historical practice. But it is not offering a causal explanation of it; it is not showing what brought it about. Thus the criterion of intelligibility in history which is actually applied by Hill in practice is not simply that of things being causally connected. As any historian should do, he recognizes more than one kind of relationship as explanatory.[9] Not that every time he invokes the notion of mere possibility in a context where explanation is being sought he is offering what might be called a "possibility" explanation. What he actually provides is often no more than a "possible" explanation — sometimes, indeed, a possible *causal* explanation. For his writings are strewn with expressions like

---

[4] Reviews of *The King's Peace*, History 41 (1956), 230, and of *The King's War*, *Spectator* 6807 (December 12, 1958), 870.

[5] Christopher Hill, "Historians on the Rise of British Capitalism," *Science and Society*, 14 (1950), 310.

[6] Christopher Hill, *The Century of Revolution* (London: Sphere Books, 1978).

[7] Christopher Hill, *God's Englishman* (Harmondsworth: Penguin Books, 1972), 123.

[8] *Op. cit.*, 69.

[9] For further consideration of this point see W. H. Dray, *On History and Philosophers of History* (Leiden: Brill, 1989), ch. 6.

"might well have been" and "probablly was," expressions that signalize, not a looseness of connection in the historical reality the historian is studying, but a tentativeness in the inference he is willing to draw about it. But although Hill does frequently employ the notion of possibility merely to soften the claims he wishes to make about the connectedness of things, he also sometimes uses it to give *content* to such claims. It might be added that his failure to recognize in theory the explanatory value of less-than-causal relationships makes it easier than it should be for him to charge narrative historians with failing in their duty to explain. For it is often the progressive revelation of a network of just such relationships that cumulatively renders the subject matter of a narrative understandable.

But the fact that, even in Hill's own writings, more than one kind of relationship is commonly regarded as explanatory is not the only thing that makes it difficult to determine precisely what he considers an historical cause to be like. For besides often assering only "possible" connections, he frequently makes it difficult to see whether it is specifically causal connections that he has especially in mind by making explicit reference only to "links," or "ties," or "associations" between the things he considers. In his *Intellectual Origins of the English Revolution*, for example, he suggests "very tentatively" that there is a "link" between the kinds of interest displayed in science and the degree of a person's political and religious radicalism, physics being more popular with Presbyterians, and chemistry with Independents.[10] But he does not say just what the "link" consists in; and in any case, by asserting it only "tentatively," thus double-hedging his thesis, he further obscures what is being claimed. In his *Century of Revolution*, with similar lack of interpretive guidance, he asserts that Puritan respect for paternal authority "corresponded" to the economic necessities of the average home.[11] Hill's vagueness about the precise nature of the connection that interests him sometimes extends even to the implied direction of the causal arrow. Most historians, he observes, now accept the thesis that there was some "connexion" between Puritanism and the proto-capitalist activities and attitudes of early Stuart merchants and certain "for-ward-looking" gentry, although it may not be clear, he adds, "which was cause and which effect."[12] In general, it could be said that, although Hill generally provides his readers with a wealth of data about similarities, spatio-temporal coincidences, social opportunities, and the like, he rather too often leaves them to work out the connection for themselves.

If the idea of explanation as Hill deploys it throws little light in the end on his idea of cause and effect in history, do any other notions appear in his

[10] Christopher Hill, *Intellectual Origins of the English Revolution* (Oxford: Oxford University Press, 1980 [c. 1965]), 119, 139.

[11] *Op. cit.*, 32.

[12] Christopher Hill, "Recent Interpretations of the Civil War," *History* 41 (1956), 68.

writings that are more promising in this regard? Three may be worth noting, especially since they have all, at times, been used by others in attempts to analyze both explanation and causal connection. These are the ideas of dialectic, of law, and of necessary and sufficient condition.[13] I will offer a brief comment on his use of each of these in turn.

Dialectic is, of course, an idea that one would expect to find in the thought of a Marxist writer, and Hill does from time to time make reference to a dialectical aspect of what he is examining, as if that rendered it somehow more intelligible. There is a "complex dialectic," he declares, in the tragic failure of Puritanism eventually to attain its goal.[14] But is this really anything more than a reminder that, to a considerable extent, Puritans brought their fate upon themselves? "By a natural dialectic," he observes in his *Century of Revolution*, "those who were most convinced that they were fighting God's battles proved the most effective fighters."[15] But is not this simply an acknowledgement of the undoubted fact that people are sometimes motivated by incoherent or even contradictory ideas? On occasion, Hill's references to dialectic seem to suggest that *the historian himself* should find a special intelligibility in what is literally contradictory, as when he implies that the Digger leader, Gerrard Winstanley, since he was a dialectical thinker, had no need to choose between belief in an immanent and a transcendent God.[16] One wonders whether it is with the idea of dialectic in mind that Hill sometimes refers to things as both causes and effects of each other — another idea that is incoherent, taken *au pied de la lettre*. For example, in his *Reformation to Industrial Revolution*, he tells us that the growing importance of the gentry in local government was "both effect and cause" of their growing importance in the House of Commons.[17] But if one can understand such a mysterious reciprocal relationship at all, one must surely understand it simply as a sum of non-mysterious and non-reciprocal causal relationships, in which different terms assume the role of cause at different times. This, however, would invoke the notion of causation to help make sense of the notion of dialectic, not the other way around.

The second idea, that of law, is a standby of conventional analyses of causal connection offered by positivist philosophers and social theorists, although one finds it also in the writings of Marxist theoreticians like Plekhanov.[18] Accord-

---

[13] For further readings on these ideas see H. Ritter, *Dictionary of Concepts in History* (New York: Greenwood, 1986), 75–79, 112–119, 146–151.

[14] Review of *Liberty and Reformation in the Puritan Revolution* by W. Haller, *English Historical Review* 71 (1956), 287.

[15] *Op. cit.*, 150.

[16] Christopher Hill, "A Rejoinder," *Past and Present* 89 (1980), 151.

[17] Christopher Hill, *Reformation to Industrial Revolution* (Harmondsworth: Penguin Books, 1969), 51.

[18] See for example, *The Role of the Individual in History*, reprinted in P. L. Gardiner (ed.), *Theories of History* (New York: Free Press, 1959) 157.

ing to such analyses, a cause is a condition which is followed by another, called its effect, in accordance with laws which render the effect predictable in principle. But although Hill from time to time states generalizations, I have not found him urging them in defence of causal judgments. Nor does he anywhere explicitly consider the possibility of there being a *logical* connection between the ideas of cause and law. In any case, some of the remarks he makes about the causes he identifies are not easy to reconcile with any straightforwardly nomological analysis of the concept. For example, he maintains that the economic crisis of the seventeenth century had quite different political results on the continent and in England. Only in England did it lead to a degree of commercial and industrial freedom; on the continent it actually produced a hardening of the old regime.[19] The implication is that, since the same cause may on different occasions have a different effect, the effect could not, in a particular case, have been predicted from what is called its cause. If prediction is possible at all, therefore, it will require knowledge of much more than a law (or laws) linking cause to effect.

Since that implies that the cause itself was, at most, a necessary, and not a sufficient condition of its effect, we are brought to consider the third of the ideas I mentioned: that of necessary and sufficient condition. This also, of course, is a staple of contemporary positivist (if not always of Marxist) thinking about causation. And, like some other historians of the period, Hill does sometimes seem to make use of the idea. For example, he warns us that neither economic nor political factors are ever in themselves sufficient causes of historical results.[20] That suggests a recognition on his part of two fundamentally different kinds of historical causes, one sufficient, the other no more than necessary for the effect. Elsewhere, however, he completely refuses to assimilate the notion of cause to that of a merely necessary condition. Geographical factors, he notes, are often conditions "without which" certain things of interest to historians do not occur, but they never, he claims, actually cause historical events.[21] The implication seems to be that necessary conditions must meet some further demand before attaining the status of causes; but we are given no hint of what this might be.[22] As for the idea of sufficient cause, if Hill thinks this viable, he at any rate gives no examples of its application. And, in fact, although conceptually clear, the idea seems to be of questionable use in history: historians simply do not ordinarily discover — or seek to discover – sufficient conditions. The conclusion we are left with is that none of the three notions considered help very much to explicate Hill's concept of causation.

[19] *Reformation to Industrial Revolution*, 14.
[20] Ibid.
[21] Ibid., 82.
[22] On such a further demand see H. L. A. Hart and A. M. Honoré, *Causation in the Law* (Oxford: Clarendon Press, 1959), chs. 1–5, or W. H. Dray, *Perspectives on History* (London: Routledge and Kegan Paul, 1980), ch. 4.

III

The difficulty of discovering in Hill's writings any clear *positive* criterion of what counts as a cause in history makes it the more interesting to find him advancing at any rate one very clear *negative* claim about the nature of the concept, a claim which is of importance not only for this particular controversy but for the theory of history generally. This is that, although, when confronted by a certain result, we sometimes quite properly find its causes in the deliberate contrivances of human agents who intended it, a successful search for causes in history does not depend on discovering such contrivances or intentions. We might say that Hill rejects, and very explicitly, a conspiratorial view of historical causation. And he believes he has a special reason to underline this rejection, given the nature of some of the recent controversy over the causes of the English Revolution. For one of the things he most objects to in the position taken by the latest wave of its re-interpreters, the so-called "revisionists," is the apparent claim that, with regard to the early phases of the Revolution at least, what occurred was "accidental": something that those caught up in it simply blundered into through a set of unfortunate mischances and confusions, hence something for which we are unlikely to find much in the way of causal explanation in the years that preceded it.[23] Revisionists generally emphasize such facts as that, when the Long Parliament met in 1640, and perhaps until just a few weeks before hostilities began in the summer of 1642, no one intended or even envisaged the possibility of such a denouement. The explanation of what happened, they insist, must therefore be found, not in such things as increasingly bitter class struggles, as contended by the Marxists, or even in the long-standing constitutional conflict more traditionally cited by the Whigs, but in the almost day-to-day actions and experiences of those who allowed themselves to slide towards an entirely avoidable catastrophe.

Hill's response to this is, in effect, to insist that there is no necessary connection between "being caused" and "being intended or anticipated" as historians employ these terms. We often speak of causal connections, he reminds us, where human intentions are not part of the subject matter at all — for example, with regard to the ordinary processes of nature. And even in human affairs, we do not equate happening accidentally with being uncaused: indeed, the very notion of an "accident" immediately conjures up images of causal inquiries into quite unintended disasters on the road or in the air in which relevant human actions, and sometimes even inactions, are quite comfortably

[23] Review of R. L. Greaves & R. Zaller (eds), *Biographical Dictionary of British Radicals in the Seventeenth Century*, *Times Literary Supplement* 4272 (February 15, 1985) 182. "Parliament and People in Seventeenth-Century England," *Past and Present* 92 (1981), 118–119, 124.

considered causes.[24] And Hill is surely right to underline this point, common-place as it is, in support of his negative thesis. Sometimes his way of putting it calls to mind another disagreement he has has with the revisionists, this time about whether what happened in England between 1640 and 1660 can be correctly referred to as a "revolution." Hill agrees with those who have argued that early seventeenth century Englishmen did not even possess the *idea* of revolution in the sense in which we now use the term.[25] The *word* existed, but, as applied to social affairs, it retained its astronomical sense of motion in a circle, therefore indicating a course of events returning to a starting point rather than a drastic and relatively permanent change of direction. The Eng-lish, in the reign of Charles I, could this hardly have *set out* to have a revol-ution as we understand it. That, however, does not mean that they could not have suffered one just the same, Hill maintains. To put it in general terms, the way the world is, even in its social aspects, does not depend on whether it is known to be that way. There may have been a revolution in our sense of the word in England in the middle decades of the seventeenth century whether or not the participants thought of what they were doing and experiencing as such. Similarly, that cluster of events referred to retrospectively as the English Revol-ution could have had the most extensive and long-standing causal origins while descending upon early Stuart consciousness like a bolt from the blue.

What Hill unfortunately does not do is tell us just what retrospectively *justifies* our regarding as causes of things like the English Revolution certain antecedent events, including actions of people who did not intend the result: he does not tell us what the *criteria* for such causal identification are. But he hardly shows full awareness either of just how strong an influence the inten-tional model of causation can have upon the way we commonly think about human affairs. Indeed, he sometimes reasons himself in ways that seem to betray this influence at work. For example, in support of his refusal to follow S. R. Gardiner in characterizing what happened in the middle decades of the century as a "Puritan" Revolution, he more than once cites Cromwell's decla-ration that "religion was not the thing at the first contested for" — as if that, assuming Cromwell to have been right, would rule out religious concerns as causes of the Civil War.[26] And he takes pains to affirm that those who were directly involved in the upheaval, notably the bourgeoisie, were almost cer-tainly a good deal less confused about what they were doing than some non-Marxist historians have been willing to grant — as if it were important for his

[24] Christopher Hill, "Forum," *History Today* 33 (March, 1983), 3; review of Conrad Russell (ed.), *The Origins of the English Civil War*, *History* 59 (1974), 470.

[25] Christopher Hill, "The Word 'Revolution' in Seventeenth-Century England," in R. Ollard & P. Tudor-Craig (eds), *For Veronica Wedgwood* (London: Collins, 1986), 148–149. See also his *Reformation to Industrial Revolution*, 191.

[26] See, for example, Christopher Hill, *Oliver Cromwell: 1658–1958* (London: His-torical Association Pamphlet 38, 1958), 28.

own position that he show at least some revolutionary proclivities on their part.[27] In both cases, Hill in effect concedes precisely the sort of conceptual connection between the ideas of intending and causing that he criticized the revisionists for accepting. Much the same can be said for a response he made to an observation by Joyce Malcolm that, whereas to the Parliamentarians the Civil War was "a religious as well as a political war," to the royalists it was "essentially a political and socio-economic conflict." This, Hill observes, "clears up some of the confusion caused by an either/or attitude towards the causes of the war"; there is no need to "assume that both sides had the same motivation."[28] But such a remark would be pointless unless a one-one relationship was thought to hold between the motives of the participants and the causes of what happened.

The precise issue separating Hill and the revisionists is in any case obscured by a degree of exaggeration that often enters into his characterization of the position he is attacking. More than once he represents his opponents as arguing that, since hostilities broke out without anyone intending it rather than in consequence of some deliberate revolutionary plan, what occurred had *no causes at all* — a view which he castigates as taking the "meaning" out of history, and which seems to him so odd that he looks for a sociological explanation of its allegedly being held, finding it in the political and social malaise of post-imperial Britain.[29] For the modern British bourgeoisie at any rate, he observes, the meaning really *has* gone out of history. But the revisionist position is not that the Revolution lacked causes; it is that its causes were short-term: abnormal events like Charles' ill-considered quarrel with the Scots, or the outbreak of rebellion in Ireland at a moment when an adequate response required an impossibly rapid resolution of a constitutional deadlock. Since Hill has so little to say about what justifies our regarding something as a cause at all, it is scarcely surprising that he does not tell us either on what principle one ought to decide *how far back* to go in looking for the causes of a given result. What does seem evident is that he is as committed as revisionists are to denying that historical causes go back indefinitely. At times, it seems to be his own view that the causes of the English Revolution go back to the dissolution of the monasteries and the consequent beginning of the rise of the gentry, the class which was to play such a large part in it. At other times, he seems inclined to find the point of causal origin as far back as the Norman Conquest — as when he argues that the idea of a "Norman Yoke" borne by the English lower orders not only had currency in early Stuart England, but actually has some

[27] See, for example, "Historians on the Rise of British Capitalism," 317.

[28] Christopher Hill, *The Collected Essays of Christopher Hill*, vol. 2, (Amherst: University of Massachusetts Press, 1986), 57.

[29] Christopher Hill, "Puritanism, Capitalism and the Scientific Revolution," *Past and Present* 29 (1964), 96–97.

historical justification. Either way, his difference with the revisionists is not about *whether* there were causes but only about *when* there were.

Hill exaggerates in still another potentially misleading way when he urges, still ostensibly against the revisionists, that the "acceptable conclusion that the English Revolution was made by events, not by the conscious wills of men, is no reason for refusing to try to analyze its causes."[30] Once again, no problem arises if all this means is that the causes of the Revolution do not have to be conspiracies to bring it about. What is problematic is the possible implication that causally efficacious "events" in history not only need not involve conspiracy, but need not involve "the conscious wills of men" at all. Of course, almost all do, either by virtue of their nature, as when continental wars cause parliamentary votes of extraordinary supply, or because of the way they bring about their effects, as when a great fire causes the rebuilding of a city. The wills of those involved in the explanatory "event" may be seen as essential to its explanatory force even if, none being the intention to bring about the result, we may for certain purposes speak of "blind forces" operating. In fact, when Hill gets down to the details of explaining anything, he is generally guided by this principle as fully as any "bourgeois" historian. His detailed exploration of the network of explanatory motives, beliefs and intentions of his actors is indeed one of the things that makes his historical writing so fascinating. Thus, although the idea of a historical cause cannot be *equated* with that of a human intention to bring about a designated result, it is difficult to separate it from the idea of human intention altogether. In this connection, Hill's practice, if not his theory, accords well enough even with the views of so-called "idealist" philosophers of history like R. G. Collingwood, who boldly identify historical causes, albeit piecemeal, with the reasons for which the relevant agents did what they did.

IV

Let me turn now from commenting on Hill's view of the *concept* of causation as he thinks it should function in historical inquiry to look at the first of the two aspects of his causal theory of the historical *process* that I mentioned earlier: the role he assigns to individual historical agents in it. My concern, I should perhaps underline, will not be whether he is (to use the current jargon) a methodological individualist rather than a holist: that is, I shall not be asking whether he would agree that, in the last analysis, group phenomena in history are just individual human beings, mainly anonymous ones, acting and reac-

[30] Christopher Hill, "Parliament and People in Seventeenth-Century England," 124.

ting.[31] What I want to do is clarify the causal role he is willing to ascribe to particular and often named individuals. I shall thus not be much concerned, either, with the interest he shows in individuals where they are not represented as causes. Hill's work is, in fact, replete with information about individuals; he is quite obsessed with individuals. In his *Change and Continuity in 17th Century England*, for example, we get a whole chapter on an obscure Welshman named Arise Evans, in whom Hill obviously takes great delight.[32] What he wants us to notice about Evans, however, seems to be less his causal powers than his causal impotence. He is seen as worth studying not because of what he himself accomplished but because of what his adventures show about other things — for example, the extent of religious toleration under Cromwell. Hill underlines the fact that even an obvious heretic like Evans might hope for a kindly hearing from his betters provided he was not seen as a political menace — as was not the case, for example, with James Naylor, the Quaker Leader, whose fate was brutally otherwise, Much of Hill's concern with named individuals, in other words, is in the service of that traditional, if always somewhat risky, historical technique of pointing to individuals in order to *exemplify* or give *evidence* of social conditions, trends or structures.

My own concern however, is with Hill's view of individual historical agents as causes. And one might naturally begin by thinking that a Marxist historian, like any student of the past who brings to it an overall causal theory formulated entirely in terms of social structures and conditions, would have some trouble finding any very important causal role for particular individuals. Hill nevertheless often ascribes to named individuals quite a crucial role. Archbishop Bancroft, for example, is said to have missed a chance to reverse the trend towards revolution by failing to resolve the conflict between ecclesiastical and common law courts; the Duke of Buckingham is said to have widened the potentially revolutionary split between court and country by the way he exercised his monopoly of patronage; and Laud's attempt to "put back the clock" in both Church and State is seen by Hill as quite as important causally as it generally is in non-Marxist writings.[33] Nor has Hill any doubt that the unfortunate character of Charles I was at least *one* of the causes of the downfall of his regime.[34] The most significant case, however, is doubtless his treatment of Oliver Cromwell, who, both in *God's Englishman* and in the earlier pamphlet Hill wrote about him,[35] is presented as a highly idiosyncratic individual, in many ways in

---

[31] For further readings on methodological individualism see J. O'Neill (ed.), *Modes of Individualism and Collectivism* (London: Heinemann, 1973).

[32] Christopher Hill, *Change and Continuity in 17th Century England* (London: Weidenfeld & Nicolson, 1974), ch. 2.

[33] *Economic Problems of the Church* 344; *Century of Revolution*, 69.

[34] *Century of Revolution*, 71.

[35] *Oliver Cromwell: 1658–1958.*

advance of his time, and quite indispensable for the course events took, both on the battlefield and in the political arena.

It should perhaps be emphasized that the issue is not whether, in his treatment of Cromwell, Hill accepts the Great Man theory of history, as at least one of his critics has insisted he very nearly does.[36] He does indeed appear to regard Cromwell as a great man — this despite his behaviour in Ireland, which Hill tries to understand without condoning, and what he considers his eventual betrayal of the Revolution.[37] But the fact that Charles is not seen in a similarly heroic light does not affect the causal role Hill ascribes to him. And no more than the virtue of the agent is the issue the degree of his control over events. Charles manifestly lacked such control. And although Cromwell was more successful, Hill, in presenting him as causally potent, no more denies that he acted within the limits of the possible than would any historian in his right mind. What is in question is indispensability, and judged by this criterion Charles and Cromwell were equally causes. We can still ask, however, how close Hill gets to regarding his causally efficacious individuals as *independent* causal variables — as not themselves fully explicable by causes of a social kind. There are some indications that, when he gets to the sticking point, he does not, or at any rate does not like to.

For example, he reminds us continually that "behind" the activities of leading individuals were, of course, economic and social forces. This could mean no more than that any adequate explanation that pointed to individuals as causes would need *also* to recognize the circumstances which allowed them to operate as they did: in the case of Charles I doubtless, among other things, the monarchial traditions established by the Tudors; in the case of Cromwell, perhaps the availability of that upwardly mobile social group — small merchants, artisans, yeomen — that made the New Model Army so formidable a military, and then a political force. To insist, however, that individuals were no more than "contributory" causes, requiring the presence of still other causes, would not undermine their claim to be considered independently necessary, and would leave any social causes in the same position. Yet, like many other social theorists of history before him, Hill wobbles in the end between this position and the claim that individuals, although truly causes and no doubt often indispensable, are themselves governed by underlying economic and social conditions. Thus, at one point, he offers something approaching a social explanation of Cromwell's violent anti-Catholicism — an outlook seen as at odds with some of his more amiable characteristics, but which accorded well enough with public opinion in England at the time.[38] And he explains Crom-

---

[36] S. E. Prall, in reviewing *God's Englishman*, *American Historical Review* 77 (1971), 168.

[37] *Oliver Cromwell*, 23.

[38] *God's Englishman*, 36.

well's increasing conservatism, once the Civil War was won, largely by reference to his concern for the propertied class to which he himself belonged.[39] On the other hand, he explicitly repudiates the view that people's actions are *determined* by their "class origins or class position";[40] and although he makes a serious effort to relate even the abstract scientific theorizing of a Newton to his alleged Puritan upbringing, he has the good sense to allow in the end that not everything in Newton's career as a scientist can be thus explained.[41] The evidence as to whether Hill thought of individuals who were causes as independent variables therefore points both ways.

All this is relevant to whether or not he can properly be called a historical determinist — or, as some prefer to say, a believer in historical inevitability. He has denied that, as a Marxist, he has any need to be an *economic* determinist — this while considering the views of Harrington.[42] But he seems to understand this notion in a rather restricted sense according to which historical events are conceived as falling under what he calls "natural" laws. This suggests either that, since history is a natural, and perhaps even a physical process, ordinary human decisions make no difference to what happens, or that it falls under laws of economic and social change which, like laws of physics and unlike the loose generalizations we derive from everyday experience, apply without exception. Yet, neither of these are positions which Hill seems really to find very comfortable. He does from time to time judge certain things to have been inevitable; but what is striking about his judgments of this sort is their being mainly small scale and short term. We are told, for example, that civil war became inevitable once the King left London in January 1642 following his failure to arrest the five members; that the restoration of the monarchy became inevitable once Cromwell had his showdown with the Levellers at Burford in 1649; that the failure of the specifically religious Revolution became inevitable once the Parliament of the Saints had to be dissolved in 1653.[43] Many such judgments may appear reasonable enough even to non-Marxist historians. But what one expects from someone equipped with Marxist theory is surely something a bit more grand: perhaps, in Hill's case, the claim that the Revolution was inevitable once the English gentry began its century-long rise to affluence and power, or once there was imposed on England that feudal system the demise of which the Revolution is represented as having been. But Hill specifically denies that the rise of the gentry "sufficiently explains" the Revolution;

---

[39] *God's Englishman*, 87, 105, 139, 197, 252–253.

[40] For example, in a revision of an earlier paper in *The Collected Essays of Christopher Hill*, vol. 3, 97.

[41] *Change and Continuity*, 251.

[42] By implication at least in his *Puritanism and Revolution* (London: Secker & Warburg, 1958), 312.

[43] *Century of Revolution* 103–104; *The English Revolution*, 52; *Oliver Cromwell*, 28.

and he has never, to my knowledge, argued that the so-called "Norman Yoke" *had* to be cast off by revolutionary means.[44]

There is still another point that I think needs noting if the limited extent of Hill's historical determinism or inevitabilism is to be made fully clear. Hill seems never to have given up the claim that what happens in history — and especially revolution — is fully explicable in terms of Marxist theory. Since that theory is formulated entirely in social terms, if the idiosyncracies of individuals are not to undermine the explanations it is taken to warrant, they must be seen as themselves explicable in social terms. As I have already pointed out, Hill does, at times, move in this direction. What he *sometimes* offers us, however, when seeking to make causally crucial individuals more understandable, is not social but *psychological* explanation. For example, he opines that Cromwell was probably a manic depressive, this sometimes making a difference not only to his private acts but to his public ones.[45] To the believer in historical inevitability, however, the intrusion of psychological determinants ought to be as embarrassing as, say, traditional belief in human free will, since it undermines no less the possibility of social prediction. What the inevitabilist needs to be able to show is that, in all relevant respects, the causally indispensable individual was "a product of his age." And this, despite his Marxism, Hill frequently admits not to have been fully so. He does want to say, of course, that causally indispensable individuals were often especially *suited* to the circumstances in which they acted, and would probably have been ineffective otherwise. Thus he notes a certain dualism in Cromwell's character which, he says, made him the ideal leader of the Independents, a group that wanted revolution, but not too much. To say that the *effectiveness* of an individual, not his *nature*, depended upon the social context, however, is not to reduce that person, after all, to the status of a dependent variable.

V

When one turns to consider ideas, one is immediately struck by how deeply Hill involves himself in intellectual history. As he admits himself in an exchange with Lawrence Stone, he has always been far more interested in ideas than in economics, and he has increasingly indulged this interest as his career has advanced.[46] In consequence, he has been applauded for having put "mind" back into history, at any rate so far as his chosen period is concerned.[47] What I want to ascertain, however, is not how much emphasis he places upon ideas as

---

[44] *Economic Problems of the Church*, 351.

[45] *God's Englishman*, 185.

[46] "Christopher Hill and Lawrence Stone discuss with Peter Burke the English Revolution of the 17th Century," *The Listener* 90 (1973), 451.

[47] Review of *Intellectual Origins*, *Economist* 215 (June 12, 1965), 1290.

a legitimate historical subject matter but how he conceives their causal efficacy, always keeping in mind his underlying Marxism. The issue is his attitude
to "ideological explanation." And with regard to this he may seem to have
made his position quite plain. Ideas, he has said, must "never be left out"; they
are not mere "epiphenomena' of the historical process, but are fully operative
within it.[48] they are analogous, he suggests, to the steam that drives the wheels
of a locomotive: the locomotive will not go anywhere without rails to take it
there; but it will not move along those rails unless the driving force of steam is
supplied. What Hill seems to be saying is that ideas are just as much required
for historical change as are factors like the state of the social environment.
Both function as indispensable contributory causes, neither providing, in itself,
sufficient explanation of the sorts of thing historians generally want to account
for. This is expecially true of revolutions, Hill maintains, which, by their very
nature, must be fought out in terms of ideas.

As in the case of individuals, however, the crucial question is whether Hill
regards ideas as *independent* causal variables in historical explanation —
whether, like Stone, who also long advocated a strictly social interpretation of
the English Revolution, he sees ideas as having "a life of their own." Does Hill
characterize ideas as indispensible elements in causally explicable change only
to add that they are themselves socially or economically determined? If he does
not — if he represents them as independently intruding into social and economic processes — he will surely have stood Marxism "on its head," as one
reviewer of his Intellectual Origins accused him of having done.[49] In fact, he does
often seem to represent ideas as themselves the products of their social environment, and hence as dependent variables, as when he says of both Milton
and Cromwell that their attitudes were "ultimately" determined by their class
background.[50] The arguments he deploys in support of this position sometimes
appear rather strange, however. For example, he more than once takes the
mere fact that ideas were held in common as evidence of their having had
social causes.[51] The most that one could legitimately infer from that, one would
think, is that they probably had common causes, the nature of the latter being
a further question. And he often moves rather easily from his own judgment
that certain social conditions provided *reasons* for holding certain beliefs to the
conclusion that what offered the reasons caused people to act accordingly.
That, for example, is the way he treats the antiquarianism ever-present in the
discussion of political affairs in the early Stuart period. Although it may seem
strange to us, this approach had a "function," he observes — as if showing that

[48] Intellectual Origins, 3; Economic Problems of the Church, 352.
[49] Review of Reformation to Industrial Revolution by J. M. Price, American Historical
Review 74 (1968), 595.
[50] Oliver Cromwell, 36.
[51] Change and Continuity, 92; Intellectual Origins, 99, 222.

ideas met a need show them to have been caused by the conditions creating that need.[52]

There is also the problem that, with reference to ideas as well as to idivi-duals, Hill seems at times to argue the other way. Calvinism, he insists — and in this largely resides its importance for early capitalist development — leads to an "ultimate anarchy of individual consciences," itself certain to encourage individualism in other than the purely religious realm.[53] To use a terminology that Hill himself employs: ideological development is here explained by refer-ence to an inherent *logic of ideas*, not by reference to something lying beyond the ideas.[54] If anything, what is exemplified is the reverse movement, the impact of ideas upon the social environment. So we come back simply to the notion of ideas and social conditions "interacting," neither depending on the other in ways the other does not depend on it. If Hill sometimes gives a contrary impression, this may be mainly because, as he says himself, he is concerned to "redress the balance," which he thinks has been skewed, es-pecially by Whiggish predecessors, in favour of ascribing independent causal influence to ideas. Relevant in this connection is the cautious way in which he sometimes characterizes his own work. Thus, in *Economic Problems of the Church*, his main aim, he says, was to underline some implications of the neglected fact that the Church, a major landowner and one of the largest employers of labour, was not *just* a religious institution, responding *only* to theological imperatives.[55]

One of the difficulties for determining Hill's precise position on the causal role of ideas lies in a certain obscurity about what he wants to contrast them with. He often talks of the influence of ideas by contrast with that of "material" factors. The contrast he has in mind in such cases is not usually with such things as the physical features of the landscape or the age and sex distribution of its inhabitants; much more often it is with social conditions, economic changes, or institutional structures — hardly "material" at all in a literal sense. But when he considers the causal efficacy of particular ideas, Hill frequently departs even further from reference to the brutely material. For example, when he says that, not ideas, but material interests, especially those related to class background, explain why certain members of the Long Parliament became revolutionaries, the implied contrast is neither with physical nor with social circumstances but, in effect, with other ideas. A well-known ambiguity in the notion of "materialism" has some relevance here. One thing this work may signalize is the assigning of a special status to what is physical rather than mental or "ideal." In such cases, the governing concern is often ontological:

[52] *Intellectual Origins*, 263.
[53] Ibid., 284–287.
[54] *God's Englishman*, 24.
[55] *Economic Problems of the Church*, x.

the contrast concerns the relative reality or potency of two sorts of things. But the reference may also be to the kind of value imputed to the seeking of one sort of goal rather than another. Motives may be seen as "material," for example, if they relate to people's selfish concerns, especially to economic ones, rather than to what might be called their principles — a term Hill himself uses in this connection.[56] Thus attention to effects on one's pocketbook would in this sense be seen as a material sort of causal factor; concern for the well-being of the commonwealth presumably would not.

All this bears especially on what Hill often has to say about religious beliefs as causal factors in the coming of the English Revolution. Religious motives, we are constantly told, were not really operative as such: they were typically cloaks or disguises for what the supposed believer was really aiming at (Hill insists repeatedly that genuine religion was nothing like as common in the seventeenth century as historians have generally assumed). Not that we should always speak of "rationalization" in this connection, Hill hastens to add; that would be too crude.[57] For the agents themselves were not always aware of the true nature of their motivations; and the overly idealistic motives they sometimes professed were often sincerely felt. In other words, the agents in question were often *self-deceived*; their actions were often guided by *unconscious motives*. Hill pushes this approach so hard, at times, that some of his more recent work has been described, apparently to his surprise, as having moved in a Freudian direction.[58] With more justification, I think, he could sometimes he accused of cynicism — a fault which, curiously enough, he warns other historians against.[59] This impression is strengthened by the fact that his reductions of ideas to expressions of interest are most often directed at segments of early seventeenth century society for which he feels little sympathy, and often great antipathy. Thus he interprets the reception of Calvinist ethics by many English merchants of the period, and particularly its presumed injunction to manifest divine election by prospering in worldly affairs, as the undertaking *as a religious duty* of what they were going to do in any case.[60] And the best he can do for seventeenth century Protestant empire-builders who professed religious motivations is to observe that, for men to whom secular pursuits could only be seen as legitimate when related to a religious goal, this was doubtless a natural way to think.[61] On the other hand, when the Presbyterian Scots, through their opposition to Charles I over the Prayer Book, were right-minded enough to

---

[56] *Economic Problems of the Church*, 352.
[57] Ibid., x; "Recent Interpretations of the Civil War," 80–81.
[58] See, for example, his exchange with Stone, *The Listener* 90 (1973), 450.
[59] *Change and Continuity*, 12. Or at any rate, he could be accused of too often being "tone-deaf" in matters of religion, as remarked by Naomi Bliven in a review of Hill's *Milton and the English Revolution*, *New Yorker* 54 (February 12, 1979), 117.
[60] *Change and Continuity*, 96.
[61] Ibid., 97.

launch the English Revolution, he makes no difficulty about taking their religious fervour at face value.[62] And he looks for no ulterior motive when he notes that, although the privileged could scarcely be expected to understand this, many seventeenth century English yeomen and artisans "genuinely believed" that God willed the equality of man.[63]

Hill's treatment of Cromwell is especially revelatory of the way he often reduces religious belief to something barely recognizable as such. He says constantly, as he does of some others, that Cromwell was a genuinely religious man. Yet he interprets what may well have been Cromwell's central religious idea, his overriding belief in Providence and his conviction that he was called to do God's work, as a rationalization of his confidence in his own powers, when properly used. Cromwell's "Providence," Hill says, was really the historical forces of his time, which he discerned more clearly than most. So we get Cromwell's notion of "waiting upon the Lord" interpreted as "waiting until the time was ripe," or even "waiting to see which way the cat would jump" — not excluding the possibility of giving the cat a little guidance at times.[64] This is hardly to ascribe an independent causal role to Cromwell's religious ideas *as such*. Yet it leaves open the possibility that the non-religious and more self-regarding motives that Hill interprets them as disguising may have played such a role. Two very different sorts of arguments are thus employed by Hill in his attempts to throw doubt on the independent causal force of ideas. On the one hand, he insists that, even when ideas function as causes, they are themselves caused in turn by conditions of other kinds and are thus not independent variables. This might be called the *underlying material cause argument*. But he also calls in question the independent causal efficacy of certain kinds of ideas by contending that they are often not quite what they seem. We might call this the *underlying material motive argument*. The latter, besides being factually unconvincing in many of its applications, clearly does nothing to show that ideas function in history only as socially dependent variables.[65]

VI

By way of conclusion, let me review some of the main contentions to which this brief analysis of Hill's causal thinking has led. I found it difficult to characterize precisely Hill's basic conception of a cause in history, partly because of his tendency, contradicted by some of his own practice, to assimilate causal judg-

[62] *Century of Revolution*, 86.
[63] *Puritanism and Revolution*, 214.
[64] *Oliver Cromwell*, 25; *God's Englishman*, 225. At any rate, this is how the "ungodly" would naturally view it, remarks Hill, with his own sympathies showing.
[65] This paper draws upon work done while a Fellow of the National Humanities Center in 1983–1984.

ment simply to giving explanation, and partly because, in his frequently rather vague talk of "links" between things, he too often leaves it unclear how, or indeed whether, these are to be interpreted causally. Nor do theoretical ideas like dialectic, law or necessary and sufficient condition, all of which appear in his writings, throw much light on his position. He does make a valid case against associating too closely the ideas of causing something and intending it, which he correctly accuses some of his opponents of having done. But he does not in his own work always escape the false implications of this association, especially when arguing against the views of others. Nor does he fully acknow-ledge the central importance of ascertaining intentions even in those cases of causal analysis where what is to be explained is itself unintended.

With regard to his view of what causes what in history, I argued that Hill assigns a larger causal role to both particular individuals and ideas than one might have expected a Marxist historian to do. On the crucial question of whether he regards either as independent variables, however, the evidence appears mixed. From time to time he judges certain results to have been inevitable; but it seems doubtful that he is a historical inevitabilist, if by that is meant someone who believes that significant historical change is fully deter-mined by antecedent social states. He may nevertheless be a determinist about the historical past in the sense of holding that everything that happened had determining conditions of some sort. A special difficulty for eliciting his position on the causal efficacy of ideas is that while the contrast he sometimes has in mind is with objective social situations and structures, at other times it is with interests. In the latter case, the real issue becomes the nature of the most causally efficacious motives, and sometimes of unconscious ones.

What has been said hardly amounts, of course, to a full and balanced ac-count of the nature of Hill's causal thinking, and still less to a full and balanced critique of it. What might nevertheless be claimed for it is that it points to ways in which such tasks may fruitfully be undertaken, ideally by historians them-selves. At the same time it serves to illustrate a kind of interest, referred to at the beginning, that philosophers of history, for their own broader epistemologi-cal purposes, are increasingly taking in the argumentation of historians, an interest which seeks to clarify the framework of ideas within which they argue out their differences about what happened in the past, and to subject it, where appropriate, to critical appraisal. There are doubtless many viable and useful ways in which interdisciplinary studies can be conceived and carried through. I should like to think that what has been done in this paper exemplifies one of them.

A View from the Vistula on the English Revolution

WILLIAM HUNT

Professor Perez Zagorin is an outstanding exception to the notorious insularity of historians of Tudor-Stuart England. In *Rebels and Rulers 1500–1650* he gave us a stimulating comparative study of political conflict in early Britain, France, Spain, and the Netherlands.[1] Since Zagorin confined his survey to Europe west of the Rhine, I should like to pay tribute to his exemplary breadth of vision by trying to widen somewhat the field of comparative analysis. In this essay I shall juxtapose the history of Britain with that of Poland during what is known, from the British point of view, as the Tudor-Stuart period. This comparison is not often made, perhaps for good reason. But its apparent oddity may suggest some new and potentially fruitful lines of argument.

First, a word about terminology: I shall for convenience' sake refer to my subjects as Britain and Poland. Both terms are inexact, and refer to entities which changed over the period in question. By "Britain" I mean the collection of lands ruled by the English monarch, who was also king of Ireland and after 1603 of Scotland as well. By "Poland" I mean lands subject to the Polish crown, which was dynastically united with the Duchy of Lithuania in 1385. The two realms were constitutionally unified in 1579 as the Polish Commonwealth (*Rzeczpospolita*), and remained united until the dismemberment of the Commonwealth by Russia, Prussia, and Austria in the late eighteenth century.[2]

Both "Britain" and "Poland" were what H.G. Koenigsberger calls "multiple monarchies": dynastic states ruling over ethnically heterogenous populations.[3] That heterogeneity was of enormous importance in shaping the history of both states in the early modern period. There is an obvious parallel, which I shall not now pursue, between the Polish Commonwealth (*Rzeczpospolita*), as this

---

[1] Perez Zagorin, *Rebels and Rulers* (2 vols., Cambridge: Cambridge University Press, 1982).

[2] The best introduction to Polish history in English is Norman Davies, *God's Playground: A History of Poland* (2 vols., New York: Oxford University Press, 1982).

[3] H. G. Koenigsberger, *Dominium Regale or Dominium Politicum et Regale: Monarchies and Politics in Early Modern Europe* (Inaugural Lecture, King's College, London 1975).

combined kingdom was called, and Great Britain under the Stuarts. Both states were plagued by regional rebellions rooted in ethnic and religious antagonisms.

Let us start by ackowledging some of the profound differences between Britain and Poland. It is well known that eastern and western Europe – roughly divided by the Elbe River — were moving in opposite directions, socially and economically, during the Tudor-Stuart centuries. West of the Elbe, commerce and urban life were, on the whole, flourishing. To the east, at least after 1600, the growth of internal markets was stunted, and towns were being strangled. Britain and Poland, moreover, represent something like the poles of this anti-nomy. In the seventeenth century England was becoming a market-based con-sumer society; Poland was mired in a retrograde seigneurialism.[4]

Alongside these enormous disparities in socio-economic development, there are nonetheless a number of intriguing analogies. Both Britain and Poland were in a sense peripheral states, located outside the former boundaries of the ancient Roman Empire. As such, they evolved in relative autonomy. To use for a moment the language of Fernand Braudel and Immanuel Wallerstein, both Britain and Poland experienced, though not simultaneously, a period of eco-nomic dependency due to their peripheral status in the evolving "world sys-tem" of European commerce.[5] The external trade of both countries depended largely on the export of a single raw material — in England's case wool, in Poland's, grain — in exchange for manufactured goods from the economic "core", especially the manufacturing region of the Low Countries.

England, to be sure, had largely escaped from this "colonial" dependency on the export of raw materials even before the acccession of the Tudors, as the export of wool gave way to that of cloth in the later middle ages. Poland's economy continued to be dominated by the grain trade throughout our period. But even under the early Stuarts, England's economy had certain "peripheral" features. Since most of her cloth was still being exported in a semi-finished condition, England remained dependent on a single relatively unsophisticated export. Both Poland and England were severely affected by the European trade slump and price depression of the 1620s.

Britain and Poland during the early modern period were also "peripheral" in relation to Roman Catholicism. Protestantism took root in both countries, and both escaped from the orbit of papal control – Poland temporarily, England for good. In both countries the religious conflicts of the period had profound political repercussions. Protestantism spread particularly among the lesser aris-tocracy, known in England as the gentry and in Poland as the *szlachta*. In each

---

[4] For useful survey of the literature see Immanuel Wallerstein, *The Modern World System: Capitalist Agriculture and the Origins of the World Economy in the Sixteenth Century* (New York: Academic Press, 1974), especially ch. 6.

[5] In addition to Wallerstein, see Fernand Braudel, *Civilization and Capitalism 15th–18th Century*, tr. Sian Reynolds (3 vols., New York: Harper and Row, 1984), especially vol. 3, *The Perspective of the World*, 39–42,

case, the fortunes of Protestantism decisively influenced the process of state formation.

It is the political parallels that are most striking. Both countries were, in the language of the day, "mixed monarchies." At a time when the medieval estates, diets, and *cortes* were declining in most of Europe, both England and Poland maintained strong representative assemblies through which the aristocracy exercised considerable political influence. Like England's Parliament, the Polish *Sejm* was bi-cameral, its Senate and Chamber of Deputies corresponding roughly to the English Houses of Lords and Commons.

Britain and Poland were the largest and most powerful "mixed monarchies" in early modern Europe. That fact alone might invite us to compare their histories. Furthermore both countries ran counter to the general early modern tendency towards absolutism. Like most of Europe, both England and Poland suffered through a "Time of Troubles" in the seventeenth century. Both countries experienced war, revolt, and governmental breakdown. In most European countries, the calamities of the seventeenth century led to the strengthening of the crown at the expense of the estates, and the centralization of administrative power at the expense of local autonomy. In both Britain and Poland, however, the opposite occurred.

By 1700 both Parliament and the *Sejm* had strengthened their control of royal finances, and thereby royal policy. To put it simply, although somewhat crudely, by 1700 both Parliament and *Sejm* were stronger in relation to the Crown than they had been two centuries earlier. Similarly, in both countries the day-to-day business of administration had devolved to the localities. Attempts by the British and Polish crowns to establish a centralized royal bureaucracy had been defeated. Real power remained in the hands of local notables, acting in England through the county Quarter Sessions and in Poland through the provincial *sejmiki*, or "dietines," which we might call "petty Parliaments."

The real social victors in both cases were the magnates — great lords exploiting their estates for commercial profit. Poland's internal economy was backward, to be sure, and these magnatial estates were cultivated by serf labor, but the Polish magnates participated fully in the European "world economy" centered in the Low Countries. They made a handsome profit shipping the grain of their estates to the urbanized west. One would hesitate to call the Polish nobility "capitalists," but they clearly contributed to, and benefited from, the growth of capitalism. If anything, they were even more "business-minded" than their English counterparts, since they exploited their estates (and their serfs) directly, rather than leasing them out and living off rents like the English aristocracy.

Nor were the Polish aristocrats necessarily inferior in culture. Indeed, by Renaissance standards — that is to say in terms of classical education — the Polish nobles were quite possibly superior to the English. English travellers to Poland often remarked with astonishment that an Englishman knowing Latin

43

could converse with noblemen throughout the country. In Poland, as in England, humanistic culture had much to do with the survival of aristocratic liberties.

Whatever may have been the case in England, there is considerable of evidence of a "rise of the gentry" in the sixteenth century Poland, and even of a "crisis" in the political fortunes of the greater aristocracy.[6] During the later sixteenth century the growing wealth and education of the Polish gentry led the more articulate of them, acting through the lower house of the *Sejm*, to challenge the power of the great magnates, represented in the Senate.

To be sure, this conflict never reached the pitch in Poland that it attained in England in 1649, when the House of Commons abolished the House of Lords and the peerage altogether. But the Polish magnates had no distinctive titles or legal status to take way. In any case the rise of the gentry was in both countries a transitory phenomenon. Both Poland and England experienced a revival of magnatial power in the later seventeenth century.

These parallels, however, only serve to highlight the colossal disparities between Poland and England. As we all know, England in the eighteenth century was headed for world hegemony, while Poland was well along the high-road to extinction. By the time England emerged triumphant from the Napoleonic wars, Poland had vanished from the map altogether.[7]

The story is familiar: perhaps too familiar. From the early nineteenth century onwards, both English and Polish historiography have been suffused with the wisdom of hindsight. England's industrial imperialism and Poland's obliteration have appeared structurally predetermined. Historians of Tudor-Stuart England have, until recently, sought to uncover in their period the roots of parliamentary democracy and industrial revolution. Their Polish colleagues have been pre-occupied with the sixteenth-century origins of national decline.

It is of course perfectly permissible to study the past with a view to later developments, and it is to some degree unavoidable. The curse of hindsight is, like the knowledge of good and evil, irrevocable. But we should guard against the facile and often fallacious assumption that what happened *had* to happen. Hindsight becomes a liability when it inhibits the imagination of alternate outcomes. Counter-factual speculation can easily degenerate into idle daydreaming. But it has its uses, if properly controlled. It is often worthwhile considering the relative plausibility of alternative scenarios, to see how much strain they place upon our imaginative capacities. It is, after all, one of history's great fascinations that much of what actually happens is highly improbable.

---

[6] For the debate about these phenomena in England, and a useful overview of English social development in comparative perspective see Barrington Moore, Jr., *Social Origins of Dictatorship and Democracy* (Bosto: Beacon Press, 1966), ch. 1. See also below, note 9.

[7] For the Polish case, see Davies, *God's Playground*, especially chapter 18.

The so-called "revisionist" historians of Stuart England were therefore right to warn against teleological determinism in the study of the English Revolution.[8] The only way to carry on this kind of discussion meaningfully, however, is through historical comparison, a method which the English revisionists have largely ignored.

For example, revisionist historians might have placed less emphasis upon English localism in explaining the Civil War if they had reflected that by European standards, England was remarkable precisely for its national cohesion, and the relative *weakness* of centrifugal tendencies. Similarly the celebrated controversy over the "rise of the gentry" might have developed in a different, and perhaps more productive manner if it had been placed in a wider comparative context.[9]

The rise (or at least expansion) of lesser aristocracies appears to have been a quite general feature of early modern European history from France to Muscovy. Virtually everywhere, including Poland, this social process worked to the advantage of the monarchy in the struggle with the magnatial nobility. Yet the English gentry controversy was premised on the assumption that a rising gentry would logically pose a *threat* to royal power, precisely the opposite of what the comparative evidence might lead one to expect.

Now it is reasonably clear that the numbers and collective wealth of Englishmen claiming gentry status increased disproportionately in the later sixteenth century. In that sense the gentry indisputably "rose," although more in the manner of a loaf of bread than a hot air balloon. The interesting question then becomes why this development did not conduce to the growth of an English absolutism. And the answer to that question, I believe, would lead us away from economic determinism into the realm of political culture, to which I shall return.

Comparative method cannot definitely establish a hypothesis – but then, as Karl Popper has shown, hypotheses can never be finally proven in the physical sciences either: they can only be *falsified* by experimental results that force

[8] The Tudor-Stuart historians loosely grouped as "revisionists" include Conrad Russell, John Morrill, Kevin Sharpe, Mark Kishlansky, and J. C. D. Clark. For critical surveys of the revisionist debate, with full bibliographical references, see Howard Tomlinson, "The Causes of War: A Historiographical Survey" in *Before the Civil War*, ed. H. Tomlinson (London: MacMillan, 1983), 7–26; Mary Fulbrook, "The English Revolution and the Revisionist Revolt", *Social History*, 7 (1982), 249–262; and Thomas Cogswell, "Coping with Revisionism in Early Stuart History" in *Journal of Modern History*, 62, no. 3 (Sept. 1990), 538–552.

[9] The best survey of the gentry controversy remains Lawrence Stone, *The Causes of the English Revolution* (New York: Harper and Row, 1972), 72–6. The celebrated and witty essay by J. H. Hexter, "Storm over the Gentry", in J. H. Hexter, *Reappraisals in History*, 2nd ed. (Chicago: University of Chivago Press, 1979), ch. 6, seriously distorts the position of R. H. Tawney, whose articles generated the debate.

their modification or replacement.[10] Comparative analysis can also serve to undermine, if not falsify, historical hypotheses. When we are dealing with a single case, it is easy to fall into a lazy *"post hoc, propter hoc"* kind of argument. When confronted with apparently similar cases which turned out quite differently, we are forced to revise and refine the hypothesis, or junk it altogether.

This is why books like Professor Zagorin's *Rebels and Rulers* are so valuable. I would cite also the work of Professor Antoni Maczak of Warsaw, whose recent book *Governors and the Governed in Early Modern Europe* (*Rządzancy i Rządzeni*) will soon appear, I hope, in English translation.[11] Since Professor Maczak writes from an Eastern European perspective, it should complement *Rebels and Rulers* in a very stimulating way.

A comparative approach would, in my opinion, inspire a fruitful reevaluation of assumptions in early modern Polish, as well as English historiography. Polish historians have proposed a number of explanations for the collapse of the Polish state in the seventeenth and eighteenth centuries. Several of the most popular arguments tend to crumble, however, when exposed to comparative analysis. Consider for example, the apparently plausible argument from geography, which attributes Poland's misfortunes to its lack of natural defenses against the predatory states of Prussia and Russia.

The problem with this argument is that the successful predators – Prussia and Russia — also lacked natural frontiers. (So for that matter did the successive waves of nomadic invaders — the Aryans, Avars, Huns, and Tatars — who poured out of Central Asia and across the Euro-Asian steppes.) In the fifteenth and sixteenth centuries, the Poles were the aggressors, not the victims, carving out Europe's largest state at the expense of the Prussians, Russians, Ukrainians, Tatars, and Turks. The Polish hussars who in the sixteenth century extended Polish power from the Baltic almost to the Black Sea were not troubled by the lack of natural frontiers.

Another, equally specious, argument lays the blame for Poland's collapse on the elective, as opposed to hereditary, nature of the monarchy. There is no question that the Polish aristocracy often chose disastrous rulers. But the lottery of hereditary succession has been known to produce disasters as well, and there is no obvious reason why an elective monarchy should be inherently inefficient or unstable. The papacy, for example, has been working tolerably well for the past millenium (and from the Polish point of view, never better than since 1979.)

In any case one can easily exaggerate the contrast between elective and hereditary monarchy. The title of Holy Roman Emperor, nominally elective,

[10] An accessible introduction to Popper's thought is provided by Brian Magee in *Popper* (London: Fontana Modern Masters, 1973).

[11] Antoni Maczak, *Rządzacy i Rządzeni* (Warsaw: Panstwowy Instytut Wydawniczy, 1986).

remained in the House of Hapsburg for almost six hundred years. In England, on the other hand, the direct hereditary succession was broken on five occasions betwen 1603 and 1715. Meanwhile the elective Polish crown remained in the Vasa line for eighty years, from 1587 to 1668. Yet it was precisely during those years that the irreversible decline of the Polish state took place.

A more plausible explanation for the debacle of the Polish state focuses on Poland's admittedly retrograde social structure. The Polish historian Konstantin Grzybowski in a very influential essay called simply "Why?" ("*Dlaczego?*"), blamed Poland's collapse on the class egotism of the Polish aristocracy, the *szlachta*.[12] To withstand the growing threat from its increasingly powerful neighbors to the east and west, Poland required a strong central state, such as had emerged in both Prussia and Russia. The *szlachta*, Grzybowski claimed, refused to tolerate the strengthening of the Crown, because they regarded a strong monarchy as a threat to their own social power. The *szlachta* feared that a strong monarchy might enlist the support of the townsmen, and (more dangerously) of the enserfed peasantry against the seigneurial order.

In Grzybowski's terms, the Polish aristocracy resisted the development of a centralized *royal* absolutism in order to preserve the petty absolutism which each noble exercised over the serfs on his own estates. From this point of view, the Polish *szlachta's* vociferous and often eloquent defense of their "golden freedom" (*złota wolnosc*) was merely an ideological veil for the fragmented despotism of the manorial system.

Grzybowski's argument had a salutary effect. By demystifying the *szlachta's* "golden freedom", he helped loosen the hold of patriotic sentimentality on the Polish historical imagination. Poland appeared less as the martyred "Christ of Nations" imagined by the nineteenth-century Romantic poets, and more as the victim of its own social injustices. But the Grzybowski thesis also fails to withstand comparative scrutiny. Absolutism, even of the most despotic kind, was perfectly compatible with the micro-despotism of manorial serfdom: witness again the cases of Prussia and Russia (and here we might add Austria and Hungary as well).

In all of these states, the monarchy essentially struck a bargain with the serf-owning aristocracy — sanctioning, indeed reinforcing, the power of the lords over their serfs in return for aristocratic support of the state. The *junkers* of Prussia and their counterparts in Russia were quite content to combine the power and perquisites of state service with those of manorial lordship. There was thus no *necessary* contradiction between royal absolutism and seigneurial power.

Moreover, the Grzybowski thesis overlooks the fact that the majority of the

---

[12] Konstanty Grzybowski, '*Dlaczego?*", reprinted (in Polish) in Robert A. and Halina Rothstein, (eds.), *Polish Scholarly Prose* (Columbus, Ohio: Ohio University Press, 1981), 95–105.

Polish *szlachta* did not own serfs. Many in fact had no lands at all. Perhaps a third of them were economically indistinguishable from the free peasantry, yet they remained fiercely attached to their "golden freedom" and their right to bear arms. One hears of impoverished nobles wearing wooden swords since they were too poor to buy steel ones. This ludicrous but poignant image effectively symbolizes the mentality of the class.

Grzybowski and his followers have been too quick to dismiss the Polish nobility's devotion to liberty as a mere ideological cover for economic self-interest. But Grzybowksi was probably right to attribute the downfall of the Polish state to the cult of golden freedom. It remains to give a more adequate explanation of why aristocratic liberty produced such disastrous consequences in Poland, when similar ideas proved compatible, in England, with a powerful and expansive state.

In the sixteenth century both the Polish *szlachta* and the English gentry were profoundly influenced by the humanistic ideal. They embraced an ideal of civic virtue, nourished by the study of classical literature. Thomas Hobbes, indeed, blamed this classical education for England's Great Rebellion. As he wrote in *Behemoth*,

> there were an exceeding great number of men of the better sort, that had been so educated that in their youth having read the books written by famous men of the ancient Grecian and Roman commonwealths concerning their polity and great actions, in which books the popular government was extolled by the glorious name of liberty, and monarchy disgraced by the name of tyranny, they became thereby in love with their forms of government. And out of these men were chosen the greatest part of the House of Commons.[13]

Whatever we think of this argument as applied to England — and I would take it more seriously than most modern historians — it fits the Polish *szlachta* remarkably well. We have only to replace the House of Commons with the Chamber of Deputies of the *Sejm*. In Poland the great authors of "the Grecian and Roman commonwealths" were invoked for two hundred years to obstruct the slightest encroachment of royal authority upon the golden freedom of the aristocracy. The Polish name for their Commonwealth — *Rzeczpospolita* – was a literal translation of the Roman "*Respublica*". The proudest boast of the *szlachta* when assembled in their *Sejm* was that they alone, of all the nations of Europe, had preserved the liberties of Republican Rome.

Humanism did not lead automatically to anarchy, however. Humanism was above all a program of education for public service. Why, then, why did it not encourage in Poland the formation of a service nobility, composed of classically

---

[13] Thomas Hobbes, *Behemoth* (London, 1840), 6.

48

trained and public-minded gentlemen? After all, the same republican ideals which Hobbes blamed for the English Revolution also inspired the framers of the most stable constitution in western history, that of the United States. A fair number of Polish aristocrats fought in the American war of Independence (Kosciuszko and Pulaski are merely the best known). On their return to Poland they incorporated these ideals into their own reformed constitution of 1791. Why were their ancestors incapable of devising a stable and defensible form of self-government during the preceding centuries?[14]

In fact, in the mid-sixteenth century, the Polish *szlachta* seemed to be doing so. The so-called "Execution of the Laws" movement represented an attempt by the lesser aristocracy — the Polish version of the "rising gentry" — to balance the imperatives of liberty and order: to strengthen the crown, limit the power of the magnates, and erect a kind of "monarchical republicanism" on the basis of humanist political principles.

Why did it fail? Any adequate answer would take us far deeper into the detailed narrative than space permits. But the main explanation would appear, at least to a historian of Stuart England, to be that the Polish gentry lacked a strong sense of national identity, such as could have sustained their efforts to reshape the state. The *szlachta* was religiously divided. For a time in the sixteenth century it seemed as if the Polish aristocracy might follow the English gentry *en masse* into Protestantism, but the Protestant tide crested in Poland around 1600 and rapidly receded thereafter.

Protestantism thus failed in Poland to provide the state with the kind of legitimating national vocation that it imparted to the English monarchy under Elizabeth and James. Nor did the resurgent Catholicism of the seventeenth-century provide a unifying focus. The Jesuits, regarded by seventeenth-century Englishmen as the congenital allies of absolutism, became in Poland the most vigorous defenders of aristocratic liberty. In any case, the decline of Protestantism was very gradual, while a significant section of aristocracy remained true to the Orthodox faith. The Commonwealth also contained Europe's largest Jewish community, who were employed and protected by the *szlachta*.[15] (Of cource the *szlachta* did so in their own interests, and treated the Jews with a mixture of condescension and contempt. But they often treated their Christian peasants considerably worse.)

Aristocratic freedom, the *zlota wolnosc*, encompassed liberty of conscience, and mandated a policy of religious toleration amongst the nobility. Therefore, religious ideology could not play a unifying role among the Polish nobility, at

[14] For the succeeding paragraphs, see Davies, *God's Playground*, chs. 10, 18 and sources cited therein.
[15] On relations between Jews and Christians in Poland, see Aleksander Hertz, *The Jews in Polish Culture*, tr. Richard Lourie (Evanston, Il.: Northwestern University Press, 1981).

least not until the decline of the Commonwealth was far advanced. It is troubling to reflect that the most attractive aspect of the Polish Commonwealth — its relative religious tolerance — may also have been a source of its fatal weakness. This indeed has been the premise of the chauvinistic (and anti-Semitic) version of Polish nationalism ever since the eighteenth century.

But matters are not so simple. England was not weakened by the Toleration Act of 1689 or by Catholic emancipation; nor has religious and cultural diversity notably hindered the growth of state power in North America. The real failure of the *szlachta* lay in its failure to evolve from its own humanist culture, a comprehensive, truly *republican* notion of citizenship, which would have given a larger proportion of the population a reason to identify with the aristocratic *Rzeczpospolita*. The barrier here lay not in the humanist tradition itself, but in the rigidly exclusive *caste* nature of the Polish nobility, which inhibited them from granting even limited political participation to subordinate strata.

The contrast with Stuart England is striking and instructive. We must avoid sentimentality here. We must not measure early modern Poland against some idealized Merrie Old England, awash in liberty, fellowship, and Real Ale. England in the seventeenth century was a hierarchical and often brutal society. The political nation — the class actively involved in political decision making — was probably smaller, as a proportion of the population, in England than in Poland. Poland's aristocracy was proportionally the largest in Europe, and its poorest members, many of whom were very poor indeed, enjoyed full political rights. If we consider as a measure of "democracy" the percentage of the population possessing the right to vote, than the aristocratic Polish Commonwealth was considerably more "democratic" than eighteenth-century England.

The aristocracy dominated the political life throughout the early modern period, and indeed down to the twentieth century. But English political culture also afforded a considerable measure of participation to groups lower on the social scale. Above all, the ethos and rhetoric of English liberty were not the exclusive property of an aristocratic caste, as was the case in Poland.

For the English aristocracy was not a caste at all. The gentry shaded off into the yeomanry and the community of literate professionals. Lawrence and Jeanne Stone have demonstrated that there was far less upward mobility into the higher aristocracy than we once believed.[16] On the other hand there was unquestionably a great deal of *downward* mobility by younger sons and daughters, which had the effect of blurring lines of cultural division, disseminating aristocratic values and claims downwards.

In Poland a man of noble descent, however wretchedly impoverished, continued to despise even his more prosperous plebeian neighbors, whom he

[16] Lawrence Stone and Jeanne C. Fawtrier Stone, *An Open Elite?: England, 1540–1880* (New York: Oxford University Press, 1984).

regarded as descendents of the Biblically accursed Ham.[17] In England, younger sons and their descendants were denied the debilitating satisfactions of caste arrogance. They could and did take pride, however, in the status of "free-born" Englishman. Dignity and liberty were theirs by right of nationality, rather than by geneology alone. I do not mean to deny, of course, that geneological snobbery remained enormously powerful in England. The point is that in England there existed a countervailing sense of national identity. Not so in Poland.

Consider the extreme but illuminating example of John Lilburne, the most theatrical of the Levellers and one of the first articulate champions of English democracy.[18] He called himself "Free-born John". Throughout his incessant legal battles against royal, episcopal, and parliamentary authority, Lilburne claimed to be defending the beleaguered liberties of all Englishmen. Yet Lilburne insisted on his own gentle origins. His father, a minor Northumbrian gentleman, was supposedly the last man in England to demand trial by combat in a dispute over real estate.

Psychological types like Free-born John Lilburne — high-minded, quarrelsome, recklessly insubordinate — were extremely common among the lower ranks of the Polish *szlachta*. But they could never have played the political role assumed by Lilburne, and they could never have endorsed the proto-democratic principles of the Putney Debates and the Agreements of the People. Nor could they have agreed with, or even understood, Colonel Rainsborough's assertion all men should have the right to vote, simply because "the poorest he that liveth hath a life to live as well as the greatest".[19] Professor Aylmer discussed the social origins of the Leveller leaders in a brief article which he entitled "Gentlemen Levellers?"[20] It is, I think, very significant that one can speak in England of *gentlemen* Levellers, even with a question mark. In Poland the species would be unimaginable.

It will be quite properly objected that even in England "Gentlemen Levellers" formed a negligible minority of their class. But the English Revolution was possible, I believe, because an important section of the English aristocracy *was* prepared to regard their social inferiors as fellow members of a Commonwealth, and to enlist their support in the defense of common freedoms.

To take one example. In 1636, the Earl of Warwick, later to command the Parliamentary navy in the civil war, defended his tenants in their refusal to pay the new royal forest fines. He explained that his tenants were for the most part old men, used to the ways of Elizabeth and James. They were unwilling, said Warwick, to go to their graves "under the stigma of having, at the end of their

[17] For this phenomenon, see Hertz, *Jews*, 72–3.

[18] On Lilburne, see Pauline Gregg, *Free-born John: a Biography of John Lilburne* (London, 1961).

[19] G. E. Aylmer (ed.), *The Levellers in the English Revolution* (Ithaca, New York: Cornell University Press, 1975), 100.

[20] G. E. Aylmer, "Gentlemen Levellers?", *Past and Present*, no. 49 (1970).

lives, signed away the liberties of the realm."[21] The language is significant. Warwick is here attributing to mere tenants a devotion to liberty which in Poland was the exclusive preserve of the aristocracy. The implications of this attitude became clear at the outbreak of the civil war, when we find this same Earl of Warwick addressing an army of apprentice volunteers as "my noble fellow-countrymen," employing the same rhetorical strategy as Shakespeare's Henry V at the Battle of Agincourt.[22]

We generally assume that revolution is a pathological phenomenon, the product (in sociological jargon) of social dysfunction. But it can also be argued, as Barrington Moore has done, that the really sick societies are those in which revolution is impossible, because they lack the cohesion to produce an effective movement of opposition.[23] One might suggest that seventeenth-century Poland suffered from just such a malady. No social group possessed a sufficient sense of civic responsibility to carry through the necessary political transformations.

In this sense the English Revolution, though not in itself a symptom of health, was made possible by the relative cohesion of English society as much as by the "multiple dysfunctions" which Lawrence Stone has sought to identify.[24] The defeat of Charles I was facilitated by the sense of national identity afforded by Protestantism, and by the ties of religious and patriotic solidarity, transecting class lines, which bound the Parliamentary cause (for a brief but decisive period) together. That this sense of national identity proved destructive of the monarchy was due largely to the failure of the early Stuarts to manipulate it effectively. The values which inspired the English Revolution could have served equally well, in my view, to support a powerful, though constitutionally regulated, monarchical state.

I would argue, then, that the English Revolution occurred not because the social order was somehow terminally ill, but because the crown was perceived to have betrayed a widely shared sense of national vocation. A revolution of this sort could occur precisely because there *was* a sense of national identity and vocation to argue, and even fight about.[25]

No such thing existed in Poland, which experienced revolts but no revolution. Polish noble consciousness remained stuck in a kind of twilight zone, a sort of ideological limbo. To put it anachronistically, the ethos of the *szlachta*

---

[21] For this episode, see William Hunt, *The Puritan Moment* (Cambridge, Mass.: Harvard University Press, 1983), 270.

[22] *A Most Worthy Speech, Spoken by the Right Honourable Robert Earle of Warwick* (1642), British Library, Thomason Tracts, E.128(30).

[23] Moore, *Social Origins*, 369, 382–4, 457–9.

[24] Stone, *Causes*, 9, 10, 14.

[25] I have argued this point at greater length in "Spectral Origins of the English Revolution", in Geoff Eley and William Hunt (eds.), *Reviving the English Revolution* (London: Verso, 1988), 305–32.

was too "liberal" to tolerate absolutism, but too "conservative" to permit the emergence of a nation of free citizens.

At the end of the eighteenth century, after centuries of colossal irresponsibility, the Polish nobility went out in a blaze of civic virtue. They proved that the humanistic culture that they had preserved since the sixteenth century was not entirely bankrupt. Faced with imminent disaster, a reforming party of the nobility worked feverishly to strengthen the central state and at the same time to extend civil liberties to the mass of the population. The result was the Constitution of May 3, 1791, which served as a sustaining source of national pride for the next two centuries. But the reforms of 1791 came too late to save the Polish Commonwealth. The prospect of a reformed (and liberal!) Polish state swiftly provoked the final partitions of Poland among its autocratic neighbors, and its virtual erasure from the map of Europe. As Polish historians have bitterly observed, Poland was crushed not because it was terminally ill but because it had begun to recover.[26]

As a consequence, the national identity which the Poles had been unable to create in freedom was achieved under foreign domination. And Polish identity has to this day retained a strong aristocratic stamp, imparted to it by the nobility in its death throes, and sustained by the intelligenstia, which has seen itself quite consciously as the carrier of *szlachta* traditions. Barrington Moore has observed that the future is often shaped by social groups that are about to be crushed by the wheel of history: such was the case with the *szlachta*.[27]

The Polish national anthem ("*Jeszcze Polska Nie Zginela*") vividly conveys the nineteenth-century sense of Polish nationality – aristocratically inspired, but democratically accessible. The anthem was originally the marching song of a legion of exiled Polish aristocrats in the service of Napoleon. Its first line declares that "Poland has not yet perished while we are alive." The soldiers vow to reconquer Poland's lost freedom by the power of the sabre, but also pledge to "link ourselves with the people". Had the Polish *szlachta* been able to speak in the sixteenth century of linking themselves with the people — thereby identifying themselves with a nation rather than an exclusive caste — they might have proved capable, like the aristocracy of Tudor-Stuart England, of reconciling aristocratic liberty with national stability and power.

[26] See Hans Roos, "The Nobility in Pre-Revolutionary Poland" in W. J. Stankiewicz, ed., *The Tradition of Polish Ideals* (London: Orbis Books, 1981).
[27] Moore, *Social Origins*, 505.

The Court and the Country Revisited

DWIGHT D. BRAUTIGAM

Just over twenty years ago Professor Zagorin published one of the more influential recent monographs in early Stuart political history.[1] In setting out to explain the roots of the English Revolution and Civil Wars, he helped spur additional research on the early Stuarts and the political, social, and religious world in which the Revolution occurred. Central to his thesis was the argument that a concerted opposition movement grew up against the Crown, or the Court, consisting of men who could collectively be called the Country. This assertion of ideological differences both enhanced and reinforced much of the "classic" work on the same period, especially that of Samuel Gardiner.

Ten years later the field of early Stuart political history was stirred up by what became known as a "revisionist" work, Conrad Russell's *Parliaments and English Politics 1621–1629* (1979).[2] Russell's "revisionism" has several significant facets, but one of its main points is that earlier historians had been guilty of a too "Whiggish" version of early Stuart politics, and that the period preceding the Revolution needed examining in its own right rather than being viewed as only a backdrop for the coming upheaval. Consequently, Russell sees English political conflict in the 1620s in terms of court factions, interpersonal disputes, "administrative breakdown" due to the fiscal difficulties of war, and other activities. For him and others, such as Sir Geoffrey Elton, there was no "high road to civil war"[3] and the facts admitted of no such interpretation.

None of this is terribly new, yet while some debate has occurred over the impact of this "revisionism",[4] and no doubt there will be more, for the most part there has been no resounding rebuttal of Russell's main ideas.[5] Further-

[1] Perez Zagorin, *The Court and the Country* (New York: Routledge and Kegan Paul, 1969).

[2] See also, preliminary to the book some of its main arguments in Russell's seminal article, "Parliamentary History in Persepctive, 1604–1629," *History*, new series, no. 61 (1976).

[3] See Elton's article of that name in his *Studies in Tudor and Stuart Politics and Government*, vol. II (Cambridge, Cambridge University Press, 1974), 164–182.

[4] See the arguments contained in the *Journal of Modern History*, March 1978. Some ideas found here had been inspired by Russell's article noted above.

[5] As noted by Thomas Cogswell, *The Blessed Revolution* (Cambridge: Cambridge University Press, 1989), 2–3. Discussion does continue, however, and there are chal-

more, the effects of revisionism are producing additional debatable conclusions in other works in the field.[6] However, some recent works indicate a growing disaffection with the revisionist approach, and a reading of some of these indicates that we should not yet canonize Russell and his interpretation. Indeed, proper historical practice requires that we demonstrate the significance of "traditional" interpretations of early Stuart history, including that found in *The Court and the Country*.

To that end I would like to embark on a modest review of some selected recent works in the field, and even add to that my own perspectives garnered from studying the 1626 Parliament. Admittedly I will omit some significant works and offend no small number of scholars, but be that as it may. In reviewing these works, I hope to demonstrate that in fact they are directly related to, if not rooted in, the interpretation Professor Zagorin first offered some two decades ago. My primary focus will be on the decade of the 1620s, both because of its tremendous interest for early Stuart historians of politics/religion/foreign relations such as myself, and because my own work gives me more familiarity with that decade. While *The Court and the Country* focuses on a later period, the things I will propose about the 1620s should strengthen

---

lenges mounting to the predominance of revisionism. For further evidence of revisionism's impact on specialists of the period, see Thomas Cogswell, "Coping with Revisionism in Early Stuart History," *Journal of Modern History* 62:3 (September 1990), 538–551.

6 There are several examples of this, but perhaps the most striking in this essay's context is Kevin Sharpe's *Criticism and Compliment: The Politics of Literature in the England of Charles I* (Cambridge: Cambridge University Press, 1987) in which he, in his opening chapter, sets out to discredit the court/country thesis, which, he feels, has been relied on too heavily by both historians and literary scholars. Concerned with connections scholars make between "decadent" Caroline literature and a trend towards absolutism, Sharpe sets out to destroy "preconceptions which though flawed in themselves have laid the shaky foundations for that superficially commanding but inherently unstable edifice on the early Stuart landscape; the thesis of a court/country polarity" (p. 11). In the argument that follows, Sharpe bases his attack on the precept that members of any "court" or "country" group shared similar attitudes about drama, literature, etc. (for the entire section, see Sharpe, 11–22). While it is difficult, and may be foolhardy, to contend with Sharpe's claim for a shared context of literature, language, and other cultural components, I cannot see how such an assertion undermines the possibility of sharp political disagreement. Sharpe ignores issues of religion/theology altogether, yet makes a claim for understanding "ideology" of particular groups based on culture. The dangerous influence of Sharpe's argument is best illustrated by the comments of one of his reviewers, who thinks Sharpe brilliant on this point: "In a series of elegant case-studies of Carew, Davenant and Townshend, the lame old court-country hobby-horse is humanely and finally (one hopes) put down" (J.S.A. Adamson, in *English Historical Review* 105:414 [January 1990], 132). Such a comment shows us much more about the reviewer's predilections than the strength of Sharpe's argument, which the rest of the essay will undermine at least indirectly.

even more the arguments Professor Zagorin made about events and attitudes in the late 1630s and the early revolutionary period.

Perhaps the basis for my assertions can best be summed up in the word "divisions." There were a variety of divisions extant in the 1620s political world, and not all of them can be characterized with the terminology of patrons and clients, courtiers both privileged and disaffected, localists vs. city men, or the other labels favored by the revisionists. While no historian of the period would deny the existence of the several divisions, the revisionists may have underestimated the significance or deep-seated nature of those divisions. In particular, I refer to the overall importance of ideology as stressed by J.P. Sommerville, which includes the religious differences of the period, the manifestations of the various divisions that appear both in Cogswell's "Blessed Revolution" of 1623–4 and my own examination of the 1626 Parliament. Especially significant in 1626 are the June remonstrance from the House of Commons to the king, his response, and the connection of the Parliament's ending to the Forced Loan controversy so well described by Richard Cust.

Before analyzing those works, however, we can gain some valuable insights by briefly reviewing the disagreement between Russell and Zagorin over early Stuart political divisions. In his *Parliaments and English Politics*, Russell, concerned that we not view seventeenth century Parliaments as incurring "divisions" in the modern sense, castigated the use of "court" and "country" as being the sort of division which MPs in the 1620s would never have accepted. In criticizing this kind of division, and specifically taking Zagorin to task for using it, Russell asserts that early Stuart historians had been "using analytical tools which are incompatible with the structure of politics in the counties." Such men could not, Russell argues, see themselves as both "opposition" members of Parliament and servants of the Crown in local positions.[7] While there are other ramifications to Russell's own understanding of these MPs, it seems clear that perhaps it is he who is artificially applying twentieth century parliamentary standards to the actions of seventeenth century men.

The problem with the revisionist argument here is pointed out succinctly by Richard Cust and Ann Hughes in the introduction to their collection of essays, *Conflict in Early Stuart England*. Cust and Hughes focus on the particular problem just illustrated in Russell's rejection of Zagorin's "court" and "country" designations. Revisionists, the authors point out, tend to overlook human perceptions of politics in favor of mechanical or structural analyses. "For example, revisionists have criticized notions of a 'court-country' split — because as a matter of practical politics many were involved in both the court and the provinces — without making sufficient allowance for the possibility that 'court' and 'country' could operate as an ideological framework within which

---

[7] Russell, *Parliaments and English Politics* (Oxford: Oxford University Press, 1979), 6–7.

people viewed politics."[8] After all, unless one participated not at all in the political system, the very nature of seventeenth century English politics meant that one was in the service of both king and country.

The crucial difference, and one that the revisionists tend to overlook, was that a person of the "country" mentality, while not a twentieth century opposition politician, was certainly not necessarily unable to oppose the policies of the king. What did pose a problem for such opponents of royal policy was finding a way to do that without appearing unpatriotic or, even worse, treasonous. One of the tactics often relied on in such a case was to oppose policy from the grounds of loyalty, arguing for the misguidance of the king by incompetent or evil advisors whose influence needed to be removed.[9] Later on we shall see how the MPs in 1626 consistently held to such an argument in their attack on Buckingham and in their June remonstrance, a document that smacks of seventeenth century political opposition. Such an argument necessitates evaluating further the importance of the "ideological framework" raised by Cust and Hughes. What sorts of ideas were motivating these Englishmen who were loyal but could nonetheless disagree with royal policy?

J. P. Sommerville's *Politics and Ideology in England 1603–1640* offers substantial illumination on the idea of such a framework. In his concern with both "principles" and "applications," he sets out to demonstrate the significance of ideology in the political climate of early Stuart England. He is particularly interested in showing the sharpness of the division within the English body politic. To that end he explores the fundamentally conflicting views of royal sovereignty and the related fears of absolutism that built among some Englishmen as the seventeenth century unfolded and the continental political scene revealed the strength of that style of kingship. He notes in particular the rise of a royal absolutist theory in the England of James I, undergirded by arguments of divine right as well as theories of sovereignty based on natural law ideas. Was the king bound by the law, or only by the natural law of God as given directly to him? Where did that put Parliament and its activities in the scheme of things? That aspect of the argument alone was enough to rouse the suspicions of some Parliament men, but the rise of royal absolutist theories also allowed for the evolution of political divisions tied to religious differences. In particular, the 1620s saw the rise of the linked anti-popery and limited monarchy move-

---

[8] Richard Cust and Ann Hughes, eds., *Conflict in Early Stuart England* (New York: Longman, 1989), 13–14. Perhaps Sharpe (fn. no. 6 above) could be rebutted by one arguing, to paraphrase Cust and Hughes, that " 'court' and 'country' could operate as an ideological framework within which people viewed culture."

[9] This was not a novel argument in the early Stuart period by any means. For example, Shakespeare has his characters in *Henry VI* make such an argument, and the theory was not novel then either. This point was well emphasized by my fellow participants and our director, Annabel Patterson, in a NEH summer seminar (1990) held at the Bread Loaf School of English in Middlebury, Vermont.

ments, while absolutism became linked with anti-Calvinism. People who opposed Charles's policies joined with men who opposed Laud's religious innovations.[10] While such an alliance did not include all members of either group, still there developed a significant number of men who saw both absolutism and Arminianism as part of a dangerous political trend.

Furthermore, absolutism was widespread, not the personal property of an English lunatic fringe. Increased clergy support for it in the early seventeenth century, coupled with Stuart belief in it, plus the frightening examples of its success on the Continent, particularly in France, had dramatic results in England. While many analogies were called upon to illustrate absolutism, in the end its supporters saw its truth in their rational understanding of natural law and God's place in granting power directly to kings.[11]

Such arguments were anathema to the anti-absolutists. For them, the purpose of royal power was to enhance the common good. This line of thinking, of course, opened the possibility that any monarch not seen to be acting in the common good could expect to encounter resistance from his subjects. "Bad government" could be deemed sufficient reason for resistance, and in the 1620s, bad government seemed to be on the rise. In that decade, and in 1626 in particular with the attack on Buckingham, parliamentary resistance took the form of criticizing royal advisors for their nefarious influence on the king. Some construed direct resistance to the king as treason, but the idea of the public good allowed one to have a basis for disagreeing, even if discreetly and indirectly.

There was also a better way of dealing with bad government instead of directly resisting the king. That was to declare the law supreme over all, and if the king's word broke the law, anyone obeying the king would be in violation of the law. This was a "milder" way of addressing the problem.[12] In 1626, the House of Commons edged toward this kind of argument, though it did not develop it fully. When Charles cleared Buckingham of some charges during the 1626 Parliament by saying he had been following the king's orders, the House was frustrated by such action. By attacking Buckingham they sought to guide the king in a different direction, but they were not, as a body, quite ready to assert the ultimate supremacy of the law. That would come out more clearly in the Petition of Right. In noting this argument based on the law's supremacy, Sommerville emphasizes the connections between English political theorists and their counterparts on the continent. Just as they feared the imitation of continental-style absolutism by the Stuart kings, so they borrowed from the

[10] J. P. Sommerville, *Politics and Ideology in England 1603–1640* (New York: Longman, 1986), 45.

[11] *Ibid*, chap. 1 *passim*.

[12] *Ibid.*, chap. 2.

continental theorists who were confronting the absolutist threat in France and elsewhere.[13]

Such were the basic "principles" Sommerville describes. When he comes to his "applications," the importance of ideology is reinforced. While absolutist theories were well known under James I, the actual practices of Charles I made his contemporaries fear for the present state of England's constitutional balance. Charles's rule was "tyrannical" when understood on the basis of the theories behind it, and so resistance of some substance was necessary.[14] Tied to this perception of the king's policies was a fear that religious policy was part of the overall absolutist trend. The main argument here is that religious resistance and opposition to Charles and Archbishop Laud was primarily constitutional resistance based on fears for the liberty of the subject and fearing the success of absolutism, rather than theological differences such as Arminianism or any other such religious quibbles.[15] Such an argument made possible the alliance of two groups whose combined numbers and influence in Parliamentary circles posed a formidable obstacle to the successful governing of the kingdom by Charles, with or without Buckingham or anyone else. As the conviction grew that it was Charles's policies and practices, *not* his advisors, that were the source of the conflict between court and country, so the ideological division deepened between those two groups.

Given that ideological scenario, how does one respond to the revisionist argument that "the structure of politics" prevented any significant division? Sommerville confronts this head on:

There was no revolutionary party, bent on overthrowing monarchy and wresting sovereign authority for the House of Commons, in any Jacobean Parliament, nor indeed in any Parliament before the Civil War. This does not show that the war was an accident resulting from a sudden inexplicable breakdown in 1642 or a little earlier. Ideological divisions did exist in James's reign, and assumed immense political importance under his son, though they were not divisions between progressives anxious to usher in Parliamentary democracy and conservatives eager to maintain the status quo. No one wanted to alter the English constitution — the ancient frame of government – but there were profound disagreements on what that constitution was. The extent to which these mattered at any time depended upon many things and not least upon recent royal actions. When absolutism was put into practice, anti-absolutists grew irritated. That is why Charles I attracted more hostility than his father. Yet as long as kings held absolutist

13 *Ibid.*, 77.
14 *Ibid.*, 117.
15 *Ibid.*, chap. 5.

views, and as long as their financial needs made it tempting to act on such views, the danger of conflict was great.[16]

In addition, Sommerville also argues that "disaffection led to administrative breakdown, not vice versa."[17] He is referring to 1638–40 here, but he could be talking about the 1620s as well. It was not only the early Stuarts', especially Charles's, inability to fight wars while managing Parliaments that gave them such trouble. That was an important factor, and Russell makes that point particularly well, but one cannot forget that the precise reason Parliaments proved difficult for James and Charles to manage was because many members were ideologically opposed to the theories (under James) and the practices (under Charles) of absolutism. The depth of such resistance should not be characterized as modern Parliamentary opposition, but neither should it be belittled as factional politics worthy of no greater origin than feuds between great lords such as Pembroke and Buckingham.[18] The conflict between early Stuarts and their subjects was ideologically based; what better terms for that conflict than "court" vs. "country"?

Cogswell's work underscores this point with his analysis of the "blessed revolution" of 1623–4 when England undertook war with Spain. Though this work is rich with intriguing points which we must ignore here, Cogswell illustrates the practical impact of political divisions in the early 1620s, both in and out of Parliament. Englishmen were enthusiastic about entering the continental war in 1624; how else does one explain the large supply the 1624 MPs provided for the effort? But when that war was fought rather differently than Englishmen expected, they turned with equal vigor on the war's overseers, especially on Buckingham (Charles being beyond direct reproach at this point). Was this a fickle swing in attitude on the part of Parliament men, or were there in fact significant political differences between Charles's government and some key Parliament men, papered over by the temporary alliance he and Buckingham had made in 1624?

The latter case is made convincingly by Cogswell, helping to explain why Charles and Buckingham found it so difficult to manage Parliament in the frustrating sessions of 1625 and 1626.[19] What about this opposition? While Cogswell agrees that one must not use nineteenth century terminology and ideas to describe seventeenth century activities, he cautions against going to the "opposite extreme" and Namierizing the era. He also wishes to modify Russell's view of "court" and "country" by noting the importance of the 1624

---

[16] *Ibid.*, 235–36.

[17] *Ibid.*, 236.

[18] Russell relies heavily on this line of argument in his *Parliaments and English Politics*, chap. 5; for a rebuttal of his argument, see Dwight Brautigam, "The Parliament of 1626," (Ph.D. diss., University of Rochester, 1987).

[19] Cogswell, *Blessed Revolution*, 309–14.

opposition, its "country" character and, behind that, the significance of ideas, just as Sommerville points out. While factional interests were significant in the politics of the decade, so were ideas.[20]

Such an understanding of the time also emerges from my own study of the 1626 Parliament. While I will not take the time here to fully summarize the events of that Parliament, I must assert that its events bear out the significant ideological differences between a majority of Commons members (and even an influential group of peers in the Lords) and the Court. While I have not specifically used the term "country" to describe these opponents of royal policy, opponents they were. Even before the Parliament's beginning, in an attempt to handicap the leadership of such opposition, the king had permitted the famous sheriff selection ploy to exclude members from the Commons. Other tactics, but for similar reasons, were employed against the peers, with the same amount of success. Early on in 1626 the members of the Commons questioned government actions, including the conduct of the war, the misspending of the 1624 subsidies, the character of Buckingham in connection with those items, and in general demonstrated a fierce independence of royal control. Both houses stood firm in defense of privileges, the Lords perhaps taking an even stronger position than the better known Commons stance.

As the session continued (and it was the longest of the decade), it became clear that ideological commitment was behind Parliamentary intransigence. Perhaps the strongest evidence for this were the *two* remonstrances the House of Commons sent Charles, the second directly precipitating the Parliament's dissolution on 15 June. This second remonstrance (the first had occurred in April) was especially interesting in light of its assertions about Buckingham's role in the mishandling of English affairs and the none too successfully veiled implication that the Commons could ask for the dismissal of the greatest subject in the land before they would cooperate in providing supply for the king's government.[21] While all this was done within the context of loyalty, as to be expected in seventeenth century politics, and while it was not the manifesto of a revolutionary party, the strength of resolve found in the June remonstrance is nonetheless revealing.[22] For a variety of reasons, both houses of Parliament in 1626 found it within themselves to resist sometimes heavy pressure from the king to perform their patriotic duty of voting supply, and instead kept returning

[20] *Ibid.*, 319–320.

[21] Cogswell reinforces this point in his recent article examining the connections 1620s Parliaments made between redress of grievances and supply. See Thomas Cogswell, "A Low Road to Extinction? Supply and Redress of Grievances in the Parliaments of the 1620s," *The Historical Journal* 33:2 (June 1990): 283–303.

[22] I will make a more detailed argument elsewhere about the significance of this June Remonstrance, which inspired the remarkable action by the lower House to give a copy to any member who wanted one. Later the king's government tried futilely to obtain every existing copy of the offending document (*Commons' Journal*, I:871).

to the distinctly nonfactional business of calling for the redress of grievances and examining their particular privileges within the constitutional system.[23] How is one to understand all this activity only within a framework of factional politics, or, for 1626, within the even narrower confines of the Pembroke-Buckingham clash, as Russell is wont to do?[24] We do little justice to that Parliament, or indeed to the Forced Loan controversy that follows it, by ignoring such sharp political divisions simply because the "structure of politics" does not seem to allow for them.

The best discussion of that Forced Loan situation occurs in Richard Cust's excellent book on the subject. His treatment reinforces my own conclusions about the 1626 Parliament, since the Forced Loan sprang from the divisive political atmosphere surrounding the June dissolution. Cust portrays Charles' view of the June Remonstrance as a direct attack on the king's prerogative, particularly in the matter of choosing his own councillors. Cust also demonstrates that Charles had inherited James I's fear of a grasping House of Commons that wished to obtain greater power. Consequently, when the Privy Council implemented the machinery to effect the Forced Loan, it was reflecting not only the government's need for money, but also an attitude reflected in Cust's assertion that "after the 1626 dissolution the government began to act as if it would never have to face Parliament again." Consequently, the Privy Council directed some of its harshest privy seal loans against Buckingham's parliamentary detractors. Though such loans were not terribly successful, their proposal indicated the depth of feeling attributable to the Duke, at least, if not also his master, the king.[25] Cust concludes that by September 1626,

> All appearance of promoting unity between Crown and subject was cast aside and instead the Council was putting itself into a position where extensive use of the prerogative was accepted as virtually inevitable. Moreover in saddling certain individuals with heavy payments, it was turning what had originally been just a scheme for raising money into a device for punishing the Duke's enemies.

This was the preparation for the tactics accompanying the Forced Loan.[26]

Cust's conclusions emphasize the growing distrust that characterized relations between Charles and his leading opponents. He sees that distrust as growing out of the period between the end of the 1626 Parliament and the

[23] The House of Commons did this fairly consistently throughout the Parliament; see Brautigam, *The Parliament of 1626, passim.* The House of Lords also proved remarkably obstinate (from Charles's viewpoint, anyway) in this area of conflict; Brautigam, chap. 5.

[24] Russell, *Parliaments,* chap. 5.

[25] Richard Cust, *The Forced Loan and English Politics 1626–1628* (Oxford: Oxford University Press, 1987), chap. 1.

[26] Cust, *ibid.*

beginning of the 1628 Parliament, but his interpretation is certainly consistent with my own understanding of the 1626 Parliament. While the distrust intensified from June 1626 on, the process clearly has roots at least as far back as the entire 1626 Parliament, as the Commons' Remonstrances of that session, along with many other events, demonstrate. Cust also argues that there were a number of "broad issues" involved in the conflict of this period, and that such conflict was not narrowly confined to the Forced Loan, though it of course did engender a lot of problems. He too emphasizes the importance of Sommerville's thinking and the ideological division that, he argues, the Forced Loan imbroglio exacerbated. He also sees the impact of religious differences growing here, as Nicholas Tyacke and others have pointed out.[27] While Cust may agree with Russell in urging early Stuart historians to look outside Parliament for important political activity, Cust provides a valuable correction in describing the significance of the political divisions both at court and in the countryside and the tactics that opponents of highhanded royal governing sharpened and used repeatedly starting in 1626. Cust might not explicitly use Zagorin's "court" and "country" terminology, but he is certainly more comfortable with that concept than the "revisionists" in the field.[28]

What conclusions can I offer, then, about such a broad subject, or array of subjects? Plainly I am no revisionist, and hence do not wish to adopt a serendipitous approach to the English Revolution and Civil War. They did not just happen. Neither, however, does anyone wish to fall into Whig determinism or even ambitiously rebuild the "high road to civil war" so vigorously destroyed (in part, anyway) by Russell, Elton, and others. In striving to clarify the picture, to offer some countering interpretation to the prevailing revisionist one, I would like for us to retain this significant and still largely accurate designation that Professor Zagorin has given us. "Court" and "country" do have special import in describing the English political scene under the early Stuarts. The terms themselves are not perfect, but neither is our understanding of those times and events that still attract us so. But if the terms are imperfect, thus far no one has offered a convincing explanation for abandoning them. Should we simply step back, throw our hands up, and explain the 1640s by saying we cannot really explain them very well at all, or best through mechanical models? Should we assume that somehow ideas, whether political, religious, social, economic, or otherwise, did not carry the force or appeal for seventeenth century Englishmen that they carry for us? Perhaps I overstate or oversimplify the case. If so, I do so only in the name of finding balance here. Balance is best served, it seems to me, by retaining terms that have served us well: the "court" and the "country."

---

[27] Nicholas Tyacke, *Anti-Calvinists: The Rise of English Arminianism c. 1590–1640* (Oxford: Oxford University Press, 1987).
[28] Cust, *Forced Loan*, 316–37.

64

The "Imperial Crown"
and the Liberty of the Subject:
The English Constitution
from Magna Carta to the Bill of Rights

JOHN GUY

This essay is about the divine right of kings and the royal prerogative in England.[1] I shall revisit the debates upon law and regality in the centuries between Magna Carta (1215) and the Bill of Rights (1689). These debates were a function of political transactions whereby subjects sought to limit the ruler's *imperium* by invoking the notion of the "rule of law". A common strategy was to link the king's coronation oath to a declaration of the "ancient" or "fundamental" laws and liberties of the kingdom; the "laws" and "liberties" which could not be abridged if the king were to respect the sanctity of his oath. These "laws" and "liberties" might be derived from customs, royal concessions or specific acts of legislation. They might be enshrined in charters, statutes or the records of the courts of law. They might even be unwritten if the "memory of man runneth not to the contrary". There was, and still is, no written "constitution" in the United Kingdom: the word "constitution" was rarely used before the mid-seventeenth century to refer to a binding political settlement. When historians speak of the English "constitution", they refer to the protocol which regulated the relations of kings with their councillors and subjects. This protocol was the subject of continual negotiation. There was no "immutable" law, nor did judicial review exist as the concept is understood in the United States. "Laws" and "liberties" could be modified or repealed by new legislation,

[1] My warmest thanks to Professor Linda Levy Peck and Dr Ronald Hutton for their comments upon an earlier draft of this paper, and to Professor J. G. A. Pocock for allowing me to read the typescript of his lectures on early-modern British Political Thought delivered in 1989 at the Villa Spelman, Florence. This chapter is a revised version of the 1990 Hinkley Memorial Lecture which I delivered at The Johns Hopkins University while the incumbent of the John Hinkley Visiting Professorship. I am extremely grateful to the History Department for the generous hospitality I was afforded during the spring semester.

or might even be emasculated politically. "Liberties" were, however, increasingly related to the possession of property and regarded as hereditary.[2]

In the later Middle Ages concepts of regality were formulated in idioms borrowed from Roman law: the ruler's prerogative was "ordinary" and "absolute".[3] By his "ordinary" prerogative he enforced juridically the privileges and "preeminences" which he enjoyed as a superior feudal lord. He might also issue pardons or mitigate the effect of statutes for the benefit of individuals. The feudal "preeminences" which the king enjoyed by the reign of Edward I were codified in the apocryphal Statute *De praerogativa regis*.[4] Again, the Statutes of Provisors and *Praemunire* prohibited the reception of papal jurisdiction into England in derogation of royal prerogative and the laws and customs of the realm.[5] These powers were integral to the common law. They helped to define what the king was king and lord over, and it was in this mode that lawyers spoke of the king's prerogative "by the order of the common law".[6]

The ruler's "absolute" prerogative was his emergency power. In time of war or revolt he could suspend the law, billet troops on householders, and levy taxation without parliamentary consent. In case of fire he might override the statutes which protected freehold property in order to demolish burning buildings. Furthermore, he was the sole judge of cases of necessity. The judges held in 1292 that "for the common utility [the king] is in many cases by his prerogative above the laws and customs usually recognized in his realm";[7] and Sir John

2   In this period the "liberty" of the subject rarely implied a natural right inhering in the human personality or an abstract conception of freedom. See, for example, J. P. Sommerville, *Politics and Ideology in England, 1603–1640* (London: Longman, 1986), 145–83.

3   The terms *ordinaria*, *ordinatia* and *regula* were variously used to signify the exercise of authority by kings and popes according to rules of positive law. But the theocratic ruler was also above the law as the prerogative of his *imperium*. In this sphere he ruled *dei gratia* and was *legibus solutus*. W. Ullmann, *Principles of Government and Politics in the Middle Ages* (London: Methuen, 2nd edn., 1966); F. Oakley, "Jacobean Political Theology: The Absolute and Ordinary Powers of the King," *Journal of the History of Ideas*, 29 (1968), 323–46; Janelle R. Greenberg, *Tudor and Stuart Theories of Kingship: the Dispensing Power and the Royal Discretionary Authority in Sixteenth and Seventeenth Century England* (University Microfilms, Ann Arbor: University of Michigan Ph.D., 1970), 37–42.

4   17 Edw. II, st. 1; F. Pollock and F. W. Maitland, *The History of English Law Before the Time of Edward I* (2 vols.; 2nd edn.; Cambridge, 1968), I, 336, 338, 339, 463 n. 1, 481.

5   35 Edw. I, st. 1; 25 Edw. III, st. 5, c. 22; and st. 6, c. 2; 27 Edw. III, st. 1, c. 1; 38 Edw III, st. 1, c. 4; and st. 2, cc. 1–4; 3 Ric. II, c. 3; 7 Ric. II, c. 12; 12 Ric. II, c. 15; 13 Ric. II, st. 2, cc. 2–3; 16 Ric. II, c. 5; 2 Hen. IV, cc. 3–4; 6 Hen. IV, c. 1; 7 Hen. IV, c. 8; 9 Hen. IV, c. 8; 3 Hen. V, c. 4.

6   W. Staunford, *An exposicion of the kinges prerogative collected out of the great abridgement of justice Fitzherbert and other olde writers of the lawes of Englande* (London, 1567); STC[2] no. 23213.

7   Ullmann, *Principles of Government and Politics*, 184 n. 2.

Fortescue, writing in the 1460s and 1470s, conceded that the dominion of the king of England was *regale* as well as *politicum*. In his "politic" role the king might not tax his subjects nor change the laws "without the grant or assent of his whole realm expressed in Parliament". But in time of emergency he was untrammelled by such restrictions.[8]

The most systematic exposition of the royal prerogative was given in 1533 when Henry VIII annexed the language of "imperial" kingship in order to break with Rome and declare his royal supremacy over the English church. Henry's political theology was proclaimed in the preamble to the Act of Appeals:

> Where by divers sundry old authentic histories and chronicles it is manifestly declared and expressed that this realm of England is an empire, and so hath been accepted in the world, governed by one supreme head and king having the dignity and royal estate of the imperial crown of the same, unto whom a body politic, compact of all sorts and degrees of people divided in terms and by names of spiritualty and temporalty, be bounden and owe to bear next to God a natural and humble obedience; [the king] being also institute and furnished by the goodness and sufferance of Almighty God with plenary, whole and entire power, preeminence, authority, prerogative and jurisdiction . . .[9]

Henry VIII defined his prerogative in terms of his *imperium*. He argued, first, that the kings of England from the second century AD had enjoyed secular *imperium* and spiritual supremacy over their kingdom and national church; and, second, that the English church was an autonomous province of the Catholic church independent from Rome and the papacy. Moreover, the use of Parliament by the Tudors to declare and enforce the royal supremacy should not be misinterpreted. The supremacy was not equivalent to a doctrine of parliamentary sovereignty. On the contrary, it was modelled upon Constantine's government of the Roman Empire after his conversion to Christianity: the Crown assumed full responsibility for the ordering of the church. Under the Tudors and early-Stuarts the supremacy was inherent in the monarch alone. Parliament simply recognized that pre-existent fact.[10]

In a striking sense, therefore, Henry VIII proclaimed the divine right of

[8] *De laudibus legum anglie* (ed.) S. B. Chrimes (Cambridge: Cambridge University Press, 1949).

[9] 24 Hen. VIII, c. 12.

[10] Alistair Fox and John Guy, *Reassessing the Henrician Age: Humanism, Politics and Reform* (Oxford: Basil Blackwell, 1986), 151–78; G. Nicholson, "The Act of Appeals and the English Reformation," Claire Cross, David Loades and J. J. Scarisbrick (eds.), *Law and Government under the Tudors* (Cambridge: Cambridge University Press, 1988), 19–30; John Guy, *Tudor England* (Oxford: Oxford University Press, 1988), 116–53, 369–78.

kings. His *imperium* was ordained by God and embraced both "temporal" and "spiritual" government. The kings of England were invested with an "imperial" sovereignty, part of which had been "lent" to the priesthood by previous English monarchs. Moreover, royal *imperium* was antecedent to the jurisdiction of the clergy and was inalienable. Despite its partial "loan" to the clergy, it could be resumed by the king at will. By exercising his *imperium* the king could redefine the duties of "his" clergy, summon church councils within his dominions, revise canon law, dissolve the monasteries and even expound the articles of faith. In particular, he could require Convocation to rule on his not infrequent matrimonial problems, and then invite Parliament to enforce this verdict by statute and common law.

Henry VIII had an extensive knowledge of law and theology. He could recite from memory extracts from Justinian's Code in order to assert the sovereignty of "emperors" who determined faith and heresy. He trawled the Old Testament in Latin and Hebrew for references to the *imperium* of rulers from Solomon onwards who appointed lay and clerical judges, disciplined their clergy, and determined spiritual and temporal affairs. Assisted by his scholars he even wrote a series of "king's books" or dissertations.

The neatest defence of royal *imperium* was culled from the *leges Anglorum*, an interpolation of the "Laws of Edward the Confessor". The crucial extract concerned Lucius I, the mythical ruler of Britain who was converted to Christianity in AD 187 and wrote to Pope Eleutherius asking him to transmit the Roman law. In reply Eleutherius explained that Lucius did not need the Roman law, because he already had the Old and New Testaments from which he might himself "take a law" for his kingdom. In a passage which became a Tudor battle-cry, Eleutherius recognized Lucius to be "vicar of God" in his kingdom; he was the superior legislator who "gave" the law and exercised *imperium* over church and state.[11]

From here it was a short step to Ulpian's thesis that the king was above the law as the prerogative of his *imperium*. The pith may be found in the notes of Henry VIII's advisers upon the most important legal treatise of the Middle Ages, Bracton's *On the Laws and Customs of England*. Whereas Bracton had stated that the king of England was "under God and the law, because the law makes the king", Henry VIII claimed that the king was "under God but not the law, because the king makes the law".[12] The question therefore became: What was the extent of the king's mystical "absolute" power? Could his *imperium* be admeasured by the common law?

The most fertile counter-thesis came from the pen of Christopher St German, a retired common lawyer who went into print to argue that it was not

[11] Fox and Guy, *Reassessing the Henrician Age*, 158–72.
[12] British Library, Cotton MS. Cleopatra E. vi, fo. 28ᵛ; Fox and Guy, *Reassessing the Henrician Age*, 159.

the "vicar of God" but the "king-in-Parliament" which was "high sovereign over the people".[13] In a reading proleptic of Richard Hooker's *Of the Laws of Ecclesiastical Polity*, St German argued that all law, whether secular or ecclesiastical, was properly made by king, lords and Commons in Parliament assembled, "for the Parliament so gathered together representeth the estate of all the people within this realm, that is to say of the whole catholic church thereof".[14] St German agreed with Henry VIII that church and state were coextensive. He therefore applied Fortescue's concept of *dominium politicum et regale* to both in order to argue that the king of England should govern in a parliamentary way. St German particularly withheld from Henry VIII the prerogative to interpret the canonical texts of scripture as supreme head of the church and thus to expound divine law. He argued that Parliament should perform this fundamental task since "the whole catholic church" came together in Parliament.[15]

Yet the politics of *imperium* were not new. Henry IV of Germany and Philip IV of France were among the medieval rulers who had wielded "imperial" vocabulary against the papacy. In the late-twelfth and early-thirteenth centuries England had herself witnessed an "experiment" in "imperial" kingship. This Angevin "experiment" was most visible in the sphere of criminal jurisdiction, where the concept of the king's peace rested on the notion that it was the king's theocratic duty to maintain law and order.[16] It was upon the platform of peace and order that such centralizing "reforms" as Henry II's "Constitutions of Clarendon" and "Inquest of Sheriffs" were presented, measures targeted against criminals and offenders, but which threatened the power of the magnates and prelates in their jurisdictions. Admittedly Henry II's dispute with Archbishop Becket cost him prestige; but the image of the king as *lex loquens* was resilient. In fact, both Glanville and John of Salisbury endorsed Ulpian's other maxim, "What has pleased the prince has the force of law". And when King John finally declared in 1202 that "regnum Angliae quasi imperio adequetur", we may reasonably ask whether his utterance was equivalent to Henry VIII's that "this realm of England is an empire".[17]

[13] *St German's Doctor and Student* (ed.) T. F. T. Plucknett and J. L. Barton (London: Selden Society, 1974), 317–40; John Guy, *Christopher St German on Chancery and Statute* (London: Selden Society, Supplementary Series, vol. 6, 1985); Fox and Guy, *Reassessing the Henrician Age*, 95–120, 179–98; John Guy, Ralph Keen, Clarence Miller and Ruth McGugan (eds.), *The Complete Works of St Thomas More*, Vol. 10: *The Debellation of Salem and Bizance* (New Haven, Conn.: Yale University Press, 1987 [1988]), xxix–xlvi, 395–417; G. R. Elton, "*Lex terrae victrix*: The Triumph of Parliamentary Law in the Sixteenth Century," D. M. Dean and N. L. Jones (eds.), *The Parliaments of Elizabethan England* (Oxford: Basil Blackwell, 1990), 15–36.

[14] St German, *An Answer to a Letter* (London, 1535), sigs. G5ᵛ–G6ᵛ; STC² no. 21558.5; Fox and Guy, *Reassessing the Henrician Age*, 199–220.

[15] *An Answer to a Letter*, sigs. G3–G6ᵛ.

[16] Ullmann, *Principles of Government and Politics*, 117–37, 155–60.

[17] Ullmann, *Principles of Government and Politics*, 159–60.

When, therefore, the barons deployed the "feudal" lexicon of politics against the "imperial" one, they protested that John governed by his "will" and not by "law", since the touchstone of "feudal" law was that its legality derived from the "counsel and consent" of the magnates. The baronial rebellion thus began with a demand for the reissue of Henry I's coronation charter, which (like Magna Carta) began with the liberties of the Church and proceeded to feudal incidents. Next, the barons and their advisers studied the "Laws of Henry I", the "Laws of Edward the Confessor" and (in all probability) Conrad II's decree concerning the "judgement" of peers to be found in the *Liber feudorum*. Their concerns were the issues of justice, judgement by peers, and baronial counselling and advice, and their final strategy was to demand the reissue of Henry I's charter and the renewal of John's coronation oath in concert as the basis of a feudal "constitutional" settlement.[18]

It is ironic that the barons glossed the identical interpolation of the "Laws of Edward the Confessor" which retailed the legend of King Lucius.[19] In the politics of 1215, however, the moral was not that Eleutherius had told Lucius that he might "take a law" for his kingdom, but that he told him to "take a law *per consilium regni vestri*" – "with the counsel of your realm". Whereas Henry VIII deployed King Lucius as a foil against the *imperium* of the pope and in defence of his own "imperial" autonomy, the barons deployed Pope Eleutherius as a foil against the *imperium* of the Angevins and in defence of the "feudal" principle of "counsel and consent".

The most celebrated chapter of Magna Carta read:

> No free man shall be taken or imprisoned or disseised or outlawed or exiled or in any way ruined, nor will we go or send against him, except by the lawful judgement of his peers and by the law of the land.[20]

The significance of this clause is disputed, but it was not Roman law, the king's law, or the customary law of villages outside the scope of the feudal compact which the barons contemplated when they spoke of *lex terrae* – the "law of the land". What they meant was feudal law, the "law" made with the "counsel and consent" of the barons.[21] Moreover, since this "law" was common to the king and his tenants-in-chief, it was in this sense "common" to the land.

---

[18] J. C. Holt, *Magna Carta* (Cambridge: Cambridge University Press, 1969); Ullmann, *Principles of Government and Politics*, 162–74; J. C. Holt, "The Ancient Constitution in Medieval England," paper read to the Liberty Fund Symposium, *Magna Carta and Ancient Constitution: Medieval and Renaissance Roots of American Liberty*, St George's House, Windsor Castle, June 15, 1988.

[19] Ullmann, *Principles of Government and Politics*, 161–2.

[20] Holt, *Magna Carta*, 326–7. I have translated the disputed *vel* as "and" not "or" for the reasons given by Ullmann, *Principles of Government and Politics*, 164–5.

[21] Ullmann, *Principles of Government and Politics*, 165–70.

Thereafter, successive confirmations of Magna Carta ensured that issues of politics and property were firmly linked to statute and common law. By an almost osmotic process "feudal" law and customary law distilled into "common law" by the beginning of the fourteenth century, and it was judges and advocates in the common law courts who interpreted the phrase "lawful judgement of peers" to mean "trial by jury"; who glossed the words "no free man" as "no man of whatever estate or condition he may be"; and who interpreted *lex terrae* to mean "due process of law", that is to say, procedure by original writ or indicting jury.[22] These definitions were incorporated into the reissued texts of Magna Carta enacted in Parliament between 1331 and 1363, and for the next two hundred years the most frequent appeals to Magna Carta were heard in pleadings designed to abridge the jurisdiction of chancery and the prerogative courts, and to confine litigation concerning freehold property to the courts of common law.[23]

It has been said that "Magna Carta sealed the fate of the monarchic king".[24] The articles that, in turn, preceded the depositions of Edward II and Richard II charged that each had ignored his feudal obligations. Moreover, the chief accusation against Richard II was that he had tried to govern by his *voluntas*. Everyone's life, goods and chattels were "at his will . . . contrary to the laws and customs of England"; he had even claimed that "the laws were in his own mouth".[25] His deposition hastened the process which culminated in Fortescue's doctrine of *dominium politicum et regale*. The king was "above the law" in the sense that he was not subject to anyone. He was the superior legislator who could not be sued in the courts of common law. Yet he could not "make" or "give" the law as the prerogative of his *imperium*. In order to legislate he required "the assent of his whole realm expressed in Parliament". Neither did he give judgement out of his own mouth in the law courts, but relied instead on the wisdom of his judges.[26] By the end of the fifteenth century the king was no longer a *lex loquens*. He had been transformed into a "limited" or "constitutional" ruler.

What could not have been predicted was that the thesis which underpinned Henry VIII's break with Rome would reactivate the theocratic component of

[22] Holt, "Ancient Constitution in Medieval England"; Faith Thompson, *Magna Carta, Its Role in the Making of the English Constitution, 1300–1629* (Minneapolis: Minnesota University Press, 1948); J. C. Holt, *Magna Carta and Medieval Government* (London: Hambledon Press, 1985).

[23] *The Reports of Sir John Spelman* (ed.) J. H. Baker (2 vols.; London: Selden Society, 1977), II, intro. 71–5, 84; Guy, *Christopher St German on Chancery and Statute*, 64–94. For a full list of citations on "due process" legislation and legal cases, see R. C. Johnson, M. F. Keeler, M. J. Cole, and W. B. Bidwell (eds.), *Proceedings in Parliament 1628* (6 vols.; New Haven, Conn., 1977–83), I, 104–36.

[24] Ullmann, *Principles of Government and Politics*, 174.

[25] Ullmann, *Principles of Government and Politics*, 182–3.

[26] *De laudibus legum anglie* (ed.) Chrimes, 23–7, 31–3, 79, 87–9, 89–91, 137.

kingship.[27] The question became: Could the king *in his new capacity as supreme head of the church* attempt what Richard II had done and get away with it? Were property rights secure? The dissolution of the monasteries and chantries under Henry VIII and Edward VI rendered this question urgent.[28] From another standpoint it was also the issue in Mary's reign, when parliamentary resistance to reconciliation with Rome was largely based on the fear that those who had purchased former religious lands would be stripped of their titles.[29] When Elizabeth's first Parliament assembled, the minority of active Protestants secured a favourable religious settlement mainly thanks to the continuing property scare.[30] By 1559 it was fully understood that the security of property transactions resulting from the dissolution of the monasteries and chantries rested exclusively upon statute and common law. Yet the superior authority of statute and common law over canon and papal law would be established only if the royal supremacy were restored. Canon and papal law had been as valid as common law under Mary, when the legitimacy of the transfer to the laity of the ex-religious lands had been disputed by the pope. In 1559 the interests of property owners were identified with the cause of the Reformation to the point where the religious settlement was enacted without a single churchman's consent.[31]

The issue of ex-religious property rights caused pens to quiver as late as the Exclusion Crisis, but a working principle was established when Henry VIII acknowledged that any significant extension of his *imperium* was in practice beyond his range. Thus, when Bishop Gardiner protested in Parliament that a *praemunire* action against the bishop of Exeter was *ultra vires* on the grounds that every bishop was "authorized" by the king, Lord Chancellor Audley retorted that he should consult the laws and customs of England, where he would "discover" that the king's *imperium* was confined to spiritual matters. " 'And [if] this were not', quoth he, 'you bishops would enter in with the king, and, by means of his supremacy, order the laity as ye listed. But we will provide . . . that the *praemunire* shall ever hang over your heads; and so we laymen shall be sure to enjoy our inheritance by the common laws, and acts of Parliament.' "[32]

Audley's formula was rhetorical, but the definitions of *praemunire* and pro-

---

[27] Fox and Guy, *Reassessing the Henrician Age*, 151–78.

[28] Guy, *Tudor England*, 143–9, 205–7.

[29] J. Loach, *Parliament and the Crown in the Reign of Mary Tudor* (Oxford: Oxford University Press, 1986).

[30] N.L. Jones, *Faith by Statute: Parliament and the Settlement of Religion 1559* (London: Royal Historical Society, 1982); Guy, *Tudor England*, 258–64; G. Alexander, "Bishop Bonner and the Parliament of 1559," *Bulletin of the Institute of Historical Research*, 56 (1983), 164–79.

[31] John Guy, "Law, Lawyers, and the English Reformation," *History Today*, 35 (Nov. 1985), 16–22.

[32] *The Acts and Monuments of John Foxe* (ed.) G. Townsend (8 vols.; London, 1843–9), VI, 43.

hibition were indeed extended to enable the common lawyers to temper not only the jurisdiction of the church courts under the Crown, but even litigation in the royal courts of equity and admiralty. The politics of this accommodation were that the Tudors needed the support of the common lawyers as well as the bishops, because the Reformation required penal enforcement until Protestantism became embedded at parish level.[33] Again, Henry VIII relied on statute and common law to assure to his coffers the proceeds of the monastic dissolutions. In return, he endorsed the common lawyers' crusade against clerical jurisdiction, which culminated in legislation whereby canon law and Convocation itself were legally subordinated to the Crown. The common lawyers won exclusive rights of audience in chancery and the prerogative courts, and by the 1560s had secured exclusive jurisdiction over real property litigation, thereby increasing their profits and professional esteem.[34]

Where friction arose was over, first, the jurisdiction of the Court of High Commission; and, second, the use of administrative patents and monopolies by the Crown in its conduct of local government. In the later years of Elizabeth's reign, "divine right" theory of monarchy and episcopacy stirred unease in Protestant circles, and the legality of the High Commission to which the queen deputed the enforcement of her ecclesiastical prerogative was challenged by those who denied the right of the bishops to deprive puritan clergy on grounds of conscience, and to fine and imprison laymen in trials by civil law procedure.[35]

In Cawdrey's Case (1591) the judges held that the queen might authorize the Commission because "by the ancient laws of this realm this kingdom of England is an absolute empire and monarchy".[36] This was the language of the Act of Appeals, and the fact that the ruler's *imperium* was now admitted by the "ancient laws of this realm" did not dislodge its theocratic component. However, the judges decided that when the High Commission rested only on the prerogative, it was obliged to observe the restrictions of existing ecclesiastical

[33] Guy, "Law, Lawyers, and the English Reformation."
[34] Fox and Guy, *Reassessing the Henrician Age*, 95–120, 179–98; G. R. Elton, *Studies in Tudor and Stuart Politics and Government* (3 vols.; Cambridge, 1974–83), II, 107–36; John Guy, *The Public Career of Sir Thomas More* (New Haven, Conn.: Yale University Press, 1980), 175–201; John Guy, *The Court of Star Chamber and its Records to the Reign of Elizabeth I* (London: Her Majesty's Stationery Office, 1985); E. Skelton, "The Court of Star Chamber in the Reign of Queen Elizabeth" (unpublished University of London, M.A. dissertation, 1931).
[35] P. Collinson, *The Elizabethan Puritan Movement* (Oxford: Oxford University Press, 1990), 385–467; P. Lake, *Anglicans and Puritans? Presbyterianism and English Conformist Thought from Whitgift to Hooker* (London: Unwin Hyman, 1988); D. MacCulloch, *The Later Reformation in England, 1547–1603* (London: MacMillan, 1990); G. R. Elton, *The Tudor Constitution* (2nd edn.; Cambridge: Cambridge University Press, 1982), 221–32.
[36] Elton, *Tudor Constitution*, 231–2.

law. And they reiterated this view in 1606, when they held that neither temporal nor ecclesiastical law could be altered by royal commission.[37] Following debate in the Parliament of 1610, James I announced that persons aggrieved by the High Commission's sentences might petition him in person for a commission of review.[38] But this was perilously close to claiming that he was a *lex loquens*.

Moreover, Cawdrey's Case precipitated a discourse in which the king's mystical divinity and emergency power were subsumed beneath a single veil. In this sphere the king was *legibus solutus*; the novelty was that his civil emergency power acquired an aura of sanctity unknown to Fortescue when he spoke of *dominium regale*. The Crown's emergency power became annexed to the "divinity" that hedges a king.

In Parliament, meanwhile, patents and monopolies provoked clashes which were the ugliest before 1628. Elizabeth was forced to annul some monopolies and allow corrupt patentees to be sued.[39] The underlying problem was that the Crown lacked the resources to match the demands of local government and economic regulation in a period of continuous warfare. Since the Tudors also failed to develop an adequate theory of sovereignty, their polity was vulnerable to corrosion. Disputes over martial law and ship money vexed the counties in the 1590s, and the Privy Council's decrees and proclamations were ignored, which encouraged a proposal to make them "of the like force as the common law or an Act of Parliament".[40] On the other hand, it was community interests and not the Crown itself which lobbied most vigorously in favour of administrative patents at this time, on the grounds that they were the way to get things done. Prominent among these sectional interests were overseas trading companies, urban corporations and Oxford and Cambridge colleges seeking to liberate themselves from inconvenient restrictions on their autonomy.[41]

The classic exposition of regality in the reign of James I was delivered by Chief Baron Fleming in Bate's Case (1606).[42] Here the king's "ordinary" power was distinguished from his "absolute" power on the grounds that these had different "laws" and "ends". The "ordinary" power was for the benefit of individuals and for the execution of justice in the ordinary courts of law. It signified the common law, which could only be changed in Parliament. In contrast

[37] J. R. Tanner, *Constitutional Documents of the Reign of James I* (Cambridge: Cambridge University Press, 1952), 146–8.

[38] J. P. Kenyon, *The Stuart Constitution* (2nd edn.; Cambridge: Cambridge University Press, 1986), 162–3.

[39] Guy, *Tudor England*, 397–403.

[40] M. A. Judson, *The Crisis of the Constitution* (New York: Octagon Books, 1976), 120.

[41] Victor Morgan, "Whose Prerogative in Late Sixteenth and Early Seventeenth Century England?", A. Kiralfy, M. Slatter and R. Virgoe (eds.), *Custom, Courts and Counsel* (London: Frank Cass, 1985), 39–64.

[42] Tanner, *Constitutional Documents of the Reign of James I*, 337–45.

"absolute" power was exercised for the general benefit of the kingdom and was *salus populi*. It was properly named "policy and government", and might be varied according to the king's discretion for the attaining of the common good.[43]

This formula was indebted to Bracton, but it sowed the seeds of a binary opposition between common law and "absolute" prerogative: first, because the latter was not confined to war or emergency as in the theory of Fortescue; and, second, because "policy and government" constituted a "law" distinct from that which had normally been understood by the words *lex terrae* since the fourteenth century. This became evident in 1613, when the Privy Council rejected the plea that the *lex terrae* clause of Magna Carta protected the subject from prerogative jurisdiction, giving as their reason the fact that "his Majesty's Prerogative and his absolute power incident to his sovereignty is also *lex terrae* and is invested and exercised by the law of the land, and is part thereof".[44]

If, however, *lex terrae* was conceivable as neither "feudal" law nor common law, it was a relatively short step to the thesis that the king's "absolute" power is *ius majestatis* or "law of state"; that when rulers act by law of state they are bounded only by the law of nature; and that the common law cannot admeasure matters of state, since when necessity of state requires it, kings may proceed according to natural equity.[45]

The counter-thesis came from the common lawyers who argued that "the king of England [is] the most absolute king in his parliament; but, of himself, his power is limited by law"; and again that the "common laws of [England] do measure the king's prerogative".[46] These were statements not incompatible with Fleming's exposition in Bate's Case, since it was usually agreed in the reign of James I that the king's "absolute" prerogative only operated outside the law when the law itself had no purchase. Royal prerogative was a supplement to common law and not an alternative; hence it is anachronistic to posit the existence of two conflicting ideologies before 1625.[47] The dissonance under

---

[43] For instances of the doctrine of "ordinary" and "absolute" prerogative in 1551 and the 1590s, see Judson, *Crisis of the Constitution*, 111–12. Fleming had previously advocated the arguments he advanced in Bate's Case in *Darcy v. Allen* (1601). I owe this information to the kindness of Professor David Harris Sacks.

[44] Judson, *Crisis of the Constitution*, 121–2.

[45] Sommerville, *Politics and Ideology in England*, 9–50; Judson, *Crisis of the Constitution*, 114–16, 135–6, 163–9; *Proceedings in Parliament 1628*, V, 281–4.

[46] S. R. Gardiner (ed.), *Parliamentary Debates in 1610* (London: Camden Society, 1st series, vol. 81, 1861), 89; E. R. Foster (ed.), *Proceedings in Parliament 1610* (2 vols.; New Haven, Conn., 1966), II, 158–9; Greenberg, *Tudor and Stuart Theories of Kingship*, 142–6.

[47] G. Burgess, "Common Law and Political Theory in Early Stuart England," *Political Science*, 40 (1988), 4–17; P. Christianson, "Royal and Parliamentary Voices on the Ancient Constitution, c. 1604–1621," Linda Levy Peck (ed.), *The Mental World of the Jacobean Court* (Cambridge: Cambridge University Press, 1991), 71–95; Conrad

James was modal, and derived from the king's conception of his prerogative in terms of divinity rather than of law. Whereas Henry VIII had joined forces with the common lawyers in order to defend his "imperial" sovereignty against the pope, James I declared that his mystical "absolute" power was "no Subject for the tongue of a Lawyer".[48]

Again, unlike Henry VIII, James vigorously asserted his personal "right" to oversee the law. He depicted himself as "Rex Pacificus" and aimed to arbitrate between "his" civil and ecclesiastical jurisdiction, between "his" bishops and common lawyers, between "his" common law and equity. He rejected Fortescue's opinion that the king interprets the law only through the mouths of his judges. And from there it was only a short step to the thesis that the king breathed life into the laws and was *lex animata*.[49]

But it was Charles I's accession which marked the watershed, for Charles was obsessive and inflexible, and his regime was exclusive. Counsellors and local magistrates were increasingly preferred on ideological grounds; the Privy Council was eclipsed by a "cabinet council"; and Charles's fiscal and religious policies were divisive.[50] In religion he stressed the visibility and catholicity of the English church and treated Calvinism as doctrinally and politically subversive. He backed so-called "Arminian" bishops, who emphasized worship and the sacraments, rejected predestination, and defined the Protestant church in terms of its Catholic antecedents. He was the first king since Henry VIII to expound an unqualified thesis of "imperial" kingship; indeed he believed that executive action in both civil and ecclesiastical government defined sovereignty. He exceeded the limits of Henry VIII's polity when he sought to advance his *imperium* beyond the limits recognized either by the common lawyers or by previous instruments imposing religious uniformity within the Church of England. His attempt to impose his ecclesiology upon England and Scotland by proclamation was idolatry in Calvinist eyes.[51]

Russell, *The Causes of the English Civil War* (Oxford: Oxford University Press, 1990), 131–60.

[48] C. H. McIlwain (ed.), *The Political Works of James I* (Cambridge, Mass.: Harvard University Press, 1918), 333.

[49] McIlwain (ed.), *Political Works of James I*, 62–3, 290–305, 306–25, 326–45; Kenyon, *Stuart Constitution*, 74–87, 158–63; L. A. Knafla, *Law and Politics in Jacobean England* (Cambridge: Cambridge University Press, 1977), 123–81; K. Fincham and P. Lake, "The Ecclesiastical Policy of James I," *Journal of British Studies*, 24 (1985), 169–207; P. Collinson, "The Jacobean Religious Settlement: The Hampton Court Conference," H. Tomlinson (ed.), *Before the English Civil War* (London: MacMillan, 1983), 27–51; W. Brown Patterson, "King James I's Call for an Ecumenical Council," G.J. Cuming (ed.), *Councils and Assemblies, Studies in Church History*, 7 (1971), 267–75.

[50] L. J. Reeve, *Charles I and the Road to Personal Rule* (Cambridge: Cambridge University Press, 1989).

[51] R. Cust, *The Forced Loan and English Politics 1626–1628* (Oxford: Oxford University Press, 1987); N. Tyacke, *Anti-Calvinists: The Rise of English Arminianism c. 1590–1640* (Oxford: Oxford University Press, 1987).

The first exchanges followed the "Arminian" defences of the forced loan of 1627 and the imprisonment of loan refusers without bail. Since England was at war it was arguably legal to levy unparliamentary taxation. But this point was obscured for two reasons. First, because Charles had dissolved the 1626 Parliament in order to save his favourite from impeachment and thereby lost taxation. Second, because the forced loan was defended in sermons and pamphlets which claimed that "tribute" was due to an "imperial" king by divine and natural law.[52]

The grievances aired in the Parliament of 1628 ranged from the forced loan, billeting and martial law to impositions and Arminianism. But tempers flared when it was discovered that Charles himself had ordered the attorney-general to pervert the legal record of the decision in the Five Knights' Case in order to establish a binding precedent for the Crown's discretionary right to imprison subjects for unknown causes without bail.[53] The debates which ensued culminated in the Petition of Right. What dictated the common lawyers' strategy was their desire to obtain a written declaration with the force of statute which outlawed forced loans and billeting of troops without the consent of householders, and which reestablished the principle that the words *lex terrae* in Magna Carta and its confirmations meant "due process" by the order of the "common law" and not procedure by "law of state", martial law, ecclesiastical law, civil law, or any other form of law unknown to the common law.[54]

In their debates the lawyers came fairly close, first, to denying the king's absolute right to act in emergencies; and, second, to saying that they mistrusted the king. They protested that they respected his prerogative, but could not understand how it could be invoked in derogation of their liberties. To which Charles replied that he would always defend his subjects' liberties but could not allow them to limit his definition of the public good.[55] Put concisely, the members of the 1628 Parliament had encountered a king who believed that the king's prerogative was to defend the people's liberties but that a function of these liberties was to strengthen the king's prerogative. In those circumstances it was unlikely that agreement would be forthcoming.

The debate centred on what "law" was specified by the words *lex terrae* in Magna Carta. Was "absolute prerogative" or "law of state" admissible? Or was *lex terrae* limited to "due process" by the common law? In this almost hermen-

---

[52] C. Russell, *Parliaments and English Politics 1621–1629* (Oxford: Oxford University Press, 1979); Cust, *The Forced Loan*, 62–5; Sommerville, *Politics and Ideology in England*, 127–40; Judson, *Crisis of the Constitution*, 171–217.

[53] John Guy, "The Origins of the Petition of Right Reconsidered," *Historical Journal*, 25 (1982), 289–312.

[54] *Proceedings in Parliament 1628*, II, 275–577; III, 3–297; Sommerville, *Politics and Ideology in England*, 145–83.

[55] Guy, "Origins of the Petition of Right Reconsidered," 298–312; Russell, *Parliaments and English Politics*, 323–89; Judson, *Crisis of the Constitution*, 218–310.

eutic exchange Charles I and his common lawyers were invoking different paradigms and speaking in different tongues. Yet, unlike the barons in 1215, the lawyers were unable to interpose a feudal shield between the "imperial" king and his landowning subjects. The reason was that feudalism no longer existed save in the realm of legal fiction. On the one hand, the vocabulary in which freehold property was ordinarily discussed was no longer that of tenures but of estates. On the other, any attempt to reconstitute feudalism in 1628 faced the problem that in feudal discourse Parliament was reduced to the status of the *curia* in which the king's vassals offered suit of court.[56] On that reading Parliament was virtually an expression of the royal prerogative which summoned and dissolved it, and the only kind of Parliament which could be imagined was one in which those who attended performed the vassal's duty to counsel the lord in his *curia* when their presence was required.

The common lawyers therefore turned to the version of English history already embedded in their consciousness. This interpreted the common law as "immemorial custom" and argued that the institutions of the common law, including Parliament, were themselves "immemorial" and comprised "the most ancient and original constitution of this kingdom".[57] The concept of an "ancient" constitution had been invoked in sixteenth-century Scotland, where it had underpinned the thesis that the people had the right to depose unsatisfactory kings.[58] It interlocked with the notion that there existed an "ancient and fundamental law, issuing from the first frame and constitution of the kingdom".[59] This "ancient and fundamental law" was that "law" which had been stated and confirmed, in turn, by Edward the Confessor, William the Conqueror, and the authors of Magna Carta. It followed that Magna Carta and its statutory confirmations incorporated this "fundamental" law, which could not be abridged if the king were to respect the sanctity of his coronation oath.[60]

Charles I assented to the Petition of Right, but its status was contested until 1641, when the Long Parliament ordered it to be strictly observed.[61] Stung by a breakdown of decorum at the dissolution of Parliament in 1629, Charles took the advice of his inner clique to govern in non-parliamentary ways, whereupon

[56] G. O. Sayles, *The Functions of the Medieval Parliament of England* (London: Hambledon Press, 1988); H. G. Richardson and G. O. Sayles, *The English Parliament in the Middle Ages* (London: Hambledon Press, 1981); J. G. A. Pocock, *The Ancient Constitution and the Feudal Law* (Cambridge: Cambridge University Press, 1957), 1–147; T. Hearne (ed.), *A Collection of Curious Discourses Written by Eminent Antiquaries upon Several Heads in our English Antiquities* (2 vols.; London, 1771), I, 281–309.

[57] Pocock, *The Ancient Constitution and the Feudal Law*, 30–90; Christianson, "Royal and Parliamentary Voices on the Ancient Constitution", 71–95.

[58] J. Wormald, *Mary Queen of Scots: A Study in Failure* (London: George Philip, 1988), 184.

[59] Kenyon, *Stuart Constitution*, 14–16.

[60] *Proceedings in Parliament 1628*, II, 188–92, 193–7, 198–202, 332–58; III, 268–97.

[61] 17 Car. I, c. 14.

the Petition was overwhelmed by the "experiment" in "imperial" kingship known as the "Personal Rule". This "experiment" at first succeeded. Charles was solvent until 1638, when the decision in the Case of Ship Money cemented his success. In the judgement of Justice Berkeley the king possessed "a monarchical power".[62] While he could not tax *de alto et basso* nor change the laws except in Parliament, he could dispense with law when necessity demanded. By his regal power he could demand supply from his subjects in cases of necessity for the defence of the commonwealth. "I never read nor heard that *lex* was *rex*", said Berkeley; "but it is common and most true that *rex* is *lex*, for [the king] is *lex loquens*, a living, a speaking, an acting law . . .".[63]

Moreover, the declaration of regality which Charles I and Archbishop Laud incorporated into the canons enacted by Convocation in 1640 was theocratic:

> The most high and sacred Order of Kings is of Divine Right, being the ordinance of God himself, founded in the prime laws of nature, and clearly established by express texts both of the Old and New Testaments. A supreme power is given to this most excellent Order by God himself in the Scriptures, which is, that kings should rule and command in their several dominions all persons of what rank or estate soever, whether ecclesiastical or civil, and that they should restrain and punish with the temporal sword all stubborn and wicked doers.[64]

This declaration was to be read from the pulpit four times a year by every minister, and it exceeded the claims of any previous official proclamation when it concluded that "tribute", taxation, "and all manner of necessary support and supply" were "due to kings from their subjects by the Law of God, Nature and Nations". While subjects had a "propriety" in their goods and estates, it was their duty to supply the king in cases of necessity.[65]

Charles was successful while he remained at peace, but the revolt of the Scottish Covenanters opened Pandora's box. When in the spring of 1640 the Short Parliament failed, the Scots' army forded the Tweed and routed the English. Whereupon twelve illustrious peers, every one of them excluded from the Privy Council, joined forces to petition Charles to summon a new Parliament where "evils" might be redressed and the "authors and counsellors" of them brought to trial.[66] The peers' petition seemed dutiful, but this was deceptive because they were in collusion with the Scots, whom they assured in

---

[62] S. R. Gardiner (ed.), *Constitutional Documents of the Puritan Revolution, 1625–1660* (3rd edn. rev.; Oxford: Oxford University Press, 1906), 115–24; Kenyon, *Stuart Constitution*, 98–103; Judson, *Crisis of the Constitution*, 136–41; Sommerville, *Politics and Ideology in England*, 160–3.

[63] Gardiner (ed.), *Constitutional Documents of the Puritan Revolution*, 116–22.

[64] Kenyon, *Stuart Constitution*, 149–53.

[65] Kenyon, *Stuart Constitution*, 151.

[66] Gardiner (ed.), *Constitutional Documents of the Puritan Revolution*, 134–6.

writing: "the enemies are all one, the common Interest one, the End is all one; a free Parliament to try all Offenders, and to settle Religion and Liberty."[67]

Charles's hand was therefore forced. He summoned the Long Parliament, which abolished the High Commission and prerogative courts. He assented to the Triennial Act, which affirmed the right of twelve or more peers to summon a Parliament should the king fail to do so.[68] But his counter-coup against the Five Members failed, and by the summer of 1642 the strategy of his opponents may be summarized in a sentence. If the king sought to be an "imperial" king, then Parliament and not the Privy Council was to be the King's Council. The argument went like this: Parliament was the king's "public" or "supreme" Council; the "privy council" was subordinate to it. Moreover, Crown appointments to the great offices of state and Privy Council required the confirmation of both Houses of Parliament. It was an audacious move, because it rehabilitated the "feudal" principle of the "counsel and consent" of the realm, while annexing to Parliament the "classical-republican" discourse of "counsel" which embodied the vocabulary of *respublica* and "civic virtue".[69] This discourse situated *imperium* and *consilium* in a conjugal relationship; it was axiomatic in this mode to speak of "the incorporation and inseparable conjunction of counsel with kings".[70] It followed that Charles had a duty to seek Parliament's advice before exercising his *imperium*, and this interpretation overcame the objection that Parliament was no more than the feudal *curia* in which the king received the service of his vassals.

In reply Charles published *His Majesty's Answer to the Nineteen Propositions of Parliament*, which itself annexed "classical-republican" vocabulary in order to overturn Parliament's claim to be the King's Council.[71] Furthermore, its authors appealed to the classical theory of the "mixed" constitution, arguing that monarchy, aristocracy and democracy coexisted in the shape of king, Lords and

[67] J. Oldmixon, *The History of England during the Reigns of the Royal House of Stuart* (London, 1730), 142–3; P. Donald, *An Uncounselled King: Charles I and the Scottish Troubles, 1637–1641* (Cambridge: Cambridge University Press, 1990), 246–7; J. S. A. Adamson, "The English Civil War of 1640," *Platt's Chronicle* (June 1989), 53–67. My thanks to Peter Donald for the reference to Oldmixon.

[68] Gardiner (ed.), *Constitutional Documents of the Puritan Revolution*, 144–55.

[69] John Guy, "The Politics of Counsel in Early-Modern England," Dale Hoak (ed.), *Tudor Political Culture* (Cambridge: Cambridge University Press, forthcoming).

[70] *The Essays or Counsels Civil and Moral of Francis Bacon, Lord Verulam* (ed). O. Smeaton (London: Dent, 1906), 62.

[71] J. Rushworth, *Historical Collections of Private Passages of State, Weighty Matters of Law, Remarkable Proceedings in Five Parliaments* (8 vols.; London, 1721), IV, 725–35; Kenyon, *Stuart Constitution*, 18–20; M. Mendle, *Dangerous Positions: Mixed Government, the Estates of the Realm, and the Making of the Answer to the Nineteen Propositions* (Tuscaloosa: University of Alabama Press, 1985); C. C. Weston and J. R. Greenberg, *Subjects and Sovereigns: The Grand Controversy over Legal Sovereignty in Stuart England* (Cambridge: Cambridge University Press, 1981), 35–86; Guy, "The Politics of Counsel."

Commons, and that it was the coordination of these components which maintained constitutional balance and equipoise. Each component possessed its own characteristic virtues and vices, and their coordination ensured that the vices did not corrupt the virtues.

For the first time, therefore, a declaration in the king's name claimed that England was a "regulated monarchy" or "mixed constitution". The traditional definition of the "body politic" was that the three estates comprised the Lords Temporal, Lords Spiritual and Commons, with the king at the head. But when the *Answer to the Nineteen Propositions* maintained that king, Lords and Commons were coordinate partners in the legislative process, the king was "incorporated" within the "body politic". Moreover, according to the *Answer*, each of the estates possessed powers with which to check the others. To prevent abuses of royal prerogative, the Commons were empowered with the raising of taxation and with the right of impeachment. The Lords were to act as a "screen and bank between the prince and people". Lastly, the "government" was entrusted to the king, according to the laws jointly made by the members of the parliamentary trinity.[72]

The *Answer to the Nineteen Propositions* was intended to make Charles I's opponents swallow a dose of their own rhetoric. By the "excellent constitution of this kingdom" the powers of the two Houses were said to be "more than sufficient to prevent and restrain the power of tyranny", whereas the king would be hamstrung if he were forced to make Parliament his "great and supreme council". He would be unable to discharge "that trust which is the end of monarchy", which would be a "total subversion of the fundamental laws" – here Charles threw his opponents' slogans in their faces. He acknowledged his duty to seek counsel, but "counselling" was a duty and not a right. As to Parliament itself, the king was as much a part of it as the two Houses, and therefore he had the right to answer freely to bills or other propositions. His answer could not be free unless he were permitted to act as his conscience dictated. Here the advantage to Charles of conceding that he was "only" one of three coordinate estates in Parliament becomes evident. It was precisely *because* the king was one of the three estates that he had the same "liberty" as the two Houses to seek and receive independent advice and to exercise his vote freely in response to bills.[73]

This is not the moment to discuss the events of the English Civil War, save to observe that as soon as Charles raised his standard at Nottingham, his opponents began levying arbitrary taxation, billeting troops on householders, and imprisoning subjects without "due process of law" in defiance of the Petition of Right. The parliamentary campaign to dominate the king's counsels raised the spectre of bicameral parliamentary absolutism, for it was a single step

---

[72] Rushworth, *Historical Collections*, IV, 728–32; Kenyon, *Stuart Constitution*, 18–20.
[73] Rushworth, *Historical Collections*, IV, 725–35.

COURT, COUNTRY AND CULTURE

from the premise that Parliament was the "great and supreme Council", which must act to secure the safety of the king and the kingdom, to the thesis that Parliament (or more accurately the two Houses) was the supreme executive council whose ordinances were more obligatory than the personal acts or resolutions of the king. That was the thesis precipitated by the Militia Ordinance, itself the immediate cause of civil war, and thereafter the vocabularies of liberty and limited government were increasingly appropriated by the "constitutional royalists" and "country" opposition, and by the more moderate Levellers.[74] By the time Charles I mounted the scaffold in 1649 he was able to pose as the ultimate guarantor of law, liberty and property, asking how it was that any free-born subject could call his life or property his own when an illegal power had "abrogated" the fundamental law of the land.[75]

When, therefore, Charles II was restored in 1660, it was well understood that the prerequisite of liberty was authority. Few conditions were required of him in his Declaration from Breda: a free pardon to all who had served against his father except those named by Parliament, full payment of the army's arrears, the confirmation of land sales since 1642, and the promise of "liberty to tender consciences".[76] However, the last and most important of these terms was emasculated by the country gentry in the Cavalier Parliament. The gentry regarded the Quakers and other religious enthusiasts of the 1640s and 1650s as a threat to property and civil order. Hence the Anglican church which the Act of Uniformity restored in 1662 was generally less comprehensive than the Elizabethan and Jacobean churches, although the High Commission and canons of 1640 were finally abrogated and inquisitorial procedure in church courts abolished.[77]

It might be argued that the Restoration left the royal prerogative intact, but the bulk of the legislation of 1641–2 remained in force. Only two acts were repealed: that excluding bishops from the House of Lords, and the Triennial Act which was diluted.[78] It is true that Charles II made strenuous efforts to suppress the doctrine of coordination embodied in the *Answer to the Nineteen Propositions*. Thus, Sir Henry Vane was convicted of treason for saying that the

[74] Gardiner, *Constitutional Documents of the Puritan Revolution*, 254–8; M. Mendle, "The Ship Money Case, *The Case of Shipmony*, and the Development of Henry Parker's Parliamentary Absolutism," *Historical Journal*, 32 (1989), 513–36.

[75] Kenyon, *Stuart Constitution*, 292–5.

[76] Kenyon, *Stuart Constitution*, 305, 331–2; R. Hutton, *The Restoration: A Political and Religious History of England and Wales, 1658–1667* (Oxford: Oxford University Press, 1985); R. Hutton, *Charles II: King of England, Scotland and Ireland* (Oxford: Oxford University Press, 1989), 127–65.

[77] I. M. Green, *The Re-establishment of the Church of England, 1660–1663* (Oxford: Oxford University Press, 1978); P. Seaward, *The Cavalier Parliament and the Reconstruction of the Old Regime, 1661–1667* (Cambridge: Cambridge University Press, 1989), 162–95; Hutton, *The Restoration*, 155–80.

[78] Kenyon, *Stuart Constitution*, 335.

two Houses shared the king's sovereignty and were empowered to "prevent and restrain tyranny" using force if necessary.[79] Again, the judges in the trials of the regicides held that the king was "*caput reipublicae*, the head of the common-wealth, [and of] the three estates." He was above the two Houses and the laws were made by him alone. He wore an "imperial Crown" and England was an "empire," as Henry VIII's Act of Appeals had stated. He was immediately subject to God, whose sole lieutenant he was.[80]

But the *Answer to the Nineteen Propositions* had seriously undermined the credibility of "imperial" kingship and of the king's mystical "absolute" prerogative. The outbreak of Civil War had detonated an explosion in the print culture and the *Answer to the Nineteen Propositions* lay at the heart of it. The vocabulary of coordination became etched on the nation's collective memory. The royalists were forced to admit that the two Houses "are in a sort Coordinate with his Majesty . . . and that they have this by a fundamental Constitution";[81] and their opponents pounced on this to argue that since the king was only one of the three estates, it followed that the two Houses might legitimately override him.[82] Again, if legislative sovereignty was equally divided among king, Lords and Commons, the king alone could not dispense the law. It could be claimed that Parliament (or rather the two Houses) was the true judge of necessity and the welfare of the kingdom. Therefore the king possessed only an "ordinary" prerogative, since as "physician of the commonwealth" it was Parliament which possessed an "absolute" prerogative.[83]

So the question was no longer: What was the extent of the king's "mystical" absolute prerogative? It had become: What was the legitimate constitution of a "mixed" monarchy?[84]

Equally important, unlike Henry VIII or even Charles I, it was difficult to envisage Charles II as the Constantine of the English church. His morals were imperfect and he did not greatly care who was appointed to bishoprics. Between 1660 and 1662 he tried to play the part of Constantine at Nicaea, only to find himself out-manoeuvred by the House of Commons in concert with the bishops.[85] During his reign the union between the "imperial" Crown and the episcopate began to dissolve. The Restoration era witnessed a burgeoning dissensus between erastian and sacerdotal visions of the church.[86]

[79] Weston and Greenberg, *Subjects and Sovereigns*, 154–7.

[80] Weston and Greenberg, *Subjects and Sovereigns*, 152–4.

[81] Judson, *Crisis of the Constitution*, 388–90.

[82] Greenberg, *Tudor and Stuart Theories of Kingship*, 196–235.

[83] Mendle, "The Ship Money Case, *The Case of Shipmony*, and the Development of Henry Parker's Parliamentary Absolutism," 532–6; Greenberg, *Tudor and Stuart Theories of Kingship*, 176–80.

[84] Judson, *Crisis of the Constitution*, 381–436.

[85] Hutton, *Charles II*, 166–213. I am extremely grateful to Dr Hutton for advice on these points.

[86] J. A. I. Champion, "The Ancient Constitution of the Christian Church: the

The most vigorous opponents of sacerdotalism in these conditions were the ex-
republicans, but this was the lobby with which Charles would not treat. In any
case, Charles was at best a man of doubtful religion, and his brother James II
was an avowed Roman Catholic. Despite the continued support of the Anglican clergy for the thesis of the divine hereditary right of kings and the sinful-
ness of resistance to their commands, Archbishops like Gilbert Sheldon and
William Sancroft increasingly found themselves interpreting the royal supremacy in terms of the counter-thesis of the "king-in-Parliament" which St
German had constructed in reaction to the theory of "imperial" kingship.

A renewed threat of civil war was finally sparked by the issue of limited
toleration for Roman Catholics and dissenters and by the attempt of Shaftesbury and the Whigs to exclude James from the succession to the throne. In
1672 Charles II issued a general Declaration of Indulgence which suspended
the penal laws. Its legality was denied by the common lawyers and House of
Commons, and the king backed down.[87] There followed an outbreak of anti-
Catholic hysteria in London, which culminated in the Popish Plot of 1678–9
and the Exclusion Crisis of 1679–81.[88] The question at first was: Could the
future supreme governor of church and state be a Roman Catholic? But the
Exclusion Crisis posed the more fundamental and dangerous question: Could
even a parliamentary monarchy alter the hereditary succession ordained by
God; and, if it did, would property rights be secure? Again: If the Exclusion Bill
passed both Houses and the king refused his assent, could the two Houses
legitimately proceed without him?

Charles II crushed his opponents, for Shaftesbury lacked support in the
Lords, while improvements in royal finances made the king less dependent on
Parliament.[89] When James II ascended the throne in 1685, the restored monarchy was at the height of its power. Yet James quickly alienated the leaders of
church and state. His policies were a fatal combination of Catholicism and
centralization.[90] When Archbishop Sancroft and six other bishops refused to
read the king's second Declaration of Indulgence from the pulpit, a crisis was
reached. If that were not enough, the seven bishops were acquitted of the
charge of seditious libel after a show trial in which their counsel pleaded the
doctrines of coordination and parliamentary sovereignty in order to maintain

Church of England and its Enemies, 1660–1730," unpublished Cambridge Ph.D. thesis (1989).

[87] J. Miller, Popery and Politics in England, 1660–1688 (Cambridge: Cambridge University Press, 1973).

[88] J. Kenyon, The Popish Plot (London: Heinemann, 1972); Miller, Popery and Politics, 154–88.

[89] C. D. Chandaman, The English Public Revenue, 1660–1688 (Oxford: Oxford University Press, 1975).

[90] Miller, Politics and Popery, 196–263; Kenyon, Stuart Constitution, 395–7, 448–9; J. R. Jones, Country and Court (London: Arnold, 1978), 225–55.

that statutes might be mitigated only in Parliament.[91] The birth of a son and heir to James proved the last straw, for it raised the spectre of an enduring Catholic succession, a prospect equally intolerable to Whigs and Tories.

The deposition of James II was accomplished through a dynastic military coup camouflaged as an "abdication" in order to avert civil war over the issue of legitimacy.[92] The actors in this drama pretended that there had been a demise of the Crown but not a dissolution of government. Or, if there had been a dissolution of government, power had not reverted to the people.[93] In some quarters it was suggested that, by virtue of the doctrine of coordination, the Lords and Commons were themselves possessed of two parts of the government, but this assertion raised many problems which it was inopportune to resolve.[94] What happened was that a group of Lords and Commons invited the Protestant Prince of Orange to invade England, and James's decision to flee the realm after William's guards were assigned to him for his "protection" made matters relatively simple; by his decision even the Tory peers could be persuaded to acquiesce.[95] After lengthy debate it was concluded that "the government of the Kingdom was extinct in a manner" by James's going, whereupon William assumed the responsibilities of government.[96]

A Convention was next summoned to legitimize these events, and a Declaration of Rights prepared to which William and Mary were asked to assent before they were proclaimed king and queen. The Declaration was then enacted as the Bill of Rights; its objectives were to define the "rights and liberties of the subject" and to settle the succession to the Crown.[97] Thus, the "suspending of laws or the execution of laws by regal authority without consent of parliament" became illegal.[98] The dispensing power as "assumed and exercised of late" became illegal, and it was further provided that in future any dispensation of statute must itself be authorized by statute. Unparliamentary taxation and prerogative fiscal devices were likewise declared illegal. Lastly, it was

[91] Kenyon, *Stuart Constitution*, 378, 396–7, 406–11; Weston and Greenberg, *Subjects and Sovereigns*, 240–6; Greenberg, *Tudor and Stuart Theories of Kingship*, 482–90.

[92] R. Beddard, *A Kingdom without a King: The Journal of the Provisional Government in the Revolution of 1688* (Oxford: Phaidon, 1988), 9–65.

[93] J. G. A. Pocock, "The Fourth Civil War: Dissolution, Desertion and Alternative Histories in the Glorious Revolution," *Government and Opposition*, 23 (1988), 151–66.

[94] Greenberg, *Tudor and Stuart Theories of Kingship*, 498.

[95] Oldmixon, *History of England during the Reigns of the Royal House of Stuart*, 763; Beddard, *A Kingdom without a King*, 58–65.

[96] Beddard, *A Kingdom without a King*, 65.

[97] J. R. Jones, *The Revolution of 1688 in England* (London: Weidenfeld, 1972); C. Stephenson and F. G. Marcham, *Sources of English Constitutional History* (London: Harrap, 1938), 599–605; Weston and Greenberg, *Subjects and Sovereigns*, 246–57.

[98] Stephenson and Marcham, *Sources of English Constitutional History*, 601; Weston and Greenberg, *Subjects and Sovereigns*, 253.

enacted that excessive bail ought not to be required, nor excessive fines imposed, nor cruel and unusual punishments inflicted.[99]

The Bill of Rights therefore emasculated "imperial" kingship as it had been defined by Henry VIII and Charles I. No longer could it be said that the king was above the law as the prerogative of his *imperium*. Instead the Bill vindicated the "sovereignty" of the king-in-Parliament, the counter-thesis which had been advanced by St German and the common lawyers, and the standpoint adopted by the Anglican bishops in the 1670s and 1680s. Again, the Bill vindicated the notion of the "mixed" constitution as expounded in Charles I's *Answer to the Nineteen Propositions*. It also vindicated the strategy of the barons in 1215. For the barons had sought the concession of a charter of liberties in concert with the renewal of John's coronation oath. Or translated into seventeenth-century vocabulary, they sought to link the king's oath to a declaration of the "ancient" and "fundamental" laws and liberties of the kingdom; the "laws" and "liberties" which could not be abridged if the king were to respect the sanctity of his oath.

A parallel may thus be drawn between the strategies of 1215, 1628 and 1689, especially between those of 1215 and 1689. Indeed, as soon as William and Mary had accepted the Declaration of Rights and before their coronation, the Convention Parliament revised by statute the text of James II's coronation oath. It claimed that it was necessary to clarify certain "doubtful words and expressions", and the effect of these changes was to expunge from the oath its residual theocratic elements.[100] At their coronation William and Mary swore to govern the people of England according to the statutes agreed upon in Parliament and according to the laws and customs of the realm. They also swore to maintain "the Protestant reformed religion established by law."[101]

As a guarantor of subjects' liberties the Bill of Rights was arguably less successful than Magna Carta. The main achievement of the Glorious Revolution was that a renewed civil war had been averted. As a "constitutional" settlement the events of 1689 were flawed, because the thesis of the "king-in-Parliament" cut two ways. St German and the common lawyers had couched it in a "populist" mode, but it was vulnerable to another reading. For it had long been recognized that the king of England was more "absolute" in Parliament than without. The break with Rome had begun this process. Henry VIII grasped the point in 1542 when he declared: "We at no time stand so highly in

[99] Stephenson and Marcham, *Sources of English Consitutional History*, 601–4; Weston and Greenberg, *Subjects and Sovereigns*, 253–4.

[100] E. Neville Williams, *The Eighteenth-Century Constitution, 1688–1815* (Cambridge: Cambridge University Press, 1960), 36–9. For an attempt in the fourteenth-century to dilute the same theocratic elements in the coronation oath, see Ullmann, *Principles of Government and Politics*, 186–9.

[101] Williams, *Eighteenth-Century Constitution*, 37–8.

our estate royal, as in the time of Parliament, wherein we as head, and you as members, are conjoined and knit together into one body politic."[102]

It is well attested that after 1689 the "executive" proceeded to cement its power in Court and country in order to assume the mantle of the "king-in-parliament". From this standpoint it might accordingly be argued that to have replaced the king by the "king-in-parliament" was to replace a tyrant with one head with a tyrant with three. Early in the reign of George III, John Douglas wrote:

> To consider the English constitution in theory, its stability would be supposed to arise from parliament. But parliaments, when once they become appendages of administration, must open the widest door to slavery. In this case, they become a mere state engine in the hands of a minister, to stamp a value on the basest metal, and to give every bad measure the sanction of national consent.[103]

That, of course, was how things could look from the other side of the Atlantic, where a clear distinction was about to be made between a constitution established by the people and unalterable by the government; and a law established by the government and alterable by the government.[104]

As to the metaphor of the "imperial" Crown, its severance from "constitutional" debates upon the royal prerogative and the Anglican Church conveniently freed it to assume the function of emblem to an expanding overseas empire. Colonists like Sir John Davies and Sir Walter Raleigh were among the first to experiment with "imperial" vocabulary along these lines in the closing years of Elizabeth I. For them, the "imperial Crown" conjured up a vision of Protestant England as an hegemonic central power ruling its dependent territories from across the oceans. But that is a different story, and another essay.

---

[102] S. E. Lehmberg, *The Later Parliaments of Henry VIII, 1536–1547* (Cambridge: Cambridge University Press, 1977), 170. See also Judson, *Crisis of the Constitution*, 86–7, 400.

[103] Cited by P. Allott, "Nice Plot, Shame about the Ending," *The Times Higher Education Supplement*, 17 March 1989.

[104] *The Federalist: A Commentary on the Constitution of the United States* (ed.) E. M. Earle (New York: Random House, n.d.), #53, 347–53.

Sir Walter Ralegh
and the Ancient Wisdom

I

The quarrel between the ancients and the moderns was inevitable whenever the ancient authors were proposed as models for imitation. So, even in antiquity itself, in the silver age for example, we can find evidence of the debate, and again during the Italian Renaissance, when we can find it even more forthrightly. In England, in the days of Queen Elizabeth when the classical authors were successfully installed in the schools after two or three generations of humanist propaganda, the quarrel began yet again. Gabriel Harvey, Samuel Daniel, and Francis Bacon all show signs of chafing under the burden of classical authority and a desire to affirm the modern accomplishment. But, as I have shown elsewhere, the quarrel soon became complicated.[1] To the issue of imitation was added now the problem of accumulation; to the question of classical precedence in the humanities and the arts was added the question of the superiority of the ancients in philosophical wisdom. And when, at the end of the seventeenth century, all this came to the boil in the famous battle of the books, it was still possible to affirm the precedence of the ancients in all matters, while the 'moderns' were still having difficulty persuading the world of the merits of their case. If this might seem improbable in the face of the new science of the Royal Society and the physics of Isaac Newton, it should be remembered that it was Newton himself who still clung to the idea that the ancients had indeed anticipated most of what was valuable in the wisdom of the west.

Just how the notion of a *prisca theologia* got abroad in Tudor England is a story that still remains to be told. To be sure, there were here, as in so many other places, medieval precedents for the idea of a translation of knowledge from antiquity to modernity, from east to west, an idea that was already familiar in ancient times. But the notion was certainly given fresh impetus by the

---

[1] I have written about the quarrel in "Ancients and Moderns Reconsidered," *Eighteenth Century Studies*, 15 (1981), pp. 72–89; in *Humanism and History* (Ithaca, 1987); and in my forthcoming *Battle of the Books: History and Literature in Augustan England* (Ithaca, 1991).

89

appearance of neoplatonism early in the century and by the obvious utility of the idea. The problem that faced the Renaissance was that knowledge of the world was either static and eternal or dynamic and (at least potentially) progressive. For the moment, there was not much appeal for the latter with its implicit relativism and there did not seem to be much evidence to support it. Europeans wanted the authority of the past to confirm their own ideas about life and the world; and they saw no reason to doubt that the same access to those ideas that was available to them (that is to say, reason and revelation) must have been available to their forebears. As a result, they were naturally predisposed to a belief in the ancient wisdom and delighted to discover in the Bible and in Plato and his followers a history of thought that seemed to demonstrate it. Thus John Woolton was pleased to find (in 1576) that the doctrine of the immortality of the soul had been "constantly receyved used and defended, not onely of al Divines, but also of the auncient and best Philosophers," especially the platonists. "The myghtye God hath letten these wise men see certen sparkes, and as it were flashes of the veritie and truth: that they might knowe him by his woorkes."[2]

Now the pathways of Renaissance platonism were many and various and it is impossible to trace them all here. Part of its appeal was to the humanists who were looking for an alternative to the scholastic Aristotle, and it is present already in that first true Renaissance generation of Erasmus, Colet and Thomas More, after which it made its way obscurely but with increasing effect until the Elizabethans began to feel its full force.[3] Poets and courtiers found its message seductive as they did in Italy, and it is no surprise to discover Baldassare Castiglione being read and admired in English, and a modern vogue for platonic love employed throughout the poetry of the entire early modern period.[4] In philosophy, neoplatonism is already present in the work of Everard Digby, whose *Theologica analytica* (1579) has some claim to being the first major philosophical treatise in Renaissance England.[5] Influence from abroad was persistent, dramatic in the appearance in England of Giordano Bruno himself, insidious in the works of such as Francesco Patrizi, whose *Nova de universis*

[2] John Woolton, *A Treatise of the Immortalitie of the Soule* (London, 1576), pp. 53v., 59. Woolton mentions Ficino, Reuchlin, and Sebastian Foxe among his sources.

[3] See Sears Jayne, "Ficino and the Platonism of the English Renaissance," *Comparative Literature*, 4 (1952), pp. 214–38. J. S. Gill, "How Hermes Trismegistus was Introduced to Renaissance England," *Journal of the Warburg and Courtauld Institutes*, 47 (1984), pp. 222–25.

[4] See John Harrison, *Platonism in English Poetry in the Sixteenth and Seventeenth Centuries* (1903); Robert Ellrodt, *Neoplatonism in the Poetry of Spenser* (Geneva, 1960). Thomas Hoby's translation of Castiglione appeared in 1561, 1577, 1588 and 1603; it was edited with an introduction by Walter Raleigh in the Tudor Translation series (London, 1900).

[5] Everard Digby, *Theoria analytica: Viam ad monarchiam scientiarum demonstrans, totius philosophiae e reliquorum scientiarum* (London, 1579).

philosophia was printed in 1593.[6] It was most accessible perhaps in the popular Protestant apologetic of Philippe Duplessis-Mornay, which was translated into English by Sir Philip Sidney and Arthur Golding and went through four editions between 1587 and 1616.[7] Even the Aristotelians, still dominant in the schools, were infected.

The work of John Case, the outstanding English scholastic of his time, lets us glimpse the progress of the ancient wisdom by the end of the century. In his magnum opus, the *Lapis philosophicus* (1599), he sets out what was fast becoming the common view.[8] Aristotle himself, it now appears, had inherited a body of truth that had come down to him from the beginning of time. Even before the flood, knowledge of the sciences had been engraved on wood, brass and stone columns. From thence it had spread first to the Chaldeans, then to Egypt and Palestine, and finally to Greece and the rest of the world. It was the Egyptian, Hermes Trismegistus, who had transmitted it to the philosophers, Thales and Pythagoras, and from them to the later Greek writers. To what extent Aristotle had improved upon this inheritance and how far the future might still bring further progress is not altogether clear. Case was clearly an 'ancient', reverent of both Aristotle and the *prisca theologia* that he had employed. Yet he was not insensitive to the modern achievement either and did not hesitate to doff his academic cap at those most wonderful contemporary inventions: printing, gunpowder, and the art of making glass from flint, not to mention the pleasure of smoking tobacco. The quarrel between the ancients and the moderns had barely begun again and we must not divide the sides either too rigidly or prematurely.

II

Surely the most ample, if not the most obvious, bridge to connect the renaissance idea of the ancient wisdom with the battle of the books was Walter Ralegh's *History of the World*. Here was an immense and expensive book, a great volume of nearly fifteen hundred folio pages, yet astonishingly popular. Ralegh wrote it for the young Prince Henry while lying in the Tower of London judicially dead, beginning probably in 1608. It was published incomplete after Henry's death with Ralegh still in the Tower and about a dozen times thereafter

[6] See especially Francis A. Yates, *Giordano Bruno and the Hermetic Tradition* (1964, reprinted New York, 1969).

[7] *A Worke Concerning the Trewness of the Christian Religion* (London, 1587). The original appeared first in Antwerp in 1581. See Jeanne Harrie, "Duplessis-Mornay, Foix-Candale and the Hermetic Religion of the World," *Renaissance Quarterly*, 31 (1978), pp. 499–514.

[8] For what follows, see Charles Schmitt, *John Case and Aristotelianism in Renaissance England* (Kingston and Montreal, 1983).

until 1687.[9] It was abridged twice, quoted often, and commended more by a host of grateful readers from Cromwell and Milton to John Locke. It was still being read, though less enthusiastically, by Hume and Samuel Johnson in the eighteenth century. Its success was due to its utility and its style. It was the one English work after the Middle Ages to try to put together the whole past on a scale sufficiently grand to include all the worthy details. No matter that Ralegh never got past the Macedonian Empire, though he certainly intended to; here at least was a great gob of the story, more than half the tale since Creation, and the most significant, if not the most immediately applicable part. Here God's providential design was most manifest and the Christian reader had most to learn, while the stately periods of Ralegh's prose were designed to ensure it — and himself – of immortality.

Ralegh's imprisonment was less a handicap than one might imagine. He had access to books and to the conversation and assistance of learned friends, some as celebrated as Thomas Harriot and Ben Jonson. The resources of the greatest library in the kingdom were available to him through the good offices of Sir Robert Cotton; and his fellow prisoner, the 'wizard' Earl of Northumberland, had brought with him to the Tower a fine collection of books. A list survives, partly in Ralegh's hand, with over five hundred titles that he seems to have assembled in the Tower to use for his history.[10] Ralegh had a chaplain, Dr. Robert Burrel, to take on some of the work, and rumour said that some of the "best wits" in England lent their help.[11] Best of all, the restless adventurer had time now on his hands, time to pursue the labyrinth of Renaissance learning even to the latest volumes of English and continental erudition; time also to assemble and arrange the thousands of interlocking pieces that were needed to lay out the grand pattern of human events.

To be sure, the genre that Ralegh attempted was an ancient one. The

[9] The book was entered in the Stationer's register, April 15, 1611. See T. N. Brushfield, "Sir Walter Ralegh and the History of the World," Transactions of the Devonshire Association, 19 (1887), pp. 389–418; "Raleghana, Part VI, The History of the World," Ibid., 36 (1904); A Bibliography of Sir Walter Ralegh, 2nd ed. (Exeter, 1908); and Charles H. Firth, "Sir Walter Raleigh's History of the World," Proceedings of the British Academy, 8 (1918), pp. 42–46. Brushfield is corrected by John Racin, Jr., "The Early Editions of Sir Walter Ralegh's History of the World," Studies in Bibliography, 17 (1964), pp. 199–209.

[10] See Walter Oakeshott, "Sir Walter Ralegh's Library," The Library, 5th ser., 23 (1968), pp. 285–327; Ralegh to Cotton, Edward Edwards, The Life of Sir Walter Ralegh, 2 vols. (London, 1868), II, pp. 321–23. G. R. Batho, "The Library of the Earl of Northumberland," The Library, 5th ser., 15 (1960), pp. 246–61.

[11] "Ben Himself had written a piece to him of the Punick warre, which he altered and set in his booke," Notes of conversations with Ben Jonson made by William Drummond of Hawthornden (1619), in Discoveries, ed. G. B. Harrison (1923, reprinted, London, 1930), p. 9. Ralegh himself refers to the "interpretation of some of my learned friends," History, pref.

SIR WALTER RALEGH AND THE ANCIENT WISDOM

Greeks had attempted universal history, although belatedly and not very satis-
factorily. Ralegh certainly knew and employed Diodorus Siculus whose *Historical Library* was especially popular in Renaissance England. But he had a better
model in the early Christian writer Eusebius, who had provided the foundation
and supplied much of the material for the many successive attempts of the
middle ages and modern times. The Eusebian Chronicle, reissued and reinforced with all the erudition of the greatest of modern scholars, Joseph Scaliger,
proved an especially valuable source for the modern Englishman.[12] Meanwhile,
throughout the sixteenth century, both Catholics and Protestants continued to
claim the past and write apologetic universal histories, among the most notable
being the chronicles of Carion-Melancthon and Gilbert Gerebrard, both of
whom served Ralegh in his undertaking. Here was one obvious place that a
Christian could claim advantage over the pagans; for not only could he hope to
detect a clear pattern in the vast heterogeneity of events, he believed he had in
the Bible access to the precise beginning and total shape of human history.
Universal history could be understood thus as perfectly comprehensive, starting from the very origin of things and embracing all human events, even to the
end of time.

It was necessary therefore to unlock the historical meaning of the Scriptures,
and there is a sense in which Ralegh's work was just another, though
astonishingly precise and detailed commentary, on the Old Testament.[13] The
problem for him, as for his predecessors, was to take the revealed account and
harmonize it somehow with all the gentile materials: the classical histories and
— to the extent that they were becoming available — the monumental remains. This required above all the assistance of chronology which was just then
coming to maturity in the work of Scaliger. It was possible now, by employing
both the new astronomy and the new philology, to formulate a more precise
account of the different calendars and the passage of years for all the ancient
civilizations and then to try to integrate the results with the Biblical narrative.
Still, the work was not, as a contemporary put it, "for everie common capacitie.
Naie it is a toile without head or taile, even for extraordinarie wits, to correct
the account of former ages so many hundred yeares received, out of uncertain-
ties to raise certainties, and to reconcile writers dissenting in opinion and
report."[14]

[12] Anthony Grafton, "From *De Die Natali* to *De Emendatio Temporum*: The Origins
and Setting of Scaliger's Chronology," *Journal of the Warbug and Courtauld Institutes*, 48
(1985), pp. 100–143. The first volume of Grafton's magisterial work on Scaliger has
appeared; the second is expected shortly, *Joseph Scaliger: A Study of the History of
Classical Scholarship* (Oxford, 1983).

[13] See Arnold Williams, *The Common Expositor: An Account of Commentaries on
Genesis 1527–1633* (Chapel Hill, 1948).

[14] Abraham Fleming in Holinshed's Chronicle (London, 1587), sig. Y6r. See G. J.
R. Parry, "William Harrison and Holinshed's Chronicles," *Historical Journal*, 27 (1984),
p. 810.

In short, the difficulties in the way of synchronism were — and are — enormous, considering how vague the Old Testament narrative is in these matters and how varied were the ancient calendars; and the problem was compounded now by the recovery not only of some of the more obscure and fragmentary works of antiquity, but of works buried within works (like the lost Berosus and Sanchuniathon quoted by Eusebius) and by forgeries early and late. "It is a great losse," Ralegh complained, "that the generall Historie of the World hath suffered, by the spoils and waste which Time hath made of these Monuments." Ralegh was well aware that the chronologists, ancient and modern, differed over many details, and he could not help but doubt the results.[15] It was Diodorus who had said, "In ancient things we are not to require an exact narration of the truth."[16] But Ralegh was undeterred and set himself to his gigantic task with characteristic gusto and independence, handicapped only by his ignorance of the ancient languages (which seems to have included Greek as well as the eastern tongues) and by his insistence on the absolute dependability of the Biblical story. He had had some recent English predecessors: for example, Ludowick Lloyd, whose *Consent of Time* was published in 1590 and dedicated to the Archbishop of Canterbury with the suggestive subtitle, *Deciphering the Errours of the Grecians in their Olympiads, the uncertaine computation of the Romans in their Penteterydes, and the building of Rome; of the Persians in the accompt of Cyrus, and other vanities of the Gentiles in fables of antiquities, disagreeing with the Hebrews, and with the Sacred Histories in consent of time*; and Edward Livelie, whose *True Chronologie of the Times of the Persian Monarchie* (1597) attempted one part of the field. "It is not to be spoken," Livelie exclaimed, "how much and clear light, the diligent study and reading of Latin and Greek writers, yield to the knowledge of holy scripture."[17] Ralegh knew and used the recent work of Thomas Lydiat that had dared to challenge the great

[15] "I may truly say with Pererius, that we ought liberally to pardon those whose feet have failed them in the slippery ways of Chronology, wherein both learning and diligence are subject to take a fall at one time or another," *History*, III, i, 6.

[16] Ralegh, *History of the World* (London, 1614), p. 417; Ernest A. Strathmann, "Ralegh on the Problems of Chronology," *Huntington Library Quarterly*, 11 (1948), pp. 129–48.

[17] Edward Livelie, *True Chronologie* (London, 1597), p. 15. Livelie also left a two-volume manuscript, *Chronologia a Mundo condito ad annum 3598*. In 1588, he tangled with another chronologist whose works were known to Ralegh, Hugh Broughton. Broughton's *Concent of Scripture* was an attempt to settle the Biblical chronology; it opened a life of scholarly controversy that is outlined by Alexander Gordon in the *Dictionary of National Biography* and suggests something of the learned labyrinths that awaited Ralegh. Ralegh could not have known the manuscript "great chronology" of William Harrison, except indirectly in Holinshed; but the discussion by G. J. R. Parry helps also to set the scene; see *A Protestant Vision: William Harrison and the Reformation of Elizabethan England* (Cambridge, 1987). There were other popular chronological works that Ralegh may have known such as John More's, *A Table from the beginning of the World to this Day* (1593).

Scaliger.[18] And as we have seen, he was fortunate to have lots of help. A contemporary gave credit to his learned chaplain, "for the greatest part of the drudgery," and Ralegh seems to have dictated his work to another, perhaps John Talbot, "one that lived with mee eleven yeares in the Tower, an excellent generall skoller and a faithfull trew man as lived."[19] For technical matters he had the assistance of his mathematician friend, Thomas Harriot.

It was in this context that Ralegh was compelled to take account of the ancient wisdom, which purported to convey (among many other things) a knowledge of the origin and meaning of human history. Indeed, it was this very same compound of disparate materials: the Scriptures and the fragmentary Greek sources — the traditional lore, speculation and fraud of Hellenistic gentiles and Jews — that appeared to furnish the best evidence both for the earliest human events and the earliest human wisdom, both for history of the world and the history of philosophy. To Ralegh it appeared that the greatest part of his work had already been done and it only remained for him to gather it up, evaluate it as far as possible, and turn it into an eloquent prose.

For the historian of the world, it was necessary to begin with the act of Creation, a moment in time that had been denied by some of the Aristotelians, who preferred to believe in the eternity of the world. Here then was familiar controversial ground, a theological problem that might be addressed either philosophically or through history. And though Ralegh was neither a theologian or a philosopher, he had a passionate interest in both. For Aristotle, however, whose authority in these matters was still intact, Ralegh had little use. "For my selfe," he wrote in the introduction to the *History*, "I shall never be so persuaded, that God hath shut up all Light of Learning within the Lanthorne of Aristotles braines." Nor did he think any better of the scholastic theologians who had considered these problems.[20] He much preferred the Platonists and their allies whom he listed with approval after his immediate source, the early sixteenth-century defender of the perennial philosophy, Agostino Steuco: Hermes, Zoroaster, Musaeus, Pythagoras, Plato, and the rest.[21] All these

[18] Ralegh, *History*, II, 25, i, pp. 592. See Thomas Lydiat's *Defensio tractatus de variis annorum contra J. Scaligeri obtrectationem* (London, 1607); Lydiat's *Emendatio temporum* appeared in 1609 and was also dedicated to Ralegh's patron, Prince Henry.

[19] "All of the greatest part of the drudgery of Sr Walter's History for Criticisms chronology and reading of greek and Hebrew authors were performed by him [Robert Burrel] for Sr W. Rawl." See Thomas Rawlins Commonplace Book, 1724–37, in Brushfield (1887), p. 10. John Aubrey seems to have heard the same thing from Burrel's widow; see Pierre Lefranc, *Sir Walter Ralegh: L'oeuvre et les idées* (Paris, 1968), p. 269.

[20] "Most of the Schoolemen were rather curious in the matter of termes, and more sutile in distinguishing upon the parts of doctines already laid downe, then discoverers of any thing hidden, either in Philosophy or Divinity," *The History of the World* (London, 1614), I. i. 7, p. 8.

[21] For Steuco, see Charles Schmitt, "Perrenial Philosophy: From Agostino Steuco

ancient writers agreed with Moses and the Bible that there was one eternal and infinite parent of the World, in short, that God had created the universe out of nothing. It was these same writers, moreover, who agreed upon the providential meaning of history so dear to Ralegh. "Besides the Scriptures," he insisted, "Hermes, Orpheus, Euripides, Pythagoras, Plato, Plotinus (in effect) all learned men acknowledge the Providence of God."[22] This argument from universal (or nearly universal) consent[23] was essentially an argument from history; and it was to remain one of the chief grounds for Christian apologetics for a very long time.

Indeed, one finds it already in Ralegh's contemporary source, Du Plessis Mornay. For the French theologian, the object was to find a defense of the essential truths of Christianity against atheists, heretics, and Jews, which he does by alternating chapters drawn from both reason and authority, that is to say from philosophy and from the traditions of the ancient wisdom. He shows that Christian wisdom was identical with the *philosophia perennis*, not only as proof for the act of Creation and God's providence, but for the immortality of the soul and even the trinity.[24] To deny any of those things, he argued, was to be both irrational and unchristian — and unhistorical.

For Ralegh, who was writing history, the argument from reason was naturally less useful for his work than the appeal to historical testimony. But this meant that he was bound to evaluate the sources in order to establish the historical facts. He begins, therefore, by answering all those who wished to object to the Mosaic account, "seeing there was no Storie thereof written, and if any such had been . . . all memorie of Antiquitie was perished in the universal floud." Ralegh preferred to believe in the old notion that there was an eye-witness account of the first human events that had been passed down from father to son in an uninterrupted tradition or cabala, from Adam to Seth, Seth to Methusaleh, and so on, down to Noah and Moses. The great age of the patriarchs meant that relatively few generations were required and their regard for the truth meant a relatively uncorrupt tradition. But besides this oral tradition, Ralegh believed that letters had been invented at the beginning of the world and that a written tradition of events, set down by Enoch on pillars

to Leibniz," *Journal of the History of Ideas*, 27 (1966), pp. 505–532; Maria Muccilo, "La *prisca theologia* nel *De perenni philosophia* di Agostino Steuco," *Rinascimento*, 2nd ser., 28 (1988), pp. 41–112.

[22] *History*, I.i.13, p. 18.

[23] "And this is certaine, that if we looke into the wisdome of all ages, wee shall finde that there were never man of solid understanding of excellent judgment: never any man whose minde the art of education hath not bended . . . but that he hath found by an unresistable necessitie, one true God, and everlasting being, all for ever causing, and all for ever sustaining. . ." None more so that the ancient Egyptian Hermes, *History*, I.vi.7, p. 96.

[24] *A Work Concerning the Truth of Christian Religion* (London, 1617), ch. 6, pp. 67–92; ch. 15, pp. 240–68.

of stone and brick (as Josephus testified) remained for Moses to see. (His authorities here are St. Augustine and the contemporary Jesuit, Pererius, whose massive commentary on Genesis was throughout a main support.) "It is not therefore strange," Ralegh concluded, "that Moses came to his knowledge of the Creation and storie of that first age, seeing hee might receive it both by tradition and letters — even if God had not directly inspired him."

In this way, Ralegh secured his principal source for the early history of the world. But Ralegh thought that there was more to it than that. Still following his neoplatonic guides (this time apparently the Florentine, Pico della Mirandola), he insisted on a second source of the ancient wisdom, a further oral tradition that Moses had passed on to his successors along with the Scriptures, a secret cabala containing a philosophical understanding of nature. It was secret because teaching these mysteries to a rude multitude would have only caused confusion and misunderstanding. Nevertheless, this philosophical wisdom, like the early history of the world, had been passed along to the gentiles as well as the Jews, both orally and in letters, these last "bearing the forme of beasties, birds, and other creatures." Ralegh here refers unmistakably to hieroglyphics, just now beginning to fascinate Europe.[25] Apparently, in the East, the ancient wisdom had been safeguarded by priests and kings: by Zoroaster, Hermes, Cadmus, and the rest, to whom it had sometimes been falsely attributed.

Thus the ancient pagan wisdom was for Ralegh and his sources no more than a derivative from the traditional knowledge of the Jews. This accounted for the surprising similarity between the ideas of the Greeks and Hebrews that had so struck Pico and Ficino — and their neoplatonic forerunners in ancient Alexandria — and continued to astonish the Christian world from the Renaissance to the battle of the books.[26] It is true that the two traditions of ancient wisdom, the Hebrew and the pagan, could be separated by claiming each of them for reason rather than revelation, a position too dangerous, however, to have much appeal to any but a deist.[27] For the while, it seemed to most thinkers during the Reformation and the Counter-Reformation that both

[25] Ralegh refers also to hieroglyphics discovered in Mexico, *History*, II, viii, 1, p. 362.

[26] The best general account remains, D. P. Walker, *The Ancient Theology* (Ithaca, 1972); for Ralegh's platonism, see Jean Jacquot, "L'élément platonicien dans l'*Histoire du Monde* de Sir Walter Ralegh," *Mélanges d'histoire littéraire de la Renaissance offerts à Henri Chamard* (Paris, 1951), pp. 347–53.

[27] According to Anthony Wood, Ralegh's friend, Thomas Harriot, was a deist who "undervalued the old story of the history of the world, and could never believe that trite position, *Ex nihilo nihil fit*. He made a philosophical theology, wherein he cast off the Old Testament . . ." Wood says Harriot told Ralegh as much while he was in the tower. If so, Ralegh clearly rejected the idea. See Wood, *Athenae Oxoniensis*, II, pp. 300–01; Earnest A. Strathmann, *Sir Walter Ralegh: A Study in Elizabethan Skepticism* (New York, 1951), p. 105.

reason and the oral tradition were too frail and inconclusive to stand on their own, and that corruption through time would account both for the inadequacies of the early pagan histories and for all those vagaries in ancient thought and religion that separated even the wisest sages from the purity of Christian conviction. This failing not only explained the need for Revelation; it explained some other puzzling things. It was through this corruption of tradition, Ralegh believed, that there had grown up a "confusion of vanities, where among the heathen themselves there is no argument or certaintie," and from which ancient polytheism and mythology had taken their rise – concealing the fact that their true origins were in the Bible. The Libyan gods and the Egyptian Osiris were thus but "crooked images of some one true historie," Saturn was in fact Adam, Jupiter was Cain, Bacchus was Noah, and so on. "It cannot be doubted, but that Homer had read over the books of Moses, as by places stolne thence, almost word for word, may appear."[28] According to Ralegh, the historian was like the chemist who sought to draw out of the poison a helpful remedy, and with sufficient skill — and the authority of the Old Testament — he could hope to reconstruct from the ancient poets and philosophers something of the story of the first ages of the world.

One by one then, Ralegh considered the claims of the ancient philosophers. Zoroaster, for example, came first, but although there was general agreement about his teaching, there seemed to be only confusion in the sources about his time and place. Ralegh could not even be sure whether the ancient sage was a Persian or Chaldean, though his Renaissance authorities (Pletho, Ficino, Pico and Steuco) all inclined to the latter. Nor was it any easier to establish his dates, although he thought that Zoroaster had probably lived after the flood. Ralegh doubted that he was Noah's son, Cham, as some claimed, or that he had invented those key sciences of the ancient world: magic (in which Ralegh includes the whole philosophy of nature) and astrology, preferring to credit the earlier Hebrews, Seth and his descendents. More likely, Zoroaster, like Abraham, had learned his science from the early Jews and passed it on to his followers, the Persian magi. Fortunately his teaching at least had come down to us intact, with a full understanding of nature's innermost powers, a true "philosophy of nature," not in any way like the "brabblings" of the Aristotelians. (Even while Ralegh was writing these words, he was himself doing alchemical experiments.)[29] Most importantly, Zoroaster had understood and preserved the genuine *prisca theologia*, "For in his *Oracles* he confesseth God to be the Creatour of the Universe: he beleeveth in the Trinitie, which he could not investigate by naturall knowledge: he speeketh of Angels, and of Paradise: approveth

---

[28] *History*, I. vi. 7, p. 93.
[29] See John W. Shirley, "The Scientific Experiments of Sir Walter Ralegh, the Wizard Earl, and the Three Magi in the Tower, 1603–17," *Ambix*, 4 (1949–51), pp. 52–66; P. M. Rattansi, "Alchemy and Natural Magic in Ralegh's *History of the World*," ibid., 13 (1966), pp. 122–38.

of the immortalitie of the soule: teacheth Truth, Faith, Hope and Love." Ralegh had read the *Oracles* for himself, "gathered and translated" by Psellus, Ficino and Patrizi. It never occurred to him to question their authority.

After Zoroaster, there was the Egyptian, Hermes Trismegistus. Once again, however, the historical record, like everything so long ago, was obscure and uncertain. Ralegh found particular trouble with the ancient chronologists such as Berosus, whose works had survived in fragments quoted at second-hand, or (worse yet) in the suspicious discoveries of the Renaissance Italian, Annius of Viterbo. Many had suspected the last, including the Spanish humanist, Juan Luis Vives, whose commentary on St. Augustine was one of Ralegh's favourite sources.[30] But the need for information about those early times, the need which Annius had so unfortunately tried to meet by inventing his sources, was over-whelming, and the Pseudo-Berosus haunts Ralegh's pages, as so many others at the time, even to putting him into conflict with the greatest scholar of the day, "that noble and learned Writer Joseph Scaliger."[31] "For mine own part," Ralegh wrote, after considering the arguments on both sides, "I believe nothing that Annius his Berosus, Metasthenes, and others of that stampe affirme, in respect of their bare authoritie; yet am I not so squeemish, but that I can well enough digest a good Booke, though I finde the names of one or two of these good fellowes alleaged in it . . . Where other Histories are silent, or speake not enough, there may we without shame borrow of these, as much as agrees with that which elsewhere we finde, and serveth to explaine or inlarge it without improbabilitie." Things that depended only on "Likelihood" could not be easily dismissed, unless the historian was content to leave a blank. Ralegh was certainly skeptical by temperament and critical by inclination but he was helpless in the end before his sources, first for lack of technique, despite his best efforts to keep up with modern scholarship, but also because, like most of his contemporaries, he could not forbear to leave empty the consecutive story which he was sure had so precise a beginning and end.

For Hermes too the sources were conflicting and deficient. Some claimed that he was Moses himself; others that he had lived earlier. Just who he was God only knew! "Envie and aged time hath partly defaced, and partly worne out the certain knowledge of him." But still the ancient doctrine had somehow survived, even more amply than with Zoroaster, and Ralegh seems to have read the text of the *Corpus hermeticum* directly in Ficino's translation, along with his commentary. Ralegh thus follows the Florentine when he writes that, Moses

---

[30] See Vives' note to Bk. xviii, ch. 7, St Augustine, *Of the Citie of God*, trans. J. Healey (London, 1610), p. 654. Livelie also attacks Annius and enumerates some other modern critics, *True Chronologie*, p. 37. For Annius, see Christopher Ligota, "Annius of Viterbo and Historical Method," *Journal of the Warburg and Courtauld Institutes*, 50 (1987), pp. 44–56.

[31] For the career of the pseudo-Berosus (the invention of Annius of Viterbo) in sixteenth-century England, see T. D. Kendrick, *British Antiquity* (London, 1950).

alone excepted, "there was never any man of these elder times that hath attributed more, and in a stile more reverend and divine unto almightie God, than he hath done." Here, in short, was the *prisca theologia* at its purest and most admirable, though not, Ralegh concludes, entirely without some traces of corruption. And here also, besides the divine wisdom, was the knowledge of mathematics, a natural science equal to the peripatetics, and a moral and political philosophy to boot.

It was from Hermes then, that the wisdom of the Hebrews had come down to the Egyptians and from them afterward to Orpheus, Pythagoras and the Greeks. Plato had clearly learned from both Hermes and Zoroaster, not to say the Bible itself. St. Augustine had once given his opinion, "that (few things changed) Plato might be considered a Christian." Nevertheless, Ralegh who was trying to conflate a great many different opinions about the transmission of knowledge from east to west, allows that the process might have begun earlier, perhaps with Prometheus who lived about the time of Moses. Despite Cicero's reservations, "the storie of Prometheus was not altogether a fiction: and that he lived about this time, the most approved Historians and Antiquaries, and among them Eusebius and St. Augustine, have not doubted."[32] It was in Mosaic times already that "Art and civilitie (bred and fostered farre off in the East and Aegypt) beganne at this time to discover a passage into Europe, and into those parts of Greece, neighbouring Asia and Judaea." Ralegh accepted as axiomatic that the course of knowledge was westward. "The Eastern people were most ancient in populacie and all humaine glorie." In the days of Alexander the Great, Rome was still barbarious, and when Babylon was triumphant, Greece had still been primitive. Ralegh's explanation was simply that Noah's ark had first come to rest further in the east — not as often thought in Armenia — and that Noah had brought directly to the Chinese the arts, sciences and letters. With this advantage, the ancient east had anticipated by many centuries even those seemingly characteristic modern inventions, printing and gunpowder, passing them on eventually to Europe. Indeed, "The farther East (to this day) the more civill, the farther West, the more salvage."[33] If Ralegh was relying to some extent on his own experience of America here, he was also recalling a recent account of Japan which claimed that it exceeded all the other kingdoms of the world. And if he had been preceded in this by Richard of Bury in the Middle ages, who preferred to start in India before ending in Paris and London, Ralegh was willing, like the 'ancients' later in the battle of the books, to extend his convictions about the course of learning to both ends of the earth.

[32] *History*, II, vi, 4, p. 317.
[33] *Ibid.*, I.vii, p. 116.

III

Much more could be said about Ralegh's use of the ancient wisdom but it is clear that he found it useful, perhaps indispensible, in recalling the early history of mankind, and he was instrumental in transmitting the notion to later times. It was useful on philosophical grounds because it demonstrated the universality and timelessness of the Christian world-view; and it was useful on historical grounds because it supplied some of the missing links in the earliest history of mankind. In many ways, Ralegh's sympathies lay with the moderns, and in several passages he specifically decried a mindless nostalgia for the past. In general, he doubted whether one time was better than another, "for good and golden Kings make good and golden ages." And he lamented with Tacitus, that "we alwaies extoll the times past, and hold the present fastidious." Both Solomon and Seneca had complained of the *laudator temporis acti*, and Arnobius had said rightly that "whatsoever is new, in time shall become old and the ancientest thinges when they tooke beginning were also new and sodaine." Somehow Ralegh was able to reconcile a genuine reverence for antiquity with an Elizabethan confidence in the present; but it is the essential timelessness of his account of history that is perhaps more to the point and that he shared with most of his contemporaries. And this, no doubt, was the best foundation for a belief in the ancient wisdom.

Yet Ralegh's history had been assembled from the bits and patches of an impressive erudition and much of its value lay in its compendiousness. It is astonishing to see how comprehensive his reading was, and his *History* offered among its many virtues a wealth of quotation, and a kind of encyclopedic guide to a vast literature, both ancient and modern, that had long been accumulating on the subject. (A later editor found over six hundred sources cited in the history.)[34] But its most attractive feature was the way in which Ralegh had been able to shape all those unwieldy materials into a coherent form and eloquent style. A century later, one of the champions of the ancients in the battle of the books praised it extravagantly for its fine writing, "the most perfect, the happiest, and most beautiful of the Age he wrote in." It seemed indeed to Henry Felton to breathe the very spirit of Athens and Rome, and he

---

[34] "He was an indefatigable reader, whether by sea or land," Robert Naunton, *Fragmenta regalia*, ed. Edward Arber (London, 1870), pp. 48–49. The 1736 edition of the *History* contains an alphabetical list of some 660 authors; but the letter to Cotton, cited above, asks to borrow thirteen titles, none of which are mentioned here. See Brushfield (1887), p. 11n. Lefranc, however, would reduce the list to something more like 200–300 authors, since many of the works were compilations, encyclopedias, etc., pp. 291–92.

thought that had Ralegh only chosen to write of his own time, he might have surpassed even Livy and Thucydides.[35]

Yet Ralegh had deliberately avoided contemporary history, and the choice of antiquity meant that he had to enter into all those abstruse and digressive matters that so facinated his contemporaries but began to try the patience of his later readers: about the size and shape of Noah's ark and the geographical location of the Garden of Eden; about the disputed chronology of his awkward sources; about the role of digression and conjecture in a narrative history.[36] And in the end, it was his scholarship that began to date his work and make it seem inadequate, although his rhetoric kept it still alive. But if that is the fate of most erudition sooner or later, it was Ralegh's destiny in particular, since his scholarship was limited by a serious inability to cope very capably with his sources. Ralegh lacked the languages and the philological training that his contemporaries, Scaliger, for example, or Seldon and Casaubon, had so painfully mastered; and he also lacked an appreciation of the importance of archaeological information (the 'antiquarian' activity of his time) which was the only hope of correcting or supplementing the defective written literature. Under the circumstances, he was bound to the fate of his defective sources: to such problematical works of antiquity as the remains collected by Annius of Viterbo and to the *Sibylline Oracles* and the *Corpus Hermeticum* which he read in translation but which were already under suspicion.

Perhaps Ralegh should have known better. One of his contemporary sources, the chronicler, Gilbert Gerebrard, the author of a very popular work which he knew and used, had already questioned the authority of the hermetic writings. As Ralegh scanned its pages, he could have seen the entry for 303 BC with its note about Hermes, arguing that the *Corpus* was written in Greek, and that the Egyptians only encountered the language after the Alexandrian conquest. In a later edition (1580), Gerebrard expanded this argument, noticing that Hermes was never mentioned by any early Greek writer; that he wrote on papyrus (according to Iamblichus) which only dates from a later period; that the first treatise in the *Corpus* known as *Pimander* mentions the sibylls who appeared long after Moses; and finally, and most tellingly, that the *Corpus* mentions the fifth-century Athenian sculptor, Phideas. Gerebrard's work was employed almost at once by the Aristotelian, Teodoro Angelucci, who tried to persuade Patrizi (another of Ralegh's sources) of the spuriousness of the hermetic writ-

---

35 Henry Felton, A *Dissertation on Reading the Classics and Forming a Just Style* (London, 1713), pp. 199–201.

36 Lawrence Echard, one of Ralegh's epitomizers, complained of "his too frequent and long Digressions and Observations . . . too many of them are wholly Foreign to his subject." See his "Advertisement to the Reader," in An *Abridgement of Sir Walter Ralegh's History of the World* (London, 1698), sig. A3v. And Hume much preferred the later parts of the work where the conjectural (and theological) matter was less evident; see Firth, p. 437.

ings. But the neoplatonist was not convinced; Patrizzi replied that the *Corpus* might have been a Greek translation of an Egyptian original (thus accounting for some of the anachronisms) and that while the reference to Phidias was surely far-fetched, it only indicted one part of the hermetic collection. Unfortunately, this argument compelled Patrizi to insist that there must have been two Hermes, grandfather and grandson, each with a son named Tat and a student named Aesclepius![37] The debate was enough certainly to raise a skeptical eyebrow but it seems somehow to have passed Ralegh by.

What he did notice was a more recent and capable criticism of the sources by the renowned classical scholar, Isaac Casaubon. Casaubon had been brought to England to adorn the court of James I with his learning, and among his heroic labors had lately taken up the task of refuting the Catholic champion, Cesare Baronius. That redoubtable scholar had tried to refute the Protestant cause with twelve great folio volumes of ecclesiastical history. Baronius was learned but not very critical, and he began his massive work with a long section showing the various gentile anticipations of the coming of Christ in which he argued in particular for the ancient authority of Hermes Trismegistus and the *Sibylline Oracles*. Casaubon was determined to meet his opponent point by point, beginning with the first volume of the *Annales*, but he was forced to give up after only half a volume by the scale of his reply. "A desultory criticism," writes his biographer, "passage by passage, of another man's book, prolonged through nearly 800 pages in folio, does not constitute attractive reading." Lancelot Andrewes, who looked the sheets over before publication, wished that Casaubon had not spent so much time with "mere questions of chronology," but it was just this sort of scholarly enthusiasm, along with his Protestant animus, that had led Causabon in the first place to question the suspicious ancient works and to try to shatter their authority. Theological prejudice made it appear unlikely to him that God would have given the Gentiles a full prevision of a revelation that he believed was unique; while philology told him that the disputed works must be forgeries. To the arguments that had been proposed by Gerebrard and Angelucci, he added now a close criticism of the style of the spurious works to show their anachronistic vocabulary. As a result, he inverted the usual opinion and demonstrated conclusively that the two works echoed rather than anticipated the writings of Plato and the New Testament. In short, they must have been the inventions of late Greek writers, Christians he supposed, passing off their platonic ideas as pious frauds. The fact that he set them a little late and exaggerated their Christian content did not by

[37] See Frederick Purnell, "Francesco Patrizi and the Critics of Hermes Trismegistus," *Journal of Medieval and Renaissance Studies*, 6 (1976), pp. 155–78; John Henry, "Francesco Patrizi da Cherso's Concept of Space and its Later Influence," *Annals of Science*, 36 (1979), pp. 549–75.

any means make his criticism less convincing to his contemporaries, nor less impressive to later times as a model of critical scholarship.[38]

Unhappily, Casaubon's work was neither as popular nor as successful as one might suppose.[39] His criticism of the Hermetic writings was buried deep in the thickets of an awkward and difficult Latin polemic. Yet Ralegh seems to have read it immediately upon its publication and it appears that he was quickly persuaded by its argument. "Of the Sibylline prediction I have sometimes thought reverendlie . . . following the common beleefe and good authoritie. But . . . that learned and excellent worke of Master Casaubon upon the Annales of Cardinal Baronius, did altogether free me from mine errour, making it apparent, that not only those prophecies of Sibyll, wherein Christ so plainly was foreshewed, but even in the bookes of Hermes, which have borne such reputation, were no better than counterfeit pieces." Nevertheless, this did not seem to matter very much to him, for he made no effort to rewrite his work, leaving the whole treatment of the ancient wisdom in the early pages of his book untouched. Of course it was late and the sheets were already in the press, but much remained to be done, cancellations were possible, and the long introduction was still to be written. (In the preface, Ralegh does not hesitate to say that Hermes lived either contemporaneously or just after Moses; in the text, he left a passage, following Ficino, that Hermes was "more ancient than Moses, because the Inventor of the Aegyptian Wisedome, wherein it is said, that Moses was excellently learned.")[40] There is no indication that suspicion of these sources was, by itself, enough to convict the ancient wisdom altogether. There remained too many ways to sidestep the consequences, as Patrizi had already indicated.

In this regard, it is interesting to find that both of Ralegh's later abridgers decided to leave his account of the ancient wisdom intact, although one of them, Alexander Ross, did not hesitate to correct Ralegh elsewhere in a set of animadversions that he printed separately. Ross actually went out of his way to defend the sibylls and Hermes against both Ralegh and Casaubon, this despite that fact that he thought that Ralegh had got the direction of ancient knowledge wrong in directing it from East to West.[41] Ross saw that the date of the

[38] For Casaubon's biography, see Mark Pattison, *Isaac Casaubon 1559–1614*, 2nd ed. (Oxford 1892); for a recent account, Anthony Grafton, "Protestant Versus Prophet: Isaac Casaubon on Hermes Trismegistus," *Journal of the Warburg and Courtauld Institutes*, 46 (1983), pp. 78–93.

[39] Yates sketches the story after Casaubon down to the Cambridge platonists, pp. 398–431.

[40] Lefranc, who notices the inconsistency points out the Angelus Vergerius, Francois de Foix and Bruno had all previously argued that Hermes was anterior to Moses, *Sir Walter Ralegh*, p. 461. For them the Mosaic revelation was thus an imperfect version of the Hermetic writings, rather than vice versa!

[41] Alexander Ross, *The Marrow of Historie: Or an Epitome of all the Historical Passages from the Creation to the End of the Last Macedonian War . . . by Sir Walter*

Corpus might be questioned but he would not allow that this must affect the doctrine. "I know the age in which hee hath lived may bee questioned, som making him no older than Diogenes, others more antient than Moyses which is likelie . . . but to question his doctrine without anie ground is not allowable."[42]

It was thus possible somehow to cling to the idea of the ancient wisdom even after the philologists had called into question its historical foundations. Indeed, as long as its use to theology and history remained, it was hard to give it up. One could even try, as a later generation of neoplatonists attempted, to call back philology to retrieve the doctrine from textual suspicion.[43] On the whole, it looks as though the defenders of the traditional wisdom were more likely to be Catholics, Arminians, or Cambridge platonists, all more or less open to the claims of reason, than the radical protestants, who were more inclined to prefer the exclusive claims of revelation. Scholarly skepticism had been provoked in the first place (and then been reinforced) — in Harrison, for example, and in Casaubon – by theological inclination; for them the claims of the *prisca theologia*, seemed to threaten both the uniqueness and the necessity of revelation. As a result, they were predisposed to disbelief and called on the new historiography to help them out. It was their successors, when the battle heated up at mid-century, who pressed the charges against the Arminians and neoplatonists that they were only deists and atheists in disguise. And perhaps they had a point, for it *was* eventually the deists (Tolland, Collins, and the rest) who became the chief supporters of the old idea.[44] By the end of the century, even orthodox Anglicans were ready to turn against the ancient wisdom, and then paradoxically it was the moderns in the battle of the books, Wotton and Bentley, who helped to finish off the criticism of the *prisca theologia*.

In short, criticism of the ancient wisdom seemed to depend on two things: theological predisposition and the advance of critical scholarship. Ralegh, needless to say, had neither the learning nor the prejudice, nor for that matter the benefit of a century's worth of argument, to bring to bear on the disputed point. It would be easier to settle the matter if we could be sure about Ralegh's religion, but the only thing that is certain is that both contemporaries and

Rawleigh (London, 1650); *Some Animadversions and Observations upon Sir Walter Ralegh's Historie of the World. Wherein his mistakes are Noted and Some Doubtful Passages are Cleered* (London, 1650). Lawrence Echard's work is noticed above, n. 36. For Ross's polemical career, see Grant McColley, "The Ross-Wilkins Controversy," *Annals of Science*, 3 (1938), pp. 153–89.

[42] Ross, *Animadversions*, pp. 68–69.

[43] The culminating work is Ralph Cudworth, *The True Intellectual System of the Universe* (London, 1678).

[44] They were preceded by Lord Herbert of Cherbury, whose posthumous work, *De Religione gentilium* appeared in 1663 and in English translation as *The Antient Religion of the Gentiles* (London, 1705). See Walker, *The Ancient Theology*, pp. 164–93; R. D. Bedford, *The Defense of Truth: Herbert of Cherbury and the Seventeenth Century* (Manchester, 1979).

modern scholars have remained baffled by it. For one thing, Ralegh had to face persistent charges of unorthodoxy throughout his career. At his trial for treason in 1603 he was flatly condemned for heathenish, blasphemous, atheistical and profane opinions.[45] Some years before (1593) there had been an inquiry into his ideas and testimony taken about his table conversation, but it is hard to make out more than that Ralegh was skeptical of traditional scholastic arguments and open to new ideas.[46] Some of his friends, like Christopher Marlowe and Thomas Harriot, did entertain some perilous notions that gained them a reputation for 'atheism'. The Catholic controversialist, Robert Parsons, went so far as to charge Ralegh with operating a school of atheism in London, "where in both Moyses and the Saviour; the olde and the new Testament are jested at, and the scollers taught amonge other thinges, to spell God backwarde."[47] And one Richard Cholmeley testified later that Marlowe told him that he had read an "atheist lecture" to Ralegh.[48] In another charge against Marlowe and his friends (the so-called *Baines Libel*), a list of heretical teachings was supplied, including several of a historical character. "That the Indians and many authors of antiquity have assuredly written of about 16 thousand yeares agone whereas Adam is proved to have lived within 6 thousand yeares. . . . That Moyses was but a Jugler and that one Heriots being Sir W Raleighs man Can do no more than he." And so on.[49] The slanders continued throughout Ralegh's life and for a long time afterward.

Of course, heresy was not welcome in Elizabethan England and caution was

[45] See the introduction to Ralegh's *History of the World*, by C. A. Patrides (London, 1971), p. 17; Jean Jacquot, "Ralegh's Hellish Verse and the Tragicall Raigne of Selinus," *Modern Language Review*, 48 (1953), pp. 1–9.

[46] The deposition by Ralphe Ironside is given in *Willobie His Avisa*, ed. G. B. Harrison (London, 1926), app. III, p. 265ff. See Leclerc, Strathmann, and John W. Shirley, *Thomas Harriot: A Biography* (Oxford, 1983), pp. 194–96.

[47] John W. Shirley, "Sir Walter Ralegh and Thomas Harriot," *Thomas Harriot: Renaissance Scientist*, p. 23; Lefranc, *Ralegh*, pp. 356–93. John Bakeless, *Christopher Marlowe: The Man in his Time* (New York, 1937), ch. XIII, pp. 195–220. Parsons' work appeared first in Latin (1592), then in English translation as *An Advertisement written to my L. Treasurers of Ingland* (1582). A whole literature has developed around the suggestions of Muriel Bradbrook that Ralegh was the center of a heretical school, including Marlowe, Chapman, and some others, satirized by Shakespeare in *Love's Labor Lost*; see Bradbrooke, *The School of Night* (Cambridge, 1936) and some of the Marlowe literature cited below.

[48] C. F. Tucker Brooke, *The Life of Marlowe* (1930, reprinted New York, 1966), p. 65; Eleanor Grace Clark, *Ralegh and Marlowe* (New York, 1941), p. 329. Paul Kocher takes the testimony seriously, *Christopher Marlowe: A Study of his Though, Learning, and Character* (1946, reprinted, New York, 1962), pp. 39–40. For some suggestions of what passed for atheism in Elizabethan England, see George T. Buckley, Atheism in the English Renaissance (Chicago, 1932).

[49] Tucker Brooke, pp. 98–100; Clark, pp. 378–80; Frederick S. Boas, *Christopher Marlowe: A Biographical and Critical Study* (Oxford, 1940), pp. 236–64.

prudent; as Thomas Harriot once explained to Kepler, it was not possible to philosophize freely.[50] It is always possible that Ralegh's religious views were more radical than they appear from the rather tenuous evidence. What does seem likely is that he was more open to skeptical or rational ideas about religion than many of his contemporaries and probably entertained some (perhaps even denying the Trinity and the divinity of Christ)[51]; but it is also true that the *History* makes a great effort to support some perfectly orthodox notions. It has all the defining characteristics that R. G. Collingwood once ascribed to Christian history: it is universal, providential, apocalyptic, and periodized. (For example, Ralegh accepts both traditional Christian schemes of seven ages and four world empires.)[52] Even Justice Montague, who sentenced Ralegh to death in 1618, was satisfied; "Your faith hath hitherto bin questioned," he told Ralegh, "but I am resolved you are a good Christian, for your booke which is an admirable worke doth testify as much."[53] Oliver Cromwell had no hesitation in recommending the *History* to his son.[54]

It appears even from the frontispiece to the work that Ralegh was determined to marry classical humanist and Christian ideas of history, to join providence with practical politics, Augustine with Cicero – perhaps even Machiavelli.[55] Such a union seemed doubtful to many then (and afterwards) and has left anomalies in the text that modern scholars have not been slow to detect.[56] It seems likely that Ralegh, locked up in the Tower, laboring over his many and sometimes irreconcilable sources, trying to put together the whole

[50] Jean Jacquot, "Thomas Hariot's Reputation for Impiety," *A Sourcebook for the Study of Thomas Harriot*, ed. John W. Shirley (New York, 1981), p. 167 (quoting from Kepler, *Opera Omnia*, II, p. 74.) There were several burnings at Norwich for socinianism between 1579–89; see Buckley, p. 57.

[51] So John Aubrey in his life of Ralegh; in *A Source Book for the Study of Thomas Harriot*, p. 182. Ralegh's Moses teaches one set of notions to the mob, another to the select few, for "to teach these mysteries which he called secretiora to the rude multitude were no other . . . then to give holy things to Dogges, and to cast pearles before swine." *History*, I, v 6, p. 78. (Lefranc finds the source in Pico, p. 458n.) Could Ralegh have been doing the same?

[52] Racin, *Ralegh as Historian*, pp. 83–92; R.G. Collingwood, *The Idea of History* (1946, reprinted Oxford, 1956), pp. 49–52.

[53] Shirley, *Thomas Harriot*, p. 443.

[54] Oliver Cromwell to his son, Apr. 2, 1650, *The Writings and Speeches of Oliver Cromwell*, ed. W. C. Abbott, (Oxford, 1939), II, p. 236. "In religion he hath shown in private talk great depth and good reading, as I experienced at his own house before many learned men," Sir John Harrington, *Nugae Antiquae*, quoted by Bradbrook, *School of Night*, p. 22. There is also a letter by Harrington testifying to Ralegh's orthodoxy; see Arthur Cayley, *Life of Ralegh*, II, pp. 456–57.

[55] For the influence of Machiavelli on Ralegh, see Lefranc, pp. 222–30; for the tension between Ralegh's juxtaposition of Machiavelli and his Christianity, ibid., pp. 250–53.

[56] Stephen J. Greenblatt furnishes a long list of contradictions and anomalies, *Sir Walter Ralegh: The Renaissance Man and his Roles* (New Haven, 1973), p. 140.

history of the world, was unable and probably unwilling to address or resolve all the problems that now concern us. Casaubon certainly alerted him to a difficulty; but it was not easy for him to see what to do about the great lacuna that would be left if the ancient pagan sources failed to fill out the narrow biblical story. His religion was open to the ancient wisdom but did not depend upon it. But his history, if it was to tell the whole tale, seemed badly to require it. So Ralegh allowed his earlier views to stand, though he left the problem open and to future generations, armed with better scholarship and different requirements, the work of sorting it all out.

In the meanwhile, his popular *History* with its many editions and two abridgements helped very much to keep the notion of an ancient wisdom alive so that it could be used by later generations to write the early history of mankind. For the learned Edward Stillingfleet, Ralegh was still "the judicious historian," and a valuable source.[57] His work appeared without interruption in eleven successive editions until 1734, and his views were still being echoed in the collaborative and authoritative *Universal History* that was printed in 1747. A generation earlier, Sir William Temple, the leader of the 'ancients' in the battle of the books, was still employing the notion of an ancient wisdom confidently and plausibly to show how everything modern that mattered had been anticipated in the ancient world.[58] We must resist the temptation to hasten the triumph of modern ideas, here as elsewhere, or the slow and uneven progress of modern historical scholarship. No doubt Ralegh was as open to modernity as anyone in his generation, but like many of the more adventurous spirits of his time, he clung to his original notion of an ancient wisdom even after some of its foundations were shaken, and to the conclusion — both rational and useful — that a knowledge of early history and of eternal matters must have existed from the beginning of time however difficult it might be to discern its transmission through the centuries.

[57] Stillingfleet, *Origines Sacrae*, 8th ed. (London, 1703), pp. 339–45, 348–49; Strathmann, pp. 189–90.

[58] A later exponent still is the Chevalier Andrew Michael Ramsay, whose *Travels of Cyrus* appeared first in French and English translation in 1727, enlarged in both languages in 1730. See Walker, *The Ancient Theology* pp. 231–63.

Benefits, Brokers and Beneficiaries: The Culture of Exchange in Seventeenth Century England

LINDA LEVY PECK

In the first two medals struck to celebrate the succesion of James VI of Scotland to the throne of England in 1603, the king portrayed himself in images that came to characterize the mental world of the Jacobean court. Conceiving the earthly court as the mirror image of the heavenly one, the early Stuart monarch and his courtiers invested their politics and culture with the symbols of antiquity and Christianity. In the first, his accession medal, copied perhaps from a miniature of Nicholas Hilliard's, King James appears clad in armor with a laurel wreath, the first representation of an English king as a Roman emperor, a god-like patron from whom all bounty flowed.[1] Secondly, at his accession, James made besants, church offerings named after Byzantine coins, both for himself and Queen Anne. In the only one to survive, King James presents himself as the grateful client, receiving favor from God, his only superior. The king kneels with uplifted hands before an altar; before him on a carpet are the four crowns of England, Scotland, France and Ireland; the besant is encircled with a quotation from Psalm 116 in which the psalmist portrays his many tribulations which have now ended with good fortune, a mirror of James's own view of his political odyssey. With the psalmist he asks "What reward shall I give unto the Lord for the benefits he hath done unto me?"[2] These two medals capture the classical and religious imagery with which the early Stuarts described the exchange of benefits central to court patronage. Together these

---

[1] See Linda Levy Peck, *Court Patronage and Corruption in Early Stuart England* (London: Unwin & Hyman, 1990), introduction and chapter one. Edna Auerbach, *Nicholas Hilliard* (London: Routledge and Paul, 1961). Jonathan Goldberg points out that James had used this Roman motif in his 1590 wedding medal in Scotland, *James I and the Politics of Literature* (Baltimore: The Johns Hopkins University Press, 1983), p. 46, and quotes Arthur Wilson who likened James to Augustus and the troubles of the reign to peace and plenty which led to dissoluteness (p. 50).

[2] British Museum, Department of Coins and Medals. See L. L. Peck, ed. *The Mental World of the Jacobean Court* (Cambridge: Cambridge University Press, 1991), plates 1 and 2.

emblems of Jacobean court culture represent the official view that the king was simultaneously the fountain of favor and part of a system of mutual benefits that flowed between king and subject as James himself had described in *The Trew Law of Free Monarchies*.[3]

Political patronage has occupied a central place in early modern historiography and the relationships between writers, artists and their patrons have dominated discussion of Renaissance and Baroque culture.[4] In seeking material or symbolic resources, the client submerged his interest in that of his patron. Or, as John Webster puts it in *The Duchess of Malfi* "Men who never saw the Sea, (yet desire to behold that regiment of waters,) choose some eminent River, to guide them thither."[5] While this practice of informal power has become a topic of great interest both to historians and literary analysts in recent years, it is usually treated either in static and/or manipulative terms. Little or no attention has been paid to the cultural meanings attached to patronage. This essay will demonstrate that the vocabulary employed by the seventeenth century English to describe patronage drew specifically on classical, especially Senecan, sources and religious, especially Catholic, imagery to invest commercial transactions with higher motives. Such classical and religious vocabulary overlapped although their emphases differed. Whether in the form of the exchange of benefits or the bestowal of God's grace, both classical and religious language emphasized the invisible aspect of exchange. While Seneca stressed that exchange took place even between those who were subordinate, such as the slave to his master, the religious language used both in the 1620s and at the Caroline court heightened the position of the court broker, to create the patron as saint. Grateful clients used classical and religious vocabulary to construct narratives of gratitude for benefits conferred. Yet the practice

[3] C. H. McIlwain, ed., "The Trew Law of Free Monarchies," in *The Political Works of James I* (New York: Russell and Russell, 1965), p. 1.

[4] See K. B. MacFarlane, *The Nobility of Later Medieval England* (Oxford: Clarendon Press, 1973) and *England in the Fifteenth Century* (London: Hambledon Press, 1981); Lewis Namier, *England in the Age of the American Revolution* (2nd ed., New York: MacMillan, 1961); R. Mousnier, *La Venalite des offices sous Henry IV et Louis XIII* (Rouen: Mangard, 1945), and *Les Hierarchies sociales de 1450 a nos jours* (Paris: Presses Universitaires de France, 1969); Conrad Russell, *Parliaments and English Politics, 1621–29* (Oxford: Oxford University Press, 1979); Kevin Sharpe, *Faction and Parliament* (Oxford: Oxford University Press, 1978); David Starkey, "From Feud to Faction: English Politics Circa 1450–1550," *History Today*, 32 (1982), 16–21; Simon Adams, "Faction, Clientage and Party, English Politics, 1550–1603," *History Today*, 32 (December, 1982), 33–39; Kevin Sharpe, "Faction at the Early Stuart Court," *History Today*, 33 (1983), 39–46; David Starkey, "The King's Privy Chamber, 1485–1547" (Ph.D. diss. Cambridge, University, 1973); and William Tighe, "The Gentlemen Pensioners in Elizabethan Politics and Government" (Ph.D. diss. Cambridge University, 1983). Stephen Orgel and Guy Lytle, *Patronage in the Renaissance* (Princeton: Princeton University Press, 1981).

[5] John Webster, *The Dutchess of Malfi* (London, 1623), dedication, lines 3–6.

of patronage during the dominance of the Jacobean favorite, George Villiers, Duke of Buckingham, sat uneasily within this framework. This reading of Buckingham's patronage shows that such narratives increasingly diverged from the reality of Jacobean commercial court transactions. As a result, the culture spoke with conflicting voices on exchange, dependency and commerce.

References to benefits are ubiquitous in the sixteenth and seventeenth century. "Benefits bind me," said Robert Cecil of his loyalty to Queen Elizabeth.[6] Sir Francis Bacon thanked his cousin Cecil for his "many effectual and great benefits" which reenforced Bacon's admiration for Cecil's "virtue and merits."[7] In his handwritten will of 1597, the Buckinghamshire gentleman, Sir John Temple, left Sir Edward Wotton his best horse. Further, he asked his heir and executor, Thomas Temple, and all of his children "to be ever thankful to him . . . for that I and my late good father deceased have all my life . . . more love, true friendship and benefits at his good fathers hands . . . and his than ever we found elsewhere in our lives."[8] But just what did benefit signify? It certainly meant more than short-term profit.

Benefit was used in English from the fourteenth century to mean a good deed, a kind action, a favor. The concept was informed by both classical and religious texts; Aristotle had discussed benefits, but the most important theoretical work was Seneca's De Beneficiis. Seneca described the good society in terms of the exchange of benefits among its members. Senecan ideas were important to early Italian humanists,[9] and neo-Stoic language and thought

6   Charles I maintained "the ill of aristocracy is faction and division, just as its good . . . is the conjunction of counsel in the ablest persons of state for the public benefit." Quoted by David Starkey, "From Feud to Faction: English Politics Circa 1450–1550," History Today, 32 (1982), 16. Sir Edward Coke used Cicero in his charge to the Norfolk bench in 1607. "He that is a judge . . . ceaseth to be a friend: for in the manner of judgement, no acquaintance, no griefs, no friends, no remembrance . . . or hope of future friendship must direct the thoughts of him that is a judge . . . in thy love to Rome's commonwealth dedicate thy labors to her public benefit." Sir Edward Coke, The Lord Coke, his Speech and Charge. With a Discovery of the Abuses and Corruption of Officers (London, 1607), B5.
7   Quoted in Chantel Rondet, "Fidelites et Clienteles dans L'Angleterre D'Elizabeth et des Stuarts," Revue du Nord, 59 (1977), 339. Bacon called Cecil "so rare and worthy a counsellor, governor and patriot." Henry Percy, ninth Earl of Northumberland, was scion of the Percies whose control of the northern borders with Scotland had marked their influence in English politics, and also the owner of Sion House described at his trial for participation in the Gunpowder Plot as "a heap of benefits." Trial of Northumberland in Star Chamber, John Hawarde, Les Reports del Cases in Camera Stellata, 1593 to 1609 (London, 1894), p. 297.
8   P.R.O. PROB 11/101, 32 Bolein, ff. 249v–251; See HEH Stowe Manuscripts, Temple Correspondence, STT 2582, STT 2583, 23 March 1591; STT 2585, 24 February 1603 for correspondence between Wotton and Temple.
9   Quentin Skinner, "Ambrogio Lorenzetti: The Artist as Political Philosopher," in Proceedings of the British Academy, 72 (1986), 1–56.

gained further circulation with the publication of Seneca's works and commentary by Justus Lipsius in the 1570s.[10] *De Beneficiis* was known in Latin in England and Seneca's works can be found in sixteenth century Cambridge book inventories.[11] But it reached a larger audience with its first translation into English in 1578 by Arthur Golding, who subtitled it "the dooing, receyving, and requyting of good turnes," and its second in 1614 by Thomas Lodge in his translation of Seneca's *Workes*.[12]

Within this Senecan tradition, duty and rights, the meat of feudal and Kantian relationships, did not exhaust the ties between people, Instead, "benefites [were] . . . a thing that most of al other knitteth men togither in felowship."[13] Moreover, what was crucial was not "the thing that is seene" no matter how lavish; such a material object was only the "badge" or signifier of the benefit; the benefit "may bee carried in hart, but it cannot be touched with hand." The freely granted good will of the benefactor, the benefit or good turn endured even when the money or office were gone.[14]

Significantly, benefits were personal, not general. "The benefyte that is bestowed upon every man without exception is bestowed upon no man." It was given freely, neither given unwillingly nor extorted. According to Seneca, "this is the foulest word in benefiting that can be, to say, pay: . . . the estimation of so noble a thing should perish, if we make a merchandise of benefits." To follow virtue "a man must tread all profit under foot . . . It is no benefit that hath reference to fortune, or hope of interest."[15]

Bounty had to be "bounded with judgement" because, "a great summe of money, if it be not given prudently, and with a will grounded on reason, is a

10 See John Salmon, "Stoicism and Roman Example: Seneca and Tacitus in Jacobean England," *Journal of the History of Ideas*, 50 (1989), 199–225.

11 E. S. Leedham-Green, *Books in Cambridge Inventories* (2 vols.; Cambridge: Cambridge University Press, 1986), II, 697.

12 See John Wallace, "*Timon of Athens* and the Three Graces: Shakespeare's Senecan Study," *Modern Philology*, 83 (1986), 350–51 and 350 n. 4. I am grateful to John Wallace for a discussion of the influence of Senecan ideas of benefits. All translations from *De Beneficiis* are from the Golding and Lodge translations where indicated, otherwise from the Loeb Library edition of Seneca's *Moral Essays*, trans. John W. Basore, vol. 3 (3 vols; Cambridge, MA: Harvard University Press, 1935).

13 *The Work of L. A. Seneca concerning Benefiting*, trans. Golding (London, 1578), book I, chapter 4.

14 *The Work of L. A. Seneca concerning Benefiting*, trans. Golding, book I, chapter 5; badge is Golding's term.

15 Seneca, *On Benefits* in *The Workes of Lucius Annaeas Seneca, both morrall and naturall*, trans. Thomas Lodge (London, 1614), book I, chapter 14; book IV, chapter 1, chapter 3. "These things which either are extorted from the giver, or seeme to fall from his hands that giveth them: although they seeme highly prized and of great appearance, yet, as I said, they are unworthy of thankes, because a gift is much more gratefully accepted and reckoned of that come from a free and liberall hand, than from a full and rich-fisted penny-father," book I, chapter 7.

treasure but no benefit."[16] A benefit could profit the giver but not if meant to profit him alone.[17] Such benefits, given freely, in moderation, and received gratefully, circulated throughout society, and constituted "the chief bond of human society."[18]

Such Senecan language of benefits was central to the language of sixteenth and seventeenth century patronage.[19] Seneca did not reject gift giving, the outward manifestation of benefits, but suggested the presentation of "such things as may continue longest, to the end that the good which we do, and gifts we bestow, may be lasting and of long continuance" so that the beneficiary might not forget it.[20] These were not abstract ideas but the common coin of contemporary discourse. Lord Burghley, for instance, urged that the patron or great man be given small gifts that would always be on view to remind him of the giver. Perez Zagorin has pointed out that this advice was often repeated by others such as Sir John Holles.[21] I suggest it is very close to Golding's transla-tion of De Beneficiis of 1578:

> But even thanklesse persones stumble uppon the remembraunce of a gift, when they see it before their eyes, so as it suffereth them not too forget it. . . because wee must never putt the receyver in mynd of them. Let the verie thyng it self revyve the remembraunce of it that was vanishyng away.[22]

---

[16] On Benefits, trans. Lodge, book I, chapter 14, 15.

[17] De Beneficiis, book 4, chapters 9, 14, book 6, chapters 12–13.

[18] Seneca, Moral Essays, trans. Basore, book I, chapter 4.

> for he who has a debt of gratitude to pay never catches up with the favour unless he outstrips it; the one should be taught to make no record of the amount, the other to feel indebted for more than the amount. To this most honourable rivalry in outdoing benefits by benefits Chrysippus urges us . . . . But teach thou me the secret of becoming more beneficent and more grateful to those who do me a service.

See John Salmon, "Stoicism and Roman Example: Seneca and Tacitus in Jacobean England," in Journal of the History of Ideas, 50 (1989), 199–225.

[19] See "Timon of Athens and the Three Graces: Shakespeare's Senecan Study," Modern Philology, 83 (1986), 349–63. See Natalie Davis's forthcoming book, From Alms to Bribes and Louis Montrose, "Gifts and Reasons: The Contexts of Peele's Araygnement of Paris," ELH, 47 (1980), 433–61.

[20] See On Benefits, trans. Lodge, book I, chapter 12.

[21] Zagorin, The Court and the Country (New York: Atheneum, 1970), p. 45.

[22] The Work of L. A. Seneca concerning Benefiting, trans. Golding, book I, chapter 12. Golding dedicated his translation to Sir Christopher Hatton, Elizabeth's favorite and privy counsellor, assimilating Seneca himself to the Elizabethan court by describ-ing the Roman as "sometyme a Courtyer, and also a Counseller of the greatest state in the worlde." Amongst the reasons Golding translated the work was so that courtiers "shalbe so much the greater Ornament too themselves, and too the place whereof they take their name as their Courtesies and Benefytes bee mo and greater towards others."

In the same way that God was the author of all benefits,[23] providing benefits was god-like because it was not done out of duty but, much as Bracton had defined gifts, freely given.[24] "The true maner of benefyting . . . maketh one like untoo God." Such language amalgamated the notion of God and the king as the original source of all bounty and the exchange of benefits.

While the language of patronage, then, was classical, Protestant Englishmen also secularized religious vocabulary borrowed from Roman Catholicism, self-consciously envisioning the patron or broker as the intercessor to the king, much like the saints. According to Catholic doctrine, intercession is a form of prayer by one who has standing before God to obtain mercy or divine benefits for another.[25] In a recent book on the theory of supererogation, David Heyd points out the important place of benefits in Catholic theology. Because the saints have accumulated benefits beyond those necessary for salvation, they enable others to be saved and indeed may intercede on their behalf. King James bestowed his bounty or his mercy freely as God granted salvation. But even Calvinists did not have to rely upon grace alone in this world; good works and the intercession of intermediaries provided access to advancement. Thus William Trumbull was advised to direct himself to the "right saint" at court.[26] In a poem about the act of writing, in which he apotheosized Ben Jonson, Robert Herrick prayed to "Saint Ben," in what he called "the language of the old religion."[27]

It must be emphasized that this language of intercession was not confined to

Thomas Lodge translated Seneca's *Workes* including *On Benefits* from Justus Lipsius's Latin edition which he dedicated to Lord Chancellor Ellesmere in 1614. Lodge dedicated the second edition of 1620 to Thomas Howard, Earl of Suffolk, after his dismissal as Lord Treasurer. By that time, the Stoic message of constancy in the face of adversity was greater than the focus on counsel and courtiership of the 1578 edition.

[23] *On Benefits*, trans, Lodge, book 4, chapter 5.

[24] Seneca's view of benefits finds an echo in the Geneva Bible's translation of The Letter of Paul to Philomen which was repeated in the Authorized Version (King James Bible): "But without thy mind would I doe nothing, that thy benefit should not be as it were of necessitie, but willingly,' *The Geneva Bible, The Annotated New Testament, 1602 Edition* (New York: The Pilgrim Press, 1989).

[25] See *The New Catholic Encyclopedia*, vol. 7 (New York: McGraw-Hill, 1967–79), pp. 566–567.

[26] Roger Lockyer, *Buckingham* (London: Longman, 1981), p. 113. "Patron" saint was one of the early usages of the word in English. OED, "patron."

[27] Robert Herrick, "His Prayer to Ben Johnson," *The Norton Anthology of English Literature* (eds), M. H. Abrams et.al. (2 vols.; New York: Norton, 1979), I, 1316. For a later manifestation see J. S. A. Adamson, "The Baronial Context of the English Civil War," *Transactions of the Royal Historical Society*, 5th series, 40 (1990), 93–120, who suggests that the Earl of Essex, Captain-General of the parliamentary army, was described in terms of "almost religious reverence" (p. 107). Such imagery was not unparalleled as Adamson argues; instead the political flattery of court favorites or "evil counsellors" and of those who attacked them was strikingly similar.

BENEFITS, BROKERS AND BENEFICIARIES

Catholics. In a series of sermons preached at court in the 1620s, the Calvinist Professor of Divinity at Oxford, John Prideaux, self-consciously and systematically borrowed images of the Baroque court and its patronage to describe God, heaven and Christ.[28] Prideaux took up themes that found resonance in his court audience sympathetic to Catholicism. In "A Plot for Preferment" Prideaux urged his listeners to turn to God for he would bring them "to the highest preferment, his eternall rest, through his deare sonne, the highest Master of Requests." Although Calvinists rejected Catholic notions of intercession, Prideaux specifically focussed on the subject of angels, one of the highest links in the Great Chain of Being leading to God. Prideaux overlaid spiritual with secular meanings. In "The Patronage of Angels," Prideaux pronounced "He cannot be slighted without great danger, who hath as it were the Angel, his Agents in the court of heaven." For angels "have perpetual access, to his glorious presence in heaven." Such images literally reflected the court before whom he preached in which royal households controlled access to the monarch. Indeed, Prideaux made the analogy concrete.

> what it is to behold the face of the Father, and in what manner these Angels are said to doe it allwaies. It seems to be a Metaphore taken from the Courts of earthly Princes, who have their attendants allwaies about them to execute their commands: as Solomon had.[29]

God's invisible grace, his "benefit," was granted through the intercession of his angels. Theology then provided a structure and meaning for court patronage that overlapped with the classical focus on benefits.

If such Stoic language and theological analogies structured narratives of English patronage and exchange, their actual practice had changed from the sixteenth century. Sir Thomas More accepted gloves from a litigant as a New

[28] John Prideaux, *Eight Sermons Preached by John Prideaux, Doctor of Divinity, Regius Professor, Vice Chancellor of the University of Oxford, and Rector of Exeter College* (London, 1621), "The Christian's Free-Will Offering as it was delivered in a sermon on Christmasse day at Christ-Church in Oxford," n.d.; *Twenty Sermons* (Oxford, 1636), "A Plot for Preferment, A Sermon Preached at the Court," "Reverence to Rulers," "The Patronage of Angels." In his letter of dedication to Dr. Bodley, Canon of Exeter, Prideaux wrote "Since buyers and sellers have broken into the Temple, Judas'es what will you give me, and Simon Magus's offering, make most bargaines for Benefices. Whereby God is dishonoured, worthy men disheartened, hirelings preferred, good lawes deluded, holy things prefaned, the Church stained, the people starved. The more remarkable therefore hath beene your free dealing with mee and your religious kinsman's M. Periam's, with Mr. Orford of our College. If such patrons might be patternes for disposing the Lords portion many in the country might be better taught, and in our Universities sooner imployued." E3–4.
[29] "The Patronage of Angels," pp. 3, 20–22. Prideaux construed Matthew 18.10, "Take heed that you despise not one these little ones, for say unto you, that in heaven their Angels doe alwaies behold the face of my Father which is in Heaven."

Year's gift but refused gold and, presented with a gilt cup, returned a more valuable, though less attractive one, to a suitor.[30] Hugh Latimer thundered at the court of Edward VI that he was glad that *munera* was now being translated as bribes not gifts. Queen Elizabeth preferred gowns to money as New Year's gifts.[31] Indeed, projects, buying and selling of office and title, memorialized in the building of Hatfield House and Audley End and the collections of York House, could fit neither into the Senecan nor the religious definition of benefits.[32]

As royal favorite from 1616 to 1628, George Villiers, Duke of Buckingham, controlled royal patronage with King James's blessing. James used Buckingham as a filter for the many demands made by suitors and officeholders upon him.[33] Although only the last of a series of Jacobean favorites, in Scotland and England, the Duke had the greatest influence on policy and the tightest control over the dispensation of favor. James I had expanded royal bounty in the form of privileges, patents and titles; many of these were marketed in order to gain revenue for the Crown. None were invented by the Duke. But Buckingham organized the dispensation of favor more thoroughly: he expanded the baronets to Scotland and Ireland; eighty-five were created in 1626 alone, most arranged by the Duke and his family.[34] He integrated their sale with the payment of royal officials and, with the king's help, extracted large payments from the customs farmers. While distributing royal bounty widely, contemporaries and later historians have noted that Buckingham demanded acknowledgement of individual dependence from his clients. That acknowledgement was a change from the earlier practice in which the language of individual dependency was belied by petition to several patrons at once. Such intercession had symbolic as well as political meaning. Prideaux's doubling of secular and theological language found its counterpart in the description of the king's favorite,

[30] See William Roper, *The Life of Sir Thomas More* (London: C. Wittingham for R. Triphook, 1822), pp. 61–62. I am grateful to John Guy for this reference.

[31] Folger Shakespeare Library Mss. Xd 428, Cavendish Talbot Mss. nos. 120, 127, 128, 130, 131.

[32] Nevertheless, as we shall see, economic debate of the 1620s continued to use language about the circle of commerce that coincided with the language about the exchange of benefits.

> . . . For money of itself (be it more or less) in whose hands so ever, without bullion to supply, is but water in a cistern taken from a spring, that by use becomes exhausted, or being let alone, consumes itself to nothing. . . So coin becomes but medals, out of use or out of fashion. For bullion being the Fountain, money is but the water, and exchange the river that serves all private turns. . . . Gerard Malynes, *The Center of the Circle of Commerce* (London, 1623), STC 17221.

[33] Lockyer, *Buckingham*, p. 28.

[34] Lockyer, *Buckingham*, p. 413; Lawrence Stone, *Crisis of the Aristocracy* (Oxford: Oxford University Press, 1965), p. 94.

Buckingham, both as angel and saint who interceded between the supplicant and the almighty monarch.

Favorites, whose power was based on the personal affection of the monarch, rather than on status or office, had existed in Europe and in England throughout the Middle Ages and the sixteenth century. Contemporaries viewed their emergence as part of the cycle of court life; the rapidity of their rise and fall was a symptom of the changing affections and unpredictable behavior of the monarch. While favorites were frequently criticized, they played an important role in the early modern court in two ways: one, insulating the monarch from incessant demands and two, substituting for a nobility whose institutional power made them a greater threat to the monarch than a favorite who was his "creature." James, it was said "strengthened himself ever with some favorite, whom he might better trust than many of the nobility tainted with this desire of oligarchy."[35] These functions were understood, indeed consciously spelled out, by contemporaries. In advising the favorite on how to organize petitions for patronage, solicit advice and handle clients, Sir Francis Bacon wrote that "the whole Kingdom hath cast their eye upon you as the new rising Star, and no man thinks his business can prosper at Court unless he hath you for his good Angel or at least that you be not a *Malus Genius* against him."[36]

Bishop John Williams advised the favorite to take up the position of Lord High Steward, pointing out that only the king's relatives, favorites or what he described as "counter-favorites (raised up of purpose to balance the great one)" had previously held the office. The position provided "very competent gettinges," and, more importantly, gave the favorite his own bounty to distribute, so that he was not merely the conduit of royal bounty. Most of all, Williams recommended "this great opportunitye, to be neerest unto the Kinge, that is, to be upon earth, as your pietye will one daye make you in heaven, an everlastinge favouritt."[37]

---

[35] Quoted in Richard Cust, *The Forced Loan* (Oxford: Oxford University Press, 1987), p. 21.

[36] James Spedding, *The Letters and The Life of Francis Bacon* (7 vols.; London: Longman, Green, Longman, 1861–1874), VI, 14. The letter of advice to Villiers exists in ms, at Trinity College, Cambridge, and was published in the 1660s. Spedding publishes two versions and analyzes their date of composition and relationship, pp. 9–56. Such a saint could also serve as a sacrificial lamb. The king was above the people's censures but his courtiers were not. Bacon advised Buckingham that "you may be offered as a sacrifice to appease the multitude." Spedding, ed. *The Letters and the Life of Sir Francis Bacon*, VI, 15.

[37] John E. B. Mayor, *Letters of Archbishop Williams with Documents Relating to Him* (Cambridge: Cambridge University Press, 1866), pp. 52–55. "It gives you opportunitye to gratifie all the Court, great and small, *virtute officij*, in right of your place, which is a thinge better accepted of and interpreted, then a courtesy from a favouritt. Because in this you are a dispenser of your owne, but in the other (saye many envious men) of the

In 1625 Williams, who had lost his position as Lord Keeper and Bucking-ham's favor, asked to be restored to life:

> I doe most humblye beseech your Grace to crowne soe many of your
> Graces former favoures, and to revive a creature of your owne, strucke
> dead onlye with your displeasure by bringing of me to kiss his Majesty's
> hand, I was never hitherto brought into the praesence of a Kinge by
> any Saint beside your selfe; turne me not over (most noble Lord) to
> offer my prayers at newe aulters.[38]

William's reading of Buckingham's patronage gave a new twist to the meaning of patron saint. By borrowing Roman Catholic language to describe his secular dependency on the royal favorite Williams played to the religious, even poss-ibly Catholic, views of the Duke and the court and, more generally, reflected a Baroque sensibility common to Protestant and Catholic European courts alike. Even if Williams's address was jesting, it was not unique. Perez Zagorin points out that Bishop Field of Llandaff wrote to Buckingham that "one blast of your Breath. . . is able to bring me to the Heaven where I would be."[39] (But how would Latimer, the great Edwardian reformer, have read these bishops's petitions?)

Buckingham's patronage can be seen in action in two examples: the negotia-tions over both the provostship of Eton and his favor to the Blundell brothers.

kinges goodnes, which wold flowe fast enough of it selfe, but that is restrayned to this pipe and chanel onelye." Williams argued that the Lord High Steward was superior to the Master of the Horse, and the Lord Admiral, urging that "if any man shall putt you in hope that the Admiraltye will fill your coffers and make you riche, call upon them to name one Admiral that ever was soe. As in times of hostilitye there is some gettinge, soe are there hungrie and unsatiable people presentlye to devoure up the same." He called attention to the example of the Earl of Leicester, "who (beinge the onely favouritt in Q. Elizabeth hir time that was of any continuance) made choise of this place onelye, and refused the Admiraltye two severall times, as being an occasion, either to withdrawe him from the Court or to leave him there laden with ignominye." Even when he gave up the Bedchamber, the office of Lord Steward would keep him close to the king, "Nowe God Almightye having given you favoure at the first, and sithence a greate quantitye . . . of witt and wise experience . . ."

[38] B. Dew Roberts, *Mitre & Musket, John Williams, Lord Keeper, Archbishop of York, 1582–1650* (London, New York: Oxford University Press, 1938), p. 110. Westminster this 7th of January 1625 (o.s.) "If I were guiltye of any unworthye unfaithfulness for the time past, or not guiltye of a resolution to doe your Grace all service for the time to com, all consideration under Heaven could not force me to begge it soe earnestlye, or to professe myselfe as I doe before God and you."

[39] Quoted in *The Court and The Country*, p. 62. Williams could milk Old Testament images of intercession too: Zagorin cites another letter from Williams to Buckingham in which he wrote "Lett all our Greatness depend . . . upon youres, the true Originall. Lett the kinge be Pharao, youre self Joseph, and lett us com after as your halfe Brethren," p. 62.

In both, the commercial transactions involved in the sale of office and title, and rent-seeking by the political elite did not quite fit into the vocabulary of benefit. The provostship of Eton was much sought after: the famous school was located near London and parents were grateful for their sons' admission. Every time the position became available during the reign of James I there was a frenzy of eager suitors each applying to one of the great patrons through court brokers.[40] In 1623 the candidates included Sir Robert Ayton, Sir Dudley Carleton, Sir Henry Wotten, Sir William Becher, and Francis Bacon, Viscount Albans.[41]

Although Becher was a diplomat and an educated man there was a general perception that he was less qualified than others contesting for the post, a suspicion based probably on social status.[42] No one but Buckingham wanted Becher for the job. Yet the Duke held to his promise to give Becher the next good post until a satisfactory financial offer was made which enabled the Duke to gratify two clients at once.

The role ascribed to the king in contemporary rhetoric as the fountainhead of favor was belied by negotiations over the provostship. While the favorite was in Spain, Lord Keeper Williams reported:

> Whomsoever your Lordship shall name, I shall like of though it be Sir William Becher (though this Provostship never descended so low). The king named unto me yesterday morning Sir Albertus Morton, Sir Dudley Carleton and Sir [blank] Aten [Sir Robert Ayton], our late Queen's secretary: but (in my opinion) though he named him last, his Majesty inclined to this Aten most. It will rest wholely [sic] upon your Lordship to name the man.[43]

It was the favorite, not the king, who would dispense this favor. Furthermore,

---

[40] See H. C. Maxwell-Lyte, A History of Eton College, 1440–1910 (London: MacMillan and Co., 1911).

[41] Maxwell-Lyte, Eton, pp. 182–184, 577–578. None met the requirements of the founder, Henry VI, that the provost be a cleric. But that requirement had been waived for Saville who had used both Essex and Sir Robert Cecil to intercede with Queen Elizabeth for him.

[42] The House of Commons, 1604–1629, ed. J. P. Ferris (forthcoming). I am grateful to the History of Parliament Trust for permission to read their biography of Sir William Becher. My thanks too to Sabrina Alcorn Baron. Sir William signed his will Becher. His grandfather was an alderman of London, his father a merchant with military contracts, and his mother daughter of a draper. Becher got his first overseas post in the household of Sir George Carew in Paris through Robert Cecil's secretary, Sir Michael Hicks, "by whose benefit I am here." Quoted in J. W. Stoye, English Travellers Abroad, 1604–1667 (New Haven: Yale University Press, 1989), pp. 70–75.

[43] B. L. Stowe Mss. 743, f. 52, 11 April 1623. "It is somewhat necessary he be a good scholar, but more that he be a good husband and a careful, provident and stayed man, which no man can be, that is so much indebted as the Lord of St. Alban's."

119

the exchange was financial. Ayton offered to forgo what he called the "benefit" of his £500 a year pension in return for the post, saying to the Duke "it is in your power. . . to strike the stroke."[44]

Sir Dudley Carleton had sought the post for ten years. At court Carleton's secretary, Edward Sherburn, was blunt: because nothing could be done without money he wanted to know how much to offer for the post.[45] Yet the commercial transaction was described in Senecan terms. Sherburn wrote "the Duke is so deeply engaged to Sir William Becher for the first good thing that should fall . . . and he had received such an obligation from that man that he should be unworthy if he made not his promises good, even in the very worst degree of unworthiness." Nonetheless, payment was clearly part of the bargain. If Carleton could "find out any means to give Sir William Becher other contentment," the Duke assured Carleton that he would carry it before any man and promised to speak with Becher about Carleton's offer.[46] But Becher turned it down because it was not "half so good as the place."[47]

Even as money played an increasingly large role in patron-client relationships in the early seventeenth century, the exchange of favor was still sealed with a gift, the outward badge of benefit, at every level of society.[48] At the Jacobean court the collecting of antique and Renaissance art had become increasingly popular and diplomats like Carleton and Wotton shaped the taste of courtiers.[49] Carleton's nephew told his uncle that Wotton had presented Buckingham with many "curious" pictures and it was thought that he aimed at the Provostship. In response, Carleton asked his nephew if this was a good time to offer Buckingham a "gate and chimney of marble?" But he urged him to "use care and discretion, for they are of too great value to be cast away, especially considering my hard estate. Wherefore first weigh with yourself how you find

[44] B.L. Add. Mss. 4107, f. 68, 10 April 1623.

[45] P.R.O. S.P. 14/92/43, 11 June 1617. Sherburn acknowledged receiving Carleton's packet of letters and distributing them. Carleton raised the issue of Eton with several people at this time. See John H. Barcroft, "Carleton and Buckingham: The Quest for Office," in Howard S. Reinmuth, *Early Stuart Studies* (Minneapolis, 1970), pp. 122–136.

[46] P.R.O. S.P. 14/153/32.

[47] P.R.O. S.P. 14/153, Oct 25, 1623, Becher thought it would weaken his pretension if he lent "an ear to any proposition."

[48] Robert Cecil took a coach and four from the Earl of Northumberland even as he argued that "gifts of value" should not pass between "those whose minds condemn all the knots that utility can fasten." Quoted in Penry Williams, *The Tudor Regime* (Oxford: Oxford University Press, 1979), p. 106.

[49] The subject of Jacobean collecting remains to be fully explored. See David Howarth, *The Earl of Arundel and his Circle* (New Haven: Yale University Press, 1985); A. R. Braunmuller, "The Earl of Somerset as Collector and Patron," in *The Mental World of the Jacobean Court*, ed. L. L. Peck, pp. 230–250.

the Duke to continue affected towards me, then what intention he hath or means to favor me."[50] Although the marble chimney appears to have been installed at York House, the Duke's London residence, Sir Henry Wotton obtained the provostship of Eton through Buckingham. But Sir William Becher had to be gratified with more than the art that Wotton had presented as gifts to the king's favorites, Somerset and Buckingham.[51] Wotton transferred to Becher his interest in a Six Clerks position in Chancery, whose profit was based on the sale and revenues of the office and the manipulation of a series of reversions, writing "all which I have been moved to do for your release of a promise which the Duke of Buckingham my noble patron had made you before my last arrival from Venice to procure for you from his Majesty the Procurator-

[50] Lockyer, *Buckingham*, p. 215. He added that Lady Carleton had gone to Middleburg to see goods that the Dutch had taken from a Spanish prize in order to make Buckingham a wonderful present.
[51] In 1613 Sir Henry Wotton had lamented his loss of two great patrons, Prince Henry and the Earl of Salisbury. *C.P.S.D. 1611–18*, p. 172, Feb. 25, 1613, Wotton to George Carleton. Wotton then turned to Robert Carr, Earl of Somerset, and, in 1614, while on a diplomatic trip to the Hague, Wotton sent Somerset a Dutch or Flemish painting, "a piece of perspective which is a very busie kinde of worke, and therefore thease patient and phlegmatique hands doe commonly excel then Italians who rather affect draughts of spirit and action: but this piece which I now send hath a little more life than ordinary by the addition of the personages which made me make choice of it for your better delectation." This landscape was tangible proof of Wotton's "fidelity" to his patron. Folger Shakespeare Library Mss. GB 10, f. 87v.

> The king hath given me leave to come home when this public business shall draw to some issue one way or other which I hope wilbe within 2 months or such. . . And then I will take Antwerp in my return for the search of some good pieces: And if I cannot serve your Lordship with judgement yet I will do it with zeal. Mr. Dowrick hath made me know besides my other obligations how much I am bound to your Lordship for the late intercession for me with the king wherein the trouble was your Lordship's, and the misfortune mine own. . . . . My comfort is now that though His Majesty's memory doth fail him as might easily among so infinite suitors, and after so long in time of silence in it, yet his goodness will never fail him, wherein when occasion serves I will build upon your Lordship's mediation and patronage, and in the meanwhile give you some demonstrations of my fidelity. In my Lord of Bruce cause I have Yet had no answer here through the absence of Monsieur Barnevelt, upon whose return I will pursue for a resolution. And so I humbly commit your Lordship to God's blessed favor.

See Logan Pearsall Smith, *The Life and Letters of Sir Henry Wotton* (2 vols.; Oxford; Clarendon Press, 1907), I, 434, Wotton wrote to Somerset on August 18, 1614, about a clerkship he thought he should be granted. By the time Wotton came home from his post in Venice, Somerset had fallen, and he himself was without funds. The king promised him the Mastership of the Rolls after Sir Julius Caesar.

ship of Eton."[52] Contemporaries estimated that Becher made at least £2000 from the deal.[53]

The Blundell brothers provide a second example. After the death in 1617 of Sir Ralph Winwood, Secretary of State to James I, his secretary and client, Francis Blundell, needed to find another patron. A younger son, he had already built up an estate through office holding in Ireland. He was fortunate enough to attach himself to Buckingham to whom he gratefully expressed his loyalty:

> By your looks such is your goodness as you make your servants happy; for the notice which you have been pleased to take of me, being observed by men of good quality in the court, hath been very advantageous unto me. . . .. For this, and your Lordship's many other favors. . . I have presumed to adventure that your lordship may see that the benefits which you have conferred upon me do not perish.

Blundell's letter provides another illuminating reading of the Duke of Buckingham's patronage. He acknowledged that he owed the favorite almost everything: Buckingham's "goodness," Blundell declared, "hath made me most of what I am."[54] He stressed the presence of onlookers as audience, an essential part of the patron-client relationship, and pledged in Senecan terms that the benefits bestowed by the Duke upon him would not perish.

The significant difference between Blundell's career before he became a client of Buckingham's and after was his increasing focus on the sale of titles both to pay royal officials and to support the Duke. The Irish baronetcy was created during Buckingham's ascendancy and Blundell was one of the first of the Irish baronets, who were created with precedence over English knights, according to John Chamberlain, to stimulate sales of the title.[55] Indeed, Blundell used his contacts to manage the sale of the title for Buckingham, marketing at least eleven between 1618 and 1622 for amounts ranging from £250 to £500.[56] To Buckingham, he described the swarm:

> I have according to your Lordship's command sent a letter to Mr Packer for the making of one Fish a Baronet of Ireland at Mr Carleton's request. . . . These being done, I hope I shall hear of no more suits of that kind until I have made up number for your Lordship, which I am now about.

[52] B.L. Egerton Mss. 860, f. 113v, Sir Henry Wotton to Sir William Becher, "dated at my lodging in King's Street this 8 of November 1624." Wotton shared his reversion with Sir Julius Caesar, Master of the Rolls.
[53] N. E. McClure, ed., *The Letters of John Chamberlain* (2 vols.; Philadelphia: American Philosophical Society, 1939), II, 572–573 and 573n.
[54] Folger Shakespeare Library Mss. Gb 10, f. 70.
[55] McClure, ed., *The Letters of John Chamberlain*, II, 316.
[56] Lawrence Stone, *The Crisis of the Aristocracy* (Oxford, 1965), p. 96.

Blundell suggested that the Irish did not recognize the importance of declaring their dependence on the favorite.

> If any man doth move your Lordship about making Sir John Fitz-gerald a viscount, I beseech you take notice of him as a man already presented to your Lordship for yourself. For I am upon terms with him but the nature of the Irish is to use several means, so as your lordship not knowing of my treaty with him, may engage your promise to some other to your own prejudice.[57]

Blundell's access to high office, title, property and project was enhanced once Buckingham became his patron and in turn he used his Irish connections to further the favorite's interests. When Lionel Cranfield as Lord Treasurer turned his investigations to Ireland, he told Blundell in 1621 that his office of Vice-Treasurer was central to the reform of Irish administration, but noted trenchantly that Blundell had not always fulfilled his responsibilities. Alluding perhaps to Blundell's role in selling the Irish baronetcies, Cranfield urged him "to do the king's service sincerely, laying aside all other thoughts for the present till the settling of this work." But Buckingham protected his client, reminding Cranfield to "continue your accustomed favor towards him [Blundell] as a man I take care of."[58]

Buckingham was also the patron of Francis's soldier brother George who was knighted in 1617. In 1623 George Blundell proposed a project by which he would supply the kingdom with new arms. Asking Secretary Conway to procure him the title of "Captain of the Arms for England and Wales," Blundell

---

[57] *Complete Baronetage*, (Exeter, 1900), I, 236. Fish had connections through his sister to Michael Boyle, Bishop of Waterford, but he obtained the baronetcy through Blundell and Dudley Carleton as Francis reported to the Duke. P.R.O. S.P. 14/124/29, Dec. 11, 1624, Blundell to Buckingham.

[58] Quoted in *Commons Debates, 1621*, ed. Wallace Notestein, Frances Relf, and Hartley Simpson (7 vols.; New Haven: Yale University Press, 1935), II, 49 n. 14, 15 January 1622. Both Cranfield and Blundell were the Duke's clients. When the Duke withdrew his favor from Cranfield in 1624, the Lord Treasurer fell to parliamentary impeachment. Afterwards, King James and Prince Charles granted him pardon. Because Buckingham was away, a member of the king's bedchamber wrote to the Duke to explain the pardon apologetically and to send the king's promises to do nothing more for Cranfield without Buckingham's approval. Cranfield was listed among Buckingham's kindred in "A schedule of the gifts and grants bestowed upon the Duke of Buckingham and his kindred" prepared perhaps for the proceedings against the Duke in the Parliament of 1626. B.L. Add. Mss. 5832. In August 1621 the Earl of Arundel asked Cranfield to write to the Lord Admiral on behalf of a kinsman of his. HMC *4th Report, Appendix*, p. 299.

promised Conway's son one shilling a piece of the first 20,000 arms sold in consideration of the father's favor.[59]

Blundell served at sea on the expeditions in the 1620s to Cadiz and the Isle of Rhé. His letters to Buckingham and to Secretary Nichols are filled both with complaints about provisioning and requests for money and favor.[60] In 1627, while serving as Serjeant Major in Plymouth, he described the dreadful situation of men, provisions and ships. He went on to say that he had heard that the Lords had settled his allowance at twelve shillings a day. Proclaiming that he would rather serve the king for nothing than receive so base a pay, he begged the Duke to put him down for forty shillings. Blundell spelled out the financial terms of court patronage, complaining that Buckingham made him a packhorse, as he put it, while others lay at court still getting sergeants or baronets to put money in their purses. Such court favor had an unfortunate end. Sir George Blundell and his son George were slain at Rhé.[61] But Sir George got his wish; he was entered on the list of the army with pay of 40 shillings a day and the wardship of his grandson was granted to his son's wife without paying the usual fine to the Crown.

In Senecan terms, Buckingham's benefits to this client did not perish. Indeed, wherever we look, Buckingham's patronage was a complex mixture of Senecan rhetoric about obligation, benefit and gift giving and commercial transactions in which royal favor was for sale, often with the king's knowledge.

In the early 1630s Peter Paul Rubens celebrated the reign of James I in his paintings for the Banqueting House ceiling based on a program probably de-

[59] P.R.O. S.P. 14/180/7. The project would create a central warehouse in London from which to provision the trained bands in the counties with arms made by poor artificers. The prices of the arms would be set by the Privy Council and members of the trained bands would be forced to buy their arms from Blundell.

Blundell feared that were James Maxwell, a member of the Privy Chamber, to return from Scotland that John Murray, Lord Annandale, long a member of James I's Scottish retinue, would insist that Maxwell get half the profits on the arms project. Claiming that he would procure arms at the lowest rates and highest quality, Blundell asked for allowances to cover the expenses of providing an armory and attendants and for sending the arms into the country. Blundell may have had connections with the Duke of Lennox because, in 1624, after the death of Esme Stuart, he wrote to an unnamed Lord, to ask despatch of his suit for £500 or £1000 saying that he kept a son of the Duke who had no other means to live. This was perhaps Sir Henry Lennox who in 1625 was granted a pension. Sir George Blundell claimed the right as part holder of the barony of Bedford to serve as Almoner at the coronation of Charles I.

[60] In 1626 Blundell asked to have a commission of a new regiment to be raised by taking one company from each regiment at Plymouth offering in exchange to forgo his pay of 20 shillings a day as Quartermaster General. He also presented a project for raising money for the king's service by the coinage of £100,000 in farthings.

[61] By putting aside a lieutenant with more service, Blundell had obtained a position for his son on his ship. CSPD 1625–1626, pp. 242, 343, 350; CSPD 1627–1628, pp. 148, 154, 159, 166, 171, 293, 348.

vised with Inigo Jones, in the 1620s. King James was presented as King Solomon, the embodiment of wisdom.[62] One of Rubens' central panels presented King James bringing the Benefits of Good Government; at its side were the figures of Royal Bounty overcoming Avarice. In this Rubens *modello*, Royal Bounty is presented in the figure of Apollo. Holding a cornucopia from which shower gold coins and crowns, the androgynous young god bestrides a crone hugging her purse.[63] The painting celebrates godlike largess and denies and denigrates self-interest. Such an image marked the ascendance of the classical theory of royal bounty and benefits and God's free gift of grace.[64]

At the same time these religious and classical meanings of benefits fused with economic meanings in contemporary debate in the 1620s. Benefits circulated swiftly resembling the circulation of money in the economy and even new notions about the circulation of the blood in the body. The economy itself was conceptualized in terms of swiftly moving benefits in the economic debates of the 1620s which served as the means to construct a new ideology based on interest, utility and the identification of private profit with virtue.[65] Sir Arthur Chichester, Lord Deputy of Ireland, had defined a commonwealth as "nothing more than a commercement or continual suppeditation of benefits mutually received and done among men."[66] Economic debate of the 1620s resonated remarkably with the classical and religious language of patronage. Gerard Malynes merged classical virtue and the sacrament of communion in this description of the economy.

> Let not your heroical virtues for the public good be blemished with private centers of commerce . . . let the procuring of bullion be your first study. . . . To be short, Bullion is the very body and blood of kings,

[62] Roy Strong, *Britannia Triumphans: Inigo Jones, Rubens and Whitehall Palace* (London: Thames and Hudson, 1980), pp. 14–20; 34–6.

[63] Julius Held, *The Oil Sketches of Peter Paul Rubens* (Princeton: Princeton University Press, 1980), pp. 214–5.

[64] While Malcolm Smuts has noted that James was represented as Apollo, the *nous* of the Platonic universe, the beautiful and androgynous young man reminds one also of Buckingham who was presented in the title page of Thomas Scot's *Vox Dei* of 1624 as overcoming bribery and faction. Because King James was lauded for the attributes of Solomon in the Banqueting Hall ceiling, Julius Held has related Rubens's image of royal bounty to the story of King Solomon and the Queen of Sheba to whom Solomon gave all of his bounty, *The Oil Sketches of Rubens*, pp. 214–215. Somerset, the previous favorite, had a painting of Solomon and Sheba, a popular subject among contemporary artists. Were Somerset and Buckingham James's Queens of Sheba? In the eighteenth century Sheba became a synonym for self-interest. J. E. Crowley, *This Sheba, Self* (Baltimore: The Johns Hopkins University, 1974).

[65] Gerard Malynes, *The Center of the Circle of Commerce* (London, 1623), STC 17221.

[66] "Letterbook of Sir Arthur Chichester, 1612–1614," *Analecta Hibernica*, VIII, 56, Chichester to the Archbishop of Canterbury, 23 October 1612.

money is but the medium between subjects and their kings, exchange the heavenly mystery that joins them both together.[67]

Commercial enterprise thus turned merchandise into benefits. The new economic theories of the circulation of benefits, however, left little room for the theological position of the angel or patron saint, unless one imagines the very visible hand of the favorite transformed into the invisible hand.

But that may not be as impossible a leap as one might think. I have argued that in the early seventeenth century classical and religious "scripts" shaped court patronage but fit only uneasily with the broadly commercial sale of office, titles, patents of monopoly that the early Stuart court and, especially, the Duke of Buckingham, engaged in. There is another script, however, in which the two were linked. In the late sixteenth century, Michel de Montaigne explicitly argued that private vice led to public good, selfish ambition brought men into public life.

> As for that fine statement under which ambition and avarice take cover — that we are not born for our private selves, but for the public — let us boldly appeal to those who are in the midst of the dance. Let them cudgel their consciences and say whether, on the contrary, the titles, the offices, the hustle and bustle of the world are not sought out to gain private profit from the public.[68]

In 1714, Bernard Mandeville wrote *The Fable of the Bees*.[69] Fusing the dis-

---

[67] Gerard Malynes, *The Center of the Circle of Commerce* (London, 1623), STC 17221.

[68] Quoted in Naneorl O. Keohane, *Philosophy and the State in France* (Princeton: Princeton University Press, 1980), p. 112, from the *Essays*, I, 39 (174); the reference is to the Ciceronian maxim frequently repeated in contemporary literature.

[69] F. B. Kaye, ed., *The Fable of the Bees: Or Private Vices, Public Benefits* (Oxford: Oxford University Press, 1924). In the prefatory poem, "The Grumbling Hive" Mandeville described:

> Their Kings were serv'd, but Knavishly
> Cheated by their own Ministry;
> Many, that for their Welfare slaved,
> Robbing the very Crown they saved:
> Pensions were small, and they liv'd high,
> Yet boasted of their Honesty.
> Calling, Whene'er they strain'd their Right,
> The slipp'ry Trick a Perquisite;
> And when Folks understood their Cant,
> They chang'd that for Emolument;
> Unwilling to be Short or plain,
> In anything concerning Gain;

There is a similarity between Mandeville's justification of venality with the modernization theorists such as Samuel Huntington.

course of seventeenth and eighteenth century French skeptics and English commercial writers, Mandeville attacked the language of virtue and corruption current among contemporary moralists and central to the Country Whig tradition inherited from seventeenth century political struggles. Arguing that selfish self-interest, self-promotion, self-seeking fostered enterprise, commercial abundance and plenty, he subtitled his book, *Private Vices, Public Benefits.*[70] At the end of *The Fable of the Bees* Mandeville argued "that private vices by the dexterous management of a skillful politician, may be turned into public benefits." Whether or not George Villiers, Duke of Buckingham, would qualify as a skillful politician either in his own time or in Mandeville's analysis may be doubted. Nevertheless, in Mandeville we hear faint echoes of the Senecan vocabulary and the economic debates of the 1620s:

> The whole Superstructure (of Civil Society) is made up of the reciprocal Services, which Men do to each other. How to get these Services perform'd by others, when we have Occasion for them, is the grand and almost Sollicitude in Life of every individual Person. To expect, that others should serve us for nothing, is unreasonable; therefore all Commerce, that Men can have together, must be a continual bartering of one thing for another.[71]

By connecting self interest and the pursuit of luxury with commercial prosperity and social improvement Mandeville transformed the tension between the values of the early Stuart court and its critics.[72] Such connections provided food for strenuous political debate in eighteenth century England and America.[73]

[70] See M. M. Goldsmith, *Private Vices, Public Benefits* (Cambridge: Cambridge University Press, 1985); Thomas Horne, *The Social Thought of Bernard Mandeville* (New York: Columbia University Press, 1978); Nathan Rosenberg, "Mandeville and Laissez-Faire," *Journal of the History of Ideas* 29 (1963), 183–96. Hector Monro, *The Ambivalence of Bernard Mandeville* (Oxford: Clarendon Press, 1975).
[71] Quoted in Rosenberg, "Mandeville and Laissez-Faire," *Journal of the History of Ideas*, 29 (1963), 193n.
[72] M. M. Goldsmith and Thomas Horne disagree on whether or not Mandeville seriously meant to place such importance on "skillful politicians." While there is an extensive debate on whether Mandeville favored mercantilism (if there was such a thing), was a forerunner of laissez-faire or occupied a position in the middle, there has been little effort to see his connection to the political and economic debates of the early seventeenth century.
[73] See for instance, J. E. Crowley, *This Sheba, Self* (Baltimore: The Johns Hopkins University Press, 1974); Werner Sombart, *Luxury and Capitalism* (Ann Arbor: University of Michigan Press, 1967); Joyce Appleby, *Economic Thought and Ideology in Seventeenth-Century England* (Princeton: Princeton University Press, 1978).

Declining Status in an Aspiring Age: the Problem of the Gentle Apprentice in Seventeenth-Century London

PAUL S. SEAVER

Even before the era of London's spectacular growth in the later decades of Elizabeth's reign, London's place both in fact and imagination was clearly exceptional. By comparison Norwich and Bristol were at best overgrown county towns, episcopal sees and provincial centers, important regionally and an object of local interest and loyalty, but not, like London, a place to dream of or fear. For the Elizabethan or Jacobean monarchy the city in the first flush of its rapid growth was seen as almost ungovernable, a sink of pestilent humours, both literal and metaphorical, an alien growth to be controlled lest it swallow up tbe body politic. However, for the young man of limited prospects, London was an English Eldorado, where, if admittedly its streets were not of gold, possibilities nevertheless seemed almost infinite. Thomas Dekker might warn against the wily coney-catcher, lurking in wait to gull the unwary country bumpkin, preying on his credulity and preparing to relieve him of his purse, but for the thousands of young people who trooped into the city every year, London must have represented an escape from the limited horizons and endless drudgery of rural existence to a life of new possibilities — of rising to who knew what heights, not by birth but by enterprise.[1]

The story of Dick Whittington's rise from a poor apprentice possessing little more than the shirt on his back and capital in the form of the cat in his arms captured precisely that combination of miracle and dream fulfillment joined to fact that put spurs to the imagination, for was not Sir Richard Whittington

---

[1] For the view that London was pestilent and potentially ungovernable, see "A Proclamation Prohibiting New Building or Subdividing of Houses, 7 July 1580", in *Tudor Royal Proclamations*, v. 2, eds. Paul L. Hughes and James F. Larkin (New Haven: Yale University Press, 466–68, and "A Proclamation Prohibiting Further Building or Subdividing of Houses in London, 22 June 1602," in *ibid.*, 3: 245–48. For Dekker, see, e.g., his *Lantern and Candlelight, or The Bellmans' Second Nights Walk* (London, 1608). For estimates of the numbers of apprentices bound in London and their place of origin, see Roger Finlay, *Population and Metropolis. The Demography of London 1580–1650* (Cambridge: Cambridge University Press, 1981), 66–67.

truly thrice Lord Mayor in fifteenth-century London? In an era in which the moralists never ceased harping on the need to remain without complaint or striving in the status to which one was born and the calling to which one was summoned by God, the story of Dick Whittington presented an alternative morality played out in that arena where the exceptional was the rule, where striving was sanctioned and rising was part of the divine plan. Whittington was, the ballad tells us,

> But of poor parentage
> . . . as we hear,
> And in his tender age
> Bred up in Lancashire.

However, unlike Robinson Crusoe, that other northern hero who differed, not in leaving home and his station in life, but in doing so in defiance of parental injunction and who was promptly shipwrecked in punishment for his presumption, Whittington's departure is simply recorded in the ballad as fact:

> Poorly to London then
> Came up this simple lad
> Where, with a Merchant-man
> Soon he a dwelling had.[2]

Conflict came not in leaving home but in deciding to remain in London. As happened so frequently in the real life of city apprentices, Whittington found himself initially engaged not in the romance of international trade but in the disillusioning drudgery of household work, in Whittington's case as a kitchen scullion, where "meat and drink [were] all his pay." And like so many London apprentices after him, Whittington decided to run away "to purchase liberty," only to be called back by "London's bells sweetly rung" telling him to

> Turn again, Whittington;
> For thou, in time, shall grow
> Lord Mayor of London.

In the moral economy of the mercantile city, success is the reward not for remaining in the station of one's birth but for faithful service to one's master, a service in no way incompatible with seizing commercial opportunities, when they are offered, even if in the unlikely form of an invasion of rats and mice, and so Whittington came back

---

2 "Sir Richard Whittington's Advancement," in A Collection of Songs and Ballads relative to the London Prentices and Trades; and to the Affairs of London Generally, ed. Charles Mackay (London, for the Percy Society, 1841), 5.

> ... with speed,
> A prentice to remain,
> As the Lord had decreed,

At least until a plague of rodents provided an opportunity to exchange his cat for gold, enabling him to leave his apprenticeship and set up as a merchant in his own right.[3]

Whittington's passage from rags to riches must have been the very stuff of young apprentices' hopes, or at least dreams, reconciling them to the inevitable long years of servitude. However, for the minority among apprentices who came of gentle blood, apprenticeship, no matter how successful the outcome in terms of riches, inevitably involved downward mobility and a conspicuous loss of social status, and the dilemmas of that situation also found literary expression, not in ballads but in tracts and on the stage.

At the beginning of Act I of *Eastward Ho*, one of those early Jacobean city comedies on which George Chapman, Ben Jonson, and John Marston all collaborated, both Master Touchstone and one of his apprentices, a young spark aptly named Quicksilver, are seen entering Touchstone's goldsmith's shop. Quicksilver is dressed in hat, pumps, short sword, and dagger and has a tennis racket trussed up under his cloak, evidence, quickly confirmed, of his fundamental frivolity. Touchstone remarks with understandable spleen: "And wither with you now? What loose action are you bound for? Come, what comrades are you to meet withal? Where's the supper? Where's the rendezvous?" To which Quicksilver retorts, "Why, sir, I hope a man may use his recreation with his master's profit. Touchstone responds to that sally in the unsympathetic fashion of the master whose limited patience is fast approaching an end. "Prentices' recreations, says he, "are seldom with their master's profit." An altercation follows in the course of which Quicksilver replies to his master with equal heat: "Why, 'sblood, sir, my mother's a gentlewoman, and my father a justice of peace and of [the] quorum: and though I am a younger brother and a prentice, yet I hope I am my father's son."[4]

A few minutes later Quicksilver is engaged in conversation with Golding, a fellow apprentice, also of gentle birth, who, when Quicksilver urges him to "be like a gentleman, be idle," replies that he has read

> Whate'er some vainer youth may term disgrace,
> The gain of honest pains is never base:

---

[3] *Ibid.*, 6–7.

[4] George Chapman, Ben Jonson, and John Marston, *Eastward Ho*, ed. R. W. Van Fossen (Manchester, England, and Baltimore, Maryland: Manchester University Press; Johns Hopkins University Press, 1979), 69–71.

From trades, from arts, from valor honor springs;
These three are founts of gentry, yea of kings."[5]

Golding's verse is, of course, the very stuff of city moralism and city pride, a theme elaborated in Richard Johnson's famous *Nine Worthies of London* and iterated again and again in the popular literature of the time, at least in that popular literature written for a London audience. Further, we, the audience, know Golding is in the right, for he will marry Touchstone's virtuous daughter. Because we know the rules of bourgeois morality, we know as well that Quicksilver will come to a bad end — but for a totally unconvincing conversion to a virtuous life in the last act.

But Quicksilver's braggarts' swagger and prickly pride are reminders of a genuine problem: the almost inevitable loss of status that the younger sons of the propertied classes experienced in almost every instance. In 1629 that impecunious gentleman, Edmund Bolton, wrote *The Cities Advocate* to refute "that pestilent error, which, having some authority for it, and many injurious partakers, lay upon the hopeful and honest estate of apprenticeship in London, the odious note of bondage and the barbarous penalty of loss of Gentry."[6] Yet it is precisely to that loss that the newly penitent Quicksilver is reconciled at the end of *Eastward Ho*, for in the last scene he warns his fellow apprentices to take a lesson from his fall:

Shun usurers, bawds, and dice, and drabs;
Avoid them as you would French scabs.
Seek not to go beyond your tether,
But cut your thongs unto your leather;
So shall you thrive by little and little,
Scape Tyburn, Counters, and the Spital.[7]

5 *Ibid.*, 76, 78.
6 Edmund Bolton, *The Cities Advocate in this case or question of honor and armes, whether apprenticeship extinguisheth gentry?* (London, 1629), Epistle Dedicatory. For Bolton and this literature in general, see Louis B. Wright, *Middle-Class Culture in Elizabethan England* (Chapel Hill: University of North Carolina Press, reissued by Ithaca, New York: Cornell University Press, 1958), 22. Bolton argues sensibly that apprenticeship cannot imply or involve bondange because the apprentice "interchangeably seales a written contract with his Master by an indented instrument . . . Let the legal and ordinarie forme of that instrument . . . be duly pondered, and it will appear a meere civill contract, which as all the world knowes, a bondman is uncapable of." Bolton concedes that citizens and gentlemen are different things, but argues that one can be both, just as the same person can be both lord and tenant. However, Bolton offers little comfort to the Quicksilvers of his world, "for neither the incorrigibly vicious, who are pestilent to morall and civill virtue; nor the incorrigibly forgetfull of their betters, whom insolencie maketh odious, have any part herein at all." *The Cities Advocate*, 9, 30, 46, and "The Epistle to the Gentlemen of England in Generall."
7 Chapman, et. al, *Eastward Ho*, 205.

As Quicksilver knew in his rakehell days, to be a gentleman is to be idle. Thriving by little and little may keep one from hanging or debtor's prison, but it is the road, not to gentility, but to the quite different life of urban respectability.

One of the many difficulties in trying to imagine the texture and feel of early modern urban life lies in coming to some sense of its social temperature, its tensions and satisfactions, its social gulfs and its sense of community. Robert Shoemaker has shown us that riots and assaults were common in the streets of early modern London but did little to rend the social fabric in any significant degree.[8] Valerie Pearl and Steven Rappaport both present London as a peaceable kingdom, a growing metropolis that nevertheless succeeded in integrating the constant stream of newcomers and managed within a remarkably stable late medieval structure to involve a high percentage of male heads of families in one or another level of civic life.[9]

Apprenticeship was a key institution both in acculturating newcomers from the countryside and the next generation of journeymen and masters to the realities of responsible economic and civic life. In some respects it is an obvious institution, performing an obvious set of social and economic functions, about as lacking in mystery as one can well imagine. On the other hand, two "facts" suggest a complexity or ambiguity that belies such apparent simplicity. First is the fact that a substantial number of young men who began an apprenticeship never completed their term of years or entered into their company's or the city's freedom. An institution that has an apparent attrition rate of close to fifty percent is puzzling on the face of it.[10] Secondly, while apprenticeship was a highly formalized institution whose rules, privileges, and obligations were spelled out in a contractual arrangement specified in the indentures, apprenticeship was also a highly personal relationship that involved the apprentice for seven years or more in the life of his master's family, a relationship that was close and intimate despite the subordination of man to master. How these two aspects — the contractual and the personal – were reconciled in practice is not readily apparent.

There must, then, have been a certain amount of tension intrinsic to this central urban institution, a tension, if not outright conflict, generated by the difference between youth and age, servant and master, discipline and freedom,

[8]   Robert B. Shoemaker, "The London 'Mob' in the Early Eighteenth Century," *Journal of British Studies* 26 (1987): 273–304.

[9]   Valerie Pearl, "Change and Stability in Seventeenth-Century London," *London Journal* 5 (1979): 3–34; S. L. Rappaport, "Social Structure and Mobility in Sixteenth-Century London, Parts I and II," *London Journal* 9 (1983): 107–35; 10 (1984): 107–34.

[10]   According to Rappaport, "approximately three-fifths" of those apprenticed in London in the sixteenth century to the fifteen companies for which records survive never finished their apprenticeships. *Worlds within Worlds: Structures of Life in Sixteenth-Century London* (Cambridge: Cambridge University Press, 312 and Table 8.6.

ambitions postponed and ambitions realized. Obviously, in some sense the institution must have worked, for it remained the dominant mechanism for learning an urban trade well into the eighteenth century and still exists in an attenuated form to this day. However, for those apprentices who sued their masters, the institution of apprenticeship had at least in those instances failed. Such litigation, is, nevertheless, worth examining, for it offers both a means of uncovering and exploring some of the tensions inherent in the institution and in urban life, and a means of providing a glimpse of the social realities that surround that rather puzzling institution itself.

For suits there certainly were, either initiated by the apprentice, or, if he was still a minor, by his guardian. In particular it is worth examining the apprenticeship litigation involving sons of gentle families, for here it may be possible to discover the real particularities behind the contemporary belief that the gently born apprentice was inevitably involved in relationships fraught with contradictions. Thomas Powell, for example, in his *Tom of All Trades*, published in 1631, purports to address the problems of a Northampton gentleman blessed by too many younger sons who, it is assumed, will in many cases become apprentices. While Powell suggests that the apprenticeship premiums, the sum agreed to be paid to the master at the time of the sealing of the indentures of apprenticeship, can be provided from the portion obtained with the eldest son's wife, and therefore at no cost to the father himself, Powell does warn that "in the next place, take heed that you put off those your sons . . . to be apprenticed, betimes, and before they take the taint of too much liberty at home."[11] Powell assumes commonsensically that the privileged freedom of a gentle upbringing conflicts with the subordination and servitude intrinsic to an apprenticeship and sensibly urges that the sons to be apprenticed should be dispatched to the city before the habits of freedom became too deeply ingrained. Golding can be taken as fictional evidence of the contemporary conviction that the gentle apprentice could succeed; Quicksilver of the conviction that the gentle apprentice was a social contradiction with at best a problematic future.

Evidence from some of the litigation involving gentle apprentices that found its way into the Mayor's Court of London is too narrow a base on which to erect definitive answers, but it may nevertheless suggest the degree to which the downward mobility of gentry sons complicated the already difficult adjustment to a new way of life in a new family in an urban setting. There are obvious problems in attempting to assess social relationships by examining evidence of their failure, and litigation represented a profound failure, for conflicts between master and apprentice rarely reached the courts in the first instance. An apprentice and master at loggerheads normally appealed to par-

---

[11] Thomas Powell, *Tom of All Trades* (London, 1631), reprinted in *Complaint and Reform in England 1436–1714*, eds. William Huse Dunham, Jr, and Stanley Pargellis (Oxford: Oxford University Press, 1938; reprinted New York: 1968), 553.

ents and friends, who, if mediation failed, frequently urged the parties in conflict to take their differences to the City Chamberlain for arbitration or judgment. Successful arbitration normally meant the return of the apprentice to his master's service; only when such attempts at conciliation failed was the apprentice, or his parents or guardian, likely to turn to the Mayor's Court for a judicial remedy.

If the apprentice and his master reached a relatively amicable parting of the ways, it was possible to proceed by what was called an "Original Bill" on the Common Law side of the Court. In an Original Bill case the aggrieved apprentice typically alleged that his master had turned him out of his service or had failed to enroll him as an apprentice before the City Chamberlain within a year of sealing the indentures as required by the custom of London. If the defendant master failed to appear after having been properly summoned thrice by the Sergeant of the Mace, the Court invariably found for the apprentice plaintiff, ordered the surrender and cancellation of his indentures of apprenticeship, and turned him over to another master in the same trade.[12] Most Original Bill litigation appears to be collusive: that is, the master did not contest the apprentice's allegation, and the litigation was presumably launched simply as a means of obtaining a legal judgment recording the termination of the contract formed by the original indentures and permitting the apprentice so freed to be turned over to a new master for the residue of his term of service.

On rare occasions the master or his attorney appeared in court, as did John Bigge, attorney for Nathaniel Wright, Citizen and Skinner, in the case of Waller and Waller v. Wright in 1657. Bigge argued that Wright's apprentice, William Waller, should not be discharged from the residue of his apprenticeship because Wright did not in fact "turn the said William out of his service and refuse to receive or relieve him any longer therein in manner and form as the said William by his petition aforesaid hath supposed. And of this he putteth himself upon the country, and the plaintiff likewise."[13] Several weeks later on 24 November 1657,

> the jurors aforesaid being solemnly called, twelve of them did appear, who being elected and tried, were sworn to say the truth in the premises. And for their verdict upon their oaths did say that the defendant on the seven and twentieth day of October in [1657] aforesaid did turn the said plaintiff out of his service and refuse to receive or retain him any longer therein in manner and form as the said plaintiff by his declaration hath alleged.

[12] See, for example, Corporation of London Records Office [CLRO], Mayor's Court [MC], Original Bill, 1/92/69.

[13] CLRO, MC 1/92/91. Spelling and punctuation here and in subsequent quotations from Mayor's Court records have been modernized.

The Court then ruled for the apprentice and turned him over to another master for the residue of his apprenticeship.[14]

It is evident that Original Bill litigation, even on the rare occasions when the plaintiff's allegations were contested, rarely revealed much about the human relationships at stake beyond the formal nature of the circumstances surrounding the termination of service. The same cannot be said of the litigation brought before the Equity side of the Mayor's Court. These cases were invariably adversarial. They took longer to litigate because they proceeded by English Bill, that is, by written complaints and answers, followed by lengthy interrogatories submitted to witnesses under oath, and finally by a written order and decree presenting the judgment of the Court. Although only fragments of this litigation survive — interrogatories without final orders and decrees, decrees without preceding interrogatories — even the fragmentary record reveals much about the conflicts between apprentices and masters, or at least much about what the litigants hoped the Court would believe about the circumstances that had led to the litigation. The truth was obviously stretched and shaped to meet the different needs of the plaintiff and defendant, but to tell the Court stories that bore no relation to ascertainable fact was to run the risk of having them falsified by the sworn testimony of those to whom the interrogatories were submitted, to say nothing of failing to survive the skepticism of the Court.

Between 1641, the date of the earliest surviving interrogatory, and May of 1671, thirty years later, files of these records of varying degrees of completeness survive for 269 cases in the Corporation of London Records Office. Of these 100 (thirty-seven percent) concern disputed apprenticeships, 23 of which were brought by apprentices claiming gentle status or their guardians. If these surviving cases are representative of seventeenth-century reality, then apprentice plaintiffs of gentry origins appeared before the court with greater frequency than their numbers among all apprentices would suggest, for Steven Rappaport found that just under ten percent of the apprentices bound in the early 1550s claimed fathers of gentry status, while W. J. Kitch found that just under fifteen percent made such a claim in the 1690s.[15] The reason for the higher rate of litigation may well be obvious. Suits, particularly if the apprentice were still a minor, required a good store of friends — parents or guardians — willing to go to law and able to afford the hiring of an attorney, for suits could cost from £5, a not inconsiderable sum, to almost twice that amount.[16] On the other hand, there was every reason to pursue litigation, if one could afford to do so, not

[14] *Ibid.*
[15] Rappaport, *Worlds within Worlds*, 23, 83. M. J. Kitch, "Capital and Kingdom: Migration to Later Stuart London," in *London 1500–1700: The Making of the Metropolis*, eds. A. L. Beier and Roger Finlay (London and New York: Longmans, 1986), 246.
[16] CLRO MC Decrees, Box 255E, Wilson v. Harris, 22 Oct. 1661; Stafford v. Cotton, 7 Oct. 1662.

simply for the sake of revenge, but more practically in the hope of recovering indentures, performance bonds, and most importantly, a substantial part of the original premium, which by the middle years of the seventeenth century was usually a sum worth fighting for: an apprenticeship to Thomas Jevon, Citizen and Draper, required a premium of £100 in the early 1650s; an apprenticeship to Robert Tempest, Citizen and Goldsmith, cost £100 plus clothing of the value of £20 a few years later; while an apprenticeship to Daniel Andrewes, Turkey merchant, carried a premium of £300 in the late 1650s.[17]

Many of the cases on the equity side of the mayor's Court reveal a pattern that might have been anticipated from an examination of the generality of the apprenticeship cases brought before that Court. The defendant masters picture their former apprentices as rude and unruly, negligent in their duties, and given to haunting taverns and gaming houses, to embezzling their master's profits to pay for such entertainment, and to returning late at night drunk and disorderly, if not actually carried home by the watch. The apprentice plaintiffs or their parents or guardians on the other hand present a picture of exploited innocence, of the provision of inadequate food and clothing, of the neglect of training, of false accusations followed by abuse and undeserved beatings, culminating in the apprentice being turned out of his master's house and shop and denied the opportunity to return to service, despite the humble submission of the apprentice and the importunate pleas of his friends.

For example, in the case brought against Randall Ellis, Hosier, by Thomas Fowke of Staffordshire, gentleman, on behalf of his son John in 1641, Master Ellis replied that he did not employ his apprentice in "servile and base employments or in any other employments than is fit and usual for apprentices," but used him well, since John Fowke was his only apprentice. Nevertheless, John Fowke did "haunt plays and lotteries and the Temple" and carried "himself very stubbornly and doggedly" and was "very negligent and stayed much abroad when he was sent on errands." Furthermore, when young John ran away, he took some of his master's goods, his indenture, and the performance bond his father had entered into for his good behavior, and he added insult to injury by leaving the shop window open when he stole away at night, exposing his master to still further losses. John Durie, Citizen and Draper, testifying for Master Ellis, confirmed Ellis' good treatment and training of young John Fowke, adding that John had confessed to him "that he had twice ventured at the lottery and had won a silver bowl the which he sold for forty shillings, and

---

[17] CLRO, MC Interrogatories, 6/49A; MC Decrees, Box 255E, Chamberlain v. Tempest, 3 July 1662; MC Interrogatories, 6/109. Richard Grassby has shown that premiums, particularly for merchant's apprentices, rose substantially particularly in the second half of the seventeenth century. "Social Mobility and Business Enterprise in Seventeenth-century England," in *Puritans and Revolutionaries*, eds. Donald Pennington and Keith Thomas (Oxford: Oxford University Press, 1978), 364–65.

did likewise confess that he had purloined and lent divers sums of money" belonging to his master. Thomas White, a neighboring apprentice, testified on oath that he "did see the said apprentice to have three pounds in gold which he said he would send into Holland for a venture and did see him sell a pair of stockings of the defendant's and put the money in his . . . pockets." Thomas White also testifed to John Fowke's expensive habits, noting that young Fowke "did spend at one reckoning at the Blue Anchor tavern in Southwark nine shillings," a sum no honest apprentice should have been able to command.[18]

If masters normally pictured their errant apprentices as unmitigated rogues, apprentices in their suits presented their masters in an equally unflattering light. When Robert Townsend sued his master, Thomas Jevon, Citizen and Draper, the principal charge was that Jevon beat him repeatedly and unmercifully before turning him out of his service. Townsend added a further charge that Jevon fed his servants "stinking and putrified meat, not fit for any Christian to eat." George Harris, another of Jevon's apprentices, swore that they were indeed served "very bad and unwholesome meat" and also confirmed that on one occasion Jevon, "being in a passionate temper, threatened the plaintiff that he would pierce him through." Peter Davys, a neighbor's servant, testified that "his master's shop being next adjoining to the defendants and but a small partition of board between, did through a little crevice see the Defendant about nine of the clock at night upon the Complainant's rising and letting the Defendant in, . . . take a yard [stick] and beat the Complainant very sorely in his shirt, so much that the Defendant broke the yard." Francis Ramm, another neighboring servant, testified that he "saw the Defendant throw the Complainant against the counter in his shop" and beat young Townsend so often "that the Defendant's wife was forced often to help the Complainant and desire her husband to forbear, whereupon the Defendant hath thrown his wife down, which hath bruised her and also the maid, she coming to help her mistress, and that once upon the Defendant's beating the Complainant's blood did issue out of the Complainant's head." Another neighbor, Alice Eaton, spinster, deposed that "the Defendant did very outrageously beat and abuse the Complainant in so much that the Defendant's wife (being then in bed) was forced to rise and open the window and cry out murder for fear least that her husband should have endangered the Complainant's life, she seeing blood issue out of his head upon the floor of the chamber, whereupon the Defendant took his wife and did throw her upon the bed."[19] Even in an age that took corporal punishment for granted, Jevon was clearly regarded by his neighbors as excessively and indiscriminately brutal.

Sometimes master and apprentice are quite unrecognizable in the stories each told the Court about the other. In 1661 the guardian of William West,

[18] CLRO, MC Interrogatories, 6/3.
[19] CLRO, MC Interrogatories, 6/49A.

apprentice and son of Robert West of Luton, Nottinghamshire, gentleman, deceased, sued Robert Restrick, Citizen and Cutler of London alleging that Restrick had failed to train young West in the art of engraving, chasing, and embossing metal, but instead had employed him "principally in carrying abroad medicines to those who complained of sore eyes." Moreover, it was further alleged that "about Shrovetide last" Master Restrick beat West "in an unreasonable manner . . . and did turn the Complainant out of his service."[20]

Ample witnesses were produced to corroborate West's version of the facts. John Brown, Citizen and Cutler, and a former apprentice of Restrick's, who had served him for a nine-year apprenticeship, testified that Restrick "did never (during the whole time aforesaid) teach or instruct him . . . in the said art nor give him any manner of directions first or last in the least, but contrariwise did as much as in him lay [to] prevent the Deponent . . . from all manner of knowledge and insight herein, and to that end, whenever he . . . had any work of his art to be done, did constantly do it all himself in a private shop which he always kept locked unto him, while he was at work." Not to be deterred by such attempts at concealment, Brown testified that "being desirous to learn the art and to live in the world did as oft as he could have opportunity . . . softly get to see and peep in a crevice and see the Defendant's manner of working and by that and other helps he acquired of some of others of the art did in the night time by himself privately practice and attain some skill."[21]

Samuel Cole, a Goldsmith, testified that he also had served as Restrick's apprentice, his apprenticeship overlapping that of young West for about a year, during which Restrick "almost altogether employed him in going of errands to and fro to persons troubled with sore eyes (the Defendant driving a great trade that way)." And to top it off, Ellen Dowse, Restrick's own servant, testifed that "about Shrovetide last past" Restrick had beaten West "upon some offense and West "came into the Kitchen (where this Deponent was) with his arm all bloody, and immediately thereupon this Deponent did hear the Defendant speak to his wife (who went into the shop to pacify the matter) that she should go and turn the said William out of doors, calling him sundry very ill names, and did swear that he . . . should never come within his doors any more."[22]

The case against Restrick certainly seemed sufficiently circumstantial, but Restrick countered with testimony equally circumstantial that told a very different story. According to Restrick, young West had "attained a very great skill in the said art of engraving . . . and might have been a great advantage to the Defendant and gained a good livelihood thereby," but for certain defects of character that became obvious in time. As one Ellen Brown, wife of Anthony Brown, Cutler, testifed, West "would frequent alehouses and such like places

[20] CLRO, MC Interrogatories, 6/111A.
[21] Ibid.
[22] Ibid.

where he met with persons of idle and vain conversation and had fiddlers and dancing night after night until many times it was very late . . . to the disturbance of the neighborhood thereabouts." William Parker, one of Restrick's apprentices, claimed that when West returned from these bouts of revelry, he "did stink of drink and would swear and curse "and throw his tools away and set himself to sleep and would declare that he should never make a workman, and that it were better for him to be a shopkeeper."[23]

Needless to say, neighbors "wondered" that the Defendant did not attempt to discipline young West for his debauched behavior, and under other circumstances Restrick undoubtedly would have, but in 1659, when West was in his first year of apprenticeship, Restrick "did then and several times since lodge and entertain divers of the king's friends and servants, as namely Major General Mason and Captain Titus and others," and as a consequence, Restrick "durst not cross the Complainant but was enforced to bear with him in sundry things for fear of being betrayed." Finally, according to his fellow apprentice, West's departure came under rather different circumstances than those previously described. In his master's absence West had taken the pattern of a seal sent by a town corporation to be engraved from his master's desk and had burnt it. When Restrick discovered this, "being somewhat moved," he told West "that he did well deserve to be beated." An altercation followed, in the course of which West seized Restrick in such a tight embrace that he injured his master's arm and would then have thrown a stool at his master, if his fellow apprentice had not prevented it. West then left the shop, only to return later in the day with his brother. When Restrick ordered him to return to work, West "would not stir, whereupon the Defendant, taking up a stick and giving the Complainant a blow or two, he the said Complainant immediately departed his service and came no more."[24]

The significant point about these cases is not that in them plaintiffs complain about brutal masters and masters counter with charges concerning the wicked behavior of their apprentices. Such charges were the staple of apprenticeship litigation before the equity side of the Mayor's Court. Differences in detail were infinite. For example, in a case brought in 1663 testimony was given that not only had the apprentice been brutally beaten, as his bruises bore witness, but the apprentice had complained in the presence of his master, which the latter did not deny, that on one occasion his master had "tied him up by his thumbs and pulled down his breeches and beaten him with a piece of whalebone," surely one of the more novel forms of punishment visited on an errant apprentice in the period.[25] Nevertheless, what is important to note is that, however various the detail, the apprentices' social status is never at issue

---

[23] CLRO, MC Interrogatories, 6/111B.
[24] *Ibid.*
[25] CLRO, MC Interrogatories, 6/171A.

in these cases, indeed is not even mentioned, and that the types of charges and countercharges noted in these cases occur just as frequently in litigation involving the apprenticed sons of rural yeomen or urban tradesmen.

Rank and status are always noted, as they are in apprentice bindings, but it appears normally as a means of identifying the father of the apprenticed son, not as an issue in the litigation itself. Hence, it is noted in the case of Paul v. Goldstone in 1669 that Rachel Paul, who sued on behalf of her apprentice son, James Paul, is widow and executrix of William Paul, late bishop of Oxford. The case, however, had nothing to do with the fact that James Paul was a bishop's son, but turned rather on whether James Paul was justified in suing out his indentures two months after William Goldstone, Citizen and Fishmonger, and James's master, had left his partnership with the older and more experienced Richard Thoroughgood. "Goldstone" and "Thoroughgood" have names that suggest the moral characteristics of characters in a Jacobean or Restoration play. Complainant Rachel Paul alleged that Goldstone relegated her son to the lowly position of junior apprentice, even after taking on a younger man, and gambled and neglected his trade as a linen draper, thus leading Thoroughgood to dissolve the partnership a year early. The real issue of the case, however, was whether James Paul the apprentice was justifed in suing out his indentures as a consequence, taking advantage of the technicality that Goldstone had omitted to enroll him before the Chamberlain at the proper time. Young James had since become Thoroughgood's apprentice, and the question before the court was whether under the circumstances the Pauls were justified in asking for the return of the bulk of the £150 given as a premium to Goldstone.[26]

Only in four of the twenty-three cases involving the sons of gentlemen, esquires, and a knight does the issue of the apprentice's gentility arise in any form, and in one of the cases it does so only inferentially. In the first case Thomas Monins of Westminster, Esquire, sued Anthony Gibbons, Citizen and Haberdasher, in 1662, on behalf of his stepson, Robert Bringfield, who had been Gibbons' apprentice. Since young Bringfield had served four years and his mother had paid a premium of £100 for the apprenticeship, much was at stake. On behalf of the apprentice it was alleged that he "was of a mild and good nature and virtuously brought up by his mother and guardian and not addicted to any ill courses when he was first bound;" in fact, it was alleged that his master had written in a letter of commendation that he found young Robert both "orderly and sensible." Further, it was alleged that the "light and wanton"

---

[26] CLRO, MC Interrogatories, 6/234 A–B. The Complainants also claimed that Goldstone was a young man, who would not have commanded a premium above £100 had he not been partner of Thoroughgood, and the Defendant suggested that Thoroughgood was simply bent on stealing his apprentice with the connivance of the Complainants, but these allegations seem to have been thrown in for good measure, since even if they were true, they would have made little difference in the determination of the case.

Mistress Ashburnham, who figures repeatedly in the ensuing testimony, was a regular customer of Gibbons' shop, a person unknown to young Bringfield until he was sent to her lodgings about his master's business. As to the note, signed by the young apprentice a year and a half after he entered service, in which he confessed to purloining £30, the suit made three countercharges: first, that "Robert, being but very young, could not spend so much as thirty pounds, or not above twenty shillings or some such small sum, which the said Robert employed in buying fruit or some such childish toys"; second, that "Robert was so watched by reason of a continual presence of the Defendant and other partners and servants that he could not (had he a will) have much opportunity of defrauding the Defendant"; and finally, that young Robert had only signed the note confessing the purloining of goods as a result of "beating or threatening that the said Robert should be carried before the Chamberlain and punished."[27]

In support of these allegations Bringfield's supporters supplied corroborative testimony. William Philips, Citizen and Clothworker, testified on behalf of the plaintiff that "about the 12th of August 1659" Bringfield had been charged by Gibbons and his partners with purloining goods to the value of £30,

> the said persons coming into the warehouse bid this Deponent write a note (as from the said Complainant's confession) of goods by him purloined to the value aforesaid. And this Deponent did thereupon write such a note, and the said Complainant set his name thereunto. And . . . Robert so soon as he had subscribed the same came to this Deponent crying, being as appeared to him very much grieved and troubled at what he had done and told him that true it was, he had set his hand to the said note, but yet that he never wronged the Defendant, his master of more than 9s. in all his time that he had been with him. And this Deponent saith that the said Complainant was then but young and as he believed could not have wronged the said Defendant of so much.[28]

In his testimony Master Gibbons countered that young Bringfield, because of his youth and small size, was virtually useless in his business, that he "was very idle, false and negligent, . . . much addicted to lying and frequenting the tavern and alehouse," and that he had embezzled money and goods from his master's shop. Robert Rocke, Mercer, testified on behalf of Gibbons that shop business was only an excuse young Robert used to explain his frequent visits to the light and wanton Mistress Faith Ashburnham, the weak and immature apprentice being transformed in this testimony into a youth of apparently insatiable sexual appetite. Mary Greatricks, Gibbons' servant, produced

27 CLRO, MC Interrogatories, 6/144A.
28 *Ibid.*

damaging testimony that young Robert "was very much addicted to lying and used to haunt taverns and alehouses and neglect the Defendant's business, and [she said that she] hath seen him return home much disguised with drink and had in his hand a woman's lock of hair, a fan and a ring and used some uncivil words to the other maid servant that attended the Defendant's children, and thereupon threw himself on the bed and slept about two hour" in what was evidently a drunken stupor.[29]

Debauched as he may have been none of this testimony specifically alleges that Bringfield's gentle birth had any bearing on the case. At most there are two pieces of testimony that may hint as much. Edward Trussell of London, Esquire, an old friend of Master Gibbons, deposed that when Robert first entered service, he "was appareled with very gaudy clothes unnecessarily trimmed with ribbons and other needless toys," which Trussell supposed may have heightened his inordinate pride. And Mary Greatricks, Gibbons' servant, remarked that once when she and Robert were alone in the kitchen, she asked Robert how it was that Gibbons would put up with his "pride, looseness of life, and the ill company that he kept," to which she alleged he replied that "he had no mind or intention ever to follow or make use of his trade, and why then should he trouble himself about it."[30]

A second case contains a similar hint. In 1654 John Browning sued the executors of his former master, Jonathan Peters, Linen Draper, apparently on the grounds that Peters' death brought an end to the apprenticeship and that under the circumstances the estate ought to repay the premium. Peters' executors countered that they had sold Peters' shop to one Master William Clift, a competent draper, who was willing to take on John Browning as apprentice for the remainder of his term. Thomas Harris, Citizen and Grocer, who testified on behalf of the executors, deposed that young Browning had no intention of completing his apprenticeship, although Harris admitted that the evidence was hearsay. Nevertheless, Harris insisted that "he hath heard from divers persons and verily believeth that the said Complainant intendeth not to follow or continue any longer at the trade of a linen draper but to go and live in the country and dispose of himself to the life of a gentleman . . . because of an estate that . . . he hath there."[31]

In a third case social status clearly played at least a contributory role, although perhaps no more than that. The suit in 1667 on behalf of Charles Bathurst was brought by a formidable group of Complainants, headed by Sir Orlando Bridgeman, baronet and Lord Keeper of the Great Seal, and including one of the barons of the Exchequer, a knight and two esquires, all trustees of the last will and testament of Dr John Bathurst, physician. Charles Bathurst,

---

[29] CLRO, MC Interrogatories, 6/144B
[30] *Ibid.*
[31] CLRO, MC Interrogatories, 6/77.

apparently with his own full consent, had been apprenticed to William Blake, Citizen and Draper, an arrangement that had soured quickly. Within a matter of months young Bathurst had run away, not merely to friends within the city but on one occasion to Oxford, and twice to Bedford, from which Master Blake had had to have the young scapegrace fetched by horse and escort at considerable expense. Contributing to Bathurst's difficulties was his father's executor, Colonel William Rosewell, Esq., who, Bathurst claimed, kept him on short commons, despite the fact that Bathurst's father had stipulated in his will that his son should have £30 in pocket money per annum during his apprenticeship. Further, it was deposed that despite Master Blake's request that they not entertain young Bathurst, Col. Rosewell had promised to pay Charles' bills at the Burning Hart in Long Acre, "near to several houses which have for many years past been reputed bawdy houses." Finally, Rosewell capped his "unhandsome dealings" by encouraging Bathurst to leave the apprenticeship, promising to save him from the penalty of breaking his indentures, and offering to arrange for him to go overseas with a merchant.[32]

Certainly if Rosewell's actions hopelessly compromised the chances of success of young Bathurst's apprenticeship, there was ample testimony that Bathurst's inflated sense of his own worth was at least a contributing factor. One of Blake's servants testified, and others corroborated, that "Charles behaved himself very proud and lofty . . . and was uncivil in his carriage and behavior to the Defendant, his wife and his fellow servants, and thought himself too good to be spoken to by them, and would constantly refuse to do anything that the Defendant bid him do in the shop that belonged to his trade." Further, when his mistress "once reproved him . . . for his ill behavior, he spoke very peremptorily to her and called her impudent whore and jade and used very many other expressions unfit for any person, much less . . . an apprentice." On another occasion when Blake had stopped his apprentice from riding off, Charles had turned on his master and called him "a jackanapes and a fool for doing so," and swore that "he would pistol any man who should serve him so." Nevertheless, Bathurst confessed on other occasions that had Col. Rosewell not deprived him of his pocket money and thus made his service "to be very irksome and as a slavery to him," he would have liked his apprenticeship with Master Blake "as well as any in England."[33] Pride of birth clearly made adjustment to servitude difficult but did not itself destroy the apprenticeship, for Blake was willing to overlook and forgive much for the love he bore Bathurst, to whom he confessed he was related.

One case alone is unambiguous, and here the issue of the apprentice's social status is central, although the Mayor's Court studiously ignored it as not germane to the issue before it. In 1661 Robert Rawlins, gentleman, guardian to

32 CLRO, MC Interrogatories, 6/217B.
33 Ibid.

Thomas Wilson, sued Wilson's master, Edward Harris, Citizen and Cloth-worker, to recover the premium of £130 paid for the apprenticeship and the indentures then sealed, so terminating the apprenticeship and freeing young Wilson. The central allegations in the case, and the only charges that the Mayor's Court took into consideration, were two. First, it was alleged that Harris, a woolen draper by trade, "did altogether neglect his said trade and betook himself for the most part to the country, little regarding the said Complainant, and left his said trade only to the management of his . . . two sons." Hence, young Wilson's training was neglected, he "having little or no instruction in the same trade." Secondly, it was charged that Wilson was unlikely to receive such instruction in the future, for Harris had "purposely omitted to enroll the said Complainant" before the Chamberlain, in consequence of which young Wilson had been forced to sue for his discharge, which the Chamberlain had granted. Although Harris admitted the facts of the case, including his frequent absences in the country, he attempted to deny their force on the grounds that his two young sons were perfectly capable of providing Wilson with the requisite training. The Court found this defense singularly unimpressive and ruled for the apprentice, requiring Harris to return £100 of the original £130, given as a premium, as well as the indentures.[34]

Quite apart from the charges of which the Court took cognizance, there was another story contained in the case that casts its meaning in an entirely different light. As John Harris, Edward Harris's twenty-four-year-old son, testified, "not long after the Complainant's coming to be the Defendant's apprentice, the said Defendant understanding that . . . [the] Complainant's older brother was dead and that he was heir to a good estate, gave him liberty to wear his hat before him." The privilege of remaining with his hat on in the presence of his master was not the only unusual feature of his new relationship, for a former servant testified that several times Harris sent for and directed Wilson to "conduct home his daughter when he hath been abroad, and to go to church with her and the like."[35] Quite evidently Master Harris saw the inevitable loss of an apprentice as more than compensated by the possible gain of a landed gentleman for a son-in-law.

However, not all young Wilsons subsequent behavior was to Harris's liking. As his son testified, on one occasion in the evening Wilson "came home so distempered with drink that, the Defendant being at prayer with his family, the said Complainant knocked with his foot, as conceiving himself to be in a tavern, calling for wine," and on another occasion took cloth from the shop without permission worth "about 25s. a yard to make him a suit and coat withall about the time of the king's coming through the city for his coronation, which suit was worth above £20." This piece of extravagance was confirmed by

34 CLRO, MC Decrees, Box 255E, Wilson v. Harris, 22 Oct. 1661.
35 CLRO, MC Interrogatories, 6/120A.

John Simpson, Citizen and Merchant Tailor, who deposed that he had indeed made the suit and coat, which involved not only the cloth "usually called superfine, but also thirty-six yards of taffeta ribbon and eight yards of expensive lining. Simpson also deposed that he had at Wilson's request made up a pair of pantaloons, which suit and pantaloons, John Harris testified, "were very unsuitable for an apprentice," so that "the neighbors living near the Defendant took very much notice of the Complainant's rudeness and extravagancies and did often say . . . that the Complainant was master." However, it is clear that what really galled the Harrises was the fact that immediately after Wilson had left his apprenticeship, he married not his master's daughter with whom he had been urged to walk abroad, but the daughter of Sir John Broughton.[36]

Thomas Wilson's behavior during his apprenticeship was clearly influenced by his status, but he was no Quicksilver, determined to live idly like a gentleman despite his apprenticeship. Soon after he was apprenticed he became a gentleman in actuality, heir to the estate of his dead father and elder brother. Further, it was his master who encouraged his presumption, obviously in the hope that he would marry his master's daughter. Finally, Wilson left his master's service, vindicated by the Mayors Court, to marry the daughter of a knight. Quite evidently no one really expected the heir to a considerable fortune to remain a servant, bettering himself "by little and little," and Master Harris himself acknowledged Wilson's change in status by permitting him to wear his hat in his master's presence.

But Wilson v. Harris is the exception that proves the rule. The apprenticed sons of the gentry were neither rakehell Quicksilvers, nor to all appearances virtuous Goldings. Like the sons of yeomen and tradesmen, apprentices of gentle birth were young men subject to a sometimes galling discipline and forced to live for years in anticipation of a far-off freedom. Like other apprentices, they were sometimes rude and disobedient; on occasion they gambled, drank too much, frequented bawds, theaters, dancing schools, and fencing masters. Like other apprentices, they liked to dress above their station, wear their hair long like a gentleman, and play the gallant. Like other apprentices, the vast bulk of them disappear in after years into the anonymous life of urban respectability. No great gulf of accent or education seems to have separated the gentle apprentice from his fellows recruited from subordinate clases.[37] Down-

---

36 CLRO, MC Interrogatories, 6/120B.

37 On the other hand, D. R. Woolf has recently argued that "the England of the later seventeenth century had become much more radically stratified, economically, socially and culturally, than that of two centires earlier," and points to evidence that "elite forms of entertainment, literature and art had grown increasingly remote from popular forms throughout the seventeenth century." "The 'Common Voice': History, Folklore and Oral Tradition in Early Modern England," *Past and Present* 120 (1988): 47. However, the Mayor's Court evidence suggests that at least some apprentices of all kinds drank to excess, gambled when they could afford to, smoked tobacco, went to the

ward mobility was and seems to have been accepted as an irreducible fact of life. Once the city apprentice entered upon his new life, social origins seem to have made very little difference.[38]

We are left with the question of why it seemed plausible to suppose that gentle birth posed a problem, if not an inevitable source of tension and trouble, for the urban apprentice. The answer may lie in the intellectual assumptions and habits of thought observers brought to the urban scene. Given the assumption, scarcely questioned until mid-century, that society was composed of discrete orders and degrees arranged hierarchically, and given the fact that the great divide was between the gentlemanly elite and everyone else, it was certainly reasonable to suppose that downward mobility was a recipe for disappointment and resentment. Given habits of thought that delighted in finding and classifying typical attributes of social types, of analyzing their humours and constructing Theophrastian "characters," a gentle apprentice must have seemed anomalous, if not exactly a freak of nature. Yet the very anomalies of his nature were perhaps typical, not of the gently born apprentice, but of the "character" of the citizen as such, for at least so he appears in the view of the future bishop John Earle, who, in "A Mere Gull Citizen," conceded that "the quality of the city hath afforded him some better dress of clothes and language, which he uses to the best advantage, and is so much the more ridiculous." Earle notes that he is "suited rather fine than in the fashion, and has still something to distinguish him from a gentleman, though his doublet cost more." However, although he does his best to undercut whatever quality he discerns in the citizen, Earle does catch the aspiring quality that London citizenship engendered: "He is one loves to hear the famous acts of citizens . . .; and the *Four Prentices of London* above all the Nine Worthies. He entitles himself to all the merits of his Company, whether schools, hospitals, or exhibitions, in which he is joint benefactor, although four hundred years ago." Yet for all his evident contempt, Earle concludes ruefully that the citizen "with all this folly . . . has wit enough to get wealth, and in that is a sufficienter man than he that is wiser."[38] To be a "sufficienter man" was perhaps what ultimately reconciled the Quicksilvers to their fate.

theater, took dancing and fencing lessons, and, if given the opportunity, wore their hair long and tried to dress in the current fashion, at least when at their leisure outside the confines and discipline of their master's shop. It may well be that the culture of the City was more powerful and seductive than the culture of origin.

[38] John Earle, *Microcosmographie, or a Peece of the World Discovered; in Essayes and Characters* (London, 1628), ed. Harold Osborne (London, n.d.), 54–55.

The Laudians and the Argument from Authority

PETER LAKE

In recent years the nexus of policies and concerns which often goes under the name of Laudianism has been much discussed. Much of the debate has centered on the subject of the alleged Arminianism of the Laudians; whether they were in fact Arminians at all, and if they were, what that meant. Was their Arminianism a new development in the church or merely a restatement of an existing tradition of thought, a necessary corrective to the growth of an aggressive and intolerant puritan Calvinism? In the course of the exchanges on this subject, Laudianism has been variously characterized. For Dr Sharpe and Dr Bernard it was just a restatement of the traditional conformist case for order and uniformity in the church, couched in an entirely traditional rhetoric of things indifferent and the authority of the church and Christian prince over things indifferent.

Other scholars have developed this position casting Laudianism as the culmination of a long maturing 'anglican' synthesis. The Laudians were the calm proponents of the tried and tested Anglican triad of reason, scripture, and tradition, guardians of that sweetly reasonable mean between Rome and Geneva, to which Hooker had pointed the way back in the 1590s. For Professor Trevor-Roper, there was rather more to it than that: Laudianism was a modernizing, liberal, rational force applying the solvent of sceptical reason and moderate reasonableness to the certainties and fanaticisms attendant upon puritan scripturalism. On this view Laudianism inhabited the anteroom to the Enlightenment; to mix the metaphor, it provided a crucial missing link in the chain of humanist scepticism linking the age of Erasmus to that of Hume or Voltaire.[1]

In this paper I want to test these interpretations not against what the Laudians did or did not say about predestination. Whether they were Arminians or not, it is difficult to argue that any scholastic development of the

---

[1] K. Sharpe, "Archbishop Laud" in *History To-day*, vol. 33, August 1983; G. Bernard, "The church of England, c. 1529–c. 1542", *History*, vol. 75, June 1990; P. White, "The rise of Arminianism reconsidered", *Past and Present*, vol. 101, 1983; H.R. Trevor-Roper, *Catholics, Anglicans and Puritans* (London, 1987).

doctrine of predestination lay at the center of the Laudians' concerns. Accordingly, I want to concentrate here on their attitude to things that they did care and care passionately about — the rites and ceremonies of the English church as they construed them and the ideal of the beauty of holiness, which for them provided those ceremonies with their *raison d'etre*. I shall not be concerned here so much with the positive content of their views on those subjects — I have dealt with them elsewhere[2] — but rather with the ways in which the Laudians' view of religion was legitimated, with the types of authority that Laudian divines mobilized to do that, and with the relative weight given to those authorities at different points in the Laudian argument.

I

Traditional conformist arguments on the rites and ceremonies of the English church were centered on the notion of things indifferent and on the assertion and defense of the power of the church and Christian magistrate to order those things guided only by general scriptural rules and prescriptions concerning order, decency, uniformity, and obedience. Once those general rules had been observed, the church's governors were free to act as they saw fit for the common good. The role of the ordinary church member was simply to do as his or her superiors ordered, safe in the knowledge that if the rites and ceremonies in question were literally matters of indifference in the eyes of God, their duty to obey the magistrate was not. The resulting ceremonies and forms were not then enforced as parts of God's worship or as having any intrinsic religious value in themselves but only for the sake of order, decency, unity, and obedience. It was only the strict observance of this limitation that protected the conformists from puritan allegations of will worship and popish superstition and that allowed even moderate puritans, in extremity, to produce elaborate justifications for conformity.[3]

The Laudians did not simply turn their backs on these traditional conformist justifications for the status quo. On the contrary, traditional conformist rhetoric echoed through a series of visitation sermons preached during the 1630s.[4]

---

2 P. Lake, "Order, uniformity and the pursuit of the beauty of holiness in the 1630s" in K. Fincham, ed., *The early Stuart church*, forthcoming.

3 P. Lake, *Anglicans and puritans? Presbyterianism and English conformist thought from Whitgift to Hooker* (London, 1988).

4 S. Hoard, *The church's authority asserted in a sermon preached at Chelmsford at the metropolitical visitation of the most reverend father in God William Laud* (London, 1636), pp. 3–9, 17, 24–5, 35–9; W. Quelch, *Church customs vindicated in two sermons preached at Kingston upon Thames, the one at the visitation of . . . Richard . . . late bishop of Winton, anno 1628, the other at the first metropolitical visitation of . . . William . . . Lord Archbishop*

II

However, the Laudian attitude concerning the beauty of holiness, defined both in terms of the beautification and refurbishment of the church fabric itself and of the ritual practice and liturgical exactitude of the church's members, went a good deal further than this. The beauty of holiness and the architectural and liturgical forms that produced it became for the Laudians essential requirements for any church, and ceremonial conformity a crucial characteristic of the true Christian. As the Laudians pressed against the confines of the traditional conformist case, seeking to emphasize the separateness of the church as a holy object from the profane world, and the necessity of ceremony and physical and ritual decorum in the service of God, they had frequent recourse to authorities other than that provided by the power of the church and the prince over things indifferent. They had recourse, in short, to divine authority in scripture and in versions of immemorial, allegedly apostolic, ecclesiastical tradition.

Thus in arguing that the church building was itself a holy place, hedged around with an aura of the sacred derived from the divine presence within it, many Laudians had recourse to texts culled from the Old Testament and to parallels with the altars and sacrifices of the patriarchs and with the tabernacle and temple of the Jews under the law. As Thomas Laurence put it in an Act sermon preached at Oxford, in 1634

> his [God's] presence is indeed everywhere but his residence especially there and though his essence be diffused through heaven and earth, in Jeremy, his glory, in Exodus, is peculiar to the tabernacle; the ladder which Jacob saw, that ascent and descent of angels, that thoroughfare betwixt earth and heaven, was at Bethel, the house of God and in Jewry the propitiatory or mercy seat was only in the temple.[5]

For Foulke Roberts the parallel between the church and temple implied not only the holiness and apartness of the building but also that a similar sanctity was attached to all the objects employed in and consecrated to God's worship. Thus, in a visitation sermon of 1631, Alexander Read cited the example of the temple as part of his critique of the disgusting state of many English churches,

of Canterbury, July 9, 1635 (London, 1636), pp. 11–12, 34; J. Featley, Obedience and submission (London, 1636), p. 25; Gilbert Ironside, Seven questions of the sabbath briefly disputed (Oxford, 1638), pp. 165–6, 188–9.

5   Thomas Laurence, Two sermons, the first preached at St Mary's Oxford, July 13, 1634, being act Sunday, the second in the cathedral church of sarum at the visitation of . . . William Archbishop of Canterbury . . . May 23 1634 (Oxford, 1635), p. 20–1; also see Thomas Laurence A sermon preached before the King's majesty at Whitehall, 7 February 1636 (London, 1637) pp. 1–4.

down to and including the filthy buckets used to fill the font and the mouldy cloth bags used to transport the communion bread. By contrast, he pointed out "all the instruments of the tabernacle were by God's own appointment so curiously covered, even the candlesticks, snuffers and snuff dishes, from the eyes of the sons of Kohath with a cloth of blue silk when they were to remove the tabernacle."[6]

The Laudians not only cited Old Testament texts to justify their vision of the church as a holy place or object, they also cited the precedent of the tabernacle and particularly the temple to prove their contention that the church's status as the house of God, a peculiarly holy and sacred space, should be reflected in the magnificence of its construction and decoration. When Robert Shelford was discoursing on the constituent parts of the holiness of God's house he chose as his first characteristic the duty to

> adorn and beautify it fit for his greatness as himself gave pattern in beautifying his tabernacle; there was gold and silver, precious stones, silks with all precious colours, the most choice woods, and all other things framed with the best cunning that God inspired Bezaleel and Aholiah and all the wise hearted of that time . . . Comeliness and holiness join hand with each other. Thus saith my text, holiness becometh thy house, O Lord.[7]

Other writers took the same tack. According to the author of *De templis* "God himself dictated to Moses the ornaments of the tabernacle." Alexander Read cited the temple at Jerusalem as a model. Walter Balcanquall, preaching at court in 1632, cited Moses "the ancientest writer we have extant" as making "the first mention of a temple, [in scripture], for God delivered unto him the pattern of the tabernacle," which in turn was "the model of the temple."[8] John Swan observed that the primitive Christians had modeled their churches on Solomon's temple "And well might they imitate such a platform . . . Their tabernacle was a pattern of their temple and their temple a type of our churches, even as all their service was a type of our Christ." Foulke Roberts repeatedly cited the ornaments and images decorating the tabernacle, the temple, and the ancient Christian churches to justify the presence in the church of stained glass windows — set not "for any matter of worship . . . but

---

[6] Foulke Robarts, *God's holy house and service* (London, 1639), p. 3–4; Alexander Read, *A sermon preached April 8 1636, at a visitation at Brentwood in Essex* (London, 1636) p. 7.

[7] R. Shelford, *Five pious and learned discourses* (Cambridge, 1635), p. 11.

[8] R. T., *De templis* (London, 1638), p. 178; Read, *A sermon preached at Brentwood*, p. 22; W. Balcanqual, *The honour of Christian churches and the necessity of frequenting of divine service* (London, 1633), p. 6.

for history and ornament" — as well as other forms of the "beauty of holiness" including church plate and music.[9]

III

If the status of the church as the house of God involved for Laudians an intense concern with the material fabric of the church defined simply as a physical structure and a heightened sense of the value of ecclesiastical ornament and decoration, it prompted an even greater stress on the ceremonial and liturgical aspects of the beauty of holiness. On this subject too the Laudians had constant recourse to patterns and principles contained in the Old Testament. Thomas Laurence told the king in 1636 that "we seldom find adoration under the law (the strictest time against superstition of any) without prostration of the body and inclination too." Indeed, Laurence went on, throughout

those sacred volumes [of the law] by a metonymia signi and a senecdoche partis . . . this [term] is frequently used alone to design the whole service of God as if all were out if this were not in, which was done with their faces towards the mercy seat, at the gate they shall worship God, saith Ezekiel . . . Nor was this guise of their devotion recorded only as a practise under the law but as a prediction concerning the gospel . . . The converted gentile falling down in the church will worship, saith St Paul, and the converted Jews falling down did worship, say the evangelists and the departed souls falling down shall worship, saith the Apocalypse. The first before an invisible the rest before a visible presence of God . . . the primitive Christians used prostration to God at their eucharistical devotions, so did they at their ordinary too.[10]

As these passages show, Laudian divines placed ceremony, and in particular bodily expressions of reverence and worship, at the very center of their vision of what a church should be like and what the outward profession of Christianity was. They did so, moreover, by deploying texts and practices culled from the Old Testament as a basis for the practices of the Christian church. In many instances their applications of these texts were general rather than particular, designed to buttress general principles about the holiness of the physical shell of the church and the objects used in and consecrated to divine worship, and the essential role in divine worship of ceremony and ritual decorum. However, not all Laudians were so cautious. Other authors used scriptural precedents to

---

[9] J. Swan *Profanomastix* (London, 1639), pp. 5, 26; Foulke Robarts, *God's holy house and service* (London, 1639), pp. 46–7.

[10] T. Laurence, *A sermon preached before the king's majesty* (London, 1637), pp. 25–8.

underwrite not merely the role of ceremony and outward reverence in the life of the church but also the specific ritual practices of the English church.

Thus Foulke Roberts, like Laurence, used prostration as a precedent for kneeling and went on to cite both "the words of the psalmist 'O come let us worship and fall down and kneel before the lord our maker'" and the "fairest precedent" of Christ himself who "kneeled down and prayed" in order to "free the gesture of kneeling in God's worship from suspicion of superstition." He also assembled a number of texts to justify the practice of standing at various points of the service.[11]

Giles Widdowes was if anything even more aggressively confident. In his 1631 tract on bowing at the name of Jesus, Widdowes expanded that claim and went into considerable detail on the relationship of church ceremony to scripture. First he described those "decent orderly signs" that were

> universal, ordained for the whole church. These are either express scripture as "imposition of hands", Heb. 6: 2. Acts 8: 17. The second is a man uncovered in the church at prayer and sermon, I Cor. 11: 4, 7. The third is loud musical instruments, Psal., hence organs and bells are used in the church. Four, bowing at the name of Jesus, Phil. 2: 10 and many such like. These are necessary ceremonies because they signify the substantial, internal duty of the catholic church.

Next came "other ceremonies . . . necessarily deducted from scripture." There followed a long list that included the ring in marriage, the surplice, the sign of the cross, kneeling to receive the communion, beating the bounds of the parish (deduced remarkably from Matt. 28: 19, "Go therefore and make disciples of all nations") standing at the reading of the creed, the four-cornered cap (deduced from the immovableness of faith in Eph. 4: 11–14 because "a four cornered body is hard to be moved") and the white penitential sheet. It was, concluded Widdowes, "more than probable that the church being rational" and "able to give a reason of her moral significant ceremonies took these scriptures etc. to be the rule and ground of her ceremonies." After these ceremonies grounded directly on scripture came a third category of "particular decent ordinary ceremonies which are not one and the same in all countries." These for Widdowes were the only genuinely indifferent ceremonies.[12]

Widdowes may have been something of an extremist, but many other Laudians used texts culled from the Old Testament to justify both the Laudian altar policy and bowing towards the altar. As Thomas Laurence explained to the court in 1637,

---

[11] F. Robarts, *God's holy house and service* (London, 1639), pp. 77–9.

[12] Giles Widdowes, *The lawless, kneeless, schismatical puritan* (Oxford, 1631), pp. 71–2; also see G. Widdowes, *The schismatical puritan* (Oxford, 1630) sig. A3v–A4r, E2v–E3r.

though the glory of the Lord filled both the tabernacle and the temple yet it filled not all alike . . . and as that distinction in holy places continued after Christ, so did the reason of that distinction too; the whole indeed is the house of God, so the apostle calls it . . . yet, though the church conceived him to be present in all parts of this house, it conceived him to be more present in one part of this house than in another.

Laurence then compared the difference between the area around the altar and the body of the church to that between the part of the temple "within the veil" and the rest of the building.[13]

The equation of God's presence at the altar with his presence in the ark or on the mercy seat in the temple was a very common Laudian conceit. John Yates and Thomas Laurence both drew a direct parallel between "an altar here" and "an oracle or ark or mercy seat there."[14] Robert Shelford agreed: "so again to this day all our churches are called sanctuaries as in many other regards so especially in regard of the Lord's table or high altar at the upper end of them which is Jesus Christ's mercy seat because there the memory of the everlasting sacrifice is made and presented to the Holy Trinity." According to Joseph Mede, "Christ is as much present here [at the altar] as the lord was upon the mercy seat between the cherubims."[15]

Just as they used the example of the temple and the tabernacle to assert the holiness and apartness of the altar, so the Laudians cited the worship of the jews toward the temple and the holy of holies within the temple to justify the practice of bowing toward the altar. Against the argument that making physical obeisance to the altar was idolatrous, the Laudians cited the practice of the jews in the Old Testament. No one was being asked, they pointed out "to give divine worship to God's table" but only "to worship God toward it."[16] Certainly to "worship God by an image" was "absolutely forbidden by the law of God." But what was being demanded here was the worship of God "towards some place and monument of his presence." This had been widely practiced by God's people. The Israelites "in the wilderness . . . worshipped God toward the cloud as the monument of his presence going with them."[17] Similarly, at the burning

13 T. Laurence, A sermon preached before the king's majesty (London, 1637), pp. 16–17

14 Ibid., p. 9; J. Yates, A treatise of the honour of God's house (London, 1637), unpaginated opening section on "the danger of an altar in the name and use."

15 R. Shelford, Five treatises (Cambridge, 1635), p. 4; J. Mede The reverence of God's house (London, 1638), p. 10; also J. Swan, Profanomastix (London, 1639), pp. 41–2. Indeed Swan went even further comparing the church triumphant to both the tabernacle and the temple and urging the church militant to confirm her practice to all three models. Ibid. p. 28–9.

16 R. Shelford, Five treatises (Cambridge, 1635), p. 19.

17 J. Swan, Profanomastix (London, 1639), p. 19.

bush Moses was commanded "to put his shoes from his feet" because "God's special presence there, specially manifested in the voice that spake and the fire which burned" had made the place "holy ground."[18] Later the Jews "looked towards the ark of the covenant or mercy seat both in the tabernacle and temple" because of the "promise made to Moses of a presence there which is enough to signify that the lord hath his throne in the places which are set apart and sanctified for his service."[19]

Thus far we have been concerned largely with texts and precedents taken from Old Testament accounts of the temple and the tabernacle, laced with passages from the New Testament to show that such injunctions and examples were still in force and had not been abrogated by the gospel. But on the issue of ceremonies and bodily gestures in divine worship many Laudians had recourse to a second body of texts, dealing not so much with the past practice of the church militant as the present and perpetual practice of the church triumphant. John Swan explained the relation between the two: "God's church is in itself but one, though the parts be two, militant and triumphant." "The church militant is a kind of heaven upon earth and therefore the congregations in it must imitate the assemblies which are triumphant." "For what better harmony can there be than that the church on earth conform herself to the church in heaven."[20] Citing a number of texts taken principally from the Revelation of St John, various authors proceded to explain just how the church on earth could be brought into line with the church in heaven. Citing Revelation 4: 10, John Browning claimed that

> the very saints and angels in heaven . . . fall down and worship and cast their crowns before the throne . . . Can anything by them used be idle or needless or superfluous? Nay rather is it not our prayer and should it not be our desire that we should so serve God as they do? That his will be so done by us as by them it is? The church (beloved) what is it but heaven upon earth? Therefore the rule of her actions can she draw from no place better than from thence.[21]

In an extended passage, Edward Boughen presented the saints in heaven as a prefect model of orderly and decent divine worship for our emulation.

[18] F. Robarts, God's holy house and service (London, 1639), p. 87.
[19] J. Swan, Profanomastix (London, 1639), p. 19; also see ibid. pp. 20–21, where King David's physical reverence and worship towards the sanctum sanctorum was cited as an example and warrant for bowing towards the altar.
[20] Ibid. pp. 27–8, 44.
[21] J. Browning, Concerning public prayer and the fasts of the church, six sermons (London, 1636), p. 26; also see Thomas Laurence, A sermon preached before the king's majesty (London, 1637), p. 27.

That the saints have white robes is decent, but that they are all clothed
with white robes is orderly. That they stand before the throne and fall
down before the throne is decent, but that they all stand together and
all fall down together is orderly. That they cry with a loud voice is
decent, that they all do so together is orderly. That they praise and
glorify God is seemly, but that they all praise God in the self same
words is . . . most agreeable to order.[22]

It is not difficult to discern in that passage the outlines of various practices
enforced in the English church. Other authors drew the parallels more explicitly even than Boughen. For instance, Giles Widdowes defended the surplice by
citing Revelation 19: 8 to the effect that "tis express scripture that tis granted
to the church to wear fine linen, white and clean" and going on to claim that
"there is a similitude between the triumphant and militant church and so an
expression of the ones glory by the others signification and is it then contrary
to decency and order to wear the surplice?"[23]
But perhaps the most obvious example of the use of texts describing the
practice of the church triumphant as a warrant for the rites and ceremonies of
the English church concerned bowing at the name of Jesus. Even William Page,
who in the main chose to defend the practice in terms of the authority of the
church over its own ceremonies, claimed, on the authority of Lancelot
Andrewes, that it may "very probably be defended even out of that text", viz.,
Philippians 2: 10. This was, Page admitted, primarily a prophecy concerned
with the last days, but

from hence, then, the church of Christ thus reasoneth; shall all knees
bow to his name at the last whether they will or no . . . then certainly
we that be Christians and look to be saved by him are bound now by
virtue of this prophesy to do his name that honour . . . so that every
good Christian heart can argue thus from these words: all shall bow,
then, therefore, I must, I ought, to bow now.

Giles Widdowes, in his tract on the subject, was a good deal more confident;
for him bowing at the name of Jesus was "express scripture . . . This bowing is
expressed enough for an obedient capacity, thus then tis a commanded duty."[24]
In a sermon preached at St Margaret's, Canterbury, during Laud's visitation of

---

[22] Edward Boughen, A sermon concerning decency and order in the church (London,
1638), p. 16; also see J. Swan Profanomastix, p. 54 where Swan cited a passage from
Revelation ("I heard a voice from heaven saith St John, as the sound of many waters
and as the sound of a great thunder") in order to justify his insistence that all Christians "use all the answers of the holy liturgy and that cheerfully and aloud, not
whispering or between the teeth nor (as some do) silently and not at all."
[23] Giles Widdowes, The schismatical puritan (Oxford, 1630), sig. E3r
[24] William Page, A treatise or justification of bowing at the name of Jesus (Oxford,

1635, Edward Boughen agreed with Widdowes. He grounded the duty to bow on the obligation of the church militant to "imitate the church triumphant, but in the church triumphant every knee bows at the name of Jesus, for so St Paul says they should do and without all peradventure they do what they should do."[25]

Some of the passages cited above, with their frequent invocation of texts from Revelations might be taken to imply that the Laudians, just like the puritans, entertained visions of a church reformed and refurbished according to an ideal type of holiness and purity based ultimately on scriptural authority and example. Where other English protestants, especially the puritans, saw the militant and triumphant churches being brought together primarily through the purity of profession and conversation achieved by the godly, the Laudians saw that same elision between the two levels of the church's existence being wrought through the ritual performance and liturgical exactitude achieved by the church of England. Accordingly, John Swan cited Bishop Williams's description of "that sacred oratory", the chapel royal, as "the vivest resemblance I know upon the earth of that harmony of the cherubins we look for in the heavens." The royal chapel was, for Laudians an oft invoked symbol of the peaks of reverent holiness of which the English church was capable, a model to which ordinary parish churches should aspire. For some of them, at least, one could go further and say that the pursuit of the beauty of holiness undertaken by Charles and Laud vouchsafed them a glimpse of heaven itself.[26]

Where direct scriptural backing for the church's practices was lacking, Laudian authors often had recourse to the traditions of the church. William Quelch, in a tract of 1636 tellingly entitled *Church customs vindicated*, asserted the right of the church to take up "a custom that tends to the furtherance of God's service" and to "stand upon it and to bind her children to conformity." According to Quelch "the customs of the church that serve for the furtherance of devotion . . . are not only humane but also divine and so may the better be stood upon."[27] John Browning agreed; "divines" he claimed, "are wont to compare obedience to Jacob's ladder: the lower part of obedience to the church stands on earth; but, as Jacob's ladder, it ends in heaven and as there so here,

---

1631), pp. 4–5, 76; G. Widdowes, *The lawless, kneeless, schismatical puritan* (Oxford, 1631), p. 17.

25 Edward Boughen, *Two sermons; the first preached at Canterbury at the visitation of the Lord Archbishop's peculiars in St Margaret's church . . . The second preached at St Paul's Cross* (London, 1635), p. 10; also see J. Swan, *Profanomastix* (London, 1639), p. 52 where he argued that "although it be in itself a duty of the text yet hath the church also interposed her authority for the more strict and decent observation of it. In which neither doth our present canon nor that injunction of Queen Elizabeth cause more to be done than what had formerly been observed in the church of God, in those ancient times which had been before."

26 *Ibid.* p. 28.

27 W. Quelch, *Church customs vindicated* (London, 1636), pp. 44, 45–6.

God stands at the top of it and, as in Jacob's ladder, no ascending to the highest but by the lowest steps. So no obedience to God unless we obey his church."[28]

This tendency to equate the authority of the church with the authority of God reached its logical conclusion in the assimilation of the customs of the church with the unwritten customs and traditions of the apostles. This was achieved through a doctrine of immemorial custom whereby church traditions to which no known historical origins could be assigned were taken to be apostolic. Both Samuel Hoard and Quelch cited in this context the saying of Augustine that "whatsoever hath been generally observed in any age and yet not prescribed in any council may be certainly believed to be apostolical." Samuel Hoard asserted the existence of "apostolic traditions, ritual and dog-matical, which are nowhere mentioned or not enjoined in the scriptures but delivered by word of mouth from the apostles to their followers." He attributed to this source "the number of canonical books, the Apostles creed, the baptism of infants, the fast of Lent, the Lords day and the great festivals of Easter and Whitsuntide". "It were to be wished," concluded Quelch,

> . . . that all the customs of the church were only such and that nothing might be used in any one but what were allowed by all the rest; when antiquity and universality meet both together in the same custom they give such credit and countenance to the practise of the church that no man can refuse to join us without suspicion of distraction.[29]

Here a position on the customs and authority of the church that could be and indeed was used to assert the sovereign authority of the church over her own ceremonies was, in fact, through the assimilation of church custom to the authority of the apostles, being turned into something rather different—so great was the Laudian impulse to lend an aura of scriptural, or, at the very least, apostolic purity and authority to the ritual practices of the church and indeed to their own versions of those practices.

IV

However, all this did not mean that the Laudians simply abandoned the exist-ing rhetoric of conformity and obedience. On the contrary they could, on occa-sion, deploy the traditional rhetoric of adiaphora with enthusiasm. On the face of it there was a clear contradiction between the Laudians' invocation of scrip-ture and of immemorial and apostolic custom, on the one hand, and their espou-sal of conventional conformist arguments, on the other. The former tendency

[28] J. Browning, *Concerning public prayer* (London, 1636), p. 61.
[29] W. Quelch, *Church customs vindicated* (London, 1636), p. 49; S. Hoard, *The church's authority asserted* (London, 1636), p. 13–14.

was clearly designed to lend an aura of religious efficacy, indeed of scriptural and apostolic necessity, to the practices and performances under discussion, practices and performances that elsewhere were described as indifferent, deriving their only necessity from the decision of the Christian magistrate to enforce them.

If we are to understand how the Laudians dealt with these apparent contradictions in their position, we need to turn to their treatment of sabbatarianism. Here was an issue on which the logic of Laudian argument appeared to run in precisely the opposite direction from that of the passages cited above. There the Laudian tendency had been to lend an aura of scriptural authority to priorities and practices, otherwise justified in terms of the power of the church over things indifferent. On the subject of the Sabbath, however, the thrust of Laudian argument was toward peeling back the authority of scripture. Instead of asserting the relevance and authority of Old Testament principles and precedents for the conduct of the Christian church, on the issue of the Sabbath the Laudians cited Christ's abrogation of the Mosaic law, the principles of Christian liberty, and the relative autonomy of the church and the magistrate in ordering things indifferent in order to show that such rules and examples did not apply to the present state of the church.

On the Sabbath the Laudians pictured themselves as locked in a battle against a simpleminded puritan scripturalism. The puritans wanted to base Sunday observance on the jewish Sabbath by construing the whole of the fourth commandment as part of the moral law and arguing that Christians as well as jews were bound to give one day in seven over to the worship of God, to rest for the entire day from all secular business and recreation. On this view, far from abrogating the Sabbath Christ had merely transferred it from Saturday to Sunday. In making such claims, the puritans were seeking to limit, if not deny, the autonomous power of the church to order the details of its own public worship and ordain holy days and festivals as it saw fit. More particularly, by elevating the Lord's day or Sabbath, as they insisted on calling it, to a uniquely scriptural status, they belittled the other holy days observed by the church and in many cases explicitly denounced them as merely human and popish superstitions. In reply to this allegedly puritan position, the Laudians construed the fourth commandment as partly moral and partly ceremonial. The ceremonial part, which had been abrogated by Christ, included the obligation to give a whole day to God's worship, to rest for the whole of that day from all secular business, and to devote the proportion of one day in seven to divine worship. The moral part, which alone was still in force, simply contained the injunction to give due and convenient time to the worship of God. What constituted due and convenient time and the nomination of specific days and times for divine worship was a matter for the relevant human authorites — the church and the Christian magistrate — to decide.[30]

---

[30] On puritan scripturalism see F. White, *An examination and confutation of a lawless*

But as ever with Laudianism, things were not quite as straightforward as all that. At one level, their case operated in terms of a simple binary opposition: the Lord's day was either a divine or an ecclesiastical institution, and since it could be founded neither on the moral law or divine positive law, it must rest solely on the authority of the church. Indeed, several authors went so far as to claim that the church could move the Lords' day to any other day of the week. However, this stark statement of ecclesiastical authority left the Lord's day bereft of any legitimating aura of scriptural or apostolic warrant. Such a position could not satisfy the Laudians for long, and each statement of the church's formal capacity to do away with Sunday worship was followed with a disclaimer, explaining why such an act would be inadvisable in the extreme. Thus according to Peter Heylin, "those powers which raised it up may take it lower if they please, yea take it quite away, as unto the time and settle it on any other day, as to them seems best". But, Heylin observed, if "the church hath still authority to change the day . . . such authority be not fit to be put in practise." Francis White expanded the point:

> the church shall do that which is offensive, if, without just, necessary and urgent cause, it presume to remove the ancient bounds or to alter the ordinance of primitive times, concerning the religious observance of the Lord's day. For the tradition of the holy apostles and of the primitive and apostolical church ought highly to be honoured and respected and (according to St Augustine's rule) it is insolent madness (unless it be done upon necessary reason) to vary from the same.[31]

In those passages, and particularly the last one, we can see the typical Laudian movement away from the unvarnished, purely legal legitimacy con-

---

pamphlet (London, 1637), pp. 33–4 and F. White, A treatise of the sabbath day (London, 1635), dedicatory epistle. For the sabbatarian assault on other holy days see John Pocklington, Sunday no sabbath (London, 1636), p. 7 and P. Heylin, The history of the sabbath (London, 1636), pt 2, pp. 254–5. On the absence of any hint of sabbatarian doctrine in natural law see J. Prideaux, The doctrine of the sabbath (London, 1634), sig.C r–v, from the translators preface by Peter Heylin. On the grounding of the sabbath in divine positive law, viz. the Mosaic law see C. Dow, A discourse of the Lord's day (London, 1636) pp. 21–25; for the abrogation of the ceremonial law of Moses, including the obligation to observe the sabbath, by Christ see F. White, A treatise (London, 1635), pp. 63, 160; for the partly moral and partly ceremonial status of the fourth commandment see P. Heylin, The History of the sabbath (London, 1636), pt 2, pp. 162–3 and G. Ironside, Seven questions of the sabbath (Oxford, 1637), p. 69. For the dependence of Sunday worship on ecclesiastical authority and its inherent mutability see P. Heylin, A history of the sabbath (London, 1636), pt 2, pp. 94–5.

[31] Peter Heylin, The History of the sabbath (London, 1636), pt 2, p. 95; J. Prideaux, The doctrine of the sabbath (London, 1634), sig.C v. from the translator's preface by Peter Heylin; F. White, An examination and confutation of a lawless pamphlet (London, 1637), p. 61.

ferred by ecclesiastical and magisterial power, to the more comforting and religiously exalted legitimacy to be derived from apostolic precedent and ancient tradition. The same move was made by a series of Laudian writers in relation to the authority of scripture itself. Thus, Christopher Dow, argued that while the proportion of one day in seven to be devoted to divine worship "cannot be said to be absolutely of the law of nature, nature being ignorant of this without the instruction of the written law" yet "that proportion of time which God himself made choice of for his own people is the fittest that can be imagined and nature informed by God cannot but acknowledge his wisdom and goodness in this choice." France White agreed: "It is consonant to the equity of the fourth commandment that one day in seven shall be an holy day wherein Christian people ought to rest and give themselves to religious exercises." And this consonance was the basis for the church's choice "both in ancient and modern times" of the Lords' day "to be a weekly day of rest from servile labour and a solemn time for divine worship." It was also the basis for the church's opinion that it was not "reasonable to alter this day".[32]

The same process of creeping scripturalism was applied to the origins of the Lord's day itself. While Christopher Dow allowed that the scriptural and patristic evidence available was not sufficient to gain the Lord's day "the reputation of divine institution," he exhorted his readers "to pitch upon that which is certain, which though it rise not so high as an immediately divine authority yet is sufficient to ground our practise upon and to exact the due observation of the day." First, then, he continued,

> it is most certain that our blessed saviour did honour this day with his most glorious resurrection and, by his often apparitions upon it to his apostles, . . . pointed out this day to his disciples as worthy to be made choice of to be celebrated in honour of him . . . Secondly, it is no less certain that the apostles (upon this ground no doubt) did observe this day and had thereon their holy assemblies . . . Thirdly that the ages of the church immediately after the apostles (whether by constitution or only in imitation of them is not known nor much material) did observe the day as the Christians' festival, styling it the Lord's day and conveyed the same practise by continual succession even to this day.[33]

Heylin took the same tack, arguing that the resurrection was "the chief reason why the Christians of the primitive times did set apart this day to religious uses" and that

---

[32] C. Dow, A discourse of the sabbath (London, 1636), pp. 21, 24–5; F. White, A treatise (London, 1635), pp. 151–2.

[33] C. Dow, A discourse of the sabbath (London, 1636), pp. 40–2.

there was some analogy or proportion which this day seemed to hold with the former sabbath, which might more easily induce them to observe the same. For as God rested on the sabbath from all the works which he had done in the creation so did the son of God also rest on the day of his resurrection from all the works which he had done in our redemption.

It was precisely because of considerations such as these that Francis White felt able to conclude that in choosing Sunday as the Lord's day "the primitive church could have made choice of no other day of the week more proper and convenient for the solemn and religious service and worship of Christ."[34]

In short, the church had power to choose any day it saw fit, but the Lord's day was so incomparably the fittest day that it almost had to choose it. The church had power to change the Lord's day but ought not to do so. Lord's day observance was not grounded in the fourth commandment, nor did it succeed the jewish Sabbath, yet Christian practice here was guided by the fourth commandment and at least ran parallel to the Sabbath of the Jews. The Lord's day was not divine or apostolic in its origins, and yet the day had been pointed out as special by Christ himself and on that basis observed as a festival by his apostles, whose own practice was in fact the basis for the church's choice of the Lord's day as a Christian festival. We have here the usual Laudian amalgam of arguments from scripture and apostolic tradition, limiting and encroaching upon a basic case founded upon the power of the church over things in themselves indifferent.

On the issue of the sabbath at least various Laudian authors went to some pains to explain how this position could be rendered coherent. What in the previous paragraph has been presented as a series of antinomies or contradictions, the Laudians presented as the result of a graded hierarchy of entirely consistent, compatible, and mutually reinforcing authorities. Thus while Francis White maintained the capacity of the church to decide on its own what might constitute "convenient and suffient time for God's public worship", he also cited as a ground and justification of the church's verdict "the general rules laid down in holy scripture for the ordering of ecclesiastical affairs . . . the precedents of the divine law in ancient time . . . the practise and example of the saints of God" as well as their own "Christian prudence". Again, White claimed that while the resurrection might operate as "a motive or cause impulsive inducing the church to make a law" it was still not "of itself any formal law."[35] In other words, Christ's resurrection might provide the occasion and cause of the church's instituting the Lord's day but the institution itself pro-

---

[34] P. Heylin, *The history of the sabbath* (London, 1636), pt 2, p. 11; F. White, *A treatise* (London, 1635), p. 270.
[35] F. White, *An examination and confutation* (London, 1637), pp. 77, 112–13.

ceeded from ecclesiastical authority, working off divine precedent rather than directly from any divine precept.

Gilbert Ironside made essentially the same point about the apostles. Only apostolic precept, and not apostolic precedent or practice could bind the conscience, and there was no record in scripture of any such precept regarding the Lord's day. Francis White admitted as much, conceding that there was no direct scriptural evidence that "the apostles ordained the sunday a weekly holy day" but arguing that such proof was not necessary in order to argue that the Lord's day was in some sense apostolic.

> The practise of the primitive church immediately and then successively after the apostles' decease argues this. For it could not possibly have come to pass that all and every apostolical church throughout the universal world should so early and in the beginning of the plantation have consented together to make the sunday a weekly service day, unless they had been thus directed by their first founders, the holy apostles themselves.[36]

This rendered the Lord's day in some sense an apostolic institution, but it did not mean that the church adopted it on the authority of the apostles. On the contrary, the church adopted it on its own authority guided but not determined or bound by apostolic precedent or practice. It was only apostolic precept, not mere practice, that could, without the interceding confirmation of ecclesiastical law, bind the conscience under pain of sin. As both Christopher Dow and Gilbert Ironside explained it, if the Sabbath had been founded by the apostles, it had been in their role as pastors rather than as part of their 'extraordinary mission to plant the gospel.' This meant that far from being a directly divine ordinance, the Lord's day, for all its apostolic origins, was 'an ordinance of the church' like any other and therefore subject to the authority of the church in later ages.[37]

In this way the Laudians were able to lend the Lord's day an aura of both scriptural and apostolic warrant while all the time defending it as just another ordinance of the church against what they took to be the spurious scripturalism of the puritans. In this way, too, they could elide the judgment and ordinances of the church with those of God himself and, through their resulting extremely exalted view of ecclesiastical tradition, confer an ever greater aura of holiness

---

[36] Gilbert Ironside, *Seven questions of the sabbath* (Oxford, 1637), p. 144; F. White, *A treatise* (London, 1635), pp. 192–3: White here cited the same passage from Augustine on the apostolic nature of immemorial ecclesiastical custom as that cited by Hoard and Quelch, see n. 29 above.

[37] G. Ironside, *Seven questions* (Oxford, 1637), pp. 160–2, 172–3; C. Dow, *A discourse of the sabbath* (London, 1636), p. 43.

on the rites and ordinances of the English church. Thus Francis White explained while

> ecclesiastical precepts and constitutions of the rulers in the church are not divine by miraculous and immediate inspiration, in such manner as the precepts of God's written law yet when they are composed according to the rules and canons of holy scripture and are apt and convenient means to the better fulfilling of the commandments of God delivered in holy scripture they are by conformity and subordination to the divine law and by divine approbation sacred and venerable. For . . . their immediate authors and composers are sacred persons, called and authorised by the Holy Ghost, to rule and order the church of Christ . . . the matter of these precepts being ordered and framed according to the apostolical rules . . . and according to precedent examples and precedents of holy scripture and the equity and analogy of former divine laws . . . and maxims and conclusions of natural reason, rectified by grace . . . and the end of such precepts being godly edification, order, decency and reverent administration of sacred and religious things. The precepts and constitutions of the church (I say) being thus qualified are sacred and venerable and their observation is an act of religion and of obedience to the general commandment of God.

From thence White extracted a very exalted vision indeed of the traditions of the church, for what else was tradition but the accreted weight of such ordinances, the collective wisdom of the universal catholic church? "Genuine traditions," White described as such as are "agreeable to the rule of faith, subservient to piety, consonant with holy scripture, derived from the apostolical times, by a successive current and which have the uniform testimony of pious antiquity." Such traditions were "received and honoured" by the English church, which owed its knowledge of "the number, integrity, dignity and perfection of the books of canonical scriptures, the catholic exposition of many sentences of holy scripture, the Apostles' Creed, the baptism of infants, the perpetual virginity of the virgin Mary, the religious observation of the Lord's day and of some other festivals as Easter, Pentecost etc" and much else to the traditions of the church.[38]

It was on the basis of this position that the Laudians were able to respond to the claim that their use of Old Testament texts on the need for and nature of external worship was illicit since it was based on the abrogated ceremonial law of the jews. In answer to that claim, Joseph Mede observed that

> in things for which we find no new rule given in the New Testament there we are referred and left to the analogy of the Old. This is the

[38] F. White, *A treatise* (London, 1635), pp. 99–100, 97–8.

apostles proof taken from hence for the maintenance of the ministers of the gospel . . . Likewise the practise of the church in baptising infants derived surely from the analogy of circumcision. The hallowing of every first day of the week, as one in every seven from the analogy of the jewish sabbath and other the like.[39]

John Swan replied to the anti-Laudian argument that while "such outward worship was requisite under the law" it was "not now required." The need for holy places consecrated to the worship of God predated Judaism, he explained: "for before Judaism began Jacob acknowledged Bethel, the house of God, to be a place of fear and reverence. He did no sooner perceive that it was an house of God but he presently began to be perplexed for fear he had not behaved himself so in it as of right he knew he ought to do in all such places." Robert Shelford agreed; for him "God's house began with an altar (as all creatures arise from small seeds) built in the place where God appeared to Abraham the father of the faithful."[40] Foulke Roberts cited the altars erected by Noah, Jacob, Abraham and Isaac as evidence that "the light of nature taught them that the place where God is to be worshipped ought to be different from other places." Indeed, he added, "the very heathen (who had no direction but from the light of nature) had their altars for their sacrifices and worship of their Gods."[41] According to Peter Heylin even Adam had had holy places set aside for worship. From the outset "nature informed them [humankind] in the main that proper and peculiar places were to be set apart to God's public worship and God himself informed them in the circumstances thereof, for the form and fashion, both when the church was moveable [in the tabernacle] and when after settled [in the temple]."[42]

Similarly, if the need for a holy place of worship predated the Mosaic law, so it had survived the abrogation of that law. John Swan drove that point home by citing Christ's action "in whipping the buyers and sellers out of the very utmost borders of the sanctuary". By doing so Christ "showed his zealous forwardness in the preserving of his father's honour and that in future times it should (of right) be as well regarded as before . . . Whereby is showed that that holiness and honour which heretofore was due to God's house and to God in his house should not die with those ending figures of the law but still abide."[43]

Joseph Mede expanded on the same point. Even under persecution the early Christians had set aside a specific space or site for the conduct of divine

---

[39] J. Mede, *The reverence of God's house* (London, 1638), p. 12.

[40] J. Swan, *Profanomastix* (London, 1639), pp. 14; R. Shelford, *Five pious and learned discourses* (Cambridge, 1635), p. 2.

[41] F. Robarts, *God's holy house and service* (London, 1639), pp. 4–5. Also see J. Mede, *The reverence of God's house* (London, 1638), p. 4.

[42] P. Heylin, *Antidotum Lincolniense* (London, 1637), section II, p. 69.

[43] J. Swan, *Profanomastix* (London, 1639), p. 24.

worship. The key Greek word that the fathers used in this context could not be translated simply as congregation or assembly, Mede insisted. It meant a separate place, a fixed physical location. In the straightened circumstances created by persecution, the church may have been no more than a room in a house, but Mede claimed this was enough to justify Eusebius' belief "the antiquity of churches or oratories of Christians to have been from the apostles times; yea to have been an apostolical ordinance." For Mede that ordinance of the apostles was in turn built on a divine ordinance taken from "the analogy of the Old Testament." Thus while the early Christians may have avoided the word "temple" to distinguish themselves from the pagans, under the word "ecclesia" or "oratory" they nevertheless enjoyed, built, and consecrated churches for divine worship.[44] John Pockington claimed that the early church had, quite rightly,

> set itself to comply with the church of the Jews in erecting, dedicating and consecrating churches and altars, ordaining of priests and levites, appointing and receiving of oblations, offering sacrifices and confirming Christ's church to be the true pattern thereof showed to Moses in the mount and lively presented in the tabernacle and temple.[45]

Thus Mede, Walter Balquancall, John Yates, Foulke Roberts, Peter Heylin, and John Pocklington were all able to present a vision of an unbroken succession of houses and habitations claimed by and provided for God amongst his people, stretching from the earliest times in the Old Testament, through the tabernacle and the temple, to the Christian churches of the present. Pocklington and Heylin in their tracts on the altar controversy went on to broaden this vision to include a similar succession of consecrated altars, sacrifices, and priests, stretching from Cain and Abel to the present.[46]

By contrast, Heylin and other antisabbatarian authors went to considerable lengths to argue that the Sabbath had not been observed by the patriarchs. They had worshiped God, at consecrated altars, made sacrifices on those altars, and done physical homage to the divine presence, but there was no evidence that they had done so regularly on a fixed day of the week. Thus while the sabbath was part of the Mosaic law and hence abrogated, the other principles

[44] J. Mede, *Churches, that is appropriate places for Christian worship* (London, 1638), pp. 15–19, 63–6.

[45] J. Pocklington, *Altare Christianum* (London, 1637), p. 128; also see J. Yates, *A treatise of the honour of God's house* (London, 1637), unpaginated opening section on "the danger of an altar in the name and use"; W. Balcanquall, *The honour of Christian churches* (London, 1633), pp. 6–7, J. Mede, *The reverence of God's house* (London, 1638), p. 4.

[46] See for instance J. Pocklington, *Altare Christianum* (London, 1637), pp. 58–60, 119–20.

inscribed in the practices of the patriarchs and jewish kings both pre and postdated the Mosaic law and hence remained of direct relevance to the church of Christ.

In this way, the authority of the church to make holy days could be vindicated from "puritan" scripturalism. At the same time the scripturalist basis claimed both for general Laudian priorities on the beauty of holiness and for particular policies such as converting communion tables to altars and bowing both to the altar and at the name of Jesus could be retained. It was retained by mediating the principles and precedents contained both in scripture and what the Laudians took to be apostolic tradition through the intervening authority of the church and ecclesiastical tradition.

V

We have then a neat hierarchy of entirely compatible and mutually reinforcing authorities, starting with the general prescriptions of natural and divine law, descending through the suggestive precedents provided by the practice of the patriarchs, the jews under the law, the apostolic and primitive churches, and indeed the practice of the church of Christ throughout its history, all coming together to form the traditions of the universal catholic church. Those traditions were then applied to meet the particular circumstances of each independent national church by the leaders of that church. On this view, while the room for maneuver left for the national church in determining its own ritual and liturgical practices was greatly constrained by the press of scriptural and ecclesiastical authority, there remained a small but distinct theoretical aperture for the exercise of the national church's sovereign power to accept and confirm what tradition and scripture passed down to it. It was that aperture that allowed the Laudians to graft on traditional arguments centred on the power of the church and prince over things indifferent to their other more exalted scripture and tradition based arguments for the beauty of holiness and the rites, ceremonies and policies that produced it.

Through their integration of the triad of scripture, church and tradition into one unitary authority the Laudians attempted at once to contain, exploit, and defuse the apparent contradictions inherent in their tendency to defend the ceremonies of the English church as both inherently indifferent and as warranted by scripture and apostolic tradition. If the scriptural injunctions concerning the decoration and design of the church, the demeanour, dress, and gestures of the clergy and laity cited by various Laudians in the passages quoted above could be construed as dealing only with necessary generalities about ceremonies and externals rather than with circumstantial specifics, then a glow of scriptural necessity could be lent to the ecclesiastical status quo without impinging on the sovereign power of the church to order its internal affairs.

That is indeed how several of these authors attempted to deal with this problem. Thus John Yates quoted various scriptural passages to the effect that "to worship the lamb is without dispensation and prostration before him admits no prohibition." But he then proceeded to construe that conclusion as a general statement on the need for outward gestures of reverence in the worship of God and to leave the choice of which gesture should be used when to the authority of the individual national church. "The ceremony before the throne" he claimed, ". . . is left us by the example of elders and angels, the manner whereof we know not exactly and therefore it is wholly left to the church to prescribe the form." Joseph Mede took the same tack, citing Jacob's response to God's presence at Bethel as evidence of the need for some outward sign of reverence before the divine presence in the church but leaving the precise content of that gesture or sign to "the discretion of our superiors and the authority of the church . . . for here as in other ceremonies the church is not tied but hath liberty to ordain (having respect to the analogy of the Old Testament) what she shall judge most suitable and agreeable to the time, place and manners of the people where she lives."[47]

This sort of distinction certainly offered a way out of the impasse if it was applied with rigor. Thus, Hoard avoided a clash between his adiaphoristic defense of conformity and his dalliance with the notion of apostolic tradition by explicitly subjugating all church customs, no matter how venerable, to the authority of particular national churches. Quelch, too, took the same line, refusing to ground his defense of the ceremonies of the English church on "fathers or councils or apostles or scriptures" but only on the customs and authority of the English church itself.[48]

Such a gloss on the passages presented above is clearly possible. But there are enough instances where the Laudian application of scriptural texts and precedents to present practices was so direct as to render it all but unthinkable that the church could legitimately refuse to follow the guidance of scripture and tradition as the Laudians' understood it. There was more than an apparent contradiction between the assertion of the sovereign autonomy of the church to decide the details of its own external worship and the assertion that, for instance, bowing at the name of Jesus was a duty of the text, or the invocation of texts describing the holy of holies in the jewish temple to justify the holiness and apartness of the Christian altar. Similarly, there was at the very least a considerable tension between the claim advanced by Gilbert Ironside that "putting religion" in "any outward observations" "as being parts and branches of God's worship" was a sin against Christian liberty established by Christ's

[47] J. Yates, A treatise of the honour of God's house (London, 1637), unpaginated opening section on "the danger of an altar in both the name and use"; J. Mede, The reverence of God's house (London, 1638), pp. 51–2.

[48] S. Hoard, The church's authority asserted (London, 1636), pp. 16–18; W. Quelch, Church custom's vindicated (London, 1636), p. 50.

sacrifice on the cross and Francis White's claim (cited above) that "the precepts and constitutions of the church . . . are sacred and venerable and their observation is an act of religion and of obedience to the general commandment of God."[49] Indeed, the contrast between those two passages is a perfect illustration of the Laudian tendency to assert the central tenets of the traditional conformist case while at the same time introducing claims to a direct religious significance and efficacy through the backdoor of scriptural and apostolic precedent, mediated by ecclesiastical tradition.

We have here, therefore, both a minimum and maximum position. The minimum position consisted of traditional arguments for conformity that had been commonplace among English protestants since at least the reign of Edward VI.[50] By quoting the Laudian version of this conventional case, Laudianism can be made to sound entirely conventional. The maximum position, however, went a good deal further than that, seeking, through the deployment of scriptural and allegedly apostolic authority, to lend an aura of religious efficacy and practical necessity to the rites and ceremonies of the English church as the Laudians understood them and indeed to the policies of the Personal Rule.

It is difficult not to see this as an attempt by the Laudians to have their polemical cake and eat it. It may be no accident that the more moderate, minimum position dominated the visitation sermons produced during the 1630s, while the rather more radical, maximum position can be found in the works of what one might call the Laudian avant garde, works often produced relatively late in the decade (some of them pseudo-official defenses of the allegedly novel aspects of the Laudian program). Thus, the initial drive toward the beauty of holiness was legitimated with a traditional rhetoric of conformity, which precisely because it was familiar, composed in large part of commonplaces, was less likely to alarm and alienate the non-Laudian members of the church whose adherence to enhanced standards of conformity was being sought. Indeed, ambitious or rabidly antipuritan Calvinists could and did invoke the traditional rhetoric of conformity in defense of the regime and could do so quite consistently. Meanwhile, on the leading edge of Laudian opinion, arguments were being used that cast the whole Laudian project in an altogether less familiar light. As we have seen, the Laudians sought to avoid the apparent logical contradictions between their adiaphoristic minimum position and their scripturalist maximum position through their account of the dynamic interaction and interdependance of the authorities of the church, scripture, and reason.

---

[49] G. Ironside, *Seven questions of the sabbath* (Oxford, 1637), p. 166; F. White, A *treatise of the sabbath day* (London, 1635), p. 100.

[50] For the centrality of the argument for obedience in things indifferent to the Elizabethan conformist case see P. Lake, *Anglicans and puritans?*, passim.

It has been argued here that they did so with only limited success and that what passed for a seamless web of mutually compatible and confirming authorities was in fact a model of authority in which the relations and connections between the constituent parts of the whole — broadly, scripture, the church and tradition — were sufficiently flexible to allow for a certain amount of play between various poles of the Laudian case, a play that the Laudians were quite capable of exploiting for polemical purposes, through the almost simultaneous deployment of the minimum and maximum cases outlined above.

This speaks to a broader ambiguity or tension in the Laudian appeal to the triad of church, scripture, and tradition and the way in which those authorities could be deployed to exalt and defend different aspects of the Laudian view of religion from attack. As we have seen, on the question of the Sabbath the whole thrust of the Laudian position had been to peel back the authority of scripture and the moral law, to reveal the question of Sunday observance as a matter for ecclesiastical authority. In this instance, their attempts to limit or mitigate the effects of this process, through a return to a more limited invocation of Old Testament, apostolic, and historical texts and precedents had been kept under control by the essentially antipuritan, antiscripturalist thrust of their position. As we have seen, the resulting stance on the Sabbath, saw the Lord's day as apostolic only in the secondary sense of having been devised by the apostles in their role as pastors and hence as continuing to be an ecclesiastical institution, subject, in theory at least, to later alteration or change by the authority of the church. The irony was that this position on the sabbath was almost identical to the position taken by some earlier conformist writers (most notably Richard Hooker) on the subject of episcopacy.[51] But on that subject the tendency among Laudians had been in entirely the opposite direction. For on episcopacy they had not simply gone with the conformist flow that had during James' reign come to see episcopacy as a genuinely apostolic institution, its place in the church now assured by divine right. On the contrary, divines like Heylin and, in one of his incarnations, Lancelot Andrewes had come to believe that the institution had been devised directly by Christ himself and by the 1630s many Laudians were talking (albeit perhaps rather loosely) as though episcopacy was essential for the being and not simply for the well-being of a true church.[52]

The same drift can be seen in Laudian attitudes to the altar and the related issues of the priesthood and sacrifice of the altar. On the subject of the Sabbath

[51] On Hooker's views on episcopacy see Lake, *Anglicans and puritans?*, pp. 220–5.

[52] For a remarkable passage on episcopacy as not merely apostolical but "of Christ's institution" which both cited a court sermon of Andrewes and sought to brand John Williams as a crypto puritan enemy of episcopacy for his opposition to this view of the matter see P. Heylin, *Antidotum Lincolniense* (London, 1637), section III, p. 8. For Laud's opinion, expressed to Joseph Hall, that "episcopacy is not so to be asserted to apostolical institution as to bar it from looking higher, from fetching it materially and

or Lord's day, Heylin and the other Laudians' position had stressed the inapplicability of examples culled from the Old Testament and the worship and practice of the Jews to the needs and experience of the Christian church. But on the subject of the altar, Heylin had been very concerned to cite such texts and precedents as a license for his use of the terms "sacrifice", "priest", and "altar" with reference to the contemporary English church. The Laudians themselves were aware of the potential contradiction here. Francis White accused the puritans of inconsistency,

> for they will not permit that the communion table shall be named an altar, no, not by an allusion or similitude because it is not so called in holy scripture and because the Romists have been superstitious in their doctrine and practise concerning the mass and because of the peril of idolatry. But again, on the other side, they style the Lord's day the sabbath day although this name is not given it in holy scripture or by any of the godly fathers of the church and although the sabbath and the Lord's day are so different as that one is legal and the other evangelical and notwithstanding the peril of jewish superstition and the heresy of Judaisants.[53]

But the argument could, of course, cut both ways.

VI

The point here is not to convict the Laudians of any greater inconsistency than that of their puritan opponents or indeed any other ideological fragment within the early Stuart church. It is rather to make several related points about their attitude to and use of authority in the conduct of religious polemic and the legitimation of what they took to be the official position of the English church. To begin with it is difficult, with Professor Trevor-Roper, to credit them with a liberal, rational, or skeptical attitude to "puritan" scripturalism. They certainly attempted to construct their opponents as simpleminded puritan scripturalists and presented themselves as reacting to that scripturalism. But, as the preceding analysis has sought to show, their relationship to the authority of scripture was on occasion not unlike that of the people they were attacking. Moreover, in the course of limiting the authority of scripture they generated a view of immemorial, ecclesiastical tradition, that was very often equated with the practice of the apostles and hardly fits the modernizing and

originally, in the ground and intention of it, from Christ himself" see P. Avis, *Anglicanism and the Christian church* (Minneapolis, 1989), p. 140. I intend to deal with this question at greater length elsewhere.

[53] F. White, *A treatise of the sabbath day* (London, 1635), p. 207.

rationalizing role that Trevor-Roper has attributed to them. This is not to deny that a critical, sceptical attitude to the claims of ecclesiastical tradition and Christian antiquity could be found among the denizens of Great Tew. John Hales, for one, certainly looked askance at any appeal to "apostolic" and ecclesiastical custom to legitimate the dogmas or ceremonies of the church.[54] The point is that such attitudes were entirely at odds with the rhetoric used to legitimate the Laudian view of the church during the 1630s and before (not to mention the attitudes of other Laudian members of the Tew circle like Henry Hammond). Secondly, the Laudians' views on these matters cannot be seen as the product of an effortlessly hierarchical, seamless web of mutually compatible and reinforcing authorities. Their position was not a logically derived and calmly stated consequence of the famous "Anglican" trilogy of reason, tradition, and scripture. On the contrary, while they could and did appeal to all those sources of legitimacy and authority the ways in which they did so and the element in the trilogy which predominated in their arguments varied from subject to subject. Finally, it will not do to see the Laudian case on the beauty of holiness, on the altar or on the sabbath as a mere restatement of traditional conformist doctrine on the subject of things indifferent, the authority of the church and the Christian magistrate, and the need for order, decency, and obedience. Certainly, the Laudians were capable of presenting their policies and priorities in that light but that was only one side of their case. The other was composed of precisely the sorts of arguments from scriptural precedent and general precept, apostolic and patristic practice and tradition that Francis White identified as informing and shaping the traditions of the church and the policies of the Laudians. These were enlisted to confer a directly religious significance on the ceremonies and observances that the Laudians placed at the center of their ideal of the beauty of holiness.

What we have in Laudianism, therefore, is a coherent and unitary vision of true religion, the visible church, and the Christian community. The internal coherence, unified aesthetic appeal, and ideological consistency of that position was not, however, necessarily reflected in the modes of argument and legitimation through which it was "sold" to a wider public. In other words the aesthetic and compositional coherence of the tableau of Laudian worship was not underpinned by an equally coherent argumentative or epistemological foundation. Different parts of the composition were given different sorts of legitimation. Sometimes the drive of Laudian argument, as over episcopacy, ran toward conferring greater and greater divine authority on some feature of the visible church; sometimes, as over the sabbath, it ran in the opposite direction. Sometimes, as over the triad of altar, sacrifice, and priesthood, the Laudians

[54] On Hales see the brief discussion in Avis' *Anglicanism*, pp. 103–109; on Great Tew see Trevor-Roper, *Catholics, Anglicans and Puritans*.

tended to emphasize the continuities between the Old and New Testaments; sometimes, as over the sabbath again, they did not. Sometimes, particularly when confronted with puritan accusations of popery or superstition, they stressed the autonomy of the church in deciding questions about its own internal organization and worship. On other occasions, they wished to emphasize the value, efficacy, and, indeed, the necessity of the beauty of holiness and the forms and observances that embodied it. Then, they placed far greater emphasis on the general scriptural injunctions and specific texts and precedents which, particularly in the Old Testament, provided both the guidelines and the legitimating warrant for the church's decisions on these matters. It is a nice question whether the resulting position, with its rather elastic notion of ecclesiastical tradition and the relations between the authorities of scripture, reason and the church, was contradictory or merely supple enough to contain and hold in creative tension a variety of contending or contradictory impulses. That question is best left to theologians. My present purpose is more modest than that; it is descriptive rather an evaluative, an attempt to document the ways in which, in different polemical contexts, the Laudians sought to sift and manipulate the legitimating authorities available to them in order to establish their vision of the visible church as a repository of the holy while negotiating their way past the fixed polemical points which the previous history of English protestant argument had left in their way. Thus, Gilbert Ironside had asserted that the Lord's day was an ecclesiastical not a divine institution, in no way enforced by the church as an integral part of divine worship. That echoed traditional conformist doctrine and headed off puritan claims of will worship. Yet he had been unwilling to leave the matter there, claiming that for all that the Lord's day was still of apostolic origin. This lent an aura of sanctity to the Lord's day all right, but Ironside had immediately to qualify just what was apostolic about Sunday worship lest he be seen to slip into what he admitted was the popish habit of inventing an apostolic tradition or warrant for any practice for which no other license or justification could be found.[55]

It was this careful balancing act between the various fixed poles of protestant argument that generated the rather different mixes between the demands of scripture, the church, reason, and tradition documented above. If historians are to make sense of the relation of Laudian attitudes to the preceding English protestant tradition, they need to bear in mind the complex, subtle, and polemically flexible synthesis that the Laudians created to defend their position.

[55] G. Ironside, *Seven questions of the sabbath* (Oxford, 1637), pp. 176–7 for the sense in which sabbath observance was apostolic and p. 172 for the popish tendency to invoke apostolic authority to justify or warrant merely ecclesiastical customs. Ironside's position here is more overtly sensitive to traditional English protestant scruples than that adopted by the other anti-sabbatarian authors discussed here.

If they do not, the bizarre misreadings with which this article started will continue and the subject will remain cloaked in controversy, as historians privilege one aspect of the synthesis over another, mistaking the part for the whole, and thus seriously distorting the significance of the view of the church, Christian community, and social order that passes, for better or worse, under the name of Laudianism.

"vesells fitt for the masters us[e]":
A Transatlantic Community of Religious Women, The Quakers 1675–1753

BONNELYN YOUNG KUNZE

In 1672 Goerge Fox, one of the preeminent leaders of early Quakerism, wrote about women's roles in the newly-emerging Quaker church:

> Friends keep your women's meetings in the power of God . . . and take your possession of that which you are heirs of, and keep the gospel-order. For man and woman were helpsmeet, in the image of God . . . before thee fell: but, after the Fall, in the transgression, the man was to rule over the wife. But, in the restoration by Christ, into the image of God and His righteousness and holiness again, in that they are helpsmeet, man and woman, as they were in before the Fall.

One distinctive feature of seventeenth-century English Quakerism was the relatively high visibility of women in public ministry. The practice of women in public religious roles was rooted in the restorationist theology of Quakerism, namely that believing men and women were spiritual equals. Although the ideal of male and female spiritual parity was not achieved in the early Quaker movement, it found at least partial expression in seventeenth- and eighteenth-century Quaker church polity. From the beginning Quaker women envisioned themselves as "vesells fitt for the master us[e]."[1]

Another distinctive feature of early English Quakerism was its repudiation of the structure, ritual, and forms of the Church of England, and indeed all other Protestant polities. As a result the Quakers encountered intermittent and sometimes heavy persecution throughout the 1650s and 1660s. By the late

---

[1] [George Fox], *Journal of George Fox*, ed. Norman Penney 1: 266–67; Box Meeting Manuscripts, Library of the Society of Friends, Friends House, London, letter #30 (hereafter the letters will be cited as BMM and the library cited as Friends House Library).

1660s in order to survive, Quakers felt the need to organize themselves into a church structure of "multi-tiered" meetings for business and worship. While men and women gathered for worship together, the early Quaker business meetings were first either conducted by the men alone or by the men and women together on a monthly basis (with the exception of London). Subsequently the business meetings were organized on a quarterly and annual basis.[2] After 1671, George Fox and his closest co-worker in early Quakerism, Margaret Fell of Swarthmoor Hall, Lancashire, oversaw the establishment of separate women's meetings for business to encourage women to participate in the Quaker fellowship. The tasks of these separate women's meetings included caring for the sick, poor, elderly, and orphans, disciplining the younger women and approving or "certifying" young couples who wished to marry. The men's and women's meetings worked as coordinates, sharing the tasks of church governance.[3]

The change in Quaker church polity was reflected in Quaker theology, which underwent significant development in this early phase of the movement. George Fox, Margaret Fell, and other early leaders (although not all) gradually moved away from a highly individualistic spiritualist stance that typified the earliest Quakers to a position where extreme individualism became subordinate to the religious experience and authority of the group. Fox's and Fell's broadened thinking on group authority in church order was reflected in the inclusion of separate women's meetings to function parallel to the men's meetings.

By the late 1660s Fell, as a forceful apologist and central figure in early Quakerism, sought to direct women toward a spiritualized group-oriented and deaconess-style ministry. In her best-known theological tract, *Women Speaking*

[2] For a discussion of the structure, degree of authority, and autonomy of Quaker women's business meetings, see Jean R. Soderland, "Women's Authority in Pennsylvania and New Jersey Quaker Meetings, 1680–1760," *William and Mary Quarterly*, vol. 44 (October 1987): 722–49. For information on the persecutions of Quakers, see Craig W. Horle, *The Quakers and the English Legal System, 1660–1668* (Philadelphia: University of Pennsylvania Press, 1988).

[3] Margaret Hope Bacon, "A Widening Path: Women in the Philadelphia Yearly Meeting, 1681–1929," in John M. Moore, ed., *Friends in the Delaware Valley* (Haverford, Pa.: Friends Historical Association, 1981), 173–99; Edwin B. Bronner, "Quaker Discipline and Order, 1680–1720 Philadelphia Yearly Meeting and London Yearly Meeting," in Richard Dunn and Mary Maples Dunn, eds., *The World of William Penn* (Pennsylvania: University of Pennsylvania Press, 1986), 323–35 (hereafter cited as WWP); Phyllis Mack, "The Prophet and Her Audience: Gender and Knowledge in the World Turned Upside Down," in Geoff Eleg and William Hunt, eds., *Reviving the English Revolution* (London and New York: Verso, 1988), 139–52; Hugh Barbour and J. William Frost, *The Quakers* (New York: Greenwood Press, 1988), 43 and chapter 6. For the origins of the London Women's Meetings, see William Beck and T. Frederick Ball, *The London Friends' Meetings* (London: published 1869).

Justified, written in 1666, Fell asserted that those who inveighed against women ministering were speaking "against Christ and his Church."[4]

In 1671 Margaret Fell gathered together her neighborhood women Friends at Swarthmoor hall to form what became the earliest continuous women's monthly meeting outside of London. The Swarthmoor Women's Monthly Meeting (SWMM), with few precedents to follow, acted as a "mother meeting" by encouraging other women to organize elsewhere in the growing, far-flung Quaker fellowship. In the 1670s the women Friends of Swarthmoor wrote an epistle on good order and discipline and sent it to other women's meetings. Although not stated explicitly, the epistle conveys the sense of a women's religious cohort at Swarthmoor which organized tasks in a quasi-independent manner. The document expressed the purpose of the separate women's meetings: "to wait upon the lord, and to hearken what the lord will say to them, and to know his mind, and will, and be ready to obey, and answer him in every motion of his eternal spirit and power." Further, it expressed the rule of this Protestant women's order in spiritualized language and metaphors common to religious groups of the period:

> And though we be looked upon as the weaker vessels, yet strong and powerful is God, whose strength is made perfect in weakness, he can make us good and bold, and valient Soldiers of Jesus Christ, if he arm us with his Armour of Light, and give us the sword of his Eternal Spirit which is the word of the Eternal God, and cover our breast with the breast-plate of righteousness, and crown us with the helmet of salvation, and give unto us the shield of Faith, with which we can quench all the fiery darts of Sathan.

The women of the Swarthmoor Quaker circle closed their epistle with the injunction:

> This is given forth for information, Instruction, and Direction, that in the blessed unity of the Spirit of grace, all friends may bee, and live

---

[4] Margaret Fell, *Women's Speaking Justified* (1666). Quoted in M. Fell, *A Brief Collection of Remarkable Passages and Occurances . . . Relating to that . . . Servant of the Lord, Margaret Fell . . .* (London: 1710), 333. In 1666 Fox also wrote about women holding their own business meetings:

> Concerning the women's meetings, encourage all the women of families that are convinced, and mind virtue, and love truth, and walk in it, that they may come up into God's service that they may be serviceable in their generation.

[George Fox]. *The Works of George Fox*, 1831 reprint (Philadelphia: AMS, 1975), 7: 283. For an overview of early Quaker theology, see Melvin B. Endy, Jr., "Puritanism, Spiritualism, and Quakerism: An Historiographical Essay," WWP, 281–301.

in the practice of the holy order of the Gospell; if you know these things happy are you if ye do them so.[5]

Within the Quaker fold there was considerable resistance to the development of separate female business meetings. The most articulate opposers of the Fox-Fell group were John Wilkinson and John Story, who led a group of Quakers in northern England into open opposition and schism in the mid-1670s over several issues. One issue was the separate women's meetings and the authority given to these meetings to certify or "clear" young couples who wished to marry. There were several attempts made at reconciliation, but this and other issues were not resolved during the lifetimes of any of the protagonists.[6] The Wilkinson-Story circle were, in Fox's view,

> dark spirits that would have no women's meetings, but as men should meet with them, which women cannot for civility and modesty's sake speak amongst men of women's matters, neither can modest men desire it, and none but Ranters will desire to look into women's matters.[7]

Although the Fox-Fell promoters of women's meetings became dominant in the early movement, the Wilkinson-Story separatists prevented women's meetings from being established everywhere in seventeenth-century Britain.[8]

The Wilkinson-Story schism did not obstruct Quaker expansion. Within a generation after Quakerism first emerged as a sect (circa 1652), it spread beyond the shores of England. George Fox and other zealous early ministers, men and women, traveled to many parts of the world to spread the message of

---

[5] Milton D. Speizman and Jane C. Kronick, "A Seventeenth-Century Quaker Woman's Declaration," *Signs* (1975): 231–45. The letter was most likely penned by Fell's middle daughter, Sarah. See also Isabel Ross, *Margaret Fell: Mother of Quakerism* (York: Ebor Press, 1984), chapter 19; Bonnelyn Young Kunze, "Margaret Fell and the Rise of Quakerism," book forthcoming.

[6] For the Wilkinson-Story view of the schism, see William Rogers, *The Christian-Quaker* (1680), Part IV.

[7] George Fox's *Epistles* letter #313 as quoted in William C. Braithwaite, *The Second Period of Quakerism* 2nd ed. Henry J. Cadbury ed. (York, England: William Sessions, 1979), 274, note 4 (hereafter the volume will be cited as SPQ).

[8] In 1692 William Penn, a staunch supporter of Fox and Fell against the separatists, wrote in response to resistance to women's meetings within Quakerism:

> But it is asked why should women meet apart? We think for a very good reason. The church increaseth, which increaseth the business of the church, and women, whose bashfulness will not permit them to say or do much, as to church affairs before men, when by themselves, may exercise their gift for wisdom and understanding, in a direct care of their own sex at least . . . while the men are upon their own business, also, as men and women make up the church, men and women make up the business of the church.

Quoted in Bacon, "A Widening Path," 175.

the Inner Light of Christ, which revealed at once human sin while it guided the rependant sinner into "Truth." Itinerant ministers who felt compelled to propagate the Truth in distant parts were usually certified by their local men's or women's monthly meetings. It is estimated that more than sixty Friends traversed the American colonies between 1651 and 1700.[9]

In 1670 George Fox, after release from an imprisonment, had an "opening" or vision to visit the new world. Fox traveled through several colonies from 1671 until 1673, organizing men's and women's meeting where he could. A number of American meetings date their origin from this time. Fox's personal visits and his epistles to these newly-formed meetings advised and encouraged both sexes to be active members of the fellowship. Communication by other traveling ministers and by letters continued on a regular basis throughout the colonial period, in an ongoing attempt to give mutual comfort, advice, and spiritual edification.[10] Thus these meetings became vehicles for the transmission of information and ideas between England and America. The British and American men's and women's monthly, quarterly, and especially the yearly meetings, preserved their correspondence. Over time it became an important function of the Philadelphia Yearly Meeting (established in 1681) to exchange letters with the London Women's Yearly Meeting (established informally in 1668).[11]

[9] Frederick B. Tolles, *Quakers and the Atlantic Culture* (Octagon Books, New York: 1980), 9. By the turn of the century Tolles estimated that there were about 50,000 Quakers in Britain and 40,000 in the New World, 24. See also Richard Vann, *The social Development of English Quakerism* (Cambridge: Cambridge University Press, 1967), 103. More recently, Hugh Barbour and G. W. Frost, *The Quakers*, 61–65, 85, have estimated that there were 40,000 to 60,000 Quakers in Britain by the 1690s. See also J. William Frost, "The Transatlantic Quaker Community Reconsidered," unpublished paper, 3–4. Frost points out that before the American Revolution, British Quaker traveling ministers visiting Pennsylvania numbered about one per annum. Because Quaker ministers often traveled in groups, there would be several in some years and none in other years. Without giving specific numbers, Frost claims that greater numbers of men than women were itinerant preachers. Margaret Hope Bacon, in "Quaker Women in Overseas Ministry," *Quaker History* 2 (1988): 93–109, has found that traveling Quaker women ministers from America to Britain in the period amounted to thirty-four percent of all traveling ministers. She claims that this is a significantly higher number of women who were traveling than has heretofore been thought.

[10] J. William Frost, *The Quaker Family in Colonial America* (New York: St. Martin's Press, 1973), 225; Tolles, *Quakers and the Atlantic Culture*, 9, 30; Bronner, "Quaker Discipline and Order," WWP, 324; Bronner points out that Fox was involved in the establishment of the London Yearly Meeting in 1668, and in the Dublin Yearly Meeting in 1669.

[11] Bronner, "Quaker Discipline and Order," WWP, 332. Bronner does not specifically describe the trans-ocean exchange of Quaker female letters. Moreover, Bacon in "Quaker Women," 177, claims the first epistle sent from the meeting was in 1699. The BMM has an epistle dated 1697 (BMM #48, see page 188). The Philadelphia Yearly Meeting included Quakers in the Delaware River Valley, west New Jersey, Pennsylva-

The transatlantic Quaker woman's meetings come to light not only through their preserved meeting minutes but also through a little-known series of letters exchanged by various Quaker women's meetings around the Atlantic rim between 1675 and 1753.[12] This series of letters was exchanged between women's monthly, quarterly, and yearly meetings in Britain, Scotland, the American colonies, and Barbados. Several aspects of the women's over-ocean correspondence endows them with a significance that transcends the experience of a single sect. The very existence of the letters raises questions about the evolution of the relationships and roles women played in seventeenth- and eighteenth-century religious sectarianism. Why were letters exchanged among these widely-separated sectarian women? How did the women present themselves in their correspondence? What type of female religious culture is described in these letters? In what ways did female Quaker religious culture depart from traditional Protestant religious life? The answers, of course, can be only partial since there are frequent and extensive gaps in the evidence. The packet of sixty-four letters is only a small sample of a vast network of Atlantic-spanning correspondence sent during the period. Several of the surviving letters lack dates and place names of origin and destination. Of the entire series, the letters that contain dates and place names number thirty-three dated before 1700 and nine dated after 1700.[13] Although the letter sampling is small,

nia, Delaware, and part of Maryland. Before 1745 it met in alternate years in Philadelphia and Burlington. According to Barbour and Frost, *Quakers*, 77, correspondence began after 1685 when the Philadelphia Yearly Meeting formally established itself.

[12] BMM, Friends House Library, London. The series contains a total of sixty-four letters that were collected in 1913 by one Mr. Crumps. It is an unbound collection of 263 pages. The precise principle of organization used by Crumps eludes definition. It appears that the collator had in mind a chronological collection of extant transatlantic women's meetings' letters. This collection is not contained in the larger collection of London Yearly Meeting epistles. See London Yearly Meetings Epistles Received, vols 1–3, 1685–1758; London Yearly Meeting Epistles Sent, vols. 1–3, 1683–1756, Friends House Library, London.

[13] The series contains sixteen letters written by George Fox giving spiritual and organizational advice to the men's and women's meetings wherever they existed. Fox's letters appear first in order in the letter series. The collection contains one letter written by Margaret Fell Fox to the London Women's Meeting after Fox's death. Of the remaining correspondence, at least six letters were sent from various counties in England to unknown destinations. Fifteen letters were written by women's meetings in the American colonies. The correspondence includes three letters from the London Women's Yearly Meeting, specifically addressing American women's meetings. The lack of place and date on many of the letters does not allow the assumption that all letters from foreign parts were destined for the London Women's Meetings. The packet includes one letter from Barbados to London, and one letter from London to Barbados. The Women's Yearly Meeting of York, England sent two printed missives to women's meetings wherever they existed, and the women's meeting in Aberdeen, Scotland sent three missives, presumably to London. One letter sent to Nottingham and another to New Jersey do not mention their origin. The collator also included three letters written

it does give us women's perspectives on Quaker women's activities and ideas in Britain and the new world over nearly a century of change. The letters speak to us of the evolution of an organization that was persecuted and that proclaimed its message in the American wilderness. They also tell us something about long-distance communication, the degree of female literacy in Quakerism and internal declension over several generations. David Cressy has found that the transatlantic letter connections between British and American family members and kin groups in the colonial period often became attenuated by the third generation, for time and distance caused family ties to dilute and become peripheral memories to the grandchildren of the first settlers. By contrast, the Quakers women's correspondence appears to have continued to function as a transatlantic letter nexus, even though it became increasingly formal and formulaic in terms of its religious expression, this despite time and distance. The tone of the letters remained affectionate, with frequent regerences that indicate that long-term separation did not obliterate their thoughts of, prayers for, and interest in one another.[14]

The early Quakers did not miss the parallel between their own newly-formed letter-writing communities and the Pauline churches among which epistles and formed a connecting link. Quaker historian Frederick Tolles suggested that the letters of the transatlantic mission were consciously styled like those of the New Testament churches around the Mediterranean, for such correspondence would foster unity, mutuality, chosenness, and clarity of doctrine, much as Paul's letters had done. One letter from Quaker women in Cumberland, England, written in 1675, expressed this spiritual unity:

> Dear Friends and well beloved Sisters; In the holly covenant [the] Father hath Begotten us; through the Power and Spirit of his Blessed son; Which He hath sent forth into our harts; by which we are Adopted children; And soe made heires, Together of the inheritance . . . and through which he hath Raised us up together.[15]

and signed by men. Some of the letters are partially illegible or too damaged to decipher.

[14] David Cressy, *Coming Over* (Cambridge University Press, 1987), 215, 285–89; J. William Frost, in "The Transatlantic Quaker Community Reconsidered," 4, contends that, "most often epistles were written in the stilted language of Quaker piety, serving as a symbol of shared faith rather than influencing change by either sender or recipient." This is true to a point. The religious salutations and exhortations were formulaic, but tucked in among these statements are numerous revealing comments on internal affairs, personal sentiments, and future plans. They also reflect a change of values over time.

[15] BMM, epistle #21; I am grateful to my former student, Mimi Daly Tipton, Colgate Rochester Divinity School, who worked on some of the BMM letters and analyzed this Pauling connection. See also Tolles, *Quakers and the Atlantic Culture*, 14.

A letter from London to Philadelphia in 1753 emphasized unity in familiar Pauline idiom: "Although we are 'strangers' in the flesh yet by Baptism we are brought into one Body and can indeed drink unto the due Spirit and Blessed by our Holy Head."[16] Other salutations in the Quaker female correspondence confirm this pattern of religious exhortation that typified not only Quaker letter but other religiously-inclined correspondence of the period. For instance, in 1697 the women's meeting of Aberdeen, Scotland, wrote to encourage the London women's meeting to bear their testimony against all odds:

> Dear friends Mothers and Sisters — Even with a measure of that pure Love which our Lord . . . hath bestowed upon us . . . hath he [been] a Supporter and Refuge in the day of trouble so that many times when the wicked one hath sought to destroy our hope his power hath been near to uphold.

Another letter from the London women's meeting to an unknown location began by stressing chosenness and unity:

> Under the influence of the true Gospel Love and a degree of that previous Union of Spirit, that Evidences to the World the real Disciples of Christ, which [?] abound in our Hearts spreads over Sea and Land, and makes one family the whole Household of Faith.[17]

After the salutation, the women's meetings reported to one another their current state of affairs. In the early years, the American meetings frequently reported an increase in membership, expressed in phrases such as, "Truth increases here." The women also expressed mutual concern over proper discipline. They seemed to accept willingly one another's exhortation to pure living and good order. In 1675 the women of Aberdeen, Scotland wrote to the London women:

> Deare Sisters; your Epistle we Received; and your motherly care; counsell and Advise; therein contained; we doe Truly Accept of and Receive; in the same love from whence it; did Proceed in you; . . . which God hath shedd abroad in your haarts; and from that Care that is weighty upon your Spirits; toward the whole Familly and Houshold of

---

[16] BMM, #62. The Rhode Island women in 1691 expressed this religious cohesiveness thusly: "This endless love of God by w[hi]ch we have been gathered near unto him and one to another in which our unitty stands . . .," BMM, #41.

[17] BMM, #18; #47. See D. Cressy, chapter 9, and especially page 222 for commentary on letter forms. The Quaker missives open with a stylized pattern of religious introduction, followed by acknowledgement of letters received, followed by statements relating to their religiously motivated activities. They close with well wishes to their distant sisters in the faith.

Faith; and Allsoe from that sincere; desire that . . . All might Be well; and nothing Amisse; or wanting in the churches of Christ; . . . we can say your godly care and Counsell; . . . hath been of great use for our confirmation and incrouragement.[18]

The women of colonial America frequently expressed a sense of isolation and loneliness as time and distance separated them from the land and religious family of their origins. A letter from the Yearly Women's Meeting in Philadelphia in 1697 or 1698 read:

Dear friends when as the Lord made many off us willing to leave our contry and kindred near and dear Relations ffriends and aquaintances to come into this Remote part off the world he also put it into their hearts . . . to pray unto him and desier off him that if his presence went not with us not to carry us thence.[19]

That same meeting wrote in a wistful tone to London sometime in the 1690s:

The glory of the Lord hath shined among his poor people in this Remote willdernesse contry . . . . And dear Sisters as you are and have been near and Dear to us so we firmly hope we shall not be forgotte by you altho we have Receiued but one epistle form you this many years; but have not fail[e]d to write to you from year to year.[20]

In 1679 the women Friends of the western branch of the "Nancimund River" in Virginia wrote to the London Women's Meeting that they wanted to be remembered to their sisters in England and at Swarthmoor, London, Bristol, and elsewhere.

We are your friends and Lovers of the truth, and do desire to be companions of all those who Love and fear the Lord . . . .. We would have you know that the Lord hath a people in this country, that are zeallous for his truth . . . and we are concerned with you in the work of the Lord.[21]

The minutes of the 1703 Philadelphia Women's Yearly Meeting express the warmth and affection felt by the women when they received these letters from abroad: "There was read at this meeting an Epistle from our beloved friends in England: as also one from our friends in Maryland: from which we were greatly comforted."[22]

---

[18] BMM, #21.
[19] BMM, #48.
[20] BMM, #49.
[21] BMM, #38.
[22] BMM, #38; Philadelphia Yearly Meeting of Women Friends: Minutes 1681–1814, 1: 9 (hereafter cited PWYMM); BMM #28.

Time and distance did however make the women strangers "in the outward [flesh]" to one another. In 1749 the women of Philadelphia reported that "we have not Received any Epistle from London for two years . . . this meeting being under a concern to revive our friendly correspondence with them . . . [will] prepare an Epistle." The London women did write a letter the next year, 1750, and explained their reason for continuing their correspondence with the Pennsylvania women:

> [We have] satisfaction to find your affectionate disposition to maintain a correspondance . . . w[hi]ch cannot fail of being both pleasant and profitable, so long as it is continu'd under ye fresh and lively dictates of that quickening Spirit, which actuated our Fr[ien]ds in ye beginning to many wholesome Doctrines and Exhortations in s[u]ch the Churches of Christ were edified.[23]

Although the Atlantic was a great barrier, the women's meetings endeavored to maintain a sense of their unity in being called out by the Lord to be a light to others.[24] Thus the London women wrote encouragingly to women at an unknown destination:

> [God] is engaging some of our Souls . . . for the glory of his great Name and the exaltation of the eternal Truth in the Churches, he has gathered by his own divine Arm, and that the borders of his Sanctuary may be enlarged, which is the earnest breathings of our Souls.[25]

Frequently the women expressed gratitude for their wide network of female fellowship where they could maintain their own testimony against worldliness. In 1700 the women of Aberdeen, Scotland wrote:

> The Lord is reaching to the hearts of many Even in this our Nation and causing them to see the Vanity and Emptiness of all evill Worthys and leting of them see the Great want there is of true and Spirituall Religion.
>
> O that wee who have known the truth and have been partakers of the life and Virtue thereof may be preserved in the same and be Examplary to them in our lives and conversations.[26]

23 BMM, #59; PWYMM, 1: 68–69.
24 An indated and unsigned letter to the London women, probably from Fox, reads, "I am to put you in mind yt you are above many of ye called of God, Set as a City upon a hill . . . ." BMM, #10; Fox was especially fond of this Matthean text and repeated it frequently.
25 BMM, #18.
26 BMM, #53.

By reading the letters aloud in the meetings, the women could discuss their spiritual conditions and cultivate a feminine approach to problems of worldly temptations consistent with their theology. Thus they were

> fully Persuaded it was the Lord's doing, in Separating . . . [their] Fore-Fathers and Elders, a People from the world. And by Vertue of his Power and holy influence made them willing to Part with everything that was offensive unto his divine Will, whereby they became exemplary One to the Other, and as Lights to the World.[27]

The women's epistles referred to the matter of declension in eighteenth-century Quakerism. Barry Levy has recently pointed out that the declension of Quaker youth in Philadelphia in the eighteenth century posed a major problem to Quaker families who had settled in the Delaware Valley. Levy contends that because Fox and Fell promulgated a radical spiritualization of the household, that subsequent family patterns went through several revolutionary changes within Quakerism. These changes in Quaker family life included an elimination of emblems of honor and deference in spouse and parent-child relations, an elevation in the value of women as "rational and self-disciplined" mothers and an "intensification in child rearing." According to Levy, these ideas were transferred to Pennsylvania and New Jersey by Quaker emigrants from northwest England, the area that saw the birth of Quakerism under the leadership of Fox, Fell, and others. Levy argues that Quaker families in Pennsylvania were deeply involved in their children's upbringing and conscientiously planned their futures from early childhood. In so doing, they attempted to shield their offspring from the corruptions of the world. This involved bringing up children exclusively in company with other Quaker children and guiding them into marriages only with other Quakers. The Delaware Valley became crowded by the mid-eighteenth century, and Quaker children began moving away and marrying outsiders. Quakers were thus confronted with a question: Should they weaken the purity and discipline of the church or disown their children who married non-Quakers?[28] Between 1750 and 1790 Delaware Valley Quakers disowned close to fifty percent of their youth. In this same period, Quakers withdrew from civil and political life and also abolished slave holding. It is noteworthy that the Quakers were a growing sect in the colonies prior to 1750. As of 1750 Quakers were the third largest religious denomination, but they declined rapidly in number after 1750, or at least they did not keep pace with the growth of other denominations.[29]

The Quaker women's letters for the years between 1700 and 1748 are missing. This gap notwithstanding, the letter evidence we do have, combined with

---

[27] From York, England, 1698, BMM, #64.
[28] Barry Levy, *Quakers and the American Family*, chapter 1.
[29] *Ibid.*, 6, 16–17; chapter 7.

the minutes of the Philadelphia Yearly Meeting of Women, suggest a growing concern over internal declension.[30] In 1749 the London women wrote to the Philadelphia women:

> Many hurtful libertys, respecting Conversation Manners, and Habit, frequently have been, and might be again Enumerated, which tend to dim the Beauty of Sion, and lessen the Brightness of her primative Appearance.[31]

In an undated letter the women of Philadelphia claimed: "Ye Lord is carrying on ye blessed work of reformation and sanctification in this citty."[32] In 1750 the Yearly Women's Meeting, which met at Burlington, wrote to their London counterpart that they were encouraged by their account of the

> care that is *reviving* upon some for restoring the Discipline established in our society which through the divine blessing has been as a Wall about us, in these places where it has been maintained.

Then they added the comment that women were not altogether useless in the church.[33]

The London women used the term "declension" to express in near-Jeremiad fashion the problem of straying from the pure spiritual path. In 1753 they wrote:

> Dear Sisters as to the Visible declension amongst us, its to be fear'd that as was formerly so now, worldly prosperity and the indulgence of rest, peace and plenty have been misapplied, and too many by placing their affection upon them are cooled towards God and his Truth.[34]

The women of pennsylvania expressed in 1714 their concern over specific youthful transgressions such as, "the unseemly and vain Conversation of some of the youth at this time . . . at Fairs." They noted that women should "be careful and keep a strict watch over all youth . . . to prevent their getting in Company either in Boat or on Horseback in the Town to the dishonour of Truth." Moreover, the Philadelphia women recorded feeling great "grieff and sorrow" when they saw Friends' children "parting the hair, pinching the caps

---

[30] See Bronner, 328–30, for a discussion of the concerns for discipline and good order, and education of Quaker children. See also Levy for his thesis on "holy conversation" as a "modus operandi" for Quaker domesticity and educational theory.

[31] BMM, #58.

[32] BMM, #55.

[33] BMM, #60.

[34] BMM, #62.

around the face; wearing pleated and Leaded sleeves, Bare Backs and Breasts, with gay Stomachers."[35]

In their struggle to keep the youth untarnished by the world, the women sought to give a gentle example of "holy conversation" rather than teaching youth by direct coercion and punishment. In this task the Philadelphia women believed that God would supply them

> with the Living Water, which will encourage, and enable us, to persevere, and hold out to the End in well doing, that so at the last an admittance may be granted, unto that Kingdom, where with the spirits of the just made perfect, who through many tribulations have washed their robes and made them White.[36]

However, in 1751 the women Friends of London were still hopefull that declension would be curbed:

> A Christian Concern still Remains on the minds of Faithful Friends, God will be Pleased in the Riches of his Love to visit their souls and like the good Samaritan bring back again those who are gone from the Truth, and that he will cause his Light so to break forth in the hearts of the Careless and Unconcern'd, that they may be brought unto his holy Hill, . . . witnessing the Benefit of the Gospel Fellowship.[37]

The Quakers of Pennsylvania and the Jerseys as early as 1703 expressed their concern over declension by preparing and circulating a document on "Order and Discipline." It subsequently became the "Book of Discipline." Monthly and quarterly meetings copied this document, circulated it, and made additions to it over the years. The Discipline enumerated rules of behavior relating to the conduct of Quaker business meetings, the oversight of marriages, and the settling of internal disputes. It also gave advice on the rearing and education of children. Although the rules sound legalistic to modern ears, Edwin Bronner has pointed out that the Book of Discipline gave as its justification "[an] exercise whereof Persuasion and gentle dealing is and ought to be our practice," and if anyone, "thro[ugh] perverseness and Stubborness" resisted reclamation, that person would undergo "Censure and Disowning" to guard "the good Reputation of the whole Body."[38]

The English Quakers devised a watch-dog method of discipline by sending a

---

[35] PWYMM, 19.

[36] BMM, #60; Barry Levy, chapter 1.

[37] PWYMM at Burlington in 1750, BMM, #61; Levy, *Quakers and the American Family*, contends that young women were programmed to remain pure through contemplation: "The inner eye that sees all secret thoughts, rather than observe all rules and restraints."

[38] Quoted in Bronner, "Quaker Discipline and Order," 328–30.

series of questions or "queries" to the monthly meetings that were to be answered and returned to their quarterly and finally their yearly meetings. American Quakers adopted this method by the eighteenth century. The women's transoceanic correspondence in the eighteenth century contains a document entitled *Queries to be observed by Women Friends in ye County of Lancashire*, penned in 1748. The author, Lydia Lancaster of Lancashire, claimed she sent the Queries to the London women,

> to show you a little of our way and manner of Proseeding in these meetings . . . [as] to walking agreable to the divers Branches of our Testimony . . . [for] the care of the church daily grows upon us.[39]

Cast in the format of seventeen questions, the disciplinary intent of the Queries is self-evident. One query reads: "Do all who profess w[i]th us keep in plainess of Language, Apparel, Dress and Furniture?" Another query expresses concern for youth:

> Are all friends who have children careful to have them religiously educated, sending them to Friends Schools to be taught in order to prevent their being corrupted by evil words; vain manners etc?

A third query points to concern for young single women:

> Are all young and unmarried women careful that they keep no disorderly company nor in any wise concern themselves upon ye account of Marriage without ye consent of Their Parents, Guardians or some faithful and judicious Friends of ye meeting they belong to?[40]

For all the early Quakers' repudiation of outward forms, these queries suggest that the trans-ocean Quaker women devised and followed through their letter network a format for order and discipline that was as strict as any written Rule of any religious group. The women seemingly found that the didactic nature of the queries and letters formed a framework for their behavior and that the reiteration and communication of this rule of living was an uppermost concern among the distaff side of Quaker religious life. In the face of declension, the letters repeatedly declared the spiritual benefits that accrued to the women who kept the discipline. The women bolstered one another with comments such as: The Lord is a "fresh taste of the hidden manna which he reserves for those who overcome through the blood of the Lamb."[41]

The letters asserted repeatedly their duty to be sober and virtuous, to do

---

[39] BMM, #57a, see page 230.
[40] BMM, #57, pages 224–27; Queries #4, 6, 7.
[41] BMM, #56.

works of charity, to defend Truth against those who spoke against it, to visit the sick, widows and orphans, and, above all, to be good examples to the youth.[42] Evangelizing declined by the mid-eighteenth century in favor of internal outreach. Quaker elders and ministers began making home visits to their own members. This change is reflected in the correspondence from the turn of the century until mid-eighteenth century. For instance, in 1697 a letter claimed that the Lord was daily giving them new "Daughters." In 1691 in language of Old and New Testament spirituality, the Quaker women's meeting at Whitby explained their peculiar mission as God's own people bringing new converts to the Gospel faith:

> The Lord is a Raiseing up many Witnessees to beare Witness against the Wickedness of this Sinfull generation and to awaken many Soules to Righteousness. Blesed be god, thinges is well with Us and truth prosperouss amongst us and many is brought into a Sense of their Lost Condition, . . . [Christ] hath Saved theire Soules by his power . . ., yea a Measure of it is felt amongst Us and we Can say ait Runs as a River, and the Streames of it Refreshes the tender Seed of our God, yea what shalal we Say the Lord is with Us and the shout of [the] Kinf is amongst Us, and he will Save his people by his Out Stretched Arme that is [s]tretched forth to Save his Israell; . . . so Dere freinds and Faithfull Sisters, it is Our prayers to god that you with Us, and we with you may be Kept in that Heavenly Unity and Fellowship that was Witnest amongst the Saints. . . .[43]

By 1751 a letter states, "In the Several Accounts brought in from our Quarterly Meetings we are Informed that amongst us, [and] the Discipline of the Church put in Practice." This seemingly reflects a change in outlook from an evangelizing stance of increasing the number of converts to an internalized sectarian view where the status quo was acceptable. It also reported that families were receiving visits.[44]

The missives and queries suggest that the women saw themselves as instructors and even rulers in their households, taking major responsibility for their children's upbringing in the faith. The women of Aberdeen, Scotland were happy to report to London that:

---

[42] BMM, see pages 53, 67, 73, 133, 135, 182, 183, 211 for statements on the women's tasks and duties.

[43] BMM, #40.

[44] BMM, #61. This letter also expressed worries over apparent declension: "we . . . Fervently Desire the . . . exercise of [the] Spirit may more generally fall upon each Particular member of our society; being fully Persuaded it was the Lord's Doing in Seperating our Fore-Fathers and Elders and People from the World."

Our young ones are Growing up in Some Measure in the love of truth, and are beginning to see the Variety and Emptiness of foolish Customs and fashions of this world so that we have good Ground to hope well Concerning them which is [a] matter of great Joy to us who are Mostly concerned in them.[45]

But in their concern to preserve the young from the "spotts of the world," their fear sometimes overcame their hope. One letter describes the "unwearied Enemy" by "hidden and subtle means" who seeks "to destroy inward life." The women braced themselves to guide "our tender offspring . . . immediate Objects of our Care, on whose account some have been ready to say, Oh! who is sufficient to discharge so weighty a Trust; Let us on their Behalf apply your Hearts unto God, in whom our Sufficiency Is . . . in case our wholsom Counsel, and repeated Admonitions have not their desired Effect."[46]

When death visited their community, the women seemingly faced it with equanimity, stressing the hope of eternal life. However, George Fox's death evinced a break from form and restraint in one letter from Rhode Island:

The deth of our Dear and worthy friend and father in the Lord G. F. hath come Exceeding neare unto us that knew him . . . Oh the great want of him that will be to severall in p[ar]ticular and the churches in generall much affects our hearts but the will of the Lord yet is Able to Supley all our wants.. . . . Even so our Consolation comes and we are Comforted in his mutiall Love for it is his and we are through it in him who is the father of [our] Spirits.. . ."[47]

The Philadelphia women's meeting tried to comfort the London women while at the same time grieving the loss of their spiritual leaders:

Yett in this are we Comforted, that if we Tread their Step's we shall in his good time Reap our Reward w[i]th them; and therefore we will not mourn as those wch have noe hope; but Rejoyce in this yt he is a fitting us for yt great Change, wch is hastening on all . . . for he is alarming the Nations, and Calling the Inhabitents of the Earth to prepare to meet him.[48]

45 BMM, #47.
46 BMM, #56; see also BMM, #23. The London Yearly Meeting published annual epistles that frequently cautioned parents against worldly influences on their children. In 1688 it sent out such advice: "when you see a libertine wanton spirit appear in your children or servants, that lusteth after the vain customs and fashions of the world, either in dressings, habits or outward adornings . . . for the good of their souls . . . help them over their temptations." (Epistle XI). Such admonitions grew more frequent in the early and mid-eighteenth century.
47 BMM, #41.
48 BMM, #52.

Fox's epistles promoting women's meetings answered a religious hunger among Quaker women for a rule of life and a fellowship geared to release their gifts of ministry. His death in 1691 eliminated an important voice favoring the ongoing separate but coordinate public ministry for Quaker women. By 1700 (two years before Margaret Fell's death), the attitude toward women's public ministry was becoming less flexible. Quaker historian William C. Braithwaite has pointed out that a less favorable attitude toward female participation in Quaker meetings existed by 1701. A minute of the London Morning Meeting reads:

> This meeting finding that it is a hurt to Truth for women Friends to take up too much time, as some do, in our public meetings, when several public and serviceable Men Friends are present and are by them prevented in their serving it's therefore advised that the women Friends should be tenderly cautioned against taking up too much time in our mixed public meetings.[49]

Although women's meetings formed early in Britain and the American colonies, and women ministers were certified and traveled abroad, a Quaker woman did not easily receive her mandate for ministry. In 1691, the youthful Elizabeth Bathhurst of London wrote of her struggle to be recognized as a public minister in the Quaker church. Bathurst traveled to Bristol, Windsor, Reading, Newberry, Malborough, and Oxford as a Quaker preacher and was imprisoned during her active ministry, yet she was not recognized by her own meeting as a bona fide minister. She wrote admonishingly to her congregation of her struggle for recognition:

> I confess I heard no publick Command for it given by any of you . . . but Prayers begun before I could so much as name my Message to you, upon request made me to be silent during Prayertime, and a promise of being heard afterward, I tarried till your Worship was ended, and then began my Mouth to open . . . but no sooner had I charged you with being out of the right way, but you made good that charge, . . . by shewing that persecuting Spirit, which infallibly marks out and deciphers the false Church . . . [b[ut] I feared not the wrath of the Adversary.[50]

---

[49] Braithwaite, SPQ, 287. As early as 1680, Mary Elson of the London women's meeting wrote: "The more opposition we have had against our women's meetings, the more we have increased in the power of the Lord, and he hath blessed our endeavours and service." *An Epistle for True Unity and Order in the Church of Christ* (London: 1680).

[50] Elizabeth Bathurst, *Truth Vindicated by the Faithful Testimony and Writings of the Innocent Servant and Hand-Maid of the Lord, Elizabeth Bathurst, Deceased* (London: T. Sowle, 1695?), 7.

Another traveling woman minister, Joan Vokins, of Berkshire, England, left her husband and children and crossed the Atlantic to the American and Caribbean colonies in 1680 and 1681. Vokins left testimony of her efforts to establish and strengthen women's meetings, and of the resistance she encountered. In her travel diary, she pleaded for women's voices to be heard:

> Oh do not strive to limit the Holy Spirit of the Lord which is but one in the Male and in the Female! . . . Oh! when will you witness that saying fulfilled, which saith . . . I will pour forth of my spirit upon all Flesh, and my Sons and Daughters shall prophesie?

Upon her return to England, sometime in 1682, to help organize the women of her own county, she wrote that she had returned

> to . . . labour for the settlement of our Womens Meetings in our country of Berkshire which was no small Cross to take up . . . the opposite Spirit did strongly strive, yet our Good Shepard did visit his Hand-maids and . . . filled us with his overcoming power, when the Mothers of Israel were so dismayed, as we were likely to have lost our Women's Meeting; but Praises . . . be ascribed unto that Almighty Power that hath set up . . . this Womens Meeting . . . and I can truly say . . . that the Lord owns our Womens Meetings . . . . He is a God of Wisdom unto the Foolish, and Strength unto the Weak, and honours his Power in contemptible Vessels.[51]

The transatlantic correspondence suggests that Quaker women perceived themselves as "vesells fitt for the masters us[e]," often emphasizing their roles as partners or helpers with one another in spreading their message and in keeping their discipline. Sentences like "Deare Sisters we salute you as being called of God to partake w[i]th us in ye heavenly inheritance of ye Saints in light and to bee fellow helpers w[i]th us in ye blessed work of ye Lord . . . ." were common in the rhetoric of the Quaker women's correspondence.[52] Moreover, the letter writers took pains to describe their meetings as being in the "heavenly order" comfortable, quiet, and peaceable.[53] In 1668 the women of the York Yearly Meeting expressed their concern for pure life and good order:

> Be . . . diligent in every [one] of your Women's Meetings, . . . do your Endeavours that nothing be practiced amongst you, but what tends to God's Honour and one another's Comfort; let nothing be indulged or connived at in any, whereby Truth is dishonoured . . . And these our

[51] Joan Vokins, God's Mighty Power Magnified and Revealed in his Faithful Handmaid Joan Vokins . . . (London: Tho. Northcott, 1691), 29–30.

[52] BMM, #17; #30.

[53] BMM, see pages 135, 163, 188, 209.

Testimonies cast not carelessly into a Corner, but sometimes . . . mark well the Advice therein, that our travail may be answered, the Lord honoured, and you reap the Benefit; and let a right Record be kept from Month to Month, and from Year to Year, of the Lord's Dealing with us, and Mercy to us, for future Ages, that from Age to Age, and one generation to another, his own Works may praise him.[54]

In spite of the internal care for close following of the women's spiritual rule, there were groups in the British branch of the Quaker church who continued to oppose women meeting separately for business. In a letter from London to Pennsylvania in 1748 the women alluded to this opposition when they noted:

The hope you express, touching an Increase of Zeal for the maintaining [of] Your Women's Meeting on its antient foundation is [a] matter of Comfort to Us . . . [we give you] Encouragement to persist in that Religious Duty; how contemptably soever some may think of it, as of other Branches of our Christian Testimony.[55]

As of 1750, the women stressed that their work was not unimportant as some were wont to see it, the Pennsylvania women telling their London counterpart:

Dear Sisters, tho our part in so weighty a Work . . . may to many appear small and inconsiderable, yet as through divine goodness some of us, with our Brethren in Christ have been made partakers of that one Baptism; . . . we esteeme it no presumption to conclude that . . . [we] are not altogether useless in the service of the Church . . . to Act for God, and his Truth.[56]

The Philadelphia Women's Yearly Meeting began in 1681 and existed until 1929 when women in American Orthodox Quakerism ceased to meet separately. The women's meeting in London gathered at the Yearly Friends meetings for worship, but they were not formally established as a separate women's yearly business meeting until 1784, and only after the London Yearly Meeting experienced some pressure from American Quakers. Despite their lack of formal structure, the London women carried on a lively correspondence with distant meetings around the Atlantic, not letting the lack of formalized authority

---

[54] BMM, #63.

[55] BMM, #56. Additionally, the same letter warned against divisiveness or disunity in the ranks: "Dear Sisters in Christ; let us watch against every appearance of Evil; especially that which would divide in Jacob, and scatter in Israel; and let not Judah vex Ephraim, nor Ephraim envy Judah; but endeavour to live in Love; demonstrating thereby the Badge of true Discipleship."

[56] BMM, #60.

195

prevent them from admonishing, counseling, and encouraging their faraway sisters.[57]

What may we conclude concerning the nature of the female religious culture described in the correspondence and the impact of these sectarian women's meetings, given the patchy evidence and the random nature of the documentation? Although much remains in shadow, the evidence we do have suggests some possible conclusions. First, the women involved reaped spiritual benefits from their meetings and correspondence. Their frequent gatherings and their epistle exchanges helped to clarify their internal problems, as it also helped to reinforce their shared goals and values. Historians have long noted a permanent potential within Christianity for the emergence of fellowship-type religious sodalities that held to rules of order and discipline, thereby distinguishing them from the world. The transatlantic Quaker women from the Restoration to the American Revolution demonstrated this type of sodality which lived by a fixed rule of discipline.

Second, there appears to be a two-fold ambiguity in the existence and influence of separate women's meeting in Britain in this period that is reflected to a lesser degree in their new world counterparts. The very existence of separate women's meetings was a subtle and implicit challenge to patriarchy. On the one hand the women, both British and American, used the deferential language of the period, referring the themselves in "weaker vessel" imagery. Further, there does not seem to have been any sense of competition between the women's and men's meetings, or any yearning on the part of the women to liberate themselves from their male coordinates. Still, the subversive potential of the women's separate meetings and networking was present. They organized, collected their own funds, and continued to meet despite considerable internal resistance. They attended to their tasks while tenaciously holding to their self-perception as parallel women's groups. This challenged patriarchy in actions if not in words. It also suggests that the women percieved themselves as equally able as men to function in their public ministries. The American women's meetings also demonstrated deferential behavior toward the men's monthly, quarterly, and yearly meetings by not challenging male dominance in questions of procedure and order.[58] However, the resistance to women's

[57] Bacon, "A Widening Path," 173–80. Early Quaker women's meetings in England maintained some financial independence. The Box Meeting had its separate funds from the beginning and the Swarthmoor Women's Monthly Meeting established its own fund or "stock" at its first meeting in 1671. The Philadelphia Women's Yearly Meeting began their separate stock in 1705. See also Bacon, "Quaker Women in Overseas Ministry," 106–107; Bronner, WWP, 326; SPQ, 287; Kunze, chp. 7.

[58] See Bacon, 177, for an example of deferential behavior of the Philadelphia Women's Meeting to the Men's Meeting there; also PWYMM, 10, 64–65; see also Susan Dwyer Amussen, *An Ordered Society: Gender and Class in Early Modern England* (Oxford: Basil Blackwell, 1988), 23, 33, cf., 91–93.

separate meetings seen in England seemingly was not replicated in colonial America.

Finally, this series of Quaker letters illuminates a surprising sectarian network of support and ongoing interest in gender-related issues that bound together the Quaker women's meetings in a fictive kinship for four generations and more. While working around gender restrictions in a patriarchal society, the women inculcated a distinctive view of radical Protestant womenhood. Thus, in the very contradictions of their activity and their discourse, the Quaker "sisterhood" illustrates a significant cultural and religious alternative in early modern England and America.

Metaphysical Implications
in Hobbes's Theory of Passions

PAOLO PASQUALUCCI

Passions are conceived by Thomas Hobbes as the "interior beginnings of our voluntary motions." These "beginnings" are motions of matter, to be explained according to the laws of motion. They are produced by our ideas, which are induced in us by our sensations. But sensations and ideas are in their turn movements too, though of a different type. The interior movements that originate our passions occur in extremely small spaces. They are infinitesimal movements or "endeavors." In explaining their characteristics, Hobbes makes use of a metaphysical assumption on the nature of motion, similar to the dichotomy paradox conceived by Zeno of Elea, though for a different purpose than Hobbes's, that is to deny motion. Zeno's argument is aimed at destroying the conceivability of any type of motion whatsoever. This paper will analyze briefly Zeno's thesis as well as Hobbes's criticism of it. Hobbes's reply to Zeno, though subtle, does not seem to be decisive, because he rejects the possibility of division of matter ad infinitum, but admits that matter is always subject to a new division. The metaphysical implications of Hobbes's theory of passions lead to an analysis of Hobbes's attitude toward the notion of the infinite and to comments on its possible contradictions.

The analysis of human passions occupies a fundamental place in Thomas Hobbes's political philosophy since he believes that "for the knowledge of the properties of a commonwealth, it is necessary first to know the dispositions, affections, and manners of men."[1] An exact knowledge of affections or passions belongs then to that part of "civil philosophy" (the object of which is given by the *civitas* or state) which is called *ethics*. The study of ethics, i.e., "of men's disposition and manners," is therefore to be considered as preliminary to that of *politics*, which covers the other section of civil philosophy, concerning "the civil duties of subjects."[2]

As a consequence of such a methodological approach, ethics is conceived of

---

[1] Thomas Hobbes, *De Corpore, English Works (EW)*, Scientia, Aalen, 1: 11; see *Opera Latina (OL)*, Scientia Aalen, 1: 10.
[2] *Ibid.*

as the result of rational knowledge in the Hobbesian sense, i.e., of a knowledge based on materialistic and mechanistic assumptions. Nonetheless, the psychological insight and the originality shown by Hobbes in exposing human passions (in the famous sixth chapter of *Leviathan*) have been often ascribed by scholars to his naturally keen capacities as an observer more than to his mechanistic theories. I do not intend to pose again the *Vexata quaestio*, whether Hobbes's definitions of the passions are substantially independent of the mechanistic tenets with which the philosopher intends to justify them.[3] Instead, I intend to consider but one among those tenets: the notion of *conatus* or endeavor, so as to be able to make some remarks on the quality of the idea of motion that it embodies.

Hobbes defines our passions as "interiour beginnings of [our] voluntary motions."[4] This definition contains a subtle distinction: passions are not just our "voluntary motions" but "their interior beginnings." What is the reason for such a distinction? "Animal" or "voluntary motion," he writes, is that type of movement that takes shape in our going, speaking, or moving "any of our limbs." It is that motion in which our will plays a decisive role,[5] so that when we move or speak, we do it "in such a manner as it is first fancied in our minds."[6]

By common sense, our voluntary movements, being conscious ones, are considered to be the product of our mind. But mind (whatever its intrinsic nature may be) is for us something in itself independent and different from the movements to which it gives origin. Mind is for us either the remote cause or one of the apparent causes of our voluntary movements, which are therefore considered as its effects. To think of the mind as in itself *movement* too would seem to dim the distinction between cause and effect.

But Hobbes's materialistic metaphysic has a peculiarity of its own and rarely coincides with the point of view of common sense. Therefore, for him our voluntary movements are *not* the product of our mind: they are only "fancied in it" by our "imagination" or "fancy," which, in itself, is but a type of motion. "That Sense, is Motion in the organs and interior parts of man's body, caused by the action of the things we See, Heare, etc. And that Fancy is but the Reliques of the same Motion, remaining after Sense, has been already sayd in the first and second Chapters."[7]

---

[3] On this point, see George Croom Robertson, *Hobbes* (Edinburgh and London, Blackwood, 1905[2]), 57; Leo Strauss, *The Political Philosophy of Hobbes*, trans. Elsa M. Sinclair (Chicago and London, University of Chicago Press, 1963), x–xi, 3–5, 6, 9, 10, 29.

[4] Thomas Hobbes, *Leviathan* (Harmondsworth: Penguin Press, 1968), 118.

[5] *Ibid.* The involuntary motions that occur in us, such as "the course of the Bloud, the Pulse, etc.," Hobbes calls "vitall motions" (*ibid.*).

[6] *Ibid.*

[7] *Ibid.* (The chapters he refers to are the first two chapters of *Leviathan*).

According to Hobbes, the process of human knowledge, conceived of as a purely material one, initiates from outside the subject and is but a graduation of related movements of matter. As the starting point of it, one must therefore take into consideration sensation or *sense*, given the fact that "there is no conception in a man's mind, which hath not at first, totally, or by parts, been begotten upon the organs of Sense."[8] *Sense*, as an act, "is caused by the action of the things we See, Heare, etc." This "action" is but motion, which invests the organs of our senses from without and in its turn generates motion in them and in our "interior parts" in general. The first stage of our knowledge of the external object results therefore from a combination of external and internal motion — the first falling upon us from matter outside; the second consisting of a whirlpool of ensuing movements belonging to the matter of which our body is composed. Furthermore, these interior movements are not instantaneous, in the sense that they are not lost in the instant in which they impress us but maintain and preserve themselves in our body, giving shape to what Hobbes calls "representation" or "imagination," "fancy," and "memory." This for him is the same as thought.[9]

In his perspective, matter can be affected by matter only, through a ceaseless movement, "for motion produceth nothing but motion."[10] But all this means that in reality there is never a place or a point where motion is absent or is going to cease. Therefore, the images of things we have in our mind cannot be conceived of as something purely mental or spiritual, as if they were in themselves something independent and different from the physical reality of motion. In Hobbes's view, they must be considered "Reliques of the same motion" that *is* the act of Sense. Memory or Imagination (i.e., our interior representation of things), is therefore "decaying sense", a sense which, though withering, has preserved itself in the interior (and to us secret) movements of matter in our body.[11]

Hobbes's reasoning, as far as this fundamental point of his doctrine is concerned, implies the acceptance of the principle of inertia (already enunciated by Galileo, Gassendi, and Descartes), and indeed he seems to be acquainted with it. He writes, in fact, "That when a thing lies still, unlesse somewhat els stirre it, it will lye still for ever, is a truth that no man doubts of. But that when a thing is in motion, it will eternally be in motion, unless somewhat els stay it . . . is not so easily assented to."[12] It seems clear, then, that Hobbes extends the

---

8 *Leviathan*, 85.
9 *Ibid.*, 85, 89.
10 *Ibid.*, 86.
11 *ibid.*, 88. "Representation," "imagination," etc., resemble what Locke defines as an idea produced by mere perception; see *An Essay Concerning Human Understanding* (London, Dent, 1965²), 1. 112), and Kant calls *Vorstellung*, see *Kritik der reinen Vernunft*, A 19, B 33.
12 *Leviathan*, 87. The law of inertia is assessed more clearly in *De Corpore*, though

principle from the physical to the spiritual domain, from the movement of the body to that of the mind. After its taking shape as a consequence of the external stimulus operating in us through "sense," we must assume, then, that imagination "will eternally be in motion" within the matter of our body, even if we are not aware of it.[13] It is the inertia inhering to motion that maintains it within us, even after its originating stimulus has disappeared, so that when we assume we know something, i.e., when we "perceive in sense" and therefore imagine something, given the overlapping of multifarious objects offered to our experience, "there is no certainty what we shall imagine next; Only this is certain, it shall be something that succeeded the same before, at one time or another."[14]

If our "representations," our thoughts, are but "reliques" of previous motion, which in the meantime has never stopped, then, we might say that for Hobbes our knowledge of things, consisting of such "reliques," is envisaged as a sort of memory, in a sort of materialistic Platonism.

But sense and its "relique," imagination, are not voluntary motions because they take shape in our mind independently from our will. Whether I want it or not, I am always imagining the reality outside me, that is, representing it in my mind, in the idea of the object perceived. How does Hobbes establish the necessary connection, then, between the notion of imagination and that one of a voluntary motion? He does it this way: "And because *going, speaking*, and the like voluntary motions, depend always upon a precedent thought of *whither, which way*, and *what*; it is evident, that the Imagination is the first internall beginning of all Voluntary Motion."[15]

The exterior movements that make up our going or speaking are never separated from a form of preceding consciousness because they take place always after "a precedent thought" or imagination of *where* we want to go, *which way*, or *what* we want to say. Our external moving is therefore consequent to an internal one since imagination is but a movement, in its turn originally provoked by the movement of matter outside. The difference between voluntary motions and the ideas or imaginations that precede them is then but a difference in the *location* of motion of matter, inasmuch as such motion takes place outside or inside us. Our imaginations do not differ from the insuing voluntary motions for the *quality* they possess (as common sense would think)

---

not yet in a rigorous form: "I have shown, that whatsoever is at rest will always be at rest, unless there be some other body besides it, which by getting into its place suffers it no longer to remain at rest. And that whatsoever is moved, will always be moved, unless there be some other body besides it, which hinders its motion" (EW 1: 205; OL, 1: 177). On this point see Frithiof Brandt, *Thomas Hobbes' Mechanical Conception of Nature* (Copenhagen-London: Levin and Monksgaard-Hachette, 1928), 282ff, 325ff.

[13] *Leviathan*, 87, 88–89, 94; *De Corpore, EW*, 1: 216 (OL, 1: 182–83).
[14] *Leviathan*, 94.
[15] *Ibid.*, 118.

but for their *quantity* only, that is, because of the position that they occupy in the general process of motion. In this process, they represent the moment in which the movement of matter in us (directly or indirectly provoked by matter outside) turns into the beginning of a conscious exterior movement of the subject. This "interiour beginning" of exterior and voluntary motion is, according to Hobbes, what men call "passion."

Hobbes's rational and materialistic approach to ethics aims at dissolving any of its moral (i.e., qualitative) connotation, so that human affections may be explained as if they were simple variations in the location and degrees of motion of matter. This way he believes he has established ethics on the firm ground of an exact, scientific knowledge. In such a perspective, the notion of the will must be also explained with the notion of movement. Contrary to the Aristotelian and Thomistic tradition, the will for Hobbes is no longer a "rational appetite," aiming at a rational goal, a goal that cannot be separated from the idea of the Good. Hobbes instead conceives it as "the last Appetite, or Aversion, immediately adhering to the action, or to the omission thereof,"[16] whatever the goal of the action or omission be. This is the will as "The Act, (not the faculty,) of Willing."[17] But our will from this perspective always appears as an act and never as a faculty. It is *the* act that takes place immediately before our action, without taking into consideration whether our "action" consists of doing or omitting to do. That act is therefore the *last* moment in the process of deliberation preceding action, a process in which "Desires, Aversions, Hopes and Fears" confront one another until we decide, one way or the other.[18] This process, as a whole, which Hobbes calls *deliberation*, consists of the sum total of all the opposite movements of attraction and aversion, our will being but the last one of them, last in time and space. In a perfect parallelism with the notion of ethics, the notion of the will likewise is then based on the all-pervading notion of movement. As such it also becomes descriptive, merely quantitative, and even naturalistic since the will is framed as a moment of the natural mental process called deliberating, as the last moment in its last segment of motion.[19]

The notion of motion, clearly employed by Hobbes to explain both the physical and the moral aspects of human nature, becomes then a universal principle according to which reality is conceived of as a whole, independently

---

[16] *Ibid*, 127.

[17] *Ibid.*

[18] *Ibid.*

[19] Stating that the will is the "last appetite or aversion" in our deliberation, Hobbes seems to deny the necessity of an object for the will. However, he admits that an object is necessary when he remarks, for instance, that when a man is transferring his right or renouncing it and considers some good he hopes to get for the transferring, this "is a voluntary act: and of the voluntary acts of every man, the object is some Good to himselfe" (*Leviathan*, 192).

from experience, on the basis of merely logical deductions. Such a notion inevitably becomes a metaphysical principle, which Hobbes, the empiricist and materialist, must defend with all his strength since the whole of his speculative system is based on it.[20] Any criticism of that notion would imperil the notion of the passions as well, especially if it denies the possibility of motion within an infinitesimal, and to us invisible, extension of matter. "And although unstudied men, doe not conceive any motion at all to be there, where the thing moved is invisible: or the space it is moved in, is (for the shortnesse of it,) insensible; yet that doth not hinder, but that such Motions are."[21] The space in which the "interiour movements" of our body are supposed to take place is so small, that it seems (to common sense) to be impossible that any real motion whatsoever might really occur in it. But "unstudied men" base their opinions just on what their sensations show them. When the thing in motion "is invisible" or when the space "it is moved in" is also invisible by reason of its "shortnesse," they think that no movement at all is there possible. But the imperceptibility of the thing moved or of the space it moves in must be ascribed to the weakness of our organs of sense, just sufficient to penetrate the mere surface of reality.

Yet the "shortnesse" of space seems in itself to confront our mind with an *objective* difficulty to conceive any motion in it, and indeed Hobbes, in replying to the fictitious "unstudied man," concentrates on it, in the following way: "For let a space be never so little, that which is moved over a greater space, whereof that little one is part, must first be moved over that."[22] The space on which a body has to move, may be as small as possible: it does not matter as far as the possibility of motion in it is concerned. Indeed, when "a greater space," of which the smaller one is part, is run through by a body, we must assume that that body must have passed through the smaller space, no matter how small. Therefore, as a general conclusion, we must admit that, no matter how large the space traversed, motion must have extended through all the possible minor spaces in which that same space can be divided. Actual motion, extending in space from one point to another, may be then conceived of as having begun in a space which is as small as possible, even much smaller than a point. And "these small beginnings of Motions, within the body of Man, before they appear in walking, speaking, striking, and other visible actions, are commonly called ENDEAVOUR."[23]

Our internal "endeavours" or "conatus" are nothing else than our very passions, divided by Hobbes in the two main and opposite fields represented by "appetite" or "desire" and "aversion," the difference depending on the direc-

---

[20] ". . . Causam omnium rerum quaerendam esse in diversitate motuum." T. *Hobbes Malmesburiensis Vita*, OL, 1: xxi. See also *Vita carmine expressa, ibid.*, lxxxix.

[21] *Leviathan*, 119.

[22] *Ibid.*

[23] *Ibid.*

tion "endeavour" takes, whether "it is toward something which causes it," or "fromward something."[24] Besides being the "interiour beginnings" of our "voluntary motions," passions are therefore endeavors or "small beginnings of motion, so small that they can be deemed to be infinitesimal. As Hobbes expresses himself in *De Corpore*, endeavor is in fact a "motion made through the length of a point, and in an instant or point of time."[25]

Hobbes's point of view is in accordance with the emerging science of nature. Galileo had indeed maintained that a body, increasing its velocity through continuous acceleration, "reaches its actual speed only after having passed through all the intervening degrees of velocity."[26] It is evident that the practically infinite degrees we may conceive of in velocity (i.e., in motion) imply the infinite divisibility of space and time, in both of which motion takes place.[27]

As far as the history of ideas is concerned, it should be noted that Hobbes's basic assumption in favor of the possibility of motion in an infinitesimal space is reminiscent of the Eleatic tenet on the divisibility of space ad infinitum, however with the decisive difference that the Eleatics admitted divisibility so as to deny the logical possibility of motion as such. This is the famous *dichotomy paradox*, the first of Zeno of Elea's four arguments against movement, traditionally consisting of the following related propositions:

A body, when in motion, must cover a certain distance. Since any distance can be divided into infinite parts, first of all we have to consider that a body must reach the half of the whole distance to be traversed, before actually covering the whole of it. Before reaching that half, a body is afterwards supposed to have crossed half that distance, and so on, over and over again. Since it is always possible to divide into two parts the extension taken into consideration, this is like saying that the halves of a given distance are infinite. Therefore, it is not possible that a body traverses infinite spaces in a time finite whatsoever.[28]

The similarity with the core of Hobbes's argument seems to me to be clear enough, whereas the conclusions inferred are completely opposite. Whatever

[24] *Ibid.*
[25] *EW* 1: 206 (*OL*, 1: 177). On Hobbes's notion of endeavor, see Brandt, *Thomas Hobbes' Mechanical Conception of Nature*, 294ff; John Watkins, *Hobbes's System of Ideas* (London, Gower, 1965), 123–24, 132–35; Brian Stoffel, "Hobbes's Conatus and the Roots of Character," in Craig Walton and Paul J. Johnson *Hobbes's "Science of Natural Justice"* (Dordrecht: Martinus Nijhoff, 1987), 123–37.
[26] Galileo Galilei, *Dialogo sopra i due massimi sistemi del mondo*, ed. Libero Sosio (Turin: Einaudi, 1970), 26–27.
[27] *Ibid.*, 28–29.
[28] Simplicius, *Physica*, 1013, 1014 quoted by Eduard Zeller-Rodolfo Mondolfo, *La Filosofia dei Greci nel suo Sviluppo Storico*, I, III, revised and enlarged Italian edition (Florence: La Nuova Italia, 1967), 378–79, fn. 20.

the distance to be covered, a body in motion must first cover half that distance. But since it is always possible to conceive the half of a given extension (that is, to dichotomize it), this is like saying that every finite extension of space, which a body in motion should traverse from one point to another, can be divided into parts (or points) ad infinitum or, which is the same, into infinite parts. Therefore, how can a body run through the infinite subdivisions, which it is possible to conceive of, in any extension of finite matter? Having to pass through infinite degrees, its movement, however progressing, should then, never be able to reach its goal.

The logical impossibility of motion is also maintained by Zeno, taking time into consideration. The time employed to cover a finite distance must in itself be a definite and therefore finite unit. But how is it possible to admit that any extension, given its divisibility into an infinite number of parts, be traversed in a finite period of time? In such a finite period, it will not be possible to traverse any given extension because space is as such divisible into an indefinite number of parts. Indeed, finite and infinite are in themselves not commensurable with one another. Therefore, if in a tract of time, it is impossible to really cover any extension at all, movement in general is not possible.

Divisibility of a finite space into an infinite number of parts proves to be Zeno's basic assumption for the definition of his paradox. But all this assumption demonstrates to Hobbes is the impossibility of any logical difficulty in conceiving motion in the parts themselves, in which finite space can be divided, since they are to be necessarily included in the distance traversed by the body in motion. What Hobbes must reject, then, in Zeno's argument is the idea that divisibility is infinite. In fact, he criticizes Zeno precisely on this point, in chapter V, paragraph 13 of *De Corpore*, arguing that "to be divided into infinite parts, is nothing else but to be divided into as many parts as any man will."[29] Therefore, Zeno's proposition, "whatsoever may be divided into parts, infinite in number, the same is infinite," is completely "false."[30] The fact that a given and limited space, and more generally, space or extension as such, may be divided into parts can by no means imply, according to Hobbes, that those parts are "infinite in number." Since the division occurs in a definite quantity, which is a finite reality, the number of parts it consists of, must be finite. This number is left to individual determination so that we might say that it is a priori indefinite; however, in no way can it effectively be infinite. The actual division of matter will therefore consist of a definite number of parts, whether we realize it or not. Thus "it is not necessary that a line should

---

[29] *De Corpore*, EW, 1: 63–64. It has been remarked that Hobbes indicates here only Zeno's general assumption for his argument against motion. See Thomas Hobbes, *Elementi di Filosofia. Il corpo—L'uomo*, trans. Antimo Negri (Turin, V.T.E.T., 1972), 123, fn. 2. In fact, Hobbes has to demonstrate that this assumption is wrong to defend the notion of motion in general and of infinitesimal motion in particular.

[30] *De Corpore, ibid.*

have parts infinite in number, or be infinite, because I can divide and subdivide it as often as I please; for how many parts soever I make, yet their number is finite."[31]

Once we have divided it into so many parts, should we say that a line is now made up of infinite parts or is in itself infinite? Zeno's thesis, in Hobbes's opinion, makes us erroneously believe that, thanks to division in parts infinite in number, a finite extension becomes in itself infinite, so that a body in motion on it never achieves its goal. But it is not possible to transmute what in itself is finite into something infinite. For Hobbes the materialist, this is not correct since every division of a finite reality into parts is always a division into a determinate and definite number of parts. Our knowledge of them may be indefinite for lack of a comprehensive view, but the parts must in themselves make up a definite and therefore finite number.

Why, then, do men call that division, a division ad infinitum? The explanation offered by Hobbes is of a nominalist type: "But because he says parts, simply, without adding how many, does not limit any number, but leaves it to the determination of the hearer, therefore we say commonly, a line may be divided infinitely; which cannot be true in any other sense."[32] The idea that every part of physical reality or this reality as a whole can be "divided infinitely" is for Hobbes a mere absurdity or just a name, a way of speaking, originating from our ignorance of how many effective parts every announced division will contain.

The core of Hobbes's criticism of Zeno seems to be in the assumption that every division into parts, no matter how small those parts, must necessarily come to an end. Once the division is made, its parts must in fact be those that have been attained, none more, none less. Whatever I am dividing, I can "make" no more parts than those I effectively make, and those parts must make up a definite, finite number. However, the statement "how many parts soever I make, yet their number is finite" does not show us, in my opinion, the reason for the finiteness of our dividing; that is, whether it comes from reality as such or from ourselves. In fact, is the number of the parts finite because our mind can operate through the calculation of finite quantities only, or because reality, being in itself finite, denies us the possibility of a division into infinite? In this last instance, there should be a point or a place beyond which we can divide no more, so that the existence of an indivisible part or element should be assumed.

But Hobbes does not believe in the existence of an ultimate, indivisible element. He is no atomist, also because the basic principle of atomism is not motion but the indivisibility of the quantum of matter.[33] Therefore, if in reality

---

[31] *Ibid.*

[32] *Ibid.*

[33] Commenting on his definition of endeavor (see fn. 25 of this paper), Hobbes writes that "by a point is not to be understood that which has no quantity, or which

nothing indivisible exists, the finiteness of our dividing must pertain to the subject that divides and not to the object divided. This means that the divisions we make are exhaustive from the standpoint of the subject who makes them but not from that of reality: objectively, there remains always the intrinsic possibility of a new division (as the development of contemporary physics has demonstrated at large). Given that possibility, should we not say, then, that an always possible new division is a division ad infinitum? If we can always calculate the half of every part we have attained, then the finite number of parts we have "made" can be endlessly subdivided without ever reaching the last half of the last part.

In the end, we have come to restate the basic assumption of Zeno's paradox on motion. Should we say, then, that Hobbes's criticism proves ineffective? To tell the truth, it seems to me that Hobbes assesses his own paradox too, in the idea that space or reality in general can be always divided, though never ad infinitum. He writes, "That which is commonly said, that space and time may be divided infinitely, is not to be so understood, as if there might be any infinite or eternal division; but rather to be taken in this sense, whatsoever is divided, is divided into such parts as may again be divided; or thus, the least divisible thing is not to be given; or, as geometricians have it, no quantity is so small, but a less may be taken."[34] If any magnitude can be divided by our calculation, and if it is in fact always divided "into such parts as may again be divided" because "the least divisible thing is not to be given," how can we deny that such a division must be conceived of as an infinite one? Otherwise, "the least divisible thing" should be given, and Hobbes should admit the existence of something that it is impossible to divide further. The contradiction, or paradox, that results from the aforesaid, originates therefore from refusing to draw the necessary conclusion in favor of the division ad infinitum after having admitted the possibility of a division in space and time "in such parts as may again be divided."

The fact is that Hobbes seems to deny the reality of infinity, not only when referred to in number but also in a substantial sense. "When we say number is infinite, we mean only that no number is expressed; for when we speak of the numbers two, three, a thousand etc. they are always finite." Therefore, when we say no more than this: "number is infinite," we use the name "number" as an "indefinite name."[35] Numbers are finite as well as the parts resulting from a division: they both indicate a definite quantity. But when we think of space

cannot by any means be divided, for there is no such thing in nature; but that, whose quantity is not at all considered, that is, whereof neither quantity nor any part is computed in demonstration; so that a point is not to be taken for an indivisible, but for an undivided thing; as also an instant is to be taken for an undivided, and not for an indivisible time" (*De Corpore, EW*, 1, 206; *OL*, 1: 177–78).

34 *De Corpore, EW*, 1: 100 (*OL*, 1: 89).
35 *Ibid.*, 99 (*OL*, 1: 87).

and time as such, how can we deny the infinite in them? Considering that when we "take or design something in our mind" in an infinite space, we give it a place. In so doing "we put an end to that space, of which we ourselves are the beginning," and the infinite comes to be determined, not in itself, but as a consequence of our mental calculation because "whatsoever any man with his mind cuts off both ways from infinite, he determines the same, that is, he makes it finite."[36]

Our "fancies" cannot contain anything infinite because infinite has for us no form whatsoever. "Whatsoever we imagine, is Finite. Therefore there is no Idea, or conception of anything we call Infinite."[37] Since we cannot have any image of it, infinite is for us like a nonbeing, about the existence of which we are not able to pose any question. "When we may question whether the world be finite or infinite, we have nothing in our mind answering to the name *world*."[38] Is then the world to be considered finite? Hobbes does not answer openly. We assume that, for him, if the world were infinite, we could never know it since all we can "imagine" is finite. And all we divide is finite too because number is finite. But how are we to interpret a statement like this: "All endeavour, whether strong or weak, is propagated to infinite distance; for it is motion."[39] If we cannot have any "idea or conception" of infinite, how can we give any meaning to the idea of a "movement" propagated to infinite distance? Furthermore, if a distance is considered to be infinite, should it not be considered divisible ad infinitum too?

The explanation of Hobbes's statement is perhaps to be found in the words "for it is motion." As we have seen, "motion produceth nothing but motion." Then endeavor, being motion, will produce endeavor, whether it occurs in void or in a space "which is filled." In fact, being motion, endeavor will cause "that which stands next in its way" to be "removed" by becoming part of endeavor itself. Endeavor will therefore multiply itself, so that matter impressed by it will "endeavor further and again remove that which stands next, and so infinitely."[40] The principle that regulates endeavor is that its propagation "proceeds infinitely," being nothing else than the propagation of motion. Of course, this propagation ad infinitum is not shown to us by experience; nonetheless it must be rationally admitted if we want to explain reality as a continuum according to rational principles. Indeed it does not matter that endeavor, "by proceeding, grows weaker and weaker, till at last it can no longer be perceived by sense; for motion may be insensible; and I do not here examine things by sense and experience, but by reason."[41]

---

36 *Ibid.*
37 *Leviathan*, 99.
38 *De Corpore, EW*, 1: 100 (OL, 1: 88–89).
39 *Ibid.*, 216 (OL 1: 182).
40 *Ibid.*, (OL, 1: 182–83).
41 *Ibid.*, 217 (OL, 1: 183), Hobbes's idea that motion propagates infinitely was

We cannot have then any image of the propagation of motion through the endless chain of endeavors. Yet, we must admit it and consider it as propagation ad infinitum. But this is like saying that the idea of the infinite, though unrepresentable, is now admitted as the logical subsidiary of the notion of infinitesimal motion. But if motion, thanks to the infinitesimal spaces it must traverse, propagates as endeavor ad infinitum, how can we deny then that those spaces be also divided "infinitely?" It seems clear that, according to Hobbes, only motion is infinite while all the rest might be finite. If infinite can be divided into parts, would we say, then, that its divisibility is not infinite? If movement be infinite, how can the space traversed by it be finite? But if that space if infinite, through endless division in parts, how can motion propagate from one point to another?

The metaphysical implications of Hobbes's theory of passions bring us back to the subtle questions posed by the first and most profound thinkers, and in what seemed to be new suddenly appears the most ancient heart of philosophy.

ridiculed by two of his enemies with the statement that "the skipping of a flea is not propagated to the Indies," to which Hobbes replied: "If I ask you how you know it, you may wonder perhaps, but answer you cannot." See Brandt, *Thomas Hobbes' Mechanical Conception of Nature*, 309–10.

Aspiring Minds: A Machiavellian Motif from Marlowe to Milton

ANTONIO D'ANDREA

The cultural prestige of Renaissance Italy met in the second half of the sixteenth century with a rising tide of English mistrust. Already in William Thomas' *History of Italy*, published in 1549, high praise for "the Italian nation which seemeth to flourish in civility most of all other at this day" is tempered by serious reservations:

> But like as I could reckon in the Italians' commendation many things more than are rehearsed, even so on the other side if I were disposed to speak of vice I might happen to find a number as ill as in any other men, which are better untouched than spoken of.[1]

Misgivings are much more pronounced in *The Scholemaster* by Roger Ascham, published posthumously in 1570. Ascham's purpose was to dissuade young English gentlemen from pursuing their education in Italy. He quotes a "common proverb," "*Inglese italianato è un diavolo incarnato*," which he interprets to mean: "You remain men in shape and fashion but become devils in life and condition." Ascham was not unaware of the importance of Italian culture, but he points out that contempt for religion and liberty to sin were the main lessons learned by English travellers, victims of "the enchantments of Circe":

> . . . they, giving themselves up to vanity, shaking off the motions of grace, driving from them the fear of God, and running headlong into all sin, first lustily contemn God, then scornfully mock his word, and also spitefully hate and hurt all well-willers thereof. Then they have in more reverence the *Triumphs* of Petrarch than the Genesis of Moses; they make more account of Tully's *Offices* than St. Paul's Epistles, of a tale in Boccaccio than a story of the Bible. Then they count as fables the holy mysteries of Christian religion. They make Christ and his gospel only serve civil policy; then neither religion cometh amiss to

---

[1] William Thomas, *The History of Italy*, ed. George B. Parks (Ithaca, NY: Cornell University press), 3, 13.

them; in time they be promoters of both openly, in place again mockers of both privily.[2]

In the last quarter of the century, the echoes of the French wars of religion, amplified by the presence in England of Huguenot exiles, together with the spread of anti-Italian Calvinist propaganda emanating from Geneva, could not fail to add to the educational worries, raised by educational travel to Italy, and to provide reasons for a deepening mistrust.[3] Despite an enduring fascination exercised by Italy and things Italian, anti-Italian sentiments became even more strident. The result, in England as well as in France,[4] was a strange mixture of attraction and repulsion, admiration and contempt, praise and condemnation for what has been called "the splendid and triumphant wickedness of Italy" — to quote from Vernon Lee's *Euphorion*.[5] The English situation was certainly different from the French. England was far from offering the bloody spectacle of internal strife offered by France. But it would be a mistake to think that the Elizabethan image of Italy could be adequately described simply in terms of a

[2] Roger Ascham, *The Scholemaster* ed. Lawrence V. Ryan (Ithaca, NY: Cornell University Press), 66, 67, 70. On the proverb, see G. B. Parks, "The First Italianate Englishmen," *Studies in the Renaissance*, 8 (1961), 197–216.
[3] Cf. my studies on: "Machiavelli, Satan, and the Gospel," *Yearbook of Italian Studies*, 1 (1971), 156–77; "Geneva 1576–78: The Italian Community and the Myth of Italy," *Peter Martyr Vermigli and Italian Reform*, ed. Joseph C. McLelland (Waterloo, Ontario: Wilfrid Laurier University Press, 1980), 53–63.
[4] For France, see Lionello Sozzi, "La polémique anti-italienne en France au XVIe siècle," in *Atti della Accademia delle Scienze di Torino*, series II, Classe di Scienze Morali, Storiche e Filologiche, vol. 106 (1972), 99–190. Sozzi calls attention to the apparent paradox of French Anti-Italianism: "Thus the century that had experienced the most wide-ranging influence in France of Italian manners, culture, literature and art; that had celebrated the monuments and majestic ruins, the flourishing cities and elegant courts of Italy; that had considered itself honoured by the presence in France of such artists as Leonardo and Cellini; that had admired the poetry of Petrarch and the prose of Boccaccio, worthy models to be followed; that had been receptive to the ideas emanating from the centres of Padua and Florence; that had seen the youth of the day cross the Alps to study in the universities of the peninsula; this same century experienced an equally strong intolerance, a rebellion, a revolt, a sharpness of criticism directed against Italy, not only extremely varied in nature and diversely motivated, but such that find no parallel in any other age" (108–09, tr. mine). Of the various aspects of anti-Italian sentiment in France, Sozzi singles out as the most important of all the competition for cultural primacy in Europe (155) — a variation on the old theme of the *translatio studii* (177, 181). No wonder the aversion for Italy reaches its highest point precisely when the influence of Italian culture is strongest. In my opinion, he makes far too little of the political and religious motives, particularly relevant in the second half of the century.
[5] Vernon Lee (pseud. of Violet Paget), *Euphorion: Being Studies of the Antique and the Mediaeval in the Renaissance* (2 vols.; London: T. F. Unwin, 1884), I, 58.

dubious taste for the outlandish and the picturesque, as it might appear, for instance, from the otherwise brilliant synthesis by John Lievsay:

> For the Elizabethan the charmed name of Italy made an appeal such as might be exercised upon the imagination of the modern American by a combination of, say, Paris, Hong Kong, and Rio de Janeiro. Italy [. . .] represented the very acme of beauty and culture, of license and corruption. With such a range of potential pleasure or disgust, it is small wonder that the Elizabethans found themselves divided in their opinions of the fascinating peninsula. Laudation and bitter attack stand side by side in the the records they have left us.[6]

More in general, the contradictory image of Renaissance Italy — the Myth of Italy — was indeed to become in succeeding centuries a paradigmatic example, at the center of discussions on the perplexing relationship between cultural values and political, moral, and religious convictions, or, more briefly put, between culture and society.[7] These ideological implications, however, would take us too far from our purpose, which is to illustrate only one small fragment of this long history.

The ambivalent attitude of the Elizabethans towards Machiavelli — "the discoursing head of a Machiavell," Ascham had written[8] — was an essential part of their overall picture of Renaissance Italy: "He horrified them, instructed them, entertained them — in fact he affected them over the whole attraction repulsion spectrum."[9] As a case in point, one could cite the Cambridge educated humanist, Gabriel Harvey, who in his published works repeatedly denounced Machiavelli, while exalting him in his *marginalia*, obviously not intended for publication: a "principal author," "Machiavelli a great writer," and so on.[10] The opposition between public and private statements ("openly" and "privily" to recall Ascham's passage already quoted) could be interpreted simply as hypocrisy and opportunism. But if this is true, especially for Harvey, it is not the whole truth, not even for him. There is more to it below the surface. Such wide swings in attitude are the symptom of a deep-seated uneasiness with a provocative writer and a disconcerting civilization. This ambivalent attitude

[6] John L. Lievsay, *The Elizabethan Image of Italy* (Ithaca, NY: Cornell University Press, 1964), 1.

[7] Cf. my article on "Alfieri e il mito dell'Italia," *Forum Italicum*, 10 (1976), 43–66.

[8] I quote from the manuscript version of *The Scholemaster*, cited by Parks, "The First Italianate Englishmen," 202.

[9] Felix Raab, *The English Face of Machiavelli* (London: Routledge & Kegan Paul; Toronto: University of Toronto Press, 1964), 67.

[10] *Gabrielis Harveij Gratulationum Valdiniensium Libri Quatuor*, Londini, Ex Officina H. Binnemani, 1578, I,7, II, 8–10. Harvey's marginal notes were collected and published only at the beginning of the twentieth century: *Marginalia*, ed. G. C. Moore-Smith (Stratford-upon-Avon: Shakespeare Head Press, 1913).

found expression in the theater, and especially in Marlowe's theater,[11] in the Machiavellian heroes of his plays, and even more specifically in a word: the verb "to aspire" and its derivatives, which forms the object of the present study.[12]

Marlowe's enthusiasm for his discovery of a new dramatic character, "the Scythian Tamburlaine" — the first of his Machiavellian heroes[13] — emerges from the Prologue to the play:

> From jygging vaines of riming mother wits,
> And such conceits as clownage keepes in pay,
> Weele leade you to the stately tent of War:
> Where you shall heare the Scythian *Tamburlaine*,
> Threatning the world with high astounding tearms
> And scourging kingdoms with his conquering sword.
> View but his picture in this tragicke glasse,
> And then applaud his fortunes if you please.
>
> (*Tamburlaine I* 1–8)

The Machiavellism of the "Scythian shepheard," in both *Tamburlaine I* and *II*, has struck critics as being quite different from that of the stock character of the Elizabethan stage.[14] Tamburlaine has too little of the fox and too much of the lion. His character is inspired by chapters 19, 20 and 21 of *The Prince*, rather than by the notorious chapters 7 and 18.[15] The endless and somewhat monotonous succession of Tamburlaine's triumphs seems to illustrate in stage terms

---

11 Cf. Marlowe's Prologue to *The Jew of Malta*, where "Machevil," who speaks the Prologue, declares: "Admir'd I am of those that hate me most." For Marlowe's works, I quote from *The Complete Works of Christopher Marlowe*, ed. Fredson Bowers (2 vols.; Cambridge, Mass.: Harvard University Press, 1973).

12 In quoting I have, therefore, always italicized this verb and its derivatives.

13 For the chronology of Marlowe's works, see John E. Bakeless, *The Tragicall History of Christopher Marlowe*, (2 vols.; Cambridge, Mass.: Harvard University Press, 1942).

14 See, for instance, Roy W. Battenhouse, *Marlowe's Tamburlaine* (Nashville, Tenn.: Vanderbilt University Press, 1941), 206–16.

15 The chapter titles are as follows: Chap. 19, *De contemptu et odio fugiendo* ("On avoiding Contempt and Hatred"); Chap. 20, *An arces et multa alia quae cotidie a principibus fiunt utilia an inutilia sint* ("Whether Fortresses and Other Things That Princes Employ Every Day Are Useful or Useless"); Chap. 21, *Quod principem deceat ut egregius habeatur* ("What is necessary to a Prince that he May Be Considered Excellent"); Chap. 7, *De principatibus novis qui alienis armis et fortuna acquiruntur* ("On new Principates That Are Obtained through the Military Power of Others and from Fortune"); Chap. 18, *Quomodo fides a principibus sit servanda* ("In What Way Faith should Be Kept By Princes"). For Machiavelli's works I have used the edition by Mario Martelli (Florence: Sansoni, 1971). The English translation is by Allan H. Gilbert (*The Prince and Other Works*, New York: Farrar, Straus, 1946).

Machiavelli's paradoxical remark that princes profit from adversity, and "rise high," as he says, "by ascending the ladder provided by their enemies."[16]

Certainly everything that Machiavelli requires of his prince to have him avoid contempt — he should not appear "variable, volatile, effeminate, cowardly, or irresolute" and must strive to show in his actions "greatness, spirit, gravity, and fortitude"[17] — is followed by Marlowe to make of Tamburlaine a hero, who for all his cruelty, violence, ruthlessness, for all the bloodshed and suffering he causes, can yet arouse the admiration of the audience. His ambiguous grandeur finds expression in the notion of "*aspyring* minds,"[18] to which he

[16] *Prince* 19 (290): "Sanza dubbio e' principi diventano grandi quando superano le difficultà e le opposizioni che sono fatte loro; e però la fortuna, massime quando vuole fare grande uno principe nuovo, il quale ha maggiore necessità di acquistare reputazione che uno ereditario, li fa nascere de' nemici, e li fa fare delle imprese contro, acciò che quello abbi cagione di superarle, e su per quella scala che gli hanno pòrta e' nimici sua, salire più alto." ("There is no doubt that princes become great when they overcome difficulties and opposition. Therefore Fortune avails herself of this, especially when she wishes to bestow greatness on a new prince, who has more need to acquire reputation than a hereditary one. For she causes enemies to rise up against him, and makes him undertake campaigns against them, that he may have the opportunity to conquer them.")

[17] *Prince* 19 (284): "Contennendo lo fa essere tenuto vario, leggieri, effeminato, pusillanime, irresoluto: da che uno principe si debbe guardare come da uno scoglio, e ingegnarsi che nelle azioni sua si riconosca grandezza, animosità, gravità, fortezza." ("Contempt is his portion if he is held to be variable, volatile, effeminate, cowardly, or irresolute. From these a prince should guard himself as from a rock in the sea. He should strive in all his actions to give evident signs of greatness, spirit, gravity, and fortitude.") See also the rest of this chapter as well as Chapter 21. In *Discourses* I.27, Machiavelli denounces the mediocrity of men, who "do not know how to be either honourably bad or perfectly good; and when evil has a certain grandeur or is somehow generous they shrink from it" (tr. mine): "non sanno essere onorevolmente cattivi, o perfettamente buoni; e, come una *malizia* ha in sé grandezza, o è in alcuna parte *generosa*, e' non vi sanno entrare" (italics mine). Machiavelli's notion of *generosa malizia* foreshadows the ambiguous grandeur of Marlowe's Tamburlaine.

[18] For the use of *aspiring* as a participial adjective, see the à *Oxford English Dictionary*. The earliest instances recorded are in 1565 and, with the same meaning as in Marlowe ("ardently desirous of advancement or distinction; of lofty aim, ambitious"), in 1577, in the English translation of Heinrich Bullinger's *Decades* (*Fiftie Godlie and Learned Sermons*, tr. "H.I. Student in Divinitie," London: Ralphe Newberrie, 1577) where we find the exact same expression: "For the honouring of Ministers of the Churches, which are the Pastors, teachers, and fathers of christian people, any things are wont to be alledged by them, who covet to reigne as Lordes, than to serve as ministers in the Church of Christe. But we which are not of that *aspiring mynde*, do aknowledge that they are given us by the Lorde, and that the Lorde by them speake to us" (italics mine). The *O.E.D.* cites also an example from Spenser (1579): "Then make thee winges of Thine *aspyring* wit" (*Shepeardes Calendar*, October, line 84). But there is no reference to the frequent occurrences of the verb *to aspire*, in its various forms (but always in the same sense), in Marlowe's works or even in Ralegh's or Milton's: see below. It might be interesting to note that the expression "aspiring mind," as used by Marlowe (pp. xxii,

resorts in an attempt to justify the murder of his ally and protector, Cosroe, and the usurpation of the Persian throne:

> Nature that fram'd us of foure Elements,
> Warring within our breasts for regiment,
> Doth teach us all to have *aspyring* minds.
> (*Tamburlaine I* II.7.18–20)

This Machiavellism, of Marlovian stripe, can be found in subsequent plays combined with the more obvious and superficial brand and its usual baggage of deceit, treachery, dissimulation, poison, that go under the name of "pollicie"; of villainous schemes, after the model of Cesare Borgia's stratagem at Senigallia; of perfidy pretending to be diabolically subtle and covert, while being instead all too obvious and even grotesque and ridiculous. The main traits of this cliché are easily recognizable in the Machiavellian characters of these other plays. Yet, in spite of the great diversity of circumstances and disparity of results, these characters are never turned, at least entirely, into simple villains: they still retain something of the heroic greatness of Tamburlaine, something of his very special Machiavellianism.

The continuity and the persistent ambivalence are underscored by the repeated occurrence of one and the same word, in the same sense. In *Tamburlaine I*, the notion of "*aspyring* minds" is foreshadowed by the words of Tamburlaine's victim, Cosroe — "What means this divelish shepheard *to aspire*" (II.6.1) — and prior to this by Tamburlaine's words to Theridamas, "And both our soules *aspire* celestiall thrones" (I.2.237). In *The Massacre at Paris*, "aspiring" always refers to the Duke of Guise: "th'*aspiring* Guise" (I.1.36), "my *aspiring* winges" (I.1.104), "*aspiring* Guise" (17.828), "his *aspiring* thoughts" (18.923). In *Edward II*, the word is used by Mortimer junior with reference to himself, "thy vertue that *aspires* to heaven" (III.1.257), without any specific reference, "Base fortune, now I see, that in thy wheele / There is a point, to which when men *aspire*, / They tumble hedlong downe" (V.6.59–61); and by others, with reference to Lancaster, "*aspiring* Lancaster" (I.1.93), and to Gaveston, "Ignoble vassaile that, like *Phaeton*, / *aspir'st* unto the guidance of the sunne" (I.4.16–17) — both suspected of having an attitude similar to Mortimer's.[19]

In all instances, the word denotes an attitude of defiance, of rebellion

---

146–48), was adopted to describe the general attitude ("the defining characteristic," p. xxiv) of the "Elizabethan younger generation" in the title of Anthony Esler's book, *The aspiring mind of the Elizabethan younger generation* (Durham, N.C.: Duke University Press, 1966; see especially pp. xxi–xxiv and 146–48).

[19] The Machiavellian protagonist of *The Jew of Malta* is an exception: the word in question is not used in his case. Barabas is not a prince nor a king, and his political machinations in the second part of the play verge on the ridiculous. The air of grandeur he has about him at the beginning only lasts until the middle of Act II.

against the established order of things, an intense and questionable desire (questionable because of its ambivalent implications)for what appears, or actually is, out of reach. In this same sense, but in a lighter vein, *aspiring* is used by Marlowe at the end of the first sestiad of *Hero and Leander*, apropos of the "fruitful wits" driven by their ambition to explore the furthest reaches of the globe:

> And fruitfull wits that in *aspiring* are,
> Shall discontent run into regions farre.   (I.477–78)[20]

Marlowe's lines seem to echo a passage in a treatise on politics, largely inspired by Machiavelli's *Prince*, though in frequent discord with it: "To cut off such as excel the rest in wealth, favour, or nobility, or be of a pregnant or *aspiring* wit, and so are fearful to a tyrant. . . ."

We have here an example of one of the devices used by "a barbarous and openly declared tyranny," listed in *The Prince, or Maxims of State, written by Sir Walter Rawleg, and presented to Prince Henry*.[21] The attribution to Ralegh has been questioned, on the basis of internal evidence,[22] with arguments I do not consider very convincing. For instance, the denunciation of the "false doctrine of the Machiavellian policy," coming as it does right after the appropriation, without citing the source, of what Machiavelli says in *Prince* 19, has led to the conclusion that the author of the *Maxims* "travaillait donc sur un canevas utilisant Machiavel à son insu et n'était pas capable de le reconnaître. Il ne peut s'agir de Ralegh." Ralegh was well versed in the works of Machiavelli. But the fact that the author of the *Maxims* "juxtapose l'exactitude, les contresens flagrants, et les attaques les plus conventionnelles sur la pensée de Machiavel," cannot be used to disprove Ralegh's authorship.[23] Inconsistencies of this kind are not very different from those we find in *The History of the World*, unquestionably by Ralegh: They are further examples of the Elizabethan ambivalence.[24]

---

[20] This is the reading to be found in the early editions. The correction 'inaspiring', meaning 'without ambition', adopted Dby some modern editors, makes it difficult to interpret the passage. The original reading has been restored by Bowers: The *Complete Works of Christopher Marlowe*, ed. F. Bowers, II, 502.

[21] *The Works of Sir Walter Ralegh* (8 vols.; Oxford: Oxford University Press, 1829), VIII, 23.

[22] Pierre Lefranc, *Sir Walter Ralegh écrivainà* (Paris: Armand Colin; Québec: Presses de l'Université Laval, 1968), 67–70. According to Lefranc (50), the *Maxims* happened to be among Ralegh's papers.

[23] *Ibid.*, 69, 68.

[24] A balanced account of Ralegh's attitude towards Machiavelli can be found in F. Raab, *The English Face of Machiavelli*, 70–73. Raab does not question the attribution of the *Maxims* to Ralegh. Lefranc's assurance is, at the very least, excessive: "Cette prévention contre Machiavel s'associait fréquemment à la méconnaissance de son

In any case, even if Raleigh is not the author of the *Maxims* and they just happened to be among his papers, the similarity between the passage in *Hero and Leander* and the passage in the *Maxims*, too close to be simply fortuitous ("fruitful wits . . . in aspiring" and "pregnant and aspiring wit," "run into regions farre" and "cut off"), establishes a connection between Marlowe and Ralegh (it is intrinsically difficult not to think of Ralegh in reading Marlowe's lines), precisely with respect to the attitude of rebellion implicit in the verb *to aspire*: an attitude and a word characteristic of Marlowe's version of Machiavellianism and of the singular grandeur of his Machiavellian heroes.

Perhaps more interesting is the use of the word in another work attributed to Ralegh, the treatise entitled *The Cabinet Council: Containing the Chief Arts of Empire and Mysteries of State*.[25] In chapter 5, "Of monarchies tyrannical," the author deals with tyrannical princes, who "do *aspire* unto greatness" and succeed in retaining power by whatever means, honest or dishonest, without respect for justice, moral conscience, or the law of nations or of nature. The passage continues as follows:

> . . . a prince by such impious means *aspired*, and desiring to hold that he hath gained, will take order that the cruelties he committeth may be done roundly, suddenly, and, as it were, at an instant. . . . Example, Dionysius and Agathocles.

The attempt here to summarize what Machiavelli says of "crudeltà male usate o bene usate," in Chapter 8 of *The Prince*, is obvious. Chapters 6, 7 and 9 of *The Prince* are condensed in Chapter 6 of *The Cabinet Council*, "Of new-found monarchies and principalities, with the means to perpetuate them." Over less than two pages, the verbà *to aspire* occurs no fewer than six times, in a variety of usages and constructions, but always apropos of the prince and his ambitions, in a context of clearly Machiavellian cast: "Some other princes are that from private estate have *aspired* to sovereignty,not by unnatural or impious proceedings, as the former, but by virtue and fortune, and being *aspired* have found no great difficulty to be maintained." "A prince being *aspired*." "The second sort of new princes are such as be *aspired* by favour or corruption, or by the virtue or greatness of fortune or friends." "A certain fortunate craft and wittiness, because he *aspireth* either by favour of the people, or by favour of the nobility." "A prince in this sort *aspired*, to maintain his estate, must first consider well by which of these factions aforesaid he is advanced; for if by favour of great men he be *aspired*, then must he meet with many difficulties."

oeuvre et à l'incompréhension de sa pensée. L'attitude de Ralegh envers le Florentin est, sur ce point comme sur tous les autres, aux antipodes de celle-ci. Les *Maxims* ne sont pas son oeuvre" (*Sir Walter Ralegh écrivain*, 70).
[25] *The Works of Sir Walter Ralegh*, VIII, 35–105; for Chapters 5 and 6 see pp. 42–44.

The word itself is not to be found anywhere in Machiavelli's text. It does derive, however, from an interpretation of his thought not unlike the interpretation that prompted Marlowe to use it in designating the Machiavellian aspirations of his characters.

The Cabinet Council was first published in 1658 by Milton, who owned the manuscript, as a work by "the Ever-renowned Knight Raleigh." Ralegh's authorship is doubtful.[26] At any rate, Milton resorted to the same word in his *Paradise Lost* to describe the pride, the ambition, the "unbounded hope" of Satan, "the proud *aspirer*" (VI.90), by antonomasia:

> ... *aspiring*
> To set himself in glory, above his peers,
> He trusted to have equaled the Most High. ... (I.38–40)[27]

> ... and from despair
> Thus high uplifted beyond hope, *aspires*
> Beyond thus high, insatiate to pursue
> Vain war with Heav'n. ...   (II.6–9)

> ... Thy hope was to have reached
> The highth of thy *aspiring* unopposed,
> The throne of God unguarded. ...   (VI.131–33)

We find it used absolutely (as in some of the quotations from *The Cabinet Council*), almost in a technical sense, to denote the kind of aspiration that led Satan to rebel against God: "some other Power / As great might have *aspired* ..." (IV.61–62). It is used again by Satan, in outlining his plan to incite Adam and Eve "to reject envious commands"designed "To keep them low whom knowledge might exalt / Equal with gods" (IV.523–26): "*Aspiring* to be such, / They taste and die" (IV.526–27). And then again by Satan, referring to himself, to designate his ambition to rise to the heights of God, the very God responsible for forcing him to stoop to the level of the lowly serpent:

> This essence to incarnate and imbrute,
> That to the height of deity *aspired*;
> But what will not ambition and revenge
> Descend to? Who *aspires* must down as low
> As high he soared. ...   (IX.166–70)[28]

[26] According to Ernest A. Strathmann ("A Note on the Ralegh Canon," *Times Literary Supplement*, 15 April 1956, 228), the author is probably Thomas Bedingfield.

[27] For the quotations from *Paradise Lost* I have used the edition by Douglas Bush: *The Complete Poetical Works of John Milton* (Boston: Houghton Mifflin, 1965).

[28] Still in *Paradise Lost*, it is used in much the same sense, with reference to the rebellious angels (III.392, VI.383, 793, 899), to Nimrod's tyrannical ambition and his defiance of God (XII.64), and to Adam's "folly to *aspire*" (XII.560) to more knowledge

The passage is reminiscent of Mortimer junior's final words in *Edward II*, V.6.59–61. In fact, the very context, metaphorical or conceptual, in which even elsewhere Marlowe employs the word, may well have suggested its application to Satan. In expounding his notion of "aspyring minds," Tamburlaine invokes the precedent of "mightie Jove," who dethroned his father to take his place, and the heavenwards flight of the soul, "Still climing after knowledge infinite," finally to conclude with "That perfect blisse and sole felicitie, / The sweet fruition of an earthly crowne." This awkward conclusion is often denounced as anticlimactic, introducing a discordance indicative of the *generatio aequivoca* of his greatness. In *Tamburlaine I*, there is also, as we have seen, "*divelish* shepheard *to aspire*," "*aspire . . . celestiall* thrones," and in *The Massacre at Paris*, "*aspiring winges*."

The lexical coincidence that links Marlowe, Ralegh, and Milton might contribute to a more accurate understanding of the ambivalent nature of Milton's Satan, "one of the most fertile — and also unsettling — characters in English literature."[29] "Both enticing and frightening,"[30] "attractive and evil, appealing and destructive,"[31] he has been the object of a controversy that goes back well beyond the Romantic period[32] between those who extolled his "high revolutionary heroism," and those who denounce his speeches "big with absurdity," his moral turpitude, his deceitfulness, his folly. "A more reasonable reaction," as has been remarked, "is to recognize that the poem is insolubly ambivalent, insofar as the reading of Satan's 'character' is concerned."[33] This seems to be a widely accepted opinion today. Now whatever biblical, theological, psychological, or even psychoanalytical explanations might be suggested for this ambivalence, whatever its esthetic or dramatic effect, whatever its conjectured sources ("no convincing single source for Milton's Satan has been found"[34]), it would be difficult not to recognize the echo of another, pre-existing ambivalence and to exclude any trace of it from the intertext of the poem.

Milton's direct knowledge of Machiavelli, at least by the time he was writing

than "this vessel can contain" (XII.559). Only in one case is it used, with no negative connotation, in a quite different context – the description of the hierarchical chain of being: "flowers and their fruit, / Man's nourishment, by gradual scale sublimed, / To vital spirits *aspire*, to animal. / To intellectual . . ." (V.482–85). The progression from the physical to the spiritual level recalls the passage in *Tamburlaine I* II.7.18–29, already referred to several times in the present study.

29 Neil Forsyth, "The devil in Milton," *Etudes de Lettres*, 2 (1989), 79.

30 *Ibid.*, 80.

31 *A Milton Encyclopedia*, ed. William B. Hunter Jr. (9 vols.; Lewisburg: Bucknell University Press, 1978–83), VII, 166.

32 J. Carey, "Milton's Satan," *The Cambridge Companion to Milton*, ed. Dennis Danielson (Cambridge: Cambridge University Press, 1989), 132.

33 *Ibid.*, 132.

34 *Ibid.*, 131.

Paradise Lost, seems beyond doubt.[35] He certainly knew *The Cabinet Council* that he himself had published, and he probably noticed the borrowings from Machiavelli and the peculiar meaning of the word that he was to use in connection with a crucial idea and a central character of his poem. Moreover, the parallels we have quoted suggest a familiarity with Marlowe's plays, not limited to *Doctor Faustus*.[36] No wonder then if his ambivalent presentation of Satan carried to the depths of hell the bewildering glory of the aspiring Machiavellian hero — a spark of the wicked splendor that Renaissance Italy had been for the Elizabethans.

[35] Milton began writing *Paradise Lost* around 1657–58 and finished it in 1665; the first edition was published in 1667: see Bush's Introduction to his edition of Milton's *Poetical Works*, pp. xxiii–xxv. On Milton and Machiavelli, see F. Raab, *The English Face of Machiavelli*, 175–81. Milton's mentions of Machiavelli, in *An Apology Against a Pamphlet Call'd A Modest Confutation* (1642), and in *The Doctrine and Discipline of Divorce* (1643), are not very telling and "indicate no necessary first-hand knowledge of Machiavelli's writings": "The seventeen entries in the *Commonplace Book*, however, dated to 1651–2, present a very different story. Milton by this time was certainly familiar with *The Discourses* and *The Arte of Warre*, both of which he had studies in an Italian edition. . . . There is no direct evidence that Milton had read *The Prince*, though circumstantially it seems unlikely that he had not" (F. Raab, *The English Face of Machiavelli*, 177).

[36] A "recollection" of *Doctor Faustus* in *Paradise Lost* IV.363–64 has been detected by J. Carey, "Milton's Satan," 140. — I wish to thank Professor Archibald E. Malloch — an old friend of mine and Perez Zagorin's — for his help with Bullinger's *Sermons* (see above note 18) and Milton's *Paradise Lost*. I am particularly happy to include his name here: a reminder of Perez's years at McGill.

Performing the Enlightenment Self: Henry Fielding and the History of Identity

EDWARD HUNDERT

> One easily forgets that human education proceeds along highly theatrical lines. In a quite theatrical manner the child is taught how to behave; logical arguments only come later. When such-and-such occurs, it is told (or sees), one must laugh. It joins in when there is laughter, without knowing why. . . . In the same way it joins in shedding tears, not only weeping because the grown-ups do so but also feeling genuine sorrow. This can be seen at funerals, whose meaning escapes children entirely. These are theatrical events which form the character. The human being copies gestures, miming, tones of voice. And weeping arises from sorrow, but sorrow also arises from weeping.
>
> Bertold Brecht,
> *Two Essays on Unprofessional Acting*

It has become something of a commonplace to refer to Hanoverian England as a society notable for the theatricality of its public life. It was one, as Roy Porter puts it, in which "grandees stage-managed a . . . studied theater of power: conspicuous menace (and mercy) from the Judge's Bench; exemplary punishment tempered with silver linings of philanthropy, largesse and selective patronage; a grudging and calculating display of *noblesse oblige*."[1]

Contemporaries often spoke in a similar language. They noticed that the distribution of rank and power seemed to depend in significantly altered ways upon the ability of individuals, especially in the metropolis, successfully to display in speech, costume, and manner the outward signs of their real or pretended status.[2] In what has been called the first consumer society,[3] an expanding market for good increasingly commercialized, and thus made unstable, the tangible symbols of hierarchy through which persons announced

---

[1] Roy Porter, *English Society in the Eighteenth Century* (Harmondsworth: Penguin, 1982), 81.

[2] Richard Sennett, *The Fall of Public Man* (Cambridge: University Press, 1976), 65–107.

[3] Neil McKendrick, John Brewer, and J. H. Plumb, *The Birth of a Consumer Society* (London: Hutchinson, 1982).

their social identities. Both in philosophy and fiction, in the writing of Mandeville and Chesterfield, of Richardson and Burke, the dramatically mobile social actor in a world of commerce became a figure symbolizing a public sphere whose altered conventions strikingly resembled those of the stage.

In what follows I will try to show how Henry Fielding's work serves as a rich point of departure for examining this concern and for understanding the interpenetration of theater, society, and the individual in the moral vocabulary of eighteenth-century intellectuals.

I

Everyday speech and behavior express what members of a culture regard as its most salient characteristics, the almost tangible elements of existence that appear as naturally embedded features of social life. These components of common-sense knowledge come to hand so readily, and without apparent effort, that an attempt to make them objects of study would appear to invite a thicket of interpretive difficulties where few need to exist. For just as a native speaker of English may find the formal study of rhetoric a supremely difficult task, and nevertheless converse with considerable fluency and effect, so too can she be a delightful dinner guest and yet be dazzled, when not driven to disbelief, upon being presented with the startlingly complex rules of behavior she had unwittingly followed.

Nevertheless, persons for whom the ordinary demands of social exchange are so habitual as to appear prereflective regularly distinguish these normal, "natural" styles of behavior from other, glaringly rule-governed practices in which they engage. The forms and strategies of dress and address at weddings and funerals, for example, may be said to stand in relation to the performances of everyday life as does a foreign language to one's native tongue. We learn the latter kind of conduct insensibly, without taking much notice of how its rules are acquired and, indeed, mostly without the awareness of rules at all. Ritual and ceremony, on the other hand, are "formal" occasions in part because we recognize the behavior that constitutes their practice as governed by dense rules whose study, as Castiglione classically observed, is required by any person seeking to perform them well. We may think it ludicrous to read a treatise on how to stroll in the garden, but at the same time hope a manual is at hand to instruct us on how to walk in St. James's Park with the Queen. Styles of behavior and formal performances that are understood as learned, and thus consciously practiced, tend uniformly to be distinguished from those other, "spontaneous" features of our interaction with others. To call any everyday performance "ritualized" is to judge that performance as unsuccessful because it is obviously rehearsed and to view the person performing it as stilted because she behaves unnaturally.

This readily acknowledged distinction between spontaneous and learned behavior, and between everyday and ritualized practices, tends to blur the further removed in time and place a society is from the culture of someone reflecting upon it. Montesquieu's Persian travelers understood this truth before it became the anthropologist's truism, while historians of the *ancien régime* have shown that the daily lives of Montesquieu's contemporaries were governed by as textured a set of unwritten behavioral ordinances as the baroque formalities Saint-Simon recorded at Versailles. We cannot now help but view the everyday speech and behaviour of a conventional Hanoverian squire as elements of a deeply inscribed system of experience and response that were features of the natural, prereflective domain of his daily existence. One might say that everyday life can be constituted as an object of study when its components have become what Iurii Lotman calls semiotized: when actions are seen as systematically encoded, spontaneous performaces of speech, gesture, and act can be understood at structured signifying units relating to the plot, style, and genre of a larger communal narrative.[4]

When historians and anthropologists attempt to account for the behavior of those they study by assuming that habitual social practices are composed of modeled performances, it is because these practices are forms of communication and because the transmission of meanings rests upon a shared, but not necessarily self-conscious, participation in specific forms of social life. Most forms of behavior are not only ways of doing something but of getting something said and thus must be undertaken with measures of tact, those degrees of emphasis given to elements of a performance that shape its meaning and so constitute the tactics of an individual's public life. The actions of a Hanoverian landlord or a popular radical are not only attemps to fulfill the socially specified requirements of a successful performance in the roles they inhabit, they are meant as well to tell a chosen audience something about the kind of persons they are and how these particular persons relate to the actions they take and the ends they seek to achieve. Yet precisely because actions are performances that transmit information about the person performing them, their success depends upon the relevant audience grasping both action and actor in their proper context. An apparently ritualized expression of sympathy to a distraught friend on the occasion of his failed romance will not only fail to move one's friend, it will cast doubt upon the quality of one's own feelings. Brecht's comment is a useful reminder that even our deepest sentiments are socially constructed, that they can only be conveyed through socially understood

---

[4] See particularly Iurii M. Lotman, "The Poetics of Everyday Behavior in Eighteenth-Century Russian Culture," in *The Semiotics of Russian Cultural History*, ed. A. D. and A. S. Nakhimovsky (Ithaca: Cornell University Press, 1985)), 67–94, and "The Theater and Theatricality as Components of Early Nineteenth-Century Culture," in *The Semiotics of Russian Culture*, ed. Ann Shukman (Ann Arbor: University of Michigan Press, 1984), 141–64.

conventions and that these conventions are learned dramaturgically. It also suggests that when performances are so understood in the course of daily life, that when apparently spontaneous, unrehearsed expressions of feeling *appear* as tactical, crafted dramatic acts, then the persons performing them take on the character of actors performing a role, of impersonating another, of offering a persona that does not match what lies behind the mask.

Moments of this kind may be the site of a crisis in personal relationships, when intimacy is destroyed by the exposure of insincerity. Such moments are also the standard materials of parody, in which the depiction of affect takes place within a strictly aestheticized, scripted, and thus utterly predictable domain. In each case what one may call a behavioral style is denaturalized and deemed theatrical as its codes become transparent, while the person performing in it is devalued as his speech and action appear to follow scripts of someone else's design. The tension here between sincere behavior on the one hand and inappropriately ritualized performance on the other has a long and intricate history, but it draws much of its contemporary force from the relatively recent notion of a person as autonomous, as a singular, indivisible subject whose words and deeds are the bearers of a unique identity.

Personal identity as a problem in philosophical discourse was virtually invented by Locke, who bequeathed to the Enlightenment the term "consciousness," which he coined to denote the appropriate existential entity whose continuity was required for the identification of a self. Its novelty required Locke's French translator heavily to annotate his edition of *The Essay Concerning Human Understanding*, since the force of the term could only with difficulty be conveyed in contemporary usage.[5] A number of writers have tried to locate the emergence of an authentic subject in the subsequent eighteenth-century exploration of consciousness, pointing to the period's unusually rich literature of self-examination as the source of the modern discovery of individuality and of the radical, irreducable privacy of an individual life.[6] Prominent features of our current self-understanding seem to be prefigured in this literature, some of whose metaphors of identity have been incorporated into our own. Yet we

[5] John Locke, *An Essay Concerning Human Understanding*, ed. P. H. Nidditch (Oxford: Oxford University Press, 1975), 2: xxvii, "Of Identity and Diversity." See, *OED*, *s.v.* "consciousness," and Emilienne Naert, "Le conscience de soi ou 'self-consciousness' chez Locke," in *Genèse de la conscience moderne*, ed. Robert Ellrodt (Paris, PUF, 1983), 175–81.

[6] Amongst the more useful pieces of a large literature, see Marcel Mauss, "A Category of the Human Mind: The Notion of a Person, the Notion of 'Self'," *Sociology and Psychology: Essays*, trans. Ben Brewster (London: Rout;edge, 1979), 57–94; Lionel Trilling, *Sincerity and Authenticity* (Cambridge Mass.: Harvard University Press, 1971); Erving Goffman, *The Presentation of Self in Everyday Life* (New York: Vintage, 1959); Thomas C. Heller, *et al.*, *Reconstructing Individualism* (Stanford: Univesity Press, 1986), and Michael Carrithers, *et al.*, eds., *The Category of the Person* (Cambridge: University press, 1985).

should beware, as Locke put it, of interpreting an author's words "by the notions of our philosophy," and restrain an impulse to view authenticity as one of the last stages of a progressive narrative of internal exploration that naturally concludes with our current sensibilities. Instead, one might usefully follow Brecht's insight and inspect the dramaturgical requirements of the figure of an "authentic person" by first retrieving the context of practices enabling the representation of self-identity as a cultural artifact. Henry Fielding's work is an exemplary source for that recovery.

II

The ancient notion of the *theatrium mundi*, a world in which persons inhabit their social roles as actors, derives much of its continuing metaphorical power from the traditions of the Western stage. Aside from church, in which attendance was compulsory, theaters were in Europe the privileged environments where virtually all social groups gathered voluntarily to form a common audience. Within these theatrical settings each group stood in a dramaturgical relation to the others. Shared styles of speech, manner, and costume set off the scene of each group's responses from those of the rest, while separate modes of intercourse distinguished the socially segregated audiences of European theaters and encouraged the analogy between the drama performed on the stage and the performances of members of each group for others. Society as a theater was a theme of Montesquieu's *Persian Letters*, as it was the motto of Petronius's *Satyricon*, because the theatricality of public life could provide an instantly comprehensible metaphor for the depiction of social space and generate compelling idioms for the examination of an individual's actions within it.

More important perhaps, the rhetorical symbiosis of the vocabularies of stage and society was further encouraged by the etymological dependence of the word "person" in Western languages on the figure of the masked actor. As Hobbes put it,

> The word Person is latine . . . , as *Persona* in latine signifies the *disguise*, or *outward appearance* of a man, counterfeited on the Stage; and sometimes more particularly that part of it, which disguiseth the face, as a Mark of Visard: And from the Stage, hath been translated to any Representer of speech and action, as well in Tribunalls, as Theatres. So that a *Person*, is the same that an *Actor* is, both on the Stage and in common Conversation; and to *Personate*, is to Act, or Represent himself, or an other.[7]

---

[7] Thomas Hobbes, "Of Man," *Leviathan*, chapter 16, ed. C. B. Macpherson (Harmondsworth: Penguin, 1968), 217–18.

Hobbes captured the truth that actions on the stage and in society have as part of their content the possibility of being variously performed and understood as features of a role. On the same occasion the same role may be filled by more than one person, while on successive occasions more than one role may be filled by the same person. Not only kings have two bodies. Since roles are filled by persons who of necessity perform them in certain ways to the exclusion of others, these performances not only invite but always demand interpretation by members of the audience to whom they are addressed. For meanings can only be generated within the relations between person, role, and audience in both decidedly social and specifically theatrical settings.

If languages of social perception and idioms of self-description are infused with inherent dramaturgical components, these components have taken on special relevance during those historical moments when the demands of inherited social roles are experienced as formally imposed constraints, as merely ritualized and thus artificial vehicles for the lives of persons inhabiting them. Lionel Trilling took Polonius's injunction, "to thine own self to true," as the starting point for his study of authenticity when he noticed that the dramatic portrayal of self-inspecting characters like Hamlet and Iago usefully could serve to represent a shift in moral attitudes toward personal repsonsibility. Trilling saw in the writing of Shakespeare's generation, and of Hobbes's, "something like a mutation in human nature,"[8] which occurred when a sudden efflorescence of the theater provided terms found uniquely appropriate for the portrayal of felt disjunctions between self and role. He understood this movement as an expression of the anxieties experienced by intellectuals and those he called "puritans" as they withheld emotional commitment from the weakened symbols of public authority and introspectively severed connections from their socially specified roles. In the next century, when the narrator of Tom Jones departed from the telling of his hero's story to reflect on the colonization of public discourse by theatrical metaphor, he could count on the reader's consciousness of role distance as a pervasive category of social perception. The "comparison between the world and the stage," he wrote,

> has been carried so far and become so general that some words proper
> to the theater and which were at first metaphorically applied to the
> world are now indiscriminately and literally spoken of both: thus stage
> and scene are by common use grown as familiar to us, when we speak of
> life in general, as when we confine ourselves to dramatic performances;
> and when we mention transactions behind the curtain, St. James's is
> more likely to occur to our own thoughts than Drury-Lane.[9]

---

[8] Trilling, Sincerity and Authenticity, 19.
[9] Henry Fielding, The History of Tom Jones. A Foundling (1749), VII, 1: "A Comparison between the World and the Stage."

Fielding accepted this theatricized public domain as his representative subject, in which "the Hypocrite may be said to be the player, [as] . . . indeed the
Greeks called them both by one and the same name." Readers of *Tom Jones*
were instructed that the characters of the novel should be considered as actors
in a double sense. Their performances enact roles understood as such by the
generalized "audience" of society, itself divided into the socially segregated
"boxes, stalls and balconies" where theatrical responses form essential aspects
of the spectacle on view. Fielding's object was conceptually to isolate these
spectators by situating them as the central and previously unconsidered characters "at this great drama." His fictions were meant to serve as appropriate
vehicles for the representation of their consciousness, one aware of the possibility of its detachment from any particular social embodiment, and for the
understanding of character as a circumscribed feature of this self-awareness.

Two texts are of particular importance here: the Preface to *Joseph Andrews*
(1742), in which Fielding sought to establish the conventions of a fictional
genre suitable for the representation of a theatricized world, and the "Essay on
the Knowledge and of the Characters of Men" (1743), in which he reflected
upon the behavioral protocols his fictions would, he claimed, for the first time
appropriately represent. Fielding wished to provide readers, conceived as the
audience at a drama in which they participated, with sets of instructions
necessary to decode its rules. The aesthetic instrument of this educative art was
"the exactest copying of nature," a representational strategy requiring the
writer to describe "not men but manners; not an individual but a species."[10]

Fielding conceived of his "comic prose epic" as a mechanism for decoding
"the ridiculous," by which he meant the figure whose source of action is
affectation and whose affectation derives from vanity and hypocrisy. His claim
that these figures demanded a new genre for their depiction was part of a larger
aesthetic enterprise of unmasking those "appearances," as a contemporary
guide to manners put it, which "give things in some measure a second existence."[11] Fielding saw in the "rational and useful pleasure" that flowed from
what he called the imitation of nature a singularly effective device for exposing
deceit within a growing, socially heterogeneous public whose relationships
were guided by newly emerging and still volatile standards of propriety.

Addison and Voltaire drew attention to the novelty in London of a public
sphere comprised of private associations like the coffeehouse, and public institutions like the stock exchange, which promoted wholly consensual forms of
intercourse between once formally stratified groups.[12] In these metropolitan
settings personalities themselves appeared as mobile as the forms of property

[10] Henry Fielding, *Joseph Andrews*, Preface.
[11] Stephen Philpot, *Polite Education* (London, 1759), 59.
[12] See, Joseph Addison, *Spectator*, 15 December 1711, and Voltaire, *Lettres Philosop-
hiques* (1732), Lettre VII, penultimate paragraph.

that occasioned their existence. Mandeville articulated this vision in *The Fable of the Bees* (1723 and 1729), and Fielding provided an exemplary history of the fugitive transformations of identity the modern city made possible in Wilson's autobiographical narrative at the structural center of *Joseph Andrews*.[13] Fielding evoked Mandeville's notorious book when he observed that men now "employed their utmost abilities to invent systems by which the artful and cunning . . . may be enabled to impose upon the rest of the world."[14] His aesthetic took as its point of departure the widely held belief that this public had, in the process of its formation, acquired fresh emotional committments as it self-consciously engaged in altered social practices. It could no longer be relied upon to respond to the inherited forms of communal moral instruction, clerical injunction, and classical tragedy, toward which its responses had "soured." Yet this burgeoning reading pubic seemed immediately responsive to the voice of satire, that staple genre of an exploding publishing industry, in which rhetorical inversions of character pointedly elevated newly crafted behavioral styles into objects demanding self-reflection. While vanity and hypocrisy had always encouraged the "affecting [of] false characters, in order to purchase applause,"[15] Fielding realized that the swelling opportunities for the conspicuous consumption of marks of esteem had within living memory propelled these vices into the forefront of an altered public consciousness. They became the artist's privileged subjects because in their fictive representations his audience would recognize themselves.

Aimed at this public of sensible spectators, Fielding's epic comedies were meant to block the reader's natural tendency to remove himself as an object of satiric representation. If satire was, as Swift put it, "a glass, wherein beholders do generally discover everybody's face but their own,"[16] the comic prose epic would further empower the moralizing function of comedy by creating a mirror of the reader's true purposes, one in which he could not help but view himself. In this project of compelling self-recognition, Fielding shared a goal in common with the most acute Augustan political commentary.[17] He saw in his own aesthetic a line of continuity with vernacular traditions of critical social realism, epitomized in the eighteenth century by Hogarth's "comic history-

---

[13] Fielding, *Joseph Andrews*, III, 3.

[14] Henry Fielding, "An Essay on the Knowledge and of the Characters of Men," *Works* (Westminster, 1899), 11: 173–216, 175. Hereafter, "An Essay."

[15] Fielding, *Joseph Andrews*, Preface.

[16] Jonathan Swift, *The Battle of the Books*, in *Prose Works*, ed. H. Davis (Oxford: University Press, 1939), 1: 140.

[17] See Dario Castiglione, "Mandeville Moralized," *Annali Della Fondazione Luigi Einaudi*, 17 (1983), 239–90, especially 257–60, and J. A. W. Gunn, *Beyond Liberty and Property. The Process of Self-Recognition in Eighteenth-Century England* (Kingston, Ontario: McGill-Queen's University Press, 1983).

paintings." Hogarth served as Fielding's visual model because his pictures "express the affections of men on canvas" by investing the figures represented with consciousness, making them *"appear to think."*[18] They were intended, Hogarth said, to absorb the spectator by placing before him outwardly referring dramatic images, in which "I wished to compose pictures on canvas, similar to representations on the stage. . . . I have endeavored to treat my subjects as a dramatic writer; my picture is my stage, and men and women my players, who by means of certain actions and gestures, are to exhibit a *dumb* show."[19]

Like Hogarth, Fielding sought to exploit the dramatic tensions between a classical order of representation and the demotic energies that found no place within the inherited hierarchy of literary genres. He parodied the neoclassical Preface by reporting that the so-called rules of the comic prose epic, supposedly originating in Homer and sanctioned by Aristotle, were now "entirely lost," but informed his readers on the title page of *Joseph Andrews* that the work before them was "Written in Imitation of The *Manner* of Cervantes." This message carried a particular meaning since the dominant contemporary understanding of *Don Quixote* was that it was the most formidable satire of social institutions in print. Sir William Temple thought the book to have caused the decline in esteem shown to the Spanish aristocracy, a view disseminated by Defoe in his *Memoirs of Capitan Carleton* (1728), whose hero is told by a Spanish gentleman that any man behaving in a noble style "found himself the jest of high and low . . . after the world became a little acquainted with [Cervantes's] notable history."[20] The 1742 English edition of *Don Quixote* was prefaced by the translator's interpretation of Cervantes as a satirist and reforming social critic, to which Pope's editor, Bishop Warburton, added an essay defending this form of vernacular literature's serious religious intentions.[21] Fielding thus drew attention to the purposes of his work by announcing its literary provenance. He would, like Cervantes, undermine the approval given to certain styles of social behavior by exposing through ridicule their dramaturgical conventions, and then extract spiritual significance from the acts of these

[18] Fielding, *Joseph Andrews*, Preface.

[19] William Hogarth, *The Analysis of Beauty* (London, 1753), quoted in Robert Halsband, "Stage Drama as a source for Pictorial and Plastic Art," in *British Theatre and the Other Arts, 1600–1800*, ed. Shirley Strum Kenny (Washington: Folger Shakespeare Library, 1984), 149–70, 155.

[20] Cited in Walter L. Reed, *An Exemplary History of the Novel* (Chicago: University Press, 1981), 124, a study of the Quixotic motif. See too A. P. Burton, "Cervantes the Man Seen through English Eyes in the Seventeenth and Eighteenth Centuries," *Bulletin of Hispanic Studies* 45 (1968), 1–15, and E. A. Peters, "Cervantes in England," *Bulletin of Hispanic Studies* 24 (1947), 226–38.

[21] William Warburton, "A Supplement to the Translator's Preface, Communicated by a learned writer, well-known in the literary world," in Cervantes, *Don Quixote*, trans. Henry Jarvis (London, 1742).

now naked actors — "stripped," as Quixote put it, "of their players' garments."[22]

In *Don Quixote* literary history itself offered the primary set of allusions, both for Quixote and his "idel reader," who was expected to recognize even minor characters as spokesmen for virtually the entire range of then-established literary genres. Quixote himself read until "his brain dried up and he lost his wits," thus becoming the projector of his textually induced fantasies. Embarked on the career of a character drawn from the *Anadis of Gaul* and *Palmerin of England*, his delirium served to isolate the *topoi* of chivalric romance as archaic delusions. Fielding found in this madness a model for what he called "biography," imaginative ethnographic records in which texts prescribing ideals of propriety are set against the lived experience of those who perform them. Such books, he said, record "the history of the world . . . , at least that part which is polished by laws, arts and sciences; and of that from the time it was first polished to this day."[23] In them, social actors become subjects whose everyday life is ordered by the gestures and motifs of their own literary experience. Yet in a world whose history had been altered decisively since Quixote's adventures, not least by the decay of those chivalric ideals Cervantes had so effectively ridiculed, literature for Fielding would have to represent a different range of behavioral possibilities.

Here Fielding participated in the wider movement of social perception that has been called "the destruction of the hero."[24] As the European warrior caste experienced an erosion of its authoritative political functions in repeated struggles with expanding monarchies, the old nobility became an object of satire as the understanding of its ethos was transformed. Even Montesquieu, the greatest defender of aristocratic privilege, conceived of these values as "false honor."[25] By the mid-eighteenth century they increasingly appeared as largely formal codes of prerogative and deference through which the ennobled exercised their vanity and self-interest. These were the very passions that most aroused Fielding's imagination. He saw the engagement of an individual's self-regarding passions with the larger imperatives of commercial societies as the site for understanding modes of self-presentation within the contemporary structures of everyday life. "The passions, like managers of a playhouse," Fielding wrote, "often force men upon parts without consulting their judgements,"[26]

---

[22] Cervantes, *Don Quixote*, III, iii.

[23] Fielding, *Joseph Andrews*, III, 1.

[24] Paul Benichou, *Man and Ethics. Studies in French Classicism*, trans. Elizabeth Highes (New York: Anchor, 1971), 98–115. See too Albert O. Hirschman, *The Passions and the Interests. Political Arguments for Capitalism before Its Triumph* (Princeton: University Press, 1977), 7–20, and Arthur O. Lovejoy, *Reflections on Human Nature* (Baltimore: Johns Hopkins University Press, 1961), *passim*.

[25] Montesquieu, *L'Esprit des Lois* (1748), VII, 7.

[26] Fielding, *Tom Jones*, VII, 1.

and so compell them to "suffer . . . private mortification [to] . . . avoid public shame."[27] In polished societies, where "the art of thriving . . . points out to every individual his own particular and separate advantage to which he is to sacrifice the interest of all others,"[28] economic opportunity had become the propulsive force driving self-regard into the foreground of self-reflection. Fielding wished to devise a morally informed genre of satiric writing specifically suited to these emotional conditions, one designed to expose the theatrically patterned hypocrisies of contemporary private aspiration.

Fielding presumed that his audience, unlike that of Cervantes, was composed not so much of elite consumers of printed texts, as of literate, middling inhabitants of a post-chivalric culture in which the standard literary genres had lost much of their power to compel. An "exact copy of nature" would suitably represent these readers as a species of self-conscious observers of actual and, as he said, metaphorical theatrical acts within roles that were adopted provisionally, as the play demanded. Joseph Andrews reports that Lady Booby "held my hand, and talked exactly as a lady does to her sweethart in a stage play, which I have seen in Covent Garden." The lady responds to what the reader knows is Joseph's genuine naiveté, itself the product of an uncritical reading of his sister's letters, as if this too must be a pose, whose "pretended innocence cannot impose on me."[29] When Joseph says that he has never done anything more than be kissed, Lady Booby gives the appropriate response of the seasoned theatergoer: "Kissing," she says, "do you call that no crime. Kissing Joseph, is as a prologue to a play."[30] Fielding took care to provide his characters with appropriate theatrical analogs, drawn from a familiar history of the stage, whose actors he named. He similarly invested these characters with a repertoire of dramatic styles through which they establish public identities, and in whose confusion "persons know us in one place and not in another and not tomorrow."[31] For in life as on the stage, "it is often the same person who represents the villain and the hero; and he who engages your admiration today, will probably attract your contempt tomorrow."[32]

Fielding's object was to effect a translation of signs and concepts formerly at home in Quixote's moral and discursive environment into the codes of a monied and mobile culture where they bore altered intersubjective meanings. The comic prose epic would be a "physic for the mind" which rendered the actions of men as performances necessarily undertaken within discrete behavioral styles, forms of public personality that the artist would represent stereo-

---

[27] Fielding, *Joseph Andrews*, III, 1.
[28] Fielding, "An Essay," 177.
[29] Fielding, *Joseph Andrews*, I, 6.
[30] *Ibid.*, I, 8.
[31] See especially, *ibid.*, II, 13: "A dissertation concerning high people and low people. . . ."
[32] Fielding, *Tom Jones*, VII, 1.

typically in order to expose their unwritten protocols. Once in conscious possession of these rules, the audience to whom performances were directed could emotionally detach itself from an involvement with the roles persons played, precisely because the performative requirements of these roles had been revealed as merely the outward conformity of otherwise free moral agents to pre-scripted social demands. Fielding sought to disperse the passionate attachments that these stylized social performances were meant to engender in an audience for whom styles of behavior had become objects of dramatic art. He wished to create what Addison had called an "impartial spectator," the participant-observer who could, in effect, systematically separate the form of an act, its socially specified and easily mimed behavioral requirements, from its ethical import, the moral sources of action upon which men ought properly to be judged.[33]

Fielding feared the demise of the classical ideal of self-sacrifice in the name of the public good because he sensed that it was fast becoming in the minds of his audience a political maxim by which the cunning advanced their private interests. Yet he sympathized with this response, for he believed that

> it is impossible that any man endowed with rational faculties, and being in a state of freedom, should willingly agree, without some motive of love or friendship, absolutely to sacrifice his own interest to that of another. . . . Thus, while the crafty and designing part of mankind, consulting only their own separate advantage, endeavor to maintain one constant imposition on the others, the whole world becomes a vast masquerade where the greatest part appear disguised . . . ; a very few only showing their own faces, who become by so doing, the astonishment and ridicule of all the rest.[34]

Here Fielding deployed one of the most ubiquitous Augustan images of social subversion and the decay of public identity.[35] It is important to notice that in the project of exposing to ridicule the moral duplicities of this "vast masquerade," he was also intent to show how even those honest souls for whom love bridged the gulf between motive and act still, of necessity, followed the dramaturgical imperatives that governed communal behavior. If these individuals

[33] *The Spectator*, 14 January 1711/1712. In *The Theory of Moral Sentiments* (6th ed., 1790), Adam Smith offered a theoretical account of an almost identical conception, the dilemmas of whose theatrical rhetoric are discussed by David Marshall, "Adam Smith and the Theatricality of Moral Sentiments," *Critical Inquiry* 10 (June 1984): 592–613.

[34] Fielding, "An Essay," 177–78.

[35] See, for example, Terry Castle, *Masquerade and Civilization. The Carnivalesque in Eighteenth-Century English Culture and Fiction* (Stanford: University Press, 1986), in which the masquerade is discussed as a destabilizing *topos*, particularly in Fielding's writings, the first of which was a poem, "The Masquerade" (1728).

were distinguished by genuinely moral, other-regarding sentiments, as social creatures they nevertheless were obliged to act within semiotized social roles, to appear in one of "those disguises" worn on "the greater stage" of society.[36] For just as Joseph Andrews mistakenly takes his sister's letters as the appropriate prompt-book of his own performances, so even the virtuous Parson Adams enacts the role of a Quixote of the ethical, a good man often deluded by the maxims of his classical education.

Of course, Fielding's purpose was to reveal the person behind the public mask, and it is of some significance that he frequently does so by creating contexts that strain his characters' scripts beyond their capacity for successful enactment. Near the end of *Joseph Andrews*, after Adams' essential goodness has been firmly established, he rebukes Joseph for being "too much inclined to passion," citing Abraham's readiness to sacrifice Isaac as his exemplary text. In the midst of this discourse the Parson receives news that his youngest son has drowned. Adams then "began to stamp around the room and deplore his loss with the bitterest agony," to which Joseph responds by attempting to give him comfort with "many arguments that he had several times remembered out of [Adams's] own discourses, both in public and private (for he was a great enemy to the passions, and preached nothing more than the conquest of them by reason and grace)." But Adams, overcome with grief and rage against his son's senseless death, "was not now at leisure to hearken to his advice. 'Child, child', said he [to Joseph], do not go about impossibilities."[37] Adams, who the reader knows as an admirer of Addison's *Cato*, "the only English tragedy I ever read," and one of the few plays "fit for a Christian to read,"[38] is the good man whose stoicism has reached its limit. At the moment when he can no longer contain his passions, he, Joseph, and Fielding's audience are made to confront the inadequacies of what was perhaps the most thoroughly inscribed Augustan role, that of the virtuous citizen, even when played by a person whose life so closely embodied its ideals. Fielding wished to show that even the best of men, Adams and Cato, must inhabit roles that shape the performance of emotional response, and thereby create a curtain behind which their passions remain hidden from view.

Yet if one maintains that all men are players, and that even the highest forms of moral sensibility remain extrinsic to the performative demands of the ethical act, how then can the theatrically embodied persons who appear on society's stage truly be known, save in those rare and privileged moments when the force of circumstance may lead to a collapse of dramaturgical ingenuity? The Augustinian severities that inspired Fielding's unmasking strategies could provide for him, as they did for the theologians Pierre Nicole and Jacques

---

[36] Fielding, "An Essay," 178.
[37] Fielding, *Joseph Andrews*, IV, 8.
[38] *Ibid.*, III, 5, and III, 11.

Esprit, little more than councils of faith and obedience in a deformed world of such moral opacity that even its greatest achievements were the unintended consequences of sinful impulses.[39] "We are like those dancers at a masked ball," Nicole wrote,

> who hold one another by the hand affectionately without recognizing one another, and part a moment later, never to see each other again. To see how men use one another one might think of human life and the affairs of the world as a serious game where any moves are permitted to seize the goods of another at our own risk, and where the lucky players despoil with all honor, the more unfortunate or less skilled."[40]

Mandeville had begun his argument by assuming the truth of this Augustinian position and then ironically transformed it into a generalized model of the moral topography of commercial societies. Fielding explicitly sought to resist the force of Mandeville's motto, "private vices, public benifits," and to deny the morally skeptical conclusions of *The Fable of the Bees* because of their licentious and atheistic implications. He argued instead that the true scene of meaningful human action, and thus of morals, was not the mere backdrop of conventional social arrangements in which, he agreed, the skillful deceived less talented players, but a universe of naturally instituted signs of divine inscription, a world populated by beings whose very features revealed their genuine moral sentiments. In such a world, even the most practiced performer could be unmasked, for

> however cunning the disguise which a masquerader wears; however foreign to his age, degree or circumstances; yet if closely attended to he very rarely escapes the discovery of an accurate observer; for Nature, which unwillingly submits to the imposture, is ever endeavoring to peep forth and show herself; nor can the cardinal, the friar, or the judge, long conceal the sot, the gamester or the rake.

[39] Hervé Madelin, "Henry Fielding and Jacques Esprit," *The Yearbook of Research in English and American Literature* [Berlin] 1 (1982), 27–74, documents Fielding's reliance on Esprit's moral philosophy. See Jacques Esprit, *The Falsehood of Human Virtue* (London, 1691).

[40] Pierre Nicole, *Essais de Morale* (Paris, 1675), 421, quoted in Nannerl O. Keohane, *Philosophy and the State in France* (Princeton: University Press, 1980), 412. In his *Traité de la Comédie* [1667], ed. Georges Couton (Paris: Société D'Edition "Les Belles Lettres," 1961), 49–59, Nicole argued that these passions were inherent in and promoted by the theater itself. See too, Dale Van Kley, "Pierre Nicole, Jansenism and the Morality of Enlightened Self-Interest," in *Anticipations of the Enlightenment in England, France and Germany*, ed. Charles Alan Kors and Paul Korshin (Philadelphia: University of Pennsylvania Press, 1987), 69–85.

In the same manner will those disguises which are worn on the greater stage generally vanish, or prove inneffectual to impose the assumed for the real character upon us, if we employ sufficient diligence and attention in the scrutiny.[41]

Fielding retained the faith of his Augustinian predecessors that truly moral acts could only be performed by genuinely virtuous actors. He believed as well that goodness was a property of the soul, given through grace, though not by the *Deus absconditus* of Pascal, Nicole, and Esprit whose workings could nowhere be seen with any certainty. Rather, Fielding believed that the purposes of an Enlightenment God "peep forth" from the "Nature" in which God inscribed them. This precept gave Fielding the courage to "defy the wisest man in the world to turn a true good action into ridicule."[42] For even if in their theatrically encoded performances all persons became fit subjects for satire, Fielding was convinced that the property of virtue was Nature's stamp, "imprint[ed with] sufficient marks"[43] on the bodies of men and permanently available for the properly instructed to decipher.

This conviction was neither an idiosyncratic idea nor simply a desperate attempt on Fielding's part to salvage transparent meanings from the resolutely opaque presentations of self dissected in his fictions. It derived from the eighteenth-century revival of the ancient art of physiognomy, a spiritually informed study of character based upon a method of reading the countenance, one supposedly possessed by Socrates and fully systematized in the next generation by the Swiss pastor, J. C. Lavater. This revived semiotics of the face gained so great a hold on the European imagination that Hegel thought it neccessary in *Phenomenology of Spirit* to refute its scientific pretentions.[44] Parson Adams spoke with Fielding's voice when he said that "nature generally imparts such a portraiture of the mind in the countenance, that a skillful physiognomist will rarely be deceived."[45]

Eighteenth-century conventions of social criticism took the passions as "Nature's never-failing Rhetoric, and the only Orators that can master our Affections."[46] Both artists and critics similarly concentrated on the repre-

[41] Fielding "An Essay," 178. The characters Fielding names are stock figures of the Restoration stage.
[42] Fielding, *Joseph Andrews*, Preface.
[43] Fielding, "An Essay," 179.
[44] G. W. F. Hegel, *The Phemomenology of Spirit*, trans. A. V. Miller (Oxford: Clarendon Press, 1977), 185–210, and see Alisdair MacIntyre, "Hegel on Faces and Skulls," in MacIntyre, ed., *Hegel: A Collection of Critical Essays* (Garden City N.V.: Doubleday, 1972), 220–36. See too Hogarth, "Of the Face," in *The Analysis of Beauty*, chapter 15. Graeme Tytler, *Physiognomy and the European Novel* (Princeton: University Press, 1982), 144–51, discusses Fielding's use of physiognomic principles in his fiction.
[45] Fielding, *Joseph Andrews*, II, 18.
[46] [Abel Boyer], *The English Theophrastus, or the Manners of the Age* (London, 1702),

sentation of the passions as the crucial element in the portrayal of character. A true "painting of the passions" was taken, as in Fielding's own criticism, to be the highest praise one could bestow on any attempt to depict the vicissitudes of human nature. An intricate set of rules provided for artists the affective conventions through which the passions could be portrayed. It was thought to be the artist's business to know the best way of representing each passion so as to make his audience appropriately respond. These conventions were in part drawn from classical authorities, but they primarily derived from recent formulations of a grammar of passions that could be represented pictorially.

The most important of these guidebooks was the *Conférence de M. Le Brun sur l'expression générale et particlière* (1667). Chancellor of the Académie Royale de Peinture et de Sculpture, Charles Le Brun codified the principles of Cartesian philosophical psychology in a catalogue of instructions, accompanied by drawings (the plates of the second edition were later reproduced in Lavater's *Fragmente*[47]) on how properly to depict the influence of each passion on the human face.[48] Each of Le Beun's illustrations was accompanied by a caption specifying the means by which the face could be drawn to express an emotion like contempt, the subject of figures 8, 9, and 10:

> Contempt is expressed by the eyebrows knit and lowering towards the nose, and at the other end very much elevated; the eye very open and the pupil in the middle; the nostrils drawing upwards; the mouth shut, with the corners somewhat down, and the under-lip thrust out further than the upper one.

The pervasive influence of Le Brun's treatise extended beyond the audience of painters to whom it was addressed. Translated into English in 1701, *A Method to Learn to Design the Passions* was reprinted throughout the century, with an expensive edition appearing as late as 1813, near the time when Wordsworth thrilled at the perfectly expressive face of the Magdalene in the Louvre.[49]

The most important non pictorial consequence of the idea that there were

301. Brewster Rogerson, "The Art of Painting the Passions," *JHI*, 14, 1 (1953): 68–94, is a rich discussion of this subject. See too Lawrence Lipking, *The Ordering of the Arts in Eighteenth-Century England* (Princeton: University Press, 1970), especially 38–65.

[47] J. C. Lavater, *Fragmente* (Leipzig, 1775–1778), 4 volumes. They were reproduced again in Thomas Holcroft's translation, *Essays on Physiognomy. For the Promotion of the Knowledge and the Love of Mankind*, 3 vols. (London, 1783).

[48] For a discussion of Le Brun, see Stephanie Ross, "Painting the Passions: Charles Le Brun's *Conférence sur L'expression*," *JHI* 45, 1 (1984): 25–47.

[49] William Wordsworth, *The Prelude*, IX, 76–80. For Le Brun's importance for the plastic arts, see Alastair Smart, "Dramatic Gesture and Expression in the Age of Hogarth and Reynolds," *Apollo* 82 (1965): 90–97, and Alan T. McKenzie, " 'The Countenance You Show Me': Reading the Passions in the Eighteenth Century," *The Georgia Review* 32 (1978): 758–73.

universal and invariant norms of expression was its effect on theatrical practices, a transmission encouraged by Shaftesbury's arguments affirming the parallels between the pictorial and dramatic arts.[50] From the acting treatises of Thomas Betterton and Aaron Hill to *The Paradox of Acting* by Diderot and Goethe's *Rules for Actors*, the stage was conceived as if it were a *tableau vivant* where actors drew upon a standardized gestural "language" for the expression of the passions. Audiences engaged with actors in a contract of performance and response in which they were presumed to be thoroughly familiar with nature's rhetoric of emotional representations. Fielding's friend and performing ideal, Garrick, said that a great actor, "by calling in the aid and assistance of articulation, corporeal motions and ocular expression, imitates, assumes, or puts on the various mental and bodily emotions arising from the various humours, virtues and vices, incident to human nature, . . . [because he knows] each humour and passion, their sources and effects."[51] These details of facial aspect, gesture, and tone of voice already began to be cataloged in 1724 in the *Thesaurus Dramaticus*, an account of the "poetical beauties" of the English stage, while Betterton's authority supported the view that the actor had to master the rules of posture and tone. Above all, he must command his face:

> Your Eye-brows must neither be immovable, nor always in Motion . . .
> but generally they must remain in the same Posture and Equality,
> which they have be Nature, allowing them their due Motion when the
> Passions require it; that is, to contract themselves, and frown in
> *Sorrow*; to smooth and dilate themselves in *Joy*; to hand down in
> *Humility*, &c.[52]

Fielding worked within this set of conventions in his satiric dramas of the 1730s, the more successful of which, like *Pasquin* and *The Tragedy of Tragedies*, repeatedly employed devices such as the play within a play so as not to allow the audience to forget that it was in the theater. Fielding's interpolated narrative, and his digressions on style and form, similarly distanced the reader of his fictions by reproducing in the novel the theater's rhetorical demands.[53] He

---

[50] Anthony Ashley Cooper, Earl of Shaftesbury, *A Notion of the Historical Draught of the Judgement of Hercules* (1732), Benjamin Rand, ed., *Shaftesbury's Second Characteristics* (Cambridge: University Press, 1914), 29–62. This point is discussed in Ronald Paulson, *Hogarth: His Life, Art and Times* (New Haven: Yale University Press, 1972), 1, 103–4. On the representation of the passions on the eighteenth-century stage, see William Worthen, *The Idea of the Actor* (Princeton: University Press, 1984), Chapter 2, and the works cited therein.

[51] David Garrick, *An Essay on Acting* (1744), in *Actors on Acting* ed. Toby Cole and Helen C. Chinoy (New York: Crown, 1954), 133.

[52] Thomas Betterton, *The History of the English Stage* (London, 1741), 98.

[53] The third-person narrator's virtual omniscience in *Joseph Andrews* is enhanced by his persona as a director who "imitate[s] the wise conductors of the stage," offering

expected his audience to be familiar with established dramatic conventions and assume a theatrical perspective on the characters he portrayed. These characters are in turn depicted within self-consciously theatrical settings where the rules of gesture and facial expression guide the meaning of the performance. When, for example, Partridge is taken by Tom Jones to see Garrick's *Hamlet*, he not only thinks that the best actor plays Claudius, but that the king does not look like a murderer. He also believes that "I could act as well as [Garrick] myself," unaware of the meaning of his own testimony that he only knew King Hamlet was a ghost when Hamlet responded to it, so great were the expressive powers of Garrick's glance. When Partridge then misquotes Juvenal's line, "*fronti nulla fides,*" he becomes the doubly satiric example of the person who consistently misreads the face and thus the meaning of the player.[54] In *Joseph Andrews* Fielding describes Mrs. Slipslop, who "flung herself into the chaise, casting a look at Fanny as she went, not unlike that which Cleopatra gives Octavia in that play," fully expecting his reader to be familiar with the characteristics signifying contempt.[55] When Fielding (correctly) quotes Juvenal in discussing the method of understanding character, he points out that the adage, "no trust is to be given to the countenance," was written by the poet in the context of his, and of Fielding's own rhetorical question, "what place is not filled with austere libertines?"[56] The theatrical transposition of Le Brun's pictorial aesthetic offered Fielding a way to answer this question by providing him with principles of unmasking the stage managers of their own public demeanors.

Nature "imprinte[ed] sufficient marks on the countenance to inform an accurate and discerning eye," and in *The Essay* and *The Journal of a Voyage to Lisbon* Fielding sought to "set down some few rules" to guide the discernment of men of open dispositions, the sure indication, he said, "of an honest and upright heart."[57] He sometimes thought that these principles, drawn from Le Brun and cited with Shaftesbury's authority, in fact offered a way for the morally worthy to remain the impartial spectators of their own social drama. These persons could achieve the critical distance necessary to comprehend the global character of theatrical behavior and then, by judging it with charity,

set-pieces of humor or satire to impede the reader's absorption in the tale before him. Brian Corman, "Congreve, Fielding and the Rise of Some Novels," in Kenny (ed.), 257–70, discusses these points.

[54] Fielding, *Tom Jones*, XVI, 5.

[55] Fielding, *Joseph Andrews*, II, 13, p. 135. The play referred to is Dryden's *All For Love*, III, 1, in which Cleopatra and Octavia meet.

[56] Fielding, "An Essay," 178, 181.

[57] Compare this quality with mere "good Breeding[,] the latter being the Art of conducting yourself by certain common and general Rules, by which Means, if they were universally observed, the whole world would appear (as all Courtiers actually do) to be, in their external Behavior at least, but one and the same Person." Henry Fielding, *The Covent-Garden Journal*, 55, 18 July 1752).

reduce the anxieties generated by their own performances. "A single bad act no more constitutes a villain in life, than a single bad part on the stage," the narrator says in *Tom Jones*: "Thus the man as well as the player may condemn what he himself acts; nay it is common to see vice sit as awkwardly on some men as the character of Iago would on the honest face of [the actor] Mr William Mills."[58] Like Tom Jones, who knows that "appearances . . . are often deceitful," but who is seldom so deceived, and unlike Jonathan Wild, author of "Maxims for the Great Man," the hypocrite's handbook, it could be hoped that good men, no matter how ordinary, might know their fellows and in that knowledge forgive them.

Yet, as the self-regarding passions drove the players of a theatricized world, they similarly distorted the judgment of its spectators, "for as affectation always overacts her part, it fares with her as with a farcical actor on the stage . . . while the truest and finest strokes of Nature, represented by a judicious and just actor, pass unobserved and disregarded."[59] Although in possession of the rules by which to decipher nature's inscriptions, men nevertheless remained prone to the passionately distorted images of their own creation and failed to encounter the man performing behind the mask. Even in a world of natural signs "a more reliable guide" was needed for their decoding. This guide, Fielding said, is to be found in "the *actions* of men,"[60] a remedy that one cannot help but think would give small relief to his discerning reader, so intimately acquainted by Fielding's own fictions with the endlessly interpretable, because never unmediated, transactions between audience and masquerade, reader and player, in what Fielding himself described as a mere pantomime of critical communication.[61] As the century's greatest mime told a philosopher who, like Fielding, sought to defend the principles of virtue and penetrate by reason the masks of vicious actors, "the man who must have a manual won't ever go far, [for] society offers many more [poses] than . . . art can imitate."[62]

[58] Fielding, *Tom Jones*, VII, 1.
[59] Fielding, "An Essay," 187.
[60] *Ibid.*, 188.
[61] Fielding, *Joseph Andrews*, III, 10, "A discourse between the poet and player."
[62] Rameau's nephew to "Lui," in Denis Diderot, *Rameau's Nephew*, trans. L. W. Tancock (London: Penguin, 1966), 76, 120. It is perhaps worthy of note that Rameau was referring to Noverre, the greatest contemporary teacher of dance, and that the dancing master was one of Fielding's preferred images for the representation of deceit, a point made by Claude Rawson in "Gentlemen and Dancing-Masters," in *Henry Fielding and the Augustan Ideal under Stress* (London: Routledge, 1972), 3–34.

III

Fielding's dilemma arose from the traditions informing his mimetic techniques. He assumed that one of the modern writer's tasks was to classify the visible signs of the invisible powers from which action sprang, providing the reader with a critical distance from his own motives by satirically rendering their effects. The rhetoric of the theater eminently suited these purposes. Fielding exploited the power of the metaphorical equation of the world as a stage as it became common lexical currency for social comprehension by persons whose expanded opportunities in an increasingly mobile world heightened the distance between their private perceptions and the requirements of public performance. The relatively stable system of expression, pose, gesture, and plot within which Fielding wrote permitted him to depict for an enlarged and diverse reading public those universal features of the human drama whose representations were previously confined to the socially elevated. His novels sought to embody the spirit of the epic under modern, prosaic conditions.

The response that Diderot placed in the mouth of Rameau's nephew serves to highlight how these representational practices, depending upon particular assumptions about what constitutes psychological realism, became problematic during the eighteenth century.[63] Fielding understood this when he rejected those "immense Romances, of the modern Novel . . . [which] without any assistance from Nature or History, records persons who never were, or will be, and facts which never did nor possibly can happen."[64] His point, here famously made against Richardson, was that the narrative of a life could only move and instruct if it placed that life in imaginative contact with those universal norms of human nature expressed on the dramatic surface of action. Hume, Smollett, and Gibbon wrote their histories from a similar perspective. Like them, Fielding thought it absurd that the peculiarities of a character's emotional response, historical or fictive, could, or should, compel the reader to "identify" with him, a usage, it is worth noting, which did not become common until late in the generation after Fielding's death.[65] Fielding, like Brecht, wanted to encourage

---

[63] Alisdair MacIntyre, *After Virtue* (Notre Dame: University Press, 1981), 35–48, gives a brilliant account of the relation between Rameau's masquerades and eighteenth-century moral philosophy. See too E. J. Hundert, "A Satire of Self-Disclosure: From Hegel through Rameau to the Augustans," *The Journal of the History of Ideas* (April–June 1986): 235–48. For the decay of the behavioral styles represented by Fielding see, Charles Pullen, "Lord Chesterfield and Eighteenth-Century Appearance and Reality," *Studies in English Literature, 1500–1800* 8 (1968): 501–15, and Michael Curtin, "A Question of Manners: Status and Gender in Etiquette and Courtesy," *The Journal of Modern History* 57 (September 1985): 395–423.

[64] Fielding, *Joseph Andrews*, Preface.

[65] *OED, s.v.* "identify." Compare Samuel Johnson on Biography in *Rambler* 60 (13 October 1750).

the reader's distance, not his or her suspension of disbelief. It was his object thoroughly to semiotize the theatrics of *all* roles, so that in an encounter with the performance of any of them one could *detach*, not identify, and so remain a self-consciously free moral agent. To observe that fielding "only" gives us the surface of characters, and regret that his characters have no convincing "inner" lives, assumes without argument that this inner life is a permanent human attribute rather than an emergent intersubjective property, a feature of the self that Fielding lacked the imagination to grasp, rather than an historical consequence of the disintegration of assumptions upon which his writing depended.[66]

When Diderot described the actor as a courtier, a puppet, a pantomime, a "nothingness" in *The Paradox of Acting*, he drew attention to the limits of the metaphor of man as an actor by taking literally the performative requirements of playing a role. If human actions are to be understood dramaturgically, then a thoroughgoing interpretation of these performances would demand that audiences presume *nothing* about the man behind the mask. There would be no criteria to establish a person's identity if that person played all roles without a genuine commitment to any of them. And if, like the professional actor, one invests his emotional energies in the role now demanded of him, then it is absurd to expect that he could still have at his disposal the resources of feeling concurrently to play other roles, the situation in which all human agents find themselves. All that we can know of actors as *actors* is the shape and fruit of their skill.

Rameau's nephew wished to bring home the point that an attempt to judge persons by seeing in their performances indelible signs of genuine sentiment mistakes for morally significant attributes of character the dramaturgical consequences of the uneven distribution of talent. So extravagant a view, and the inability of Diderot's *philosophe* adequately to respond to it, suggests that the representational project typified by Fielding's work was approaching a point of exhaustion. For what both Rameau and his interlocutor desired, and neither adequately could express, were precisely those features of an individual life that would define it as comprehensible and unique against the background of *any* behavioral style, against a commonly recognized catalogue of dramatic narratives of the person, both historical and fictive. The realization that *every* social performance could be represented as an enactment of thoroughly inscribed, fully semiotized, theatrical injunctions had become for them, as it was not for Fielding, the source of a need to discover a different axis of signification. They sought to devise representative practices expressive of an inner life that some-

---

[66] The first judgment is Ian Watt's in *The Rise of the Novel* (London: Perigrine Books, 1963), 282, 286; the second is Ronald Paulson's in *Satire and the Novel in Eighteenth-Century England* (New Haven: Yale University Press, 1967), 126.

how resisted all attempts to encode it, and because it remained unencoded, singular, and because it was singular, self-defining.

Yet as Brecht reminds us, such a project must forever remain incomplete since this imagined life, no matter how exceptional, would, like every other, require patterns of performance for its social comprehensibility and thus for its appropriate enactment. This is equally true for Richardson's Pamela, as it was for Werther or Napoleon, subsequent emblems of individuality. It is significant that the most pervasive model for this new role of the unique, self-defining subject was crafted by the greatest admirer of Richardson, Fielding's antagonist. "I know my own heart and understand my fellow man," Rousseau began *The Confessions*: "I am made unlike any one I have ever met. I will even venture to say that I am like no one in the whole world. I may be no better, but at least I am different." Like Fielding's novels, Rousseau's autobiography and its startling importance for his readers' conception of themselves ought to pose problems in understanding how he and they came to represent this difference, and how this difference entailed for them transformed patterns of emotional response and self-understanding. But even this extraordinary, self-dramatized life, elements of whose narrative constitute the fable of Romantic identities, should not underwrite the presumption that it was also a discovery about the timeless structure of our own. Hegel, who first gave philosophical statement to a conception of self largely transformed by the myth of that life, and of Pamela's, Werther's and Napoleon's, grasped this issue with some clarity by metaphorically locating it in the theater. "It is manifest that behind the so-called curtain, which is supposed to conceal the inner world, there is nothing to be seen unless *we* go behind it ourselves, as much in order that we may see, as that there may be something behind there which can be see."[67] This remark can stand, I think, as a relevant interpretive principle, both for the comprehension of Henry Fielding's strategy for the representation of identity and for the subsequent transformation in the conception of self signaled by its collapse.

[67] Hegel, *The Phenomenology of Spirit*, 103.

Selected Publications of Perez Zagorin

A History of Political Thought in the English Revolution, London, Routledge and Kegan Paul, 1954, 2nd ed., 1966.

The Court and the Country, London, Routledge and Kegan Paul, 1969, New York, Atheneum, 1970.

Changing Views on British History, Harvard University Press, 1966. (contributor)

Social Change and Revolution in England, 1540–1640, London, Longmans, 1965. (contributor)

Revolutions in Modern Europe, N.Y., Macmillan, 1966. (contributor)

Seventeenth-century England. A Changing Culture, vol. 2: Modern Studies, Ward Lock and Open University Press, London, 1980. (contributor)

The Revolution That Wasn't. A Contemporary Assessment of 1776, Kennikat, N.Y., 1981. (contributor)

"The Authorship of Mans Mortallitie," The Library, Transactions of the Bibliographical Society, 1950.

"The English Revolution 1640–1660," Journal of World History, 2 parts, June, October 1955.

"Professor Becker's Two Histories: A Skeptical Fallacy," American Historical Revie, October 1956.

"The Social Interpretation of the English Revolution," Journal of Economic History, September 1959.

"Historical Knowledge," Journal of Modern History, September 1959.

"The Court and the Country," English Historical Review, April 1962.

"English History 1558–1640, A Bibliographical Survey," American Historical Review, January 1963.

"Sir Edward Stanhope's Advice to Thomas Wentworth, Viscount Westworth: An Unpublished Letter, 1631," Historical Journal, September 1964.

"Thomas Hobbes," International Encyclopedia of the Social Sciences, 1964.

"Theories of Revolution in Contemporary Historiography," Political Science Quarterly, March 1973.

Prolegomena to the Comparative History of Revolution in Early Modern Europe," Comparative Studies in Society and History, April 1976.

"Thomas Hobbes's Departure from England in 1640," Historical Journal, June 1984.

Culture and Politics from Puritanism to the Enlightenment, ed. with introduction, Berkeley, University of California, 1980.

Rebels and Rulers (1500–1660), Cambridge University Press, 2 vols., 1982.

"Vico's Theory of Knowledge" A Critique," Philosophical Quarterly, January 1984.

"On Vico: Reply to Sir Isaiah Berlin," *Philosophical Quarterly*, July 1985.

"Clarendon and Hobbes," *The Journal of Modern History*, December 1985.

"Did Strafford Change Sides?", *English Historical Review*, January 1986.

Revueltas y Revoluciones en la Edad Moderna, v. 1. *Movimientos campesinos urbanes*, v. 2. *Guerras revolucionarias*, Catedra, Madrid, 1986.

"Cudworth and Hobbes on Is and Ought". (forthcoming)

Ways of Lying: Dissimulation, Persecution, and Conformity in Early Modern Europe, Harvard University Press, 1990.

Religion, Philosophy, and Science in the Seventeenth Century (co-editor: to be published by the Cambridge University Press, 1991.

"Hobbes on Our Mind," *Journal of the History of Ideas*, 1990.

"Historiography and Postmodernism: Reconsiderations," *History and Theory*, 1990.

Notes on Contributors

DWIGHT BRAUTIGAM is Assistant Professor of History at Huntington College. He has presented papers on the Parliament of 1626 and the conflict within it, and on the ideological clash between Puritans and Arminians in early Stuart England. He is currently revising his book-length monograph on the 1626 Parliament, while also working on articles about the Puritan/Arminian clash and the House of Commons June 1626 Remonstrance to Charles I.

ANTONIO D'ANDREA is Professor Emeritus of Italian at McGill University and Fellow of the Royal Society of Canada. He has published *Il nome della storia* (1982), and numerous articles on the notion of historical truth and the meaning of literary criticism, particularly relating to Italian literature. Professor D'Andrea is also co-editor with Pamela D. Stewart of the critical edition of Innocent Gentillet's *Discours contre Machiavel* (1974).

WILLIAM H. DRAY is Professor Emeritus of Philosophy and History at the University of Ottawa and Fellow of the Royal Society of Canada. His publications include *Laws and Explanation in History* (1957 and 1979), excerpts of which have been reprinted in English and translated into Italian (1974), German (1977), and Hebrew (1985). His book *Philosophy of History* (1964), has been translated into Spanish (1965), Japanese (1968), Portuguese (1969), Italian (1969), and French (1982). He is also the author of *Perspective on History* (1980) and *On History and Philosophies of History* (1989). Professor Dray is currently completing a monograph to be titled *History as the Re-enactment of Past Experience*.

JOHN GUY is Professor of Modern History at the University of St Andrews and Fellow of the Royal Historical Society. He is author of numerous books and articles, including, most recently, *The Court of Star Chamber and its Records to the Reign of Elizabeth I* (1985), *Tudor England* (1990), "Thomas Cromwell and the Intellectual Origins of the Henrician Revolution" in *Reformation, Humanism and Revolution: Proceedings of the Folger Institute Center for the History of British Political Thought*, ed. Gordon J. Schochet (1990), and "Henry VIII and his Ministers" in *Henry VIII*, ed. D. Starkley, forthcoming. Professor Guy is currently working on a survey of English Political Thought from Fortescue to Hobbes and on a study of the Tudor Privy Council.

EDWARD J. HUNDERT is Associate Professor of History at the University of British Columbia. He is author of numerous articles on seventeenth and eighteenth century history of literary criticism, the most recent of which are, "The Thread of Language and the Web of Dominion: Mandeville to Rousseau and Back" (1988); "Rousseau in Mandeville's Shadow" (1989), and "Sexual Politics and the Allegory of Identity in Montesquieu's *Persian Letters*" (1990).

WILLIAM HUNT is Professor of History at St. Lawrence University. He has published *The Puritan Moment: The Coming of the Revolution in an English Country* (1983), and is co-editor, with Geoff Eleg, of the volume, *Reviving the English Revolution* (1988). He has contributed an article, "Civic Chivalry and the English Civil War" to the volume, *The Transmission of Culture in Early Modern Europe* (1990), edited by Anthony Grafton and Ann Blair. Currently, Professor Hunt is working on a book-length study, "Prince Henry's Ghost: Cultural Origins of the English Revolution."

BONNELYN YOUNG KUNZE is Visiting Assistant Professor of History at Colgate Rochester Divinity School. Her published articles on early English Quakerism include, "Religious Authority and Social Status: The Friendship of Margaret Fell, George Fox, and William Penn," *Church History* (1988) and " 'Poore and in Necessity': Female Quaker Philanthropy in Northwest England in the 1670s," *Albion* (1990). Her book-length monograph "Margaret Fell and the Rise of Quakerism" is forthcoming. Professor Kunze is currently conducting research on the transatlantic Quaker women's communities.

PETER LAKE is Lecturer in History at Royal Holloway and Bedford New College in the University of London. His publications include, *Moderate Puritans and the Elizabethan Church* (1982) and *Anglicans and Puritans? English Conformist Thought from Whitgift to Hooker* (1988). He has coedited, with Maria Dawling, *Protestantism and the National Church in Sixteenth-Century England* (1987). Professor Lake is currently doing research on English conformist thought from Hooker to Laud.

JOSEPH LEVINE is Professor of History at Syracuse University and is a Fellow of the Royal Historical Society. His publications include *Elizabeth I* (1969), *Humanism and History: Origins of Modern English Historiography* (1986), and *The Battle of the Books: History and Literature in the Augustan Age*, (1991). He is also writing a book-length monograph, "Between the Ancients and Moderns: From Humanism to Neoclassicism."

PAOLO PASQUALUCCI is Professor of Philosophy of Law at the University of Perugia, Italy. He has written a two-volume study on Rousseau and Kant, *Rousseau e Kant* (1974 and 1976), together with several essays and articles on the history of ideas and the theory of law. For some years he has been conducting research on Thomas Hobbes.

LINDA LEVY PECK is Professor of History at Purdue University, and is a Fellow of the Royal Historical Society. Professor Peck has co-edited with Professor John Guy the *Bibliography of British History 1500–1700* (RHS). Professor Peck's publications include *Northampton: Patronage and Policy at the Court of James I* (1982), *Court Patronage and Corruption in Early Stuart England* (1990), and she is the editor of *The Mental World of the Jacobean Court* (1991). One of her current research projects includes "Britain and the Baroque: Politics, Political Theory and Court Culture in Seventeenth-Century England, Scotland and Ireland."

GORDON J. SCHOCHET is Professor of Political Science at Rutgers University. He has published *The Authoritarian Family and Political Attitudes in Seventeenth-Century England* (1988). He is editor and contributor to the multi-volume series titled, *Proceedings of The Folger Institute Center for the History of British Political Thought* (1990). Professor Schochet is currently working on the subject of religious toleration in seventeenth-century England and completing a book titled, "John Locke and the Politics of Religious Toleration."

PAUL S. SEAVER is Christensen Professor of History at Stanford University and Director of the Program in Cultures, Ideas and Values at Stanford. His publications include *The Puritan Lectureships 1560–1662* (1970), *Wallington's World: A Puritan Artisan in Seventeenth Century London* (1985), and numerous articles in edited books and academic journals. He has also contributed several articles to *The Biographical Dictionary of British Radicals in the Seventeenth Century*, eds. Richard L. Greaves and Robert Zaller, 3 vols (1982–84). Professor Seaver is currently doing research on London apprentices in the seventeenth century.